THE OFFICIAL
PRICE GUIDE TO

COLLECTOR HANDGUNS

ALSO BY THE AUTHOR

The Official Price Guide to Antique and Modern Firearms
The Official Guide to Gunmarks

THE OFFICIAL® PRICE GUIDE TO

COLLECTOR HANDGUNS

ROBERT H. BALDERSON

FIFTH EDITION

HOUSE OF COLLECTIBLES • NEW YORK

Important Notice. All of the information, including valuations, in this book has been compiled from the most reliable sources, and every effort has been made to eliminate errors and questionable data. Nevertheless, the possibility of error, in a work of such immense scope, always exists. The publisher will not be held responsible for losses that may occur in the purchase, sale, or other transaction of items because of information contained herein. Readers who feel they have discovered errors are invited to *write* and inform us, so they may be corrected in subsequent editions. Those seeking further information on the topics covered in this book are advised to refer to the complete line of *Official Price Guides* published by the House of Collectibles.

Published by: House of Collectibles
201 East 50th Street
New York, NY 10022

Distributed by Ballantine Books, a division of Random House, Inc., New York, and simultaneously in Canada by Random House of Canada Limited, Toronto.

http://www.randomhouse.com

Manufactured in the United States of America

ISSN: 0747-7570

ISBN: 0-676-60038-7

Cover design by Kristine V. Mills-Noble
Cover photo by George Kerrigan

Fifth Edition: December 1996

10 9 8 7 6 5 4 3 2 1

CONTENTS

Acknowledgments vii
Introduction...3
History of the Handgun..3
Handgun Designers and Inventors...9
Legal Classifications of Firearms 13
Factors That Determine Value 14
Investment Opportunities 17
How to Buy and Sell Handguns...17
Limited Edition Handguns...21
Restoring and Refinishing Handguns 23
Pistol and Revolver Cartridges...28
Scope of the Book...34
How to Use This Book...35
Listing of Manufacturers and Models (A–Z)..........................36
Glossary 510
Abbreviations 517
Model Index..521

ACKNOWLEDGMENTS

Many people share the credit for this book—fellow collectors, dealers, clients, and friends who have contributed their information, time, and support over many years.

I extend sincere gratitude to the following:

Orvel L. Reichert
James Ferrell
Butterfield & Butterfield
Stephen H. McKelvain
Interarms
Tom Motter
Michael Krause
Mitchell Luksich
Victor Juskauskus
Peter Hischier

Del Denny
Nick Todd
Stan Lukowicz
Michael McHugh
R.E. Magruder
Frank Just
Bob Burton
Smith & Wesson
AMT
Fulton Court

A special thanks goes out to David Byron, whose research this book is based upon; and to my agent, Dorothy Crouch, for her determined success in bringing this work to fruition.

SPECIAL NOTE TO THE READER

The *Official Price Guide to Collector Handguns* is continually revised and expanded with new factual material. Reader's comments and suggestions are respectfully solicited. The author is interested in previously unpublished data and photographs for inclusion in future editions. BE OFFICIALLY ACKNOWLEDGED! In return for your information, you will become a member of our Board of Contributors and will be acknowledged in print for your efforts. Please write to the author with your ideas.

Robert H. Balderson
P.O. Box 254886
Sacramento, CA 95865

COLLECTOR HANDGUNS

INTRODUCTION

Like most books, this one was created to fill a need: in this case, to be an identification reference manual on current or widely used out-of-production handguns. The format of this book was chosen specifically with firearms technologists, collectors, and dealers in mind. It provides an easy-to-use rapidly accessible reference to over two hundred different models of handguns. We have attempted in our research for this book to provide a wide amount of information about each model. However, throughout the book, you will notice that there are sometimes gaps in this information. These omissions are either a result of manufacturer's records being somewhat haphazard or possibly a result of the fact that many manufacturers consider such information as this to be proprietary and therefore refuse to release it. In such cases, we have attempted to reconstruct this missing information to the best knowledge of available sources. Where this information is highly inconclusive, or where expert sources disagree, then we have left that section blank and hope in future editions to be able to clear up the problem.

HISTORY OF THE HANDGUN

The origins of the modern handgun are lost in the mists of time. They date back to the time of the invention of gunpowder, which in itself is quite a mystery. There are as many theories as to the development of gunpowder as there are to the development of the firearm and since gunpowder is the primary ingredient of firearms, we should examine some of the various theories.

The most popular European theory is that a monk in Freiberg known as Black Berthold, also known as Berthold Schwarz, was the inventor of gunpowder. Indeed, in many of the gun books there are beautiful old woodcuts depicting the Black Monk in his lab mixing away at his chemical formulas until coming up with this explosive, blasting off the top of the mortar and flinging the unfortunate monk to the ground. But that is only theory, and a theory based on some of Bacon's writings.

Much more to the point and somewhat more factual, a Chinese manuscript describes cannons that were employed in the siege of Pienkingu in the 15th century B.C. and how these cannons, which were known as the Huopao, fired projectiles and made a horrible noise that set the fortifications of a town bright with fire. Supporters of this theory believe that gunpowder was probably brought by the Mongols to Europe.

Another hypothesis is that gunpowder was invented even earlier than that, but in India, with some writers going so far as to claim that Alexander the Great was even using it in his campaigns. Another theory is that gunpowder was introduced in Spain by the Moors. The secret was discovered by the Byzantine Greeks. They were the ones who then brought it to other European countries.

All of these theories notwithstanding, there are some facts that still remain. Most modern experts and students of military history conceded that in the Far East, explosives and primitive bombs were used very early on. But they do not believe they were firearms as we understand them, that a tube using a powder to obtain expanding gasses and forcing a projectile outward with some degree of relative accuracy was used by these ancients. What does appear, however, is that these ancients, on up to maybe the 12th century, were using similar compounds but were using them as flares or propulsion methods for rockets. The late-12th-century book *Liber Ignium ad Comburendos Hostes*, which literally means "the book of fires for consuming the enemy," purportedly written by a Marcus Graecus, contains several formulas, which though comprising the same constituents as classical gunpowder, are mixed in the wrong proportions, which would produce only strong flares.

The first actual manuscript setting down the actual proportions for gunpowder was *Epistola Desecretis Operibus Artis Et Naturae*, which was written by Roger Bacon sometime toward the middle of the 13th century. Unfortunately for most historians, because of the time that Bacon lived in, had he written the formula in plain language, he probably would have been one of the first to feel its effects, presumably as he would have been tied to a wooden stake. Therefore, his entire treatise consists of anagrams and riddles, and it wasn't until about a hundred years ago that it was effectively translated. So the question is, who invented gunpowder? Was it the ancient Chinese? The Mongols? The Moors? Black Berthold? Or Bacon? Nobody seems to know, and it will probably remain one of the great riddles of mankind.

Actual firearms are only slightly easier to pinpoint. It appears that during the third quarter of the 1200s, the Moors decided to defend their cities in Spain, and they used what look like round buckets, about a foot across and about two feet deep, and what they did was stuff a couple of pounds of gunpowder, with a few pounds of rocks on top of it, and then, thrusting a red hot wire in a little touch hole at the bottom, would watch it send the rocks up in the air, hopefully to land on some horrible enemy, much like a modern mortar.

From this developed a wonderful hand cannon, which was essentially short tubes attached to long wooden poles. You stuck the pole into the ground, filled the tube with powder, put a few rocks in it, set it off, and the long stick would absorb the recoil. These seemed to be quite popular during the 1300s, and most people using firearms, tending to be rather conservative, stuck with this general system until the mid-1400s, when an immense breakthrough occurred, and the matchlock was developed. This meant that instead of having to hold the weapon in one hand and hold the match or a piece of hot wire in the other hand, both were combined, and all you needed was one hand to hold the weapon as well as fire it. The matchlock was a simple device that consisted of a barrel attached usually to a wooden stock, and an S-shaped piece of iron holding the slow match and looping down to where we would consider the trigger position to be. The arm was loaded as modern muzzle loaders are, with a little bit of powder sprinkled over a touch hole. You waited until you saw your target, and then slowly lowered the match into the touch hole, by means of the S-shaped metal flange. The system worked rather well, so long as you made sure that you did not go out in the rain, since you always had to have a burning wick.

Utilizing this system, barrels were refined, and actions were developed, some of them getting quite complex and quite ornate. In order to overcome the problem of always having a lit match on hand, and especially on your gun, the great geniuses of the day set their minds to developing a system to overcome this problem, and again, firearms development being what it is, it wasn't until the early 1500s that Johann Kiefuss in Nuremburg, Germany, finally developed a system called the *wheellock*. This operated quite like a modern cigarette lighter. You had a piece of pyrite that would rest against a serrated wheel. The wheel was wound up by spring pressure. A trigger would unlock the wheel, setting it to spin, causing sparks to fly and hopefully causing them to fly in the direction of a pan containing a little bit of priming powder, setting that off, and then setting off the main charge inside the barrel. It was quite a nice system, and you could even use it in the rain. Unfortunately, without machinery to produce the firearms, and everything being handmade, a very limited number of gunsmiths had the capability and the technical expertise to actually put one of these together. Instead it was left to skilled artisans with clockmaking ability; a sad situation, since only wealthy people could afford them. And kings, sometimes being rather penurious, could not afford to equip entire armies with them. That development had to wait until the invention of the Miquelet lock.

The Miquelet lock was the predecessor of the flintlock, and lacking grace, most of the working parts were located on the outside of the firearm. This development transpired in the mid-1500s, which for firearms was rather rapid development. In the early 1600s, this lock was improved and became the flintlock, with working parts on the inside of the lock, a waterproof cover over the priming compound, and a real trigger and hammer, allowing for excellent aiming capabilities. Things stayed for quite a while at this point in development.

It wasn't until 1807 that a Scottish minister by the name of Alexander Forsyth developed a compound that exploded when struck. His fulminating compounds were the basis of a revolution in firearms, for they were to provide the power to ignite the powder charge, rather than having to wait until an arbitrary mechanical device provided a spark. This is the beginning of the percussion system.

The first firearms using his invention were pill locks, so called because the fulminate was ground and made into small pellets, and a pellet holder held those pellets until you were ready to use them. You then lowered it onto a small anvil, got everything out of the way, and let the hammer fly, which crushed the pellet, exploding it and sending fire into the powder chamber, igniting the main charge. This was an excellent system so long as you did not turn the firearm one way or the other and let the pellets slip off the anvil.

In order to prevent the pellets from slipping off the anvil, around 1814 someone dreamed up the idea of placing the fulminating chemicals inside a small metal cap. To make it waterproof, a small bit of foil was placed underneath it and sealed with shellac. That cap then fit over a projecting tube, with a hole in the center leading to the powder chamber, and when struck by a hammer, it went off! This was an incredibly efficient system. Not only could you use it in all weather, but you could tilt the firearm in any manner you chose, and because of the interference fit over the tube, the cap would not fall off. The only problem with this system was that it was slow. You had to stop what you were doing and pick up a cap and put the cap in place, and so inventors had a field day trying to devise methods to place fulminating charges over these tubes in rapid succession without having to do it manually.

First there came tape primers, which looked like modern-day children's caps that they put in cap guns. This was invented in 1845 and, being paper, was susceptible not only to damage from humidity but also to jamming. In 1852, Christian Sharps invented disk primers that were thrown forward by the action of the hammer itself. Being made of copper, they were not affected by moisture. However, they did not always get thrown forward, and once again, as you may have noticed, we went through almost the entire 1800s without a major development or change from the percussion system, but the inventors were trying.

The first thing that everyone tried to do was get a self-contained charge; that is, try to avoid having to first pour powder down a long tube (the barrel), then stuff wadding material in, followed by stuffing a projectile in, and possibly more wadding material to prevent the projectile from rolling out, then having to stop what you were doing and prime the whole thing so that you could fire it. After this entire drill, you were ready to take aim at your target, which was supposedly rushing at you at great speed!

The first idea that came along for a self-contained cartridge was something called a *volcanic*. In this system you had a hollowed-out bullet, loaded from the rear, which contained not only the powder charge, but also the fulminating compound at its base. When struck by a firing pin, the entire assembly went flying down the barrel. Unfortunately, like most of these early breech loaders, there was nothing to seal the gas within the breech, and even with the finest machining available eventually erosion took place, gas started to escape, and the arm became dangerous.

The breakthrough finally came when the rimfire cartridge was developed. It consisted of a thin, metal tube with folds at the rear that not only held it in place in the chamber, but also were lined with fulminating powder, so that wherever the rim was crushed, it would detonate the powder, igniting the main charge. Not only was this an efficient way to carry the entire charge and bullet and a way to ignite it, it also had the secondary feature of being able to provide a gas seal at the breech of the weapon, holding the expanding gasses in check, preventing erosion and escaping of gas through the breech and allowing the bullet to travel on its way expeditiously.

For a time, from the mid-1800s through the turn of the century, inventors had a field day! In rapid succession, after the rimfire cartridge was developed, in order to get around its patents, came the annular rim cartridge, which was very similar except that the rim containing the fulminate was one-third of the way up the base of the cartridge toward the waist. Then came lipfire, in which a small tab of fulminating compound was sticking up at the base of the cartridge, rather than an entire rim; teatfire, in which a small projection out of the rear of an otherwise rounded based cartridge held the fulminate, a cup primer that had a hollowed out or concave base and the walls of the concave cavity contained the fulminate; a pinfire cartridge, which was a cartridge that had a pin sticking out the side of the case, and when the pin was hit by the hammer, it would hit a primer located on the inside of the case with just a small bulbous area sticking out; and finally the centerfire cartridge, starting with the Martin, which had a primer wrapped around the center of the base of the cartridge. The first modern development was the reloadable-type centerfire with what essentially is a percussion cap stuck into the base of the cartridge. Only this cartridge style and the rimfire have withstood the test of time.

The firearms employing these cartridges were extremely diverse, and in development we saw more changes from the third quarter of the 1800s to the second quarter of the 1900s than all the previous times since the 1300s, when firearms had been invented. If the development of ammunition that was capable of being rapidly reloaded provided the means by which this development took place, then it still must be remembered that the real pressure came from the military looking for a firearm that was either rapidly loadable, or repeatable, in order to have greater mass fire. As early as the 16th century in Nuremburg, Germany, multi-shot firearms were being developed, with the first revolver being invented around 1600. An interesting aside is that in the British Royal United Service Museum in Whitehall there is a six-shot, 50-caliber Snaphaunce revolver which had been made in Holland. On one of his voyages to England as a sailor, Sam Colt may have seen this particular weapon, because the rotation system on it is identical to his 1836 revolver patent.

Because of the lack of sophisticated machinery, the most popular method of achieving multiple fire was through multiple barrels. Around 1800, flintlock handguns with multiple barrels known as *pepper boxes* started to come on the market. This development was followed in slow succession by pistols with superimposed charges—that is, a person would load the pistol in the conventional manner, put the wadding over the projectile, and then start putting more powder in, followed by another projectile, possibly followed by more powder, followed by another projectile, and the lock was sliding. It pushed to the forward position where the vent hole ignited the first powder charge, hopefully not disturbing the powder charges behind it. As you slid the lock backward, you would ignite each powder charge in succession, still hopefully not igniting them all at once!

The fast changes began with the percussion locks. First, of course, all of the systems developed in the flintlock were continued, the repetitive chamberings and the pepper boxes being prime examples, as well as the multiple-barrel pistols. The great development, however, was still Samuel Colt's marketing genius with his revolver. Colt was a genius, not as a mechanic and inventor, but rather as a developer of a complete marketing system as well as modern manufacturing techniques for firearms. He enhanced Eli Whitney's ideas for interchanging parts by adding modern production methods well before any of his competitors. His true fame can be said to be drawn to his ability to attract expert mechanics and designers as well as his penchant for publicity. As far as revolvers went, for almost half a century Colt led the way. His real competition came at the hands of Smith & Wesson and their breech-loading revolver, based on the Rollin White patent.

Smith & Wesson achieved a lock on the design whereby a self-contained cartridge was inserted from the rear of the cylinder and then fired singly by rotating the cylinder and bringing it in line with the barrel and the hammer. At the time Colt's entire production was based on percussion arms. Sensing the possible market for the cartridge firearm, most arms manufacturers scrambled to try to meet the demand and overcome the Rollin White patents by inventing all sorts of cartridges; hence the rapid development in cartridges. The fact that they are not still with us stems from the fact that they were merely stopgaps, something by which a manufacturer could put a firearm on the market and say, "I'm using the metallic cartridge," and still not be in violation of Smith & Wesson's Rollin White patent. But when that patent expired in the late 1860s, the rush was on. It seemed that overnight, everyone started making revolvers, from the cheap, so-called *Saturday Night Specials*, which sold for 50¢ or $1.00 and had all sorts of fanciful names such as "Bonanza," and "Big Bang," all the way up to the finer makers, including Colt in 1870.

But still the search was on for something faster than a revolver. After all, with a revolver, even with double action, you had to pull the trigger for each shot, which manually rotated the cylinder containing the cartridge and required a great deal of force, which could throw off your aim in a rapid-fire action. And loading was still slow; you had to load each chamber, one at a time. So inventors started turning their sights to yet faster methods of loading and firing a handgun. Pioneers in this work, starting in about 1870, were inventors such as Plesner, Lutze, and Paulson who were all trying to invent semiautomatic revolvers. About thirty years later, the groundwork that they would lay down resulted in the development of the Webley-Fosberry automatic revolver. The true semiautomatic pistols were not developed until the 1890s by such pioneers as Dormus, Schonberger, Cromer, Schwarzlose, Cherola, and Bittner. Finally, the factories of Bergmann and Mauser came out with semiautomatic pistols that could be mass marketed and even found military use. Toward 1900 these were followed in quick succession by pistols designed by Krnka, Borchardt, Mannlicher, Luger, and Browning.

Between 1898 and 1910 an immense variety of automatic pistols appeared on the market, many using extremely complex actions of possibly extremely heavy cartridges and therefore not successful. By the end of World War I, the reliable designs had sorted themselves out, and it is from these few designs, primarily the Browning-based designs, that all of today's automatic pistols stem.

In looking at firearms from the period of 1914 until today, aside from cosmetic differences, there have been very few new developments. We are once again at that point of history where we were in the 1600s with the flintlocks. The next great development in firearms is going to have to be radical, but no one seems to know what it will be. And it is important for us, as current-day observers, not to confuse minor design changes in a single type of action with the sweeping type of change that would occur when the entire action is updated, such as when it went from flintlock to percussion or from percussion to cartridge. We do know partially what the future holds in store. We do know that material advances are going to occur; we now have firearms made out of lightweight, high-strength and nonmetallic materials. Will the next great step be toward lasers or particle beam weapons? I don't know. But it sure will be interesting to find out!

HANDGUN DESIGNERS AND INVENTORS

All too often when we hold a common object that we are used to in our hands, we forget who invented it . . . what genius of strange inclination put together this mechanical marvel. Very few people remember who invented objects that we utilize in everyday existence, much less those objects of beauty and design that we are enthralled with. This section is dedicated to those historical arms makers who led the way in the development of modern cartridge handguns.

ADAMS, ROBERT. A partner in the London firm of Dean, Adams and Dean, in 1851 Robert Adams patented the first double-action revolver. Even though this was a percussion revolver, the design was recognized by many to be so advanced that it wasn't long before virtually every nation that used a revolver in the military had to have a double-action revolver rather than a single-action, which had been used previously. By the 1870s the only nation that used a single-action revolver was America. It was the combination of the Adams patent, the Rollin White patent, and the Colt patent of 1836 that made the modern revolver possible.

ALBINI, AUGUSTO. Born in 1850 in Genoa, Italy, Albini is a little-known genius who is most remembered for being an admiral in the Italian navy and for designing a breech-loading infantry rifle, which, though turned down by the Italians, won an English trial in 1866 and was adopted by Belgium, Bavaria, and Wurttemberg. But in my opinion, his true claim to fame is that in 1869 he patented in Great Britain a swing-out cylindered revolver with simultaneous manual extraction, with the extractor also incorporating a cylinder ratchet. It was a system virtually identical to that used by Colt 20 years later. Albini lived until 1909 but he never did receive the credit for this invention that he should have received.

BERDAN, HIRAM. Though his name is most associated with the Berdan rifle, a very early bolt-action breech loader that was used by the Russians in the 1870s and with a priming system for center-fire cartridges that carries his name, this former Civil War colonel should be best remembered for the fact that he designed the center-fire fixed cartridge with a brass case. First designed in 1865, patents were obtained for this in 1868 and 1869.

BORCHARDT, HUGO. Born in 1850 in Germany, Bochardt immigrated to the United States in about 1865. He was an engineering genius who during his lifetime accumulated a string of patents for his designs, including rock drills, gas burners, ball bearings, as well as repeating and automatic firearms. He is best remembered for designing the pistol on which the Luger is based. During his career he worked for such firms as the Pioneer Breech Loading Arms Company, the Singer Sewing Machine Company, Colt, Sharpes

Rifle Company (where he developed the Sharpes-Borchardt hammerless dropping block rifle), and Winchester, where he designed a revolver with a swing-out cylinder. In 1882 he returned to Europe and joined the Hungarian Femaru Fegyver es Gepgyar. He remained with them until around 1890. In 1892 he joined the German firm of Ludwig Loewe and Company (that firm later became D.W.M.) Borchardt died in 1921.

BROWNING, JOHN MOSES. This genius could almost be called the father of the automatic weapon. Born in 1855 in Ogden, Utah, of a gunsmithing family, Browning became one of the most prolific and successful arms inventors of all time. He designed every style of weapon from breech loaders to heavy machine guns. His arms are made by such firms as Fabrique Nationale, Remington, Winchester, and Colt, and designs that are now 80 years old are still not only considered classic but the epitome of what a firearm should be. There has not been a time since the turn of the century when firearms that he has patented have not been made, nor is there any other inventor in arms history whose work has been relied on by so many other inventors in developing their firearms. His handguns include the simple blowback .25 automatics on up to the venerable Colt 1911 system and Browning High-Power system. He died in 1926 in Liege, Belgium.

COLT, SAMUEL. Born in 1814, Colt is probably the best known handgun manufacturer in history, which is in no small amount due to his great expertise as a showman. Even though there is some dispute as to whether he actually invented the revolving-cylinder, multiple-chambered handgun with a single barrel, or whether he saw it in a museum in London in its flintlock version, there is no disputing that he was the first not only to patent the device but to exploit it to its full market potential. The public acceptance of this principle, coupled with the Adams patent for the double-action revolver and White's patent for the throughbred cylinder to allow rear loading, are the basis on which the modern revolver has been built. And though for the last hundred years the fame of Colt has been built on revolvers such as the single-action "Peacemaker," and the double-action revolvers built on the "Police Positive" design, Colt never lived to see them. He died in 1862.

DERINGER, HENRY. Born in 1789 in Pennsylvania, this gunsmith of German descent is probably best known for his short and concealable single-shot pistol. While he was an excellent mechanic, his greatest claim to fame lies in giving his name to all future generations of small, concealable, non-repeating handguns. Deringer died in 1868, but his fame lives on.

FROMMER, RUDOLF. Born in 1868, Frommer was another of the firearms engineering geniuses. He spent his entire career with the Arms and Machinery Company Ltd., which he joined in 1896, until he retired in 1935. He was a pioneer in the early semiautomatic pistol field, designing all sorts of firearms, primarily using the long recoil system. By the time he died in 1936, Frommer had more than 100 patents issued to him.

KRNKA, KAREL. Born in 1858 of a gun-making family, Krnka became one of the most prolific and important inventors of this century. A great believer in automatic mechanisms and an early proponent of automatic and semiautomatic firearms, some of the devices that he has patented are still being used today, such as double-action triggers for semiautomatic pistols and rotary locking systems. He is perhaps best known for the pistols that he designed for G. Roth Company, such as the Roth-Steyr pistol, and later, for his designs for Ceska Slovenska Zerogovka (C.Z.). He died in Prague in 1926.

LUGER, GEORG. Though never known as a really great firearms inventor, Luger, born in 1849, has his name permanently etched in the minds of all firearms enthusiasts and is perhaps even more widely known than any other firearms figures other than Winchester and Colt. His great claim to fame lies not in the redesign of the Borchardt pistol to make it lighter and more manageable, and more applicable to military use, but rather in the invention of the 9mm Parabellum cartridge, which appears to be the ultimate as far as maximum power and lightness of cartridge are concerned. Luger died in 1923.

MANNLICHER, FERDINAND RITTER VON. Born in 1848, Mannlicher was another of a generation of arms geniuses and has succeeded in bringing the world away from percussion and into cartridge firearms of modern type. From the 1880s until he died in 1904, Mannlicher designed a series of semiautomatic weapons. His most profound influence on modern firearms, however, lies in his magazines, many styles of which are still being used.

MARGOLIN, MICHAEL. Margolin is a Russian designer who specializes in international-style target pistols. An amazing thing about this man is that he has been blind since 1923, and he has to build his prototype models by touch.

MAUSER, PETER PAUL. Born in 1838, Mauser became perhaps one of the most influential designers of the early part of this century. Though best known for his rifle designs, he and his brother Wilhelm also designed the famous Mauser Zig-Zag revolver. After Wilhelm's death in 1882, Paul Mauser continued to run the factory and continued to invent new systems of weapons. In the handgun field, he is best known for the C-1896 pistol, which through the years has become known to us as the "Broom Handle," or the "Bolo Mauser." Mauser died in 1914.

MYSKA, FRANTISEK. Myska is another inventor whose pistols are widely known and highly regarded but whose name nobody recognizes. Probably the major reason for this in Myska's case is the fact that his entire career has been spent with either the Praga Arms Factory, the Skoda Works, or with Ceska Zbrojovka, all in Czechoslovakia. Among his designs are the Nickl style pistols, best known as the CZ-24 and CZ-27s, as well as a wide range of .25 automatic pistols, such as the CZ-36 and the CZ-45. Another military pistol of his was the VZ-38.

NAGANT, EMILE, AND NAGANT, LEON. These gentlemen were the Nagants of the company Nagant Freres. Together, these brothers invented and marketed a revolver system utilizing a gas seal cylinder, in which at full-cock position the cylinder was actually pushed forward against the barrel, and the cartridge case, which extended slightly outward from the cylinder and beyond the nose of the bullet, actually sealed the space in between the rear end of the barrel and the forward face of the cylinder, thus allowing for greater velocities in the revolver cartridge. Even though there were copies of the Nagant revolver made, this was the only revolver that was ever truly successful as a gas seal, and although it was adopted by Norway, Sweden, Luxemburg, and Belgium as a military revolver, it is probably best known for its service in the Russian army.

NECAS, AUGUSTIN. Necas is another Czechoslovakian arms designer who specializes in target pistols and revolvers.

PIEPER, NICOLAS. Nicholas Pieper was one of the early manufacturers of both revolvers and semiautomatic pistols. Inheriting the very successful firm of Ancienes Etablissements Pieper from his father, Henry Pieper (Henry Pieper was also a well-known firearms designer), Nicolas continued the family tradition. Many of his early designs for automatic pistols, though, were not produced by his own company; rather they were produced by Waffen Fabrik Steyr in Austria. Nicolas Pieper should probably be best remembered for the very wide range of handguns that he not only invented but also manufactured.

SANFORD, HARRY. The father of the Auto Mag pistol, Harry Sanford was another in the very small group of advanced thinkers who created a successful pistol to handle an immensely powerful cartridge safely. Like his predecessors, who invented monsters such as the Mars, Sanford's Auto Mag, even though an extremely reliable and functional pistol, became relegated to becoming a collector's delight, due to the woes of the marketplace.

SCHMEISSER, LOUIS. Born in 1848, Schmeisser's name, sadly, is connected more with his submachine gun than it is with his brilliant automatic pistols. He was one of the first inventors of the semiautomatic handgun in the early 1890s, and much of what we have today is based on his early thoughts. The pistols that he designed were marketed under the names Bergmann and Dreyse. Schmeisser died in 1917.

SCHWARZLOSE, ANDREAS WILHELM. Born in 1867, Schwarzlose is best known for his machine guns, a fact he played on by using a tripod-mounted machine gun as part of his trademark and putting it on the sides of his automatic pistols. In the handgun field, he is probably best remembered for inventing the only *blowforward* pistol that ever worked. That is, instead of a slide reciprocating backward, the barrel moved forward and stripped a new round into the chamber of the magazine on its return. Schwarzlose died in 1936, probably saddened because nobody wished to adopt the blowforward barrel for military use.

STEVENS, JOSHUA. Born in 1814 and trained by Colt's factory, he became famous with a factory of his own called J. Stevens Arms and Tool Company, which by the turn of the century had become one of the largest producers of sporting firearms in the United States. He was best known in the handgun field, with several revolver designs, and his famous single-shot, hinged-barrel pistols. Stevens died in 1907, and his company was later absorbed by Savage Arms.

TOKAREV, FEODOR VASSILEVICH. Born in 1871, Tokarev apprenticed out to become a gunsmith and then went on to become a military armorer. During the 1920s he designed various weapons that would later bear his name, one of the most famous of which was the TT-30 (Tula-Tokarev) pistol, which was adopted by the Soviet army.

TOMISKA, ALOIS. Born in 1867, Tomiska was another of the famous designers who worked at the Ceska Zbrojovka factory during the period between the two world wars. He invented a style of double-action trigger mechanisms for semiautomatic pistols that was later followed through and used in the Walther, Mauser, and Sauer pistols. Tomiska died in 1946.

WHITE, ROLLIN. Born in 1817, Rollin White was one of the great geniuses of firearms design. While his patent of 1855 covered a revolver that could never be a commercial success, one detail of the patent stood out and set him apart from all of the other designers of the day. In his cylinder he called for chambers to be drilled all the way through, from front to back, so that loading of the cartridge could be accomplished from the rear. In those early days when cartridges were almost unknown, this incredible development was not instantly recognized for the great advance that it was. In fact, when White approached Colt to try and sell it to them, they immediately rejected the idea. Daniel Wesson and Horace Smith, however, saw the potential, and during the life of that patent they had a virtual monopoly on what could be termed "modern revolvers." We can credit the existence of the revolver as we know it today to Rollin White, Robert Adams, and Samuel Colt.

LEGAL CLASSIFICATIONS OF FIREARMS

For better or worse, handguns have been classified by federal government legislation into four categories. Collectors can take a look at a firearm, draw a fine line and say, "If it was made before this point it was definitely an antique," or they can say that it is definitely a curio. With other forms of collectibles, one can say that it is a classic, whereas the definition of "antique" is open for debate.

The following are the four definitions of the classification terms used by the Bureau of Alcohol, Tobacco, and Firearms of the Treasury Department.

Antique: Any firearm manufactured in or before 1898, and replicas that do not fire rim-fire or center-fire cartridges readily available in commercial trade. Antiques are exempt from federal regulation.

Modern: Firearms manufactured after 1898, excluding Replica Antiques, and with special regulations for Class III arms.

Curios and Relics: Certain modern firearms that can be sent interstate to licensed collectors.

Class III Arms: This includes machine guns, silencers, short (under 18") shotguns, short (under 16") rifles, modern smooth-bore handguns, and modern arms with a rifled bore diameter greater than .50".

Any firearm may be legally owned, notwithstanding federal regulations and local restrictions. If you are in doubt, contact your local office of the Bureau of Alcohol, Tobacco, and Firearms.

A SPECIAL NOTE ABOUT
THE LEGAL CLASSIFICATIONS

Curios: This is a subdivision of "modern" and pertains to arms that may be sent interstate to licensed collectors. However, there is a great deal of confusion as to what constitutes a "curio." The Bureau of Alcohol, Tobacco, and Firearms issues a yearly list of arms so classified, which is always changing.*

The following is the Treasury Department's guideline to use to determine if your specific firearm is a "curio." To be a curio it must

1. have been manufactured at least 50 years prior to the current date, but not including replicas thereof; or
2. be certified by the curator of a municipal, state, or federal museum that exhibits firearms to be curios or relics of museum interest; or
3. derive a substantial part of its monetary value from the fact that it is novel, rare, bizarre, or from the fact of its association with some historical figure, period, or event.

If you wish to obtain a curio or relic determination on your handgun from the A.T.F., you should submit a letter to the Chief of Firearms Technology Branch, Bureau of Alcohol, Tobacco, and Firearms, Washington, D.C. 20226. Your letter should include a complete physical description of your gun, or ammunition, stating the reasons that you believe that the firearm or ammunition in question merits such classification, and supporting data concerning the firearm or ammunition, including production figures if available and market value.

FACTORS THAT DETERMINE VALUE

DEMAND

Demand is defined as desire for a commodity. Additional to the desire is ability to pay; combined they form what economists call "effective demand." We will assume all demand to be effective demand. Demand is required for an item to have value. No demand equals no value. High demand creates high value. Demand affects value relative to supply, which is covered in the next section.

Attempting to forecast future demand, or any consumer behavior, is an art at best. It is characterized as inconstant, unsteady, fluctuating, and erratic; it is influenced by geographic location, historical association, esthetics, quality,

---

*See *The Official Guide to Gunmarks* from House of Collectibles for more complete information.

transportability, and buyer whim. To emphasize the importance of demand in the value equation, visualize the following situation. During an appraisal of a gun collection, an appraiser explains to the client that a piece of great rarity has little value because "the only thing more rare than the gun is a buyer." Regardless of rarity, without demand, an item will have a low value and be difficult to sell.

SUPPLY

Supply is defined as the quantity of goods available at a given time and place. In the realm of collecting many times supply is referred to as rarity, scarcity, and availability. Supply is the counteracting factor to demand in determining value. Given a set demand, the lower the supply the higher the value.

Supply estimation is more complex than simply researching the quantity manufactured. Some weapons suffer a much higher attrition rate than others. Military weapons produced during a period of war will have a low survival rate, and therefore, be less common than those made during peace time. Again, experience comes into play—knowing the frequency with which a specimen is encountered.

SUPPLY AND DEMAND	VALUE
High Supply / High Demand	Normal Value
Low Supply / High Demand	High Value
High Supply / Low Demand	Low Value
Low Supply / Low Demand	No Market Value

CONDITION

A significant factor in assessing a firearm's worth is, naturally, the shape it is in. Use, abuse, wear, and aging all affect the value of the gun. The degree of this effect is dependent on the amount of damage to it as well as the collectibility of the arm itself. Because of the difficulty of describing the condition of a gun to another person without actually having the firearm present to examine, this has led to several different standardized guidelines, the most prevalently used being the N.R.A. condition guidelines. The N.R.A. guidelines fall into two different sets of standards—one for modern guns, and one for antique guns. Antique, in this case, is the federal definition of having been manufactured in or before 1898.

N.R.A. CONDITION GUIDELINES

This set of standards applies to "modern" firearms as follows:

NEW: Not previously sold at retail, and in the same condition as current factory production.

NEW-DISCONTINUED: Same as new, but discontinued model.

The following definitions will apply to all secondhand articles:

PERFECT: In new condition in every respect.

EXCELLENT: New condition, used but little, no noticeable marring of wood or metal, bluing perfect (except at muzzle or sharp edges).

VERY GOOD: In perfect working condition, no appreciable wear on working surfaces, no corrosion or pitting, only minor surface dents or scratches.

GOOD: In safe working condition, minor wear on working surfaces, no broken parts, no corrosion or pitting that will interfere with proper functioning.

FAIR: In safe working condition but well worn, perhaps requiring replacement of minor parts or adjustments, which should be indicated in advertisement, no rust but may have corrosion pits that do not render article unsafe or inoperable.

Another set of standards applies to "antique" arms as follows:

FACTORY NEW: 100% original finish and parts, everything perfect.

EXCELLENT: All parts and 80%–100% finish original; all letters, numerals, designs sharp; unmarred wood, fine bore.

FINE: All parts and over 30% finish original; all letters, numerals, designs sharp; only minor wood marks, good bore.

VERY GOOD: Up to 30% original finish, all original parts; metal surfaces smooth, with all edges sharp; clear letters, numerals, designs, wood slightly scratched or bruised; bore on collector items disregarded.

GOOD: Only minor replacement parts; metal smoothly rusted or lightly pitted in places; cleaned or reblued; principal letters, numerals, designs legible; wood refinished, scratched, bruised, or with minor cracks repaired; mechanism in good working order.

FAIR: Some major parts replaced; minor replacements; metal may be lightly pitted all over, vigorously cleaned or reblued; edges partly rounded; wood scratched, bruised, cracked or repaired; mechanism in working order.

Another set of standards has sometimes been used with handguns, established by collectors and dealers selling handguns. Using their system, you would first figure the surface area of the firearm and then with tracings, the exact surface area of wear or blemishes on your particular handgun. From that you would determine an exact percentage scale. However, this system leaves open to the describer such information as refinishing or replacement of major parts, and only comments on percentage of blue or finish remaining. The most accurate description of condition would be the combination of the N.R.A. and N.A.P.C.A. guidelines.

INVESTMENT OPPORTUNITIES

The best bets in handguns have always been the highly embellished top-of-the-line handguns from major manufacturers. Not only are handguns with beautiful engraving and ornate gold inlay work a delight to look at, but they will always be very rare. These are virtually always special-order guns made by the factory for a particular individual; and a sad fact of life is that few of us can afford to have this type of work done, or if we can afford it, we will probably procrastinate and not order it until after the model is out of production, and then we have missed the boat. The best buy would be ornately decorated arms of the type that are not ordinarily suited for being high grade. An example of this would be pistols that are thought to be strictly for combat use.

At the other end of the spectrum, a great hedge against inflation has been found by collectors who purchase arms with low serial numbers from new gun companies that might have novel designs or unique ideas. If the marketing experiment works, then you own a low-serial-number firearm, which is collectible. If it does not go over, then you own a scarce, limited-production firearm. Always look for nonstandard calibers, special sights, and special markings whenever you are buying firearms of this type for investment.

HOW TO BUY AND SELL HANDGUNS

BUYING COLLECTIBLE HANDGUNS

Where to buy

It is estimated, depending on the source, that there are somewhere between 50 and 100 million handguns in private hands in the United States. It sounds like an enormous amount, but you have probably picked out the special kind of handguns that you wish to collect, and in looking for them, you have noticed that you can't find them anywhere. So where do you go to get them? There are several sources.

Mail Order. Even though federal law prohibits the mailing of firearms to individuals, the mail order gun business is alive and doing very well.

However, the method of doing business is a little bit different because of the current laws and the nature of the firearms business. According to federal law, only licensed gun dealers may ship and receive modern firearms. But many dealers, for a very small fee, will be happy to receive the gun you ordered and transfer it to you. Another alternative for the collector is to get a federal collector's license from the Bureau of Alcohol, Tobacco and Firearms. This license allows you to receive and send interstate shipments and modern firearms that are classified as curios or relics to another firearms licensee. For more information about licenses, contact your local office of the B.A.T.F.

If you follow the few rules, mail order is legal and fairly simple. But most important, it is an excellent way to build your collection and take advantage of prices that may be more competitive outside your local area. Most specialist mail order dealers are very reputable, and they offer an inspection period so that you may return the gun in the same condition as it arrived if you're not satisfied. Almost all of the dealers of collectible guns advertise, and many have regular lists of handguns offered for sale, and you can subscribe to these lists at a nominal rate. Many gun magazines and collector newsletters have classified sections that provide excellent leads.

Gun Shows. There are gun shows held in all parts of the United States with great frequency. They provide a good opportunity to examine large numbers of collectible firearms, all at one place, and a chance to compare them with others of the same type to examine them for possible defects and flaws, and to recognize quality. A gun show also provides a chance to bargain with the owners of the guns for a better price.

Gun Shops. Gun shops and pawn shops offer an exciting chance to find a collector's item at an excellent price because they may not have a market to sell some of the more interesting items. As a result they sometimes buy very low and sell very low in order to turn their inventory.

Private Individuals. This category includes stores that don't normally sell guns, as well as individuals, and this is the area where real caution has to be exercised. Although bargains may be found, many times people have an inflated idea of the value of their handgun, and very often the article for sale is misidentified, as well as misgraded. Remember, knowledge is power!

What to look for

Refinished Guns. A refinished gun can be beautiful. Unfortunately, it also drastically reduces the value of a collector's item, so it's valuable to know how to do spot refinishing. Most of the time when a gun is reblued or replated it must be heavily polished to remove small pits. A good craftsman will keep all of the edges sharp, will try to preserve the lettering, and will try to avoid a "ripple" effect, that is, waves polished into the gun in places where the metal should be dead flat. Poor craftsmen will grind off the lettering, round the edges, and in general remove too much metal. The finish on a good job will be even and bright; on a poor job it will look splotchy and uneven. If you suspect that a gun has been refinished, look for these signs: the lettering will have "drag-out marks" (one edge of the letter will be furrowed from polishing); the quality of finish doesn't match the original factory job; some parts may have been finished to a different color than original factory. Remember, most factories did an excellent job of finishing.

Upgrades. Upgrading means to take a normal gun that is in fairly good condition and engraving or otherwise embellishing it so that it is more valuable. In many cases a good upgrade comes within 60% to 70% of the value of the factory original if the job is done very well. But beware of guns that people try to pass off as original. The best defense is education. If you're interested in a high-grade gun, try to examine as many known factory originals as you can to get a feel for the factory's style and quality, or enlist the aid of an expert to help you.

Fakes. It seems that counterfeits have always been with us, and as with many items of value, low-cost reproductions have been made and passed along as the real thing. There are all kinds of reproductions, from the crude kitchen table conversion with the uneven lettering stamps to the ultra-sophisticated copy made with some original parts. Fakes include complete reproductions of antique guns down to ⅛″ police stamps on World War II German pistols. Once again, knowledge is power. Learn all you can before buying, and on valuable items, buy from someone that you can trust. Most dealers of collectible guns are honest.

Condition Descriptions. The N.R.A. guidelines should always be used by dealers and collectors when describing their guns. Many times there will be descriptions such as "95% blue" or "near mint," which, while they sound good, sometimes mask a multitude of problems. Remember, just because somebody uses either vague descriptions or their own grading system does not necessarily mean that they're trying to hide something. Sometimes dealers get entrenched in their ways. It does pay to ask a few questions to make sure that everything is functioning as it should and that all the parts are there. Accurate percentage descriptions are an acquired skill and when used in conjunction with the N.R.A. description can give an accurate picture, but be sure that you have complete information.

SELLING COLLECTIBLE HANDGUNS

Just as important as buying is the ability to sell what you have, and there are many ways to do this. The primary consideration when you want to sell your firearms is how fast you want to turn them over and how much you want for them. The two are not necessarily mutually exclusive, but usually if you want the top price, you have to compete with the dealer and that takes time. Always remember the choice of what you are willing to take for them is yours and will be based on your own abilities of salesmanship.

Where to sell

Gun Stores. Your local gun dealer generally cannot pay you a top price on a collectible gun unless he has a good market for it. Even then he must make a profit. But this is a good place to sell your handguns quickly.

Specialists and Mail Order Dealers. Many times these people will pay a somewhat higher price and work on a slimmer margin because they have a built-up customer list gathered over years, and they may have a guaranteed resale on your gun.

Your Own Ad. This may be the way to get the most for your firearms, but it also takes the longest and requires the cooperation of a gun licensee for shipping. There is usually a four- to eight-week time lag between the time you place the ad and the time it is in print and the publication is distributed. Additionally, you also have the cost of the ad to consider as well as the cost of packaging and shipping.

Gun Shows. This can provide not only a place to sell your guns but a great meeting ground for fellow collectors. Of course, here again your salesmanship is of prime importance to get your best price, but you will get to meet people with similar interests who may be very interested in buying what you have.

Auctions. This is the most uncertain venture of all. In an unreserved auction the highest bid wins, and if there is a bad crowd, your guns could go for very little; and to add insult to injury you will have to pay a commission. In a reserved auction you are allowed to set a reasonable bottom figure, and if the firearm does not reach that amount, you will get it back. However, you will generally have to pay a small commission to have it returned on reserve. But the other side of the coin is that people sometimes get carried away at an auction, and many times firearms fetch a much higher price than what is expected. With auctions you have to be lucky.

IDENTIFYING FIREARMS

There are several points to look for when trying to figure out just who made the gun that you are holding in your hand. The most basic, of course, is if the manufacturer in question actually stamped the gun to identify that he made it, and virtually all guns do fall into this category. Unfortunately for the collector, there are always those guns that either are trade labeled or, if they were made before World War II, may not even have makers' names on them. When such items are encountered, there are several approaches, the first being to follow all the class characteristics and try to find a photograph of something that resembles your gun. This can be an extremely tedious procedure, especially when there may be hundreds if not thousands of firearms that fall into your classification. Therefore, the best starting point is to first examine any markings that may be found on the gun. Now there are several types of marks to be found on firearms, the most regulated among them being proof marks. Many countries, with the amazing exception of the United States, require that all firearms be proofed; that is, that they be fired with overload charges to make sure that they do not blow up. In the United States, proof is left to the individual manufacturer, and in many cases, that manufacturer not only proofs that gun but has his own private stamp to show it. Other markings that may be found to help pinpoint your firearm are the marks put on by the manufacturers themselves or the ultimate end seller. These fall into three categories. First is trade names. These were devised not only to draw distinctions between guns made by the same firm but also to assist in advertising and promotion for the manufacturer. Second is the practice of contract manufacturing, whereby guns are made for large retailers under contract agreement with one or more gun makers. For example, Western Field Firearms were sold by Montgomery Ward but actually made by subcontractors. And third is the fact that sometimes distributors and retailers mark guns that were sold through them, even though the guns were not made directly under contract for them or by them.

Besides the name identification, other marks that will be found on guns are trademarks, a distinctive symbol, usually pictoral but sometimes monogramic, either by the manufacturer or by the end seller; importer's mark, which is required by some countries; serial number, which is required by virtually all countries; and on military articles, code numbers of sometimes regimental names. While this book encompasses descriptions of many marks found on guns, a companion volume entitled *The Official Guide to Gunmarks*, also by Robert H. Balderson, is the best source for this type of identification.

Once a firearm is determined to be of a certain type or manufacture, then it is best to go and find a description of that arm, broken down by manufacturer and then by class characteristics; that is, whether it is a pistol or a revolver, if it is single action, double action, etc., and what type of finish it came with. An excellent book for this purpose, describing well over 30,000 firearms, is *The Official Price Guide to Antique and Modern Firearms*, by Robert H. Balderson, also published by House of Collectibles. In it, all firearms are first listed by manufacturer and then broken down by class characteristics and model. For easy reference, there is an index further breaking down each firearm by each type of class characteristic.

LIMITED EDITION HANDGUNS

This category of collectible handguns can be subdivided into several major categories: commemoratives, special purpose, or short production. Virtually all popular firearm companies at one point or another have made weapons that fall into one of these three categories. The primary consideration in judging a weapon of this type is that all deviations from the standard firearm be factory original.

COMMEMORATIVES

The start of the commemoratives firearms craze can be accurately traced to two models of gun, both made by Colt. The first is the Sheriff's Model Single Action Army, made in 1961, which, although most collectors list it as a commemorative, is more accurately defined as a short production gun. However, for the interests of brevity, we will continue to list it as a commemorative. The other gun, and the one that most popularized collecting commemoratives and made the firearm companies aware that there could be a vast market for the commemoratives, was the Geneseo Anniversary Colt Derringer, which was commissioned by Cherry's Sporting Goods, a company later to become famous as *the* expert dealers of commemorative firearms.

In the years since 1961, literally millions of commemorative firearms have been issued. They range anywhere from editions of 50 guns, highly embellished and custom made by the factory, costing thousands of dollars each, on down to standard production guns with possibly an extra digit on the serial number or an extra stamp on the side of the barrel. If you are considering getting into a commemorative collecting field, a very important question you should ask yourself is, is this firearm something special? Did the factory actually make something special, in limited production and completely different in style and embellishment from the standard weapon? If so, then you have a commemorative that will rise in value, probably showing the most marked appreciation within the first two to three years and then leveling off to a little bit better than the inflation rate. If the firearm, a special edition, has just a token extra stamp or perhaps a different finish, and was pretty well mass-produced, then appreciation on it would be quite slow, with the possibility that its actual market value might take some time before it reaches the suggested retail price. The best way to maintain the value of your commemorative is to keep it wrapped in factory packaging and keep it in new condition with all papers and accessories. Shooting your firearm, and the subsequent wear involved, will drastically affect the price.

SPECIAL PURPOSE MARKINGS

Various levels of government agencies and law enforcement groups, as well as stores, have ordered factories to put special markings on guns. If you wish to collect guns in this subcategory, you should first look for firearms that are already collectible, with the best bets being rare markings on already very scarce guns. However, caution is very advisable, since this particular market is quite limited and highly specialized. Remember, with rare items, when you get out of your depth, it is always best to consult an expert in the field. Police or agency markings, in lieu of regular marks (not overstamps or extra stamps added), can add 30% to 50% to the price of your gun. Likewise, trademarks of stores in exotic locales might add 50% or more to the price of your gun. Scarce foreign military stampings should add another 50%. The absence of stamps, upside-down stamps, and improper markings add value to firearms as well as to postage stamps, and could more than double the price of the gun, depending on the collectibility of the firearm itself. At times, governmental groups, especially law enforcement agencies, will order firearms from the factory with special features. This might be anything from special grips to perhaps cutouts of the trigger guard or special sights. Firearms in this category should bring an extra 50% to 100% over the standard model.

SHORT PRODUCTION

Arms in this category should be unique models unto themselves, rather than just a simple adaptation of a standard model; for instance, the Colt Camp Perry Model Target Pistol, which even though based on the Officer's Model Match frame, was quite unique from it. On the other side of the coin, the Colt Model .357 was simply the predecessor of the Colt Trooper, and all that was involved was a name change. Remember that the older a firearm is, the greater the production quantity that collectors will allow and still call the firearm short production. The primary factor in judging this is survival rate. An example of this would be the PAF Junior Pistol; although as many as 10,000 may have been made, only 2,000 to 3,000 probably now exist. Arms in this category will probably appreciate at a faster rate than other limited editions, as long as the arm itself was well made and is collectible.

RESTORING AND REFINISHING HANDGUNS

All collector handguns should be preserved in original condition, at least until evaluated by an expert. Firearms, unlike collectible automobiles and furniture, are *not* improved by restoration; in fact all collector value may be lost and the gun will reduce to its utility value. To the gun collector what counts is originality, not always beauty.

Always be careful to differentiate between restoration and refinishing. In firearms, restoration means that any imperfections present on a firearm are eradicated, and the entire arm is brought back to original factory finish, including all accessories. Refinishing means that the arm is merely cleaned up, and either reblued or replated, or that the finish is changed; that is, a blued gun may be nickled. In restoration, any pitting that is present on the firearm must be filled and then ground down and polished, with the polishing marks exactly duplicating the factory job. On refinishing, any pitting that is present may be ground down and then polished with no respect for where the original surface of the metal was. The primary objective is that the arm just looks good.

RESTORATION

Metalwork

While actual finishing is best left to an expert, there are many things that you can do to restore your gun. The greatest enemy of firearms is rust, which is an iron oxide and spreads like cancer. And yet rust removal is fairly simple to accomplish; it only takes patience. First, disassemble your firearm, making sure that it is unloaded. Put the parts in a bin and soak them for at least two to three days in either kerosene or in a rust-removing oil such as JB-BO. Under no circumstances use rust removers that are commercially available, such as the trade-name product Naval-Jelly. Such chemicals, rather than just removing rust, will also etch the metal, ruining your gun. After the parts have soaked for a sufficient length of time, you will notice that the rust has been softened and loosened from the surface. At this point, take either very fine steel wool, 000 or 0000, or a thin wire steel carding brush, which resembles a steel toothbrush, and gently wipe the rust away. After carding, wipe down all metal parts with rags and return the parts to a fresh solution of rust-removing oil. After waiting another several days, repeat the process, and then clean thoroughly. By this time all of the rust should be removed, and many times the arm is in sufficiently good condition so as not to warrant further finish restoration.

Burred metal

Many times, on old firearms, people have used screwdrivers that did not fit the screw slots, and in doing so, the screw was fairly well torn up and jagged pieces of metal left protruding to catch on everything. But before getting out your file and getting rid of the jagged edges, remember that the screw was soft enough for the metal to burr in the first place. So after setting the screw in a vise and utilizing a clean, polished ended pin punch, very gently tap the offending edges until they are level again with the head of the screw. This will generally push the metal down and close up your slot slightly. Then take a very thin pillar file or screw slot file, and open that slot up again. You will then have a very clean-looking screw rather than one that looks as if it was butchered.

Missing parts

This is a rather ticklish question. Many times it is quite simple to pick up a fairly rare firearm at a ridiculously low price simply because it is missing *one* or *two* parts. However, the seller knows full well that the reason he is getting rid of the piece is that he cannot find those one or two parts. This is where some real detective work sometimes pays off. There are a few specialist part dealers in the United States.

Wood and grips

It is not uncommon for grips to be cracked or even for small pieces to be missing. Both conditions can be repaired. Broken grips, where all pieces are present, can be joined. On porous grips, such as wood, use epoxy cements to bond them together. On nonporous grips, such as plastic or hard rubber, use alphasyano-acrilate. It sells under trade names such as Eastman 910 or Superglue. When chips are missing, take some epoxy glue and grind up a similar compound, mixing it in so that you get a matching color. You can then spread it on the offending surface, sand it down, and use a small checkering tool or engraving tool to match the contour on the checkering lines. When properly done, this type of repair is virtually invisible. Wood grips sometimes have deep dents in them. Rather than file the entire grip down to match the contour of the newly formed dent, instead take a small sewing needle and punch small holes throughout the dent. Moisten a patch, warm an iron, and touch the iron to the patch, releasing steam into the area of the dent. Repeat this four or five times, and the dent will rise back up to the former surface. The grip can then be lightly sanded, and a small amount of finishing oil can be put on to restore the finish.

Refinishing

Many aspects of refinishing can be carried out by the home gunsmith. For metalwork, some of the new cold blues are particularly effective, and while not matching the darkness or the depth of the color provided by hot blues done professionally, they do a very good job if used properly. When cold-bluing a gun, make sure that all metal surfaces are absolutely clean. The normal steps to take are:

1. Polish. This can be accomplished by using various grits of wet or dry sandpaper and going all the way down to 600 grit in incremental steps. For instance, if there is light pitting and you start with 220 grit, then go the route of 320, 400, then 600. Every time you make a pass with the sandpaper, use a slightly different direction when you change grits. For instance, if you are rubbing straight with the 220, then when you use the 320, go at about a 45-degree angle. Whenever possible, always use a backing surface on the sandpaper to assure flat edges.

2. Clean. At the end of sanding and polishing, or when you have reached 600 grit, then thoroughly clean the metal with alcohol or another similar degreaser. Remember, after you clean with alcohol or the other degreaser, *do not touch the metal again with your bare hands.* Your skin contains oils that will inhibit the effect of the cold blues.

3. Applying blue. Many of the commercially prepared cold blues work more efficiently on warm metal. Therefore, it is sometimes wise to warm your metal parts under hot running water before applying the cold blue. As long as you do not leave those bare pieces of metal wet for more than a few minutes at a time, you needn't worry about further rusting. After applying the cold blue and letting it dry according to label directions, card off the remaining bluish-tinted fuzz that develops with a 0000 steel wool.

It sometimes might be necessary to repeat the entire process three or four times in order to achieve the depth of blue that is satisfactory, and after the final rust carding, reclean and oil your gun before reassembling.

Refinishing wood

Wood is similar to metal in that it has to be slightly sanded to achieve a smooth finish. However, unlike metal you need to go down to at most 320 grit. It is especially important on wood that you back the sandpaper with something other than your fingers. The reason for this is wood has varying hardnesses, depending on the direction of the grain and the type of grain involved. Finger pressure behind the sandpaper provides an even pressure on a yielding surface, which means that the softer areas of the wood will be ground more deeply than the harder areas of the wood, and you will have a rippled effect. After sanding, you have a wide variety of finishing choices. Do you want a completely filled, shiny surface, or do you prefer the unfilled look and just having it sealed to protect it against the elements? If your preference is the latter, then stop after the first step, which is to seal the grip in either a sanding sealer or with an oiled finish. Resins recommended for this stage would be either thinned exterior varnish or material such as true oil or linseed. To achieve a high finish, apply thin coats of whatever finishing material you have chosen and allow each coat to dry before applying the next. After about three thin coats, use your fine-grit sandpaper and completely sand down the surface of the wood, not going below the surface. This should fill the grain pores. Apply another three coats and repeat. This time you should have an absolutely even surface with no shininess in any of the pores. Apply two to three more coats, and after the last is thoroughly dried, wipe down with 0000 steel wool, which will smooth the surface and give you what is called a "satin" finish. To achieve a semigloss, use any of the rubbing compounds commercially available. To achieve a high gloss, use the fine furniture polishes or preparations that are widely available, such as Birchwood Casey's Stock Sheen and Conditioner.

INSPECTION FOR FUNCTIONING

There are several things that everyone who uses a handgun should know how to do. Besides knowing proper safety procedures, know how to inspect your firearm to make sure that it is functioning properly.

Revolvers. Timing is crucial to safe operation on a revolver. This means that as the cylinder rotates, it must index precisely with the barrel at the moment of firing. This is accomplished usually by a pawl turning the cylinder, and on the outside periphery a small locking lug snapping into a notch at the moment of alignment. There are two things that you should do to check the safety of this function. One is to very, very slowly cock the hammer and bring it back to full cock position. At this point, lightly touch the cylinder and see if there is rotation in either direction. If there is, proceed to the next step, and holding the hammer, very lightly pull the trigger until the hammer releases. Again, check the cylinder for rotation in either direction, or for play or slop. Next, either cock the hammer rapidly, or if it is a double-action arm, pull the trigger rapidly once or twice to see if the cylinder rotates beyond the point where it should be caught by the cylinder stop. In the former case, if the cylinder did not rotate far enough to be locked at the moment that the hammer would drop, that is called *undertiming*. If the cylinder went beyond the position where it should have been locked, that is called *overtiming*. Both instances may be unsafe, and the gun should be sent to a gunsmith or the manufacturer for repair.

Another check that you can perform on your revolver is if the cylinder does lock up, is it indexed properly? To perform this test you will need a range rod, usually made from a cleaning rod or even a wooden dowel. Turn the diameter of the plug so that it is just slightly smaller than your bore size, and attach it to the end of your dowel or cleaning rod. Making sure that your gun is unloaded at all times, cock the hammer and pull the trigger, and then slowly move the rod through the bore and into the cylinder. If there is improper alignment on any cylinder location, then the dowel will not be able to move from the bore into the cylinder. In that case, you do not have proper indexing and the arm once again should be repaired.

Should a revolver be actually fired with improper indexing, or out of time, then you get a condition known as *lead shear*. That is, the bullet will be hitting one side of the barrel, and small pieces of lead will be sliced off to fly out in a direction perpendicular to your cylinder. If your gun is sufficiently out of time, it could create a very dangerous situation in which most of the bullet's force is spent on the side of the barrel. On break-top revolvers always check to see whether the latch is sufficiently strong or tight. Look for old repairs, flame cutting from shooting, or any looseness at either the toggle joint or at the catch.

Semiautomatic Pistols. Of great concern here is, will the pistol double? That is, will it fire more than one shot with each pull of the trigger. It is possible for a malfunctioning semiautomatic pistol to empty the entire magazine at the first shot. To check for this, always remembering to make sure, of course, that your gun is unloaded, cycle the slide, pull the trigger, and keeping the trigger pulled, cycle the slide again with your other hand. On this second cycle, pull the slide all the way to the rear and let it go, so that it snaps forward under the impetus of the recoil spring. Then, slowly let the trigger go, and listen for the sound of the disconnector snapping into place. Pull the trigger again, and if the hammer falls, then your disconnector is functioning. This is a test that should be tried several times, and if at any time the hammer has already fallen from the force of the slide closing, then take the gun to your friendly gunsmith to have it examined for proper sear angle, disconnector wear, or proper spring tension. Another common problem with semiautomatic pistols is failure to feed and jamming. This can be caused by several things. A jam on initial cycling—that is, a cartridge coming out of the magazine and being caught between the barrel and the slide, or stovepiping—usually indicates either (1) the magazine lips are bent or (2) the angle of the barrel ramp is improper for the bullet shape of the cartridge you are using. If the jam comes during firing, and it appears that you have a spent cartridge case impinging against the fresh round that is trying to get up into the chamber, then your problem is one of extraction and/or ejection. If your pistol functions well with dummy cartridges and does not function on actual firing, then you probably have a rough chamber, which can be cured by polishing. On all of the cycling problems, unless you have the tools and equipment to cure these ailments and the dangers inherent in grinding and proper angles, this had best be left to your local gunsmith.

GUN CLEANING

There are quite a few things that can go wrong with a handgun. It can start jamming, it can misfire, and it can otherwise malfunction. Virtually every one of these problems can sometimes be traced to a single cause, that being lack of cleaning. By cleaning I do not mean running a patch through the bore making sure that it is shiny. I mean complete disassembly of the entire gun and complete cleaning of every single part. On a weapon that is used, this should be done at least every year or two. On a weapon that is kept stored, it should be done every four to five years. Even with the best of maintenance, your gun should be completely stripped of all old oil. The reason for this is that many of the oils on the market (excluding JB-86[1]) used on firearms will dry to a very hard varnish after a year or so. This acts like a glue and completely freezes some internal working parts. If you do not feel that you are qualified to disassemble your firearm completely, then by all means don't. It is a wise man who knows his own limitations, and in such a case always refer your gun to a professional. In the long run this could be much less expensive as well as much less embarrassing than bringing a bag of parts to your gunsmith and saying, "Here's my gun, can you help me?" In order to remove old dried oil, there are two methods that should be tried after the normal alcohol treatment fails. One is boiling in an oakite solution, or running it under 1,1,1 trichlorolethylene. Remember when using caustic

---

1. Justice Brothers Car Care Products. Available from your local dealer, or write to RB Distributors, 2830 Arden Way, Sacramento, CA 95825.

solutions or aromatic solutions, always follow safety precautions. Normal cleaning will not involve such heavy-duty swabbing.[2] The average cleaning job can be conducted with a few clean rags, cleaning rod or brush, and an old toothbrush. Use such common bore cleaners as Hoppes No. 9 to clean your gun completely.

PISTOL AND REVOLVER CARTRIDGES

2.7mm KOLIBRI AUTO. This is the smallest center-fire cartridge that was ever commercially manufactured. It was used for the miniature Kolibri Semi-Automatic pistol introduced around 1914. The cartridge design was as a rimless, semiautomatic, straight-walled case. It had a muzzle velocity of about 650 f.p.s. with an energy of about three ft./lbs. and fired a 3-gr. bullet.

3mm KOLIBRI. This cartridge is virtually identical to the 2.7mm with the exception that it is slightly larger, bullet diameter being .120″ as opposed to .107″ for the 2.7mm. The cartridge lengths were identical as well as the power.

4mm M-20 UBUNGSMUNITION. This is a reduced load, center-fire cartridge designed for indoor target practice utilizing Lothar Walther adapters in either pistols or revolvers. The case is one piece, resembling a shotgun primer; the projectile is a round, lead ball. It is designed for indoor use, has low noise, and the bullet can be stopped by a small telephone book.

4.25mm LILIPUT AUTO. This is another automatic, straight-walled, rimless cartridge case made for miniature European pistols, the two most popular being the Liliput and the Erika. The muzzle energy on this monster is 17 ft./lbs. with a muzzle velocity of 800 f.p.s. and a bullet weight of about 12 gr.

5mm CLEMENT. This cartridge boasts a bottleneck case and a rimless design, firing a 36-gr. bullet. The muzzle velocity was about 1030 f.p.s. with an energy of about 78 ft./lbs. This cartridge was made for the Charola-Anitua pistol as well as the Clement and was made from about 1904 until just before World War II.

5mm BERGMANN. This is another of the collector series of cartridges made only for a few years primarily for the Bergmann #2 pistol about 1895. It came in two variations, both consisting of straight-tapered, rimless cases. The earliest variation, however, has no extractor groove. It fired a 37-gr. bullet at just under 600 f.p.s. and yielded a muzzle energy of about 28 ft./lbs.

5.5mm VELODOG REVOLVER. From the turn of the century until just before World War II, this was an extremely popular cartridge in Europe, and a wide variety of inexpensive handguns were chambered for it. It is a center-

---

2. Always test any cleaner on a small area first.

fire .22 caliber of a little less power than a 22 long rifle and has a similar shape. It has a straight case and large rim. The European loading consisted of a 45-gr. load bullet with a muzzle velocity of about 650 f.p.s. and an energy of about 40 ft./lbs.

.22 REMINGTON JET. This is a rimmed, tapered neck, center-fire cartridge, which was developed in 1961 for the Smith & Wesson .22 Jet Revolver. The factory loading called for a bullet of 40 gr. with a muzzle velocity of 2460 f.p.s. and a muzzle energy of 535 ft./lbs.

.221 REMINGTON FIREBALL. This is a rimless, necked center-fire cartridge, which was developed in 1963 for the Remington XP-100 Fireball Pistol. In factory loading it fired a 50-gr. bullet, with a muzzle velocity of 2650 f.p.s. and a muzzle energy of 780 ft./lbs.

.25 A.C.P. Also known as the 6.35mm automatic pistol, this cartridge was introduced in about 1906 for the Browning design FN Pocket Pistol. Since that time hundreds of guns have been designed to fire this cartridge. It has a semirimless, straight-walled case, and in factory loading fires a 50-gr. bullet, with a muzzle velocity of about 810 f.p.s. and a muzzle energy of 73 ft./lbs.

.256 WINCHESTER MAGNUM. First marketed in the early 1960s, this cartridge has a rimmed, straight-walled, necked case, fired a 60-gr. bullet, had about 220 f.p.s. with a muzzle energy of 650 ft./lbs.

6.5mm BERGMANN. Developed about 1894, this cartridge is similar to the 5mm Bergmann, in that it is also a rimless, tapered-neck cartridge, and in some variations is made without an extractor groove. It fired a 65-gr. bullet with a muzzle velocity of about 780 f.p.s. and a muzzle energy of about 93 ft./lbs.

7mm NAMBU. Developed for the Baby Nambu Pistol in the early 1920s, this cartridge has a rimless, necked case and fired a 56-gr. bullet at about 1250 f.p.s. with a muzzle energy of 195 ft./lbs.

7.62mm TOKAREV. Developed around 1930 for the Tokarev Model TT-30 and TT-33 pistols, this cartridge has been used throughout the communist world. It is a rimless, necked cartridge with an 87-gr. bullet fired at 1390 f.p.s. with a muzzle energy of 365 ft./lbs.

7.62mm NAGANT REVOLVER. This is an unusual, straight-walled, rimmed cartridge, which was developed in 1895 for use in the Nagant and Pieper revolvers. In factory loading, the 108-gr. bullet is seated completely inside the case mouth, so that the cartridge can move forward and create a gas seal between the cylinder and the valve. The bullet moved at about 725 f.p.s. with an energy of about 125 ft./lbs.

7.63mm MAUSER. Also known as .30 Mauser, this was used in both the Borchardt pistol and the early Mauser Broomhandles. In factory loading it fired an 86-gr. bullet, with about 1400 f.p.s. and a muzzle energy of 375 ft./lbs.

7.65mm BORCHARDT. Also known as the .30 caliber Borchardt, this cartridge was the predecessor of the .30 Mauser and was used in the Borchardt pistol. It fired an 85-gr. bullet, 1280 f.p.s., with a muzzle energy of about 310 ft./lbs.

7.65mm MANNLICHER. Also known as the 7.63mm Mannlicher, this cartridge was developed by Mannlicher for their series of automatic military pistols, the models 1900, 1901, and 1905. It was a straight-walled, rimless cartridge which fired an 85-gr. bullet at about 1025 f.p.s. with a muzzle energy of about 200 ft./lbs.

7.65mm LUGER. Known also as the .30 Luger. This cartridge was developed from the .30 Borchardt for the early Luger pistols. It fires a 93-gr. bullet at 1220 f.p.s. with an energy of 307 ft./lbs.

7.65mm FRENCH. Also called 7.65mm N.A.S. This is a straight-walled, rimless cartridge developed for the Petter pistols, known as the model 1935A and 35S. It fired an 85-gr. bullet at 1120 f.p.s. with an energy of 240 ft./lbs.

7.65mm ROTH-SAUER. This cartridge was developed for the Roth-Sauer pistol around the turn of the century and has a rimless, straight-walled case, and fired a 70-gr. bullet, about 1000 f.p.s., with an energy of about 180 ft./lbs.

.32 A.C.P. Also known as 7.65mm Automatic Pistol. This was another in the series of cartridges developed by John Browning. A straight-walled case with a semirim, this has been a very popular police cartridge in Europe. In factory loading it uses a 71-gr. bullet that travels at 905 f.p.s. with an energy of about 129 ft./lbs.

.32 SMITH & WESSON This straight-walled, rimmed, center-fire cartridge has been with us since the late 1870s. It fires an 85-gr. bullet at 705 f.p.s. with an energy of 97 ft./lbs.

.32 SMITH & WESSON LONG. This cartridge, developed around the turn of the century, is the same as the .32 Smith & Wesson except that the case is .32" longer. It fires a 98-gr. bullet at 780 f.p.s., with an energy of 132 ft./lbs.

.320 REVOLVER. In the United States, this cartridge was known as the .32 Short Colt. It was first used about 1870, and fired an 80-gr. bullet 550 f.p.s., with an energy of about 53 ft./lbs.

.32 LONG COLT. Developed in the mid-1870s, this was essentially the same cartridge as the .32 Short Colt but with a longer case. It fired an 82-gr. bullet at 790 f.p.s. with an energy of about 114 ft./lbs.

.32 WINCHESTER. Also known as the .32-20. This is a center-fire, rimmed, necked cartridge that was first developed in the 1880s for Winchester rifles and then later used in revolvers. It fires a 100-gr. bullet at 1030 f.p.s. with an energy of 271 ft./lbs.

.35 SMITH & WESSON AUTO. Introduced just before World War I on the Clement design, this cartridge fired a 76-gr. bullet at 109 f.p.s. with an energy of about 110 ft./lbs.

7.5mm SWISS ARMY. This straight-walled, rimmed, center-fire cartridge was introduced in 1882. It fires a 102-gr. bullet at about 708 f.p.s. with an energy of about 114 ft./lbs.

7.5mm SWEDISH NAGANT REVOLVER. A rimmed, tapered-wall, straight cartridge, for the Husqvarna 1887 Revolver. This cartridge fired a 104-gr. bullet at about 725 f.p.s. with an energy of about 120 ft./lbs.

8mm NAMBU. A rimless, bottleneck cartridge that was developed just after the turn of the century for the Japanese Military Nambu Pistol. It fired a 102-gr. bullet at about 960 f.p.s. with an energy of about 200 ft./lbs.

8mm LABEL REVOLVER. A center-fire, rimmed, straight-walled cartridge that was developed for the French 1892 Ordnance Revolver. This cartridge fired a 102-gr. bullet at 625 f.p.s. with an energy of about 103 ft./lbs.

8mm ROTH-STEYR. This center-fire, rimless, straight-walled case was developed for the 1907 Roth-Steyr Pistol. It fired a 116-gr. bullet at 1090 f.p.s. with an energy of about 309 ft./lbs.

8mm RAST-GASSER. This straight-wall, rimmed cartridge was developed in the mid-1870s for the Austrian Military Revolver. It fired a 115-gr. bullet at 750 f.p.s. with an energy of about 154 ft./lbs.

9mm GLISENTI. This cartridge was for the Italian Glisenti in Brixia automatic pistols. It fired a 124-gr. bullet at 1050 f.p.s. with an energy of about 309 ft./lbs.

9mm STEYR. Developed for the 1911 and 1912 Steyr pistols, this rimless, straight-walled cartridge fired a 116-gr. bullet at 1250 f.p.s. with an energy of about 370 ft./lbs.

9mm PARABELLUM. Also known as 9mm Luger. Developed as an outgrowth of the Borchardt and first made in 1902 for the Luger pistol, this cartridge has now become the most popular handgun cartridge in the world. It fires a 115-gr. bullet at 1155 f.p.s. with an energy of about 341 ft./lbs.

9mm MAUSER. Made for the export model Mauser Automatic Pistol around the turn of the century. This cartridge fired a 125-gr. bullet at about 1300 f.p.s. with an energy of about 475 ft./lbs.

9mm BROWNING LONG. Developed for the 1903 FN Military Pistol as well as the 1907 Husqvarna Automatic Pistol, this cartridge fired a 110-gr. bullet at 1100 f.p.s. with an energy of about 300 ft./lbs.

9mm BAYARD. First developed for the 1910 Bergmann-Bayard Pistol, this rimless, straight-walled cartridge had a 125-gr. bullet that traveled at 1120 f.p.s. with an energy of about 350 ft./lbs.

9mm MAKAROV. This is a current Russian military cartridge that is used both in the Makarov Pistol and the Stechkin. It is a rimless, straight-walled cartridge that fires a 94-gr. bullet at 1115 f.p.s. with an energy of about 260 ft./lbs.

9mm WINCHESTER MAGNUM. Introduced in 1979 for the Wildey Gas-Operated Magnum Pistol. This cartridge develops 1475 f.p.s. with a 115-gr. bullet, and impacts 556 ft./lbs of energy.

.357 MAGNUM. Developed in 1935 for the Smith & Wesson Model 27 Revolver, this straight-walled, rimmed cartridge has become the most popular police cartridge in the United States. It fires a 158-gr. bullet at 1235 f.p.s. with an energy of 535 ft./lbs.

.380 REVOLVER. Developed in the early 1870s for the Webley Revolver, this straight-walled, center-fire, rimmed cartridge had a 124-gr. bullet that traveled at 625 f.p.s. and had an energy of 110 ft./lbs.

.38 LONG COLT. This was the U.S. Army caliber from 1892 until 1911, when it was superseded because of its lack of stopping power. It is a straight-walled, rimmed case that held a 150-gr. bullet that traveled at 770 f.p.s. with an energy of 195 ft./lbs.

.38 SMITH & WESSON SPECIAL. Also known as .38 Special and .38 Colt Special. A very popular police cartridge, this straight-walled, rimmed case has a 158-gr. bullet that travels at 855 f.p.s. with an energy of 256 ft./lbs.

.38 SMITH & WESSON. Developed in the late 1870s, this straight-walled, rimmed cartridge has a 200-gr. bullet that traveled at 630 f.p.s. with an energy of 176 ft./lbs.

.38 A.C.P. Also known as .38 Colt Automatic, developed about 1900 on the John Browning design, this rimless, straight-walled cartridge used a 130-gr. bullet which travels at 140 f.p.s. with an energy of 312 ft./lbs.

.38 COLT SUPER AUTOMATIC. Developed in the late 1920s, this cartridge uses the same case as the .38 A.C.P. but to a much more powerful loading and should not be used interchangeably. It has a 115-gr. bullet that travels at 1300 f.p.s. with an energy of 431 ft./lbs.

.380 A.C.P. Also known as .380 Automatic and 9mm Kurz. This is a very popular European police cartridge and another in the John Browning series. It fires a 95-gr. bullet, 955 f.p.s., with an energy of 192 ft./lbs.

.38-40 WINCHESTER. This rimmed, bottleneck cartridge was very popular in single-action revolvers. It fires a 180-gr. bullet, 975 f.p.s., with an energy of 380 ft./lbs.

.41 LONG COLT. Developed in the late 1870s, this rimmed, straight-walled cartridge had a 200-gr. bullet that traveled at 730 f.p.s. with an energy of 231 ft./lbs.

.41 MAGNUM. Also known as .41 Smith & Wesson Magnum or .41 Remington Magnum. A center-fire, rimmed, straight-walled cartridge, it fires a 210-gr. bullet that travels at 1500 f.p.s. with an energy of 1050 ft./lbs.

10.4mm ITALIAN REVOLVER. Also known as 10.4mm Glisenti. This is a military service round that was developed in the mid-1870s. It fired a 177-gr. bullet, 810 f.p.s., with an energy of 250 ft./lbs.

.44 SMITH & WESSON AMERICAN. Developed in the late 1860s, this straight-walled, rimmed, center-fire cartridge fired a 205-gr. bullet that traveled at 682 f.p.s. with an energy of about 610 ft./lbs.

.44 WEBLEY. Also known as .442 Royal Irish Constabulary. This cartridge, developed in the late 1860s, fired a 200-gr. bullet about 715 f.p.s. with an energy of about 230 ft./lbs.

.44 AUTOMAG. A straight-walled, rimless cartridge, developed in the early 1970s, that fired a 240-gr. bullet, 1300 f.p.s., with an energy of almost 900 ft./lbs.

.44 SMITH & WESSON RUSSIAN. Also known as .44 Russian. Developed in 1870 for the Russian Model Smith & Wesson Revolver, this cartridge used a 246-gr. bullet that traveled at 770 f.p.s. with an energy of 324 ft./lbs.

11mm FRENCH ORDNANCE REVOLVER. Developed for the 1873 Revolver, this cartridge used a 180-gr. bullet that traveled at just under 700 f.p.s. with an energy of 190 ft./lbs.

11mm GERMAN SERVICE REVOLVER. Developed for the 1879 and 1883 Riechs Revolvers. This cartridge had a 262-gr. bullet that traveled at 700 f.p.s. with an energy of 290 ft./lbs.

.44-40 W.C.F. Also known as .44 Winchester. This cartridge, though designed primarily for rifles, was very popular in single-action pistols. It uses a 200-gr. bullet that travels at 975 f.p.s. with an energy of 420 ft./lbs.

.44 SMITH & WESSON SPECIAL. Also known as .44 Special. Developed just after the turn of the century, this popular revolver cartridge uses a 246-gr. bullet that travels at 755 f.p.s. with an energy of 311 ft./lbs.

.44 COLT. Between 1871 and 1873 this was the official army cartridge. It used a 225-gr. bullet that traveled at 640 f.p.s. with an energy of 207 ft./lbs.

.44 REMINGTON MAGNUM. Also known as .44 Smith & Wesson Magnum or .44 Magnum. Developed in the mid-1950s, this is a popular revolver and rifle cartridge. It uses a 240-gr. bullet that travels at 1625 f.p.s. with an energy of 1406 ft./lbs.

.44 BULLDOG. Developed by Webley about 1880, this cartridge used a 168-gr. bullet that travels at 460 f.p.s. with an energy of just under 80 ft./lbs.

11.75mm MONTENEGRIN REVOLVER. Developed for the Montenegrin Gasser Revolver about 1870, this huge cartridge had a 282-gr. bullet that traveled at about 700 f.p.s. with an energy of about 328 ft./lbs.

.45 WINCHESTER MAGNUM. Developed about 1979 for the Wildey Magnum Pistol, this cartridge uses a 230-gr. bullet that travels at 1400 f.p.s. with an energy of 1001 ft./lbs.

.45 A.C.P. Also known as .45 Automatic. Another of the John Browning cartridges that was developed about 1905 and adopted by the U.S. government as its standard cartridge in 1911. This rimless, straight-walled, cased cartridge uses a 230-gr. bullet that travels at 850 f.p.s. with an energy of 369 ft./lbs.

.45 AUTO-RIM. Developed just after World War I for use in military revolvers that had been chambered for .45 A.C.P., using half-moon clips to retain the cartridges. This cartridge has an exceptionally thick rim and has the same ballistics as .45 A.C.P.

.45 COLT. Adopted by the army in 1875, this was our official handgun cartridge until about 1892. It uses a 250-gr. lead bullet that travels at 860 f.p.s. with an energy of 410 ft./lbs.

.45 SMITH & WESSON. Developed in 1875 for the Smith & Wesson Schofield Revolver, this cartridge used a 250-gr. bullet that traveled at 710 f.p.s. with an energy of 283 ft./lbs.

.45 WEBLEY. Developed by Webley in the mid-1870s, this revolver cartridge used a 230-gr. bullet that traveled at 550 f.p.s. with an energy of 150 ft./lbs.

.450 REVOLVER. This British cartridge was developed in the late 1860s for the Adams Revolver, and used by the military. It had a 225-gr. bullet that traveled at 700 f.p.s. with an energy of 245 ft./lbs.

.455 WEBLEY AUTOMATIC. This cartridge was developed just before World War I for the .455 Webley Self-Loading Pistol. It used a 224-gr. bullet that travels at 700 f.p.s. with an energy of 247 ft./lbs.

.455 COLT. Also known as .455 Revolver MK-1. This cartridge was developed in the early 1890s and used by the British military in their Webley series of revolvers. It used a 265-gr. bullet that travels at 757 f.p.s. with an energy of 337 ft./lbs.

.455 REVOLVER MK-2. Also known as .455 Webley MK-2. Interchangeable with the MK-1 and also used in the Webley revolvers, this cartridge used a 265-gr. bullet that travels at 600 f.p.s. with an energy of 220 ft./lbs.

.476 ENFIELD MK-3. Also known as .476 Elee, also known as .455/.476. Used by the British military from about 1881 to 1891, this cartridge used a 260-gr. bullet that traveled at 675 f.p.s.

SCOPE OF THE BOOK

As denoted by the book's title, this work covers collector handguns. A "collectible" is an item that has attained significant collector interest to create a market, and realize a value beyond its mere utility. Firearms that are simply "used," with their value a function of the price of a new comparable piece, may not be listed. Discontinuance of production in and of itself does not deem the existing items to be collectible. Generally, the items of highest demand by collectors were expensive and the "best" when new. For omissions the reader does feel exist, please write to the author with your information for inclusion in future editions.

This book represents an analysis of prices for which collectible handguns have actually been selling during the preceding period. Although every reasonable effort has been made to compile an accurate and reliable guide, the prices of firearms vary significantly depending on such factors as the locality of the sale and changing economic conditions. Accordingly, no representation can be made that firearms listed may be bought or sold at the prices indicated, nor shall the author be responsible for any error made in compiling and recording the prices.

The reader is reminded to comply with all local, state, and federal firearm laws. The legality of ownership, transfer requirements, and firearms classifications change, and vary from one jurisdiction to another. If in doubt, contact the Bureau of Alcohol, Tobacco and Firearms or your local law enforcement agencies.

As comprehensive as this work is, by no means is it a complete coverage of collector handguns; and the data and prices are intended to be applied as a guide. For specific information and valuation on an individual gun, the reader is advised to seek a professional appraisal. The author offers this service at a nominal fee. Please write: Robert H. Balderson, P.O. Box 254886, Sacramento, CA 95865.

HOW TO USE THIS BOOK

All firearms in this book are listed alphabetically by manufacturer, and under each manufacturer are again listed first alphabetically and then numerically by model designation. Additionally, the model may be referenced directly in the model index.

We have listed the manufacturers of the various firearms and their addresses, how the firearm works, the available calibers, barrel lengths, the finish. Where known, we have listed the manufacturing dates, the types of stocks that the firearm came with, the rifling specification where it is standardized for the model, the unloaded weight in the most popular caliber or barrel length, and sights that were available. When the information is proprietary, we have included what serial number data we could research, as well as the location of the serial number on the firearm. Where a model has gone through various stages and progressions, we have tried to include those under "Variations." For ease of identification, also listed are markings on the most common variant. The prices reflect the current market value of the firearm. Occasionally, certain categories will be left blank. The reason is that information regarding that category is either sketchy, incomplete, or contradictory; and the author feels it best to say nothing rather than include possibly erroneous information.

LISTING OF MANUFACTURERS
AND MODELS (A–Z)

AMT
(Arcadia Machine & Tool)
6226 Santos Diaz Street
Irwindale, CA 91702

Model: Back Up

Action Type: semiautomatic, blowback operated.

Caliber(s): .380 A.C.P., .22 L.R. (disc. in 1987).

Barrel Lengths: 2½″.

Finish: stainless steel.

Manufacturing Dates: 1977 to date.

Stocks: wood or plastic.

Rifling: 8R.

Weight, Unloaded: 17 oz.

Sights: fixed.

Serial Numbers: n/a.

Serial Number Location: about trigger on left side of frame.

Major Variations: TDE marked.
 OMC marked.
 AMT marked.

Markings: manufacturer's initials in circle on left side of slide followed by caliber, Back up, El Monte, Calif.
on right side of frame: initials of manufacturer in circle followed by El Monte, Calif.
on right side of slide: Stainless, Made in U.S.A.

Price(s):
 .380 A.C.P., $150.00–$225.00
 .22 L.R.R.F., $200.00–$250.00

History: The Back Up pistol is the brainchild of Harry Sanford, the inventor of the Auto Mag, and it might be called a case of going from one extreme to the other, from one of the largest pistols in the world to one of the smallest; and like the Auto Mag, the Back Up exhibits Sanford's mark of genius. First samples were put together while he was at TDE (Trust Deed Estate), which at the time was manufacturing the Auto Mag pistol. Once the Back Up was fully developed, a separate corporation was formed called OMC (Ordnance Manufacturing Corporation) and then was finally transferred to AMT (Arcadia Machine & Tool Company), the current manufacturer. It is currently the smallest .380 automatic made in the United States.

Mechanical Functioning: The Back Up pistol is a straight blowback operated, semiautomatic pistol utilizing a concealed hammer and a detachable 5-shot box magazine with the magazine catch located at the bottom rear of the frame. It is of all stainless steel construction, and possesses a manual safety located on the left side of the frame forward of the grip, which locks the sear, and a grip safety located on the rear gripstrap. Field stripping is not carried out in the run-of-the-mill manner; instead it is a good exercise in basic gunsmithing. Tools that will be handy include a pin punch to fit the breechblock retaining pin and a small screwdriver. A small nonmarring mallet and a short length of wood dowel would be handy. Takedown is accomplished by first making sure that the gun is unloaded and removing the magazine. Make sure the pistol is cocked by pulling the slide to the rear to cock the internal hammer. Then, using a proper-size pin punch, drift the retaining pin located just above the slide serrations from left to right. Now the breechblock can be removed, either by lightly rapping the slide with a nonmarring mallet or by tapping it through the magazine well with a suitable object. Once the breechblock is out, reach through the recess with a screwdriver and push the hammer down slightly while pushing the slide forward and past the hammer. Lift the slide slightly and run off the end of the frame. The recoil spring and its guide can now be lifted out. Reassemble in the reverse order. When resetting the breechblock, make sure that it's fully seated before trying to replace the drift pin.

AMT Back Up .380 A.C.P.

Advantage Arms U.S.A., Inc.
St. Paul, MN

Model: 422

Action Type: double-action-only, top-break, four-barreled pistol.

Caliber(s): .22 L.R., .522 W.R.M.

Barrel Lengths: 2½″.

Finish: nickel, blue, or Q.P.Q.™ black.

Manufacturing Dates: 1986–1987.

Stocks: walnut.

Rifling: 4R.

Weight, Unloaded: 15 oz.

Sights: fixed.

Serial Numbers: n/a.

Serial Number Location: n/a.

Major Variations: n/a.

Markings: left barrel flat:
Advantage Arms USA Inc.
Advantage 422™ .22 Cal.
St. Paul Minnesota.

Price(s):
blue, very good—$100.00; excellent—$125.00
nickel, very good—$125.00; excellent—$150.00
QPQ black, very good—$150.00; excellent—$175.00

History: Advantage Arms U.S.A., Inc., was formed in 1982 to manufacture this pocket handgun, which appears to be based on the Mossberg Brownie design and the Tanfoglio Fabbrica D'Armi (E.I.G.) pistol of similar pattern. The primary changes seem to be in materials used in the construction—namely, 4140 steel, which is formed by investment casting—the addition of a ventilated rib, and the use of spring-loaded extractors in place of manual extraction. The designated market for this pistol seems to be the law enforcement community; however, they are not ignoring the possibly greater demand for a compact pistol of this type in these calibers by the average outdoorsman. This design, caliber, and size is ideal for use as an emergency camp gun or for the tackle box, and should perform well with shot cartridges against snakes. The Model 422 is fairly thick, about 1″, and is very hand-filling even though its overall size is quite diminutive. This is an advantage when actually shooting; however, it makes the pistol a bit bulky if it must be carried concealed. The sights are fixed, and the sight radius is quite short; combined with a double-action trigger, it makes accurate aimed fire difficult. However, within the average combat distance of seven yards it should do well for point shooting.

Mechanical Functioning: The Advantage Arms Model 422 is a hinged-frame, double-action-only pistol with four fixed barrels, each fired sequentially by means of a rotating firing pin. The action is locked by means of a T-shaped latch located at the top of the breech securing the rear face of the barrels against the breechface. This latch is opened by depressing the rear sight, which pivots, raising the spring loaded T-latch and allowing the barrels to pivot downward for cleaning, extraction, or loading. The firing pin consists of a cylinder with a raised rimfire-style striking surface of chisel type extending from the periphery of the cylinder toward the center and is about the length of the radius. The assembly rotates in a clockwise direction, turning to align with each chamber as the trigger is pulled in a manner similar to the way a hand rotates the cylinder of a revolver. Force is imparted to the firing pin, as well as functioning the entire lockwork, when the trigger is pulled. A true double action, the Model 422 compresses the mainspring, rotates the firing pin, and overrides the sear, allowing the pistol to fire when the trigger is pulled all the way to the rear. There is no provision for single action (cocking). The overall length is 4½″, the height is 3¼″, and the thickness is almost 1″.

Advantage Arms Model 422

American Derringer Corp.
127 N. Lacy Drive
Waco, TX 76705

Model: 1, 7, and 3

Action Type: single-action, double-barreled Remington design.

Caliber(s):
.45 Colt, .45 A.C.P., .45 Winchester Magnum, .45 × 2½″,
.44 Magnum, .44 Special, .44-40, .41 Magnum, .357 Magnum,
.38 Super, .38 Special, .380 A.C.P., 9mm Luger, 30/30 W.C.F.,
.223 Remington, .22 L.R.R.F., .22 W.M.R.,
.32 Smith & Wesson Long, .32 A.C.P., .25 A.C.P., .45/70

Barrel Lengths: 3″.

Finish: high-polish stainless steel, satin-finish stainless steel, combat gray, sandblast stainless steel.

Manufacturing Dates: introduced in 1979.

Stocks: plastic, rosewood, zebrawood, mother-of-pearl, ivory, stag.

Rifling: varies, but generally 4R.

Weight, Unloaded: 15-oz. Model AD; 18-oz. Model ADS, 7½-oz. Model ADL.

Sights: fixed.

Serial Numbers: start at 25,000.

Serial Number Location: right side of frame.

Major Variations:
Model 1—standard Remington pattern Derringer.
Model 7—lightweight Remington pattern Derringer.
Model 3—single-shot Remington pattern Derringer with dummy top barrel.

Markings: engraved models available, as well as dual caliber on special order.
American Derringer Corp. on right side of barrel.
"P" denotes that the gun has been proof tested.
"PP" on heavy calibers denotes double proofing.

Price(s):
Model 1—$100.00–$225.00
Model 7—$160.00–$450.00
Model 3—$75.00–$125.00

History: American Derringer Corp. was founded in 1979 by Bob Saunders, who was also the designer of the various models produced by the company. The first guns came off the assembly line in 1980. Many variations are available on special order, including nonstandard calibers.

Mechanical Functioning: Single-action Remington-style superposed double-barreled Derringer with an additional hammer blocking manually operated safety that disconnects upon cocking. On larger calibers a spring-loaded cocking system is employed. Warning: severe recoil is experienced on the following calibers: .45 A.C.P., .45 × 2½″, .44 Special, .44-40, .357 Magnum, .38 Super, and the .223 Remington. Extreme recoil is experienced on the .45 Winchester Magnum, .44 Magnum, .41 Magnum, and .30/30 W.C.F.

American Derringer Corp. Model 7

Gaspar Arizaga
Eibar, Spain

Model: Mondial

Action Type: semiautomatic, blowback operated.

Caliber(s): 6.35mm.

Barrel Lengths: 2½".

Finish: blue.

Manufacturing Dates: circa 1920s.

Stocks: hard rubber.

Rifling: noted in the lower serial ranges as 6R, in the higher ranges as 6L.

Weight, Unloaded: 12 oz.

Sights: fixed.

Serial Numbers: n/a.

Serial Number Location: right rear of frame.

Major Variations: Model I has a grip safety.

Markings: on left top of slide: Manufacture of Firearme "Mondial."
left side of frame above trigger: Cal 6.35.

Price(s):
Mondial, very good—$150.00
Mondial, excellent—$200.00

History: Gaspar Arizaga was an active producer of semiautomatic pistols in Eibar, Spain, during the 1920s, and he was taking advantage of the fairly wild firearms market prevalent in Europe at the time. Most of his product line was fairly standard Eibar pattern pistols with not much to recommend them. This is quite understandable since it seems that the Eibar gunmakers were able to make a living by cranking out guns of which all that could be said was that they shot. Arizaga was one of the multitude of Spanish gunmakers put out of business by the Civil War. It appears that Arizaga must have appreciated the Savage pistols because he tried his best to duplicate the appearance of them. He did this on several models, but the Mondial is the most pronounced imitation. From outward appearances, the Mondial seems to be a copy of the Savage automatic pistol Model 1907 with very similar-appearing frame cuts. It was nicely machined, and it is an interesting pistol because of its exterior design. However, the Savage appearance is only external. The interior of the gun more closely resembles the standard Eibar product. An early version of this pistol with a grip safety had been recorded; however, to date, this author has neither seen the pistol nor photographs to confirm its existence. At some point during the manufacture of this pistol, Arizaga must have changed barrel makers, for the early models of this pistol have been seen with a rifling with a right-hand twist, whereas later examples show rifling with a left-hand twist.

Mechanical Functioning: The Mondial is a straight blowback, semiautomatic pistol that is striker-fired. It contains a detachable box magazine holding seven rounds that is inserted through the gripframe and is retained by a spring-loaded catch located at the bottom of the butt toward the rear. The safety is mechanical and is located on the left rear side of the frame and works to block the sear. The trigger is of the pivoting type and is linked to a sear connector. The disconnector works by lowering the sear connector until the slide is at battery, and then it allows the sear connector to rise and engage the sear. The grips are inserted from the rear into a milled out area. They are then tacked down with a single screw. Takedown can be accomplished in normal Eibar pattern. First make sure that the pistol is unloaded and remove the magazine. Then pull the slide to the rear and observe the cutout area in the slide through the ejection port for the barrel lugs to be rotated into. When the slide is pulled back to the proper alignment, turn the barrel and allow the slide to be run forward and off of the frame. The recoil spring, firing pin, and striker spring can now be removed. The barrel can be turned to have the lugs pointing toward the bottom of the slide again, and then it is pulled down and out from the rear. Assembly is carried out in the reverse order.

Mondial Model II

Arminex Ltd.
7882 East Gray Road
Scottsdale, AZ 85260

Model: Tri-Fire

Action Type: semiautomatic, recoil-operated, M1911-type action.

Caliber(s): .45 A.C.P., 9mm Luger, .38 Super.

Barrel Lengths: 5″.

Finish: blue or electroless nickel.

Manufacturing Dates: 1981–1985.

Stocks: smooth walnut.

Rifling: n/a.

Weight, Unloaded: 38 oz.

Sights: adjustable rear with interchangeable front.

Serial Numbers: n/a.

Serial Number Location: right frame above trigger.

Major Variations: standard model comes in a black canvas case. presentation model comes in a fitted wooden case. accessories available: conversion kits in .45 A.C.P., .38 Super, or 9mm Luger, fixed rear sight, and ambidextrous safety.

Markings: n/a.

Price(s):
Standard, very good—$275.00; excellent—$375.00
Target, very good—$300.00; excellent—$400.00

History: The Arminex Tri-Fire is a modernized version of the Browning/Colt design for the Government Model of 1911 and only slightly differs in several respects. Since the stated purpose of this pistol is to be used primarily as a combat weapon, the trigger guard was redesigned to provide a gripping surface for a comfortable two-handed hold. The grip safety has been eliminated, and the user must rely on the manual safety for carrying in the loaded condition. By the way, in common parlance for carrying the M1911 "condition 1" means loaded magazine, chamber empty; "condition 2" means loaded magazine, round in chamber, and hammer down resting on the firing pin retainer; "condition 3" refers to having a full magazine, a round in the chamber, and the hammer cocked with the safety on. Condition 3 is also known as "cocked and locked." A common affliction that many M1911 users suffer is "hammer bite," which is caused by the hammer pinching the web of the hand between the thumb and forefinger if the shooter is incautious enough to allow that part of the hand to protrude over the rear tang. To eliminate this problem the rear tang was elongated to prevent the hand from riding up the gripframe when shooting. This gun was designed to fill the need for a rugged pistol that can be used for combat as well as target work.

Mechanical Functioning: This is a recoil operated semiautomatic pistol based on the Browning/Colt M1911 system with some modifications. The hammer style is a la Commander, with a rounded top and a hole through the center. The trigger is Gold Cup style, wide and adjustable for overtravel. The front sight can be readily interchanged for target or combat work, and the front sight is adjustable. The extractor and ejector are of pivoting type and are spring loaded rather than fixed. The M1911 safeties have been eliminated and instead have been replaced by a slide-mounted safety that intercepts the firing pin in a manner similar to the Walther PPk, but without the provision to automatically lower the hammer. While it can be slightly unnerving to carry a weapon in condition 3 (cocked and in this case, unlocked) without a mechanical block to prevent the hammer from falling, with the slide safety functioning and in the on position, discharge from an accidentally falling hammer can be prevented. However, this author would prefer condition 2 (round in the chamber, hammer down and resting on the firing pin retaining plate, safety off) with the Arminex Tri-Fire. This pistol can be converted to other calibers easily. To accomplish this, the user replaces the barrel, magazine, extractor, and slide stop. Standard M1911 magazines can be used, and all parts are made from 4140 steel.

Arminex Tri-Fire

Hijos de Calixto Arrizabalaga
Eibar, Spain

Model: Sharp Sooter

Action Type: semiautomatic, blowback operated.

Caliber(s): 6.35mm, 7.65mm, 9mm C.

Barrel Lengths: 3¹/₁₆″.

Finish: blue.

Manufacturing Dates: circa 1924.

Stocks: wood with inlaid medallion.

Rifling: 6R.

Weight, Unloaded: about 16 oz.

Sights: fixed.

Serial Numbers: n/a.

Serial Number Location: left side of frame above trigger.

Major Variations: none.

Markings: left side of slide: Sharp Sooter Patent No. 68027.
left side of frame: caliber and Made In Spain.

Price(s):
Sharp Shooter, very good—$275.00
Sharp Shooter, excellent—$325.00

History: As you may have guessed, "Sharp Sooter" is a misspelling. The true name of this pistol is "Sharp Shooter," and it was made by the Hijos de Calixto Arrizabalaga of Eibar, Spain, and was marketed in Spain by Ojanguren y Vibosa and by Aldazabal. They are essentially the same exact pistol as the Jo-Lo-Ar, with the exception that the Jo-Lo-Ar has an extractor and the Sharp Shooters do not. The Sharp Shooter was available in 6.35mm and 7.65mm and has been reported in 9mm K. On the other hand the Jo-Lo-Ar was made in 9mmK and 9mm Bergmann, and was reported in 6.35mm. Since the only difference in the two models of guns is the existence of an extractor, the reporting of these odd calibers may just be an error in examination; but the possibility exists that the factory may have made an odd gun to satisfy a special requirement, and thus is a collector's delight. Somewhere a rare variant may exist! The total production life seems to have spanned the years from about 1920 to about 1930. They are interesting pistols. The Sharp Shooters were of somewhat standard looks and had trigger guards, while the Jo-Lo-Ars were larger and of necessity bulkier, but they had no trigger guards. Rather they had what appear to be sheathed spur triggers at first glance, but the "sheath" is somewhat cut away. Neither the Sharp Shooter nor the Jo-Lo-Ar had grooves on the slide to load the pistol. Instead you were supposed to pop up the pivoting barrel and drop your first cartridge in. Blowback operation was supposed to load the rest via the clip. These pistols may have been the basis for the Le Francais series of pistols, which were built with the same mechanical philosophy. One item to note about the Jo-Lo-Ars: They did have a means of reciprocating the slide in the form of a large lever mounted on the right side of the slide. It was long because the strong recoil spring necessitated using your full grip to work the slide.

Mechanical Functioning: The Sharp Shooter automatics are blowback-operated, semiautomatic pistols utilizing a detachable box magazine inserted through the gripframe and retained by a spring-loaded catch at the base of the butt. An unusual feature of these pistols is the tip-up barrel. There are two barrel lugs, one of them drilled through, mounted on an axial pin in the front of the frame; the other lug is engaged by the safety, which, when rotated fully around, releases the barrel to spring upward for cleaning or for loading. The recoil spring is located beneath the barrel and the slide has been cut out from the breech face forward so that it rests only on the sides and underneath the barrel. There is an external hammer with a half-cock notch, and the arm operates in single-action mode only. On the Jo-Lo-Ar style pistols with the extractor there may also be a cocking lever located on the right side of the frame, which is used to draw the slide back.

Sharp Sooter

Astra-Unceta y Cia., S.A.
Apartado 3
Guernica, (Vizcaya) Spain

Model: A-80

Action Type: semiautomatic, recoil operated.

Caliber(s): 9mm Luger, .38 Super, .45 A.C.P.

Barrel Lengths: 3³/₄".

Finish: blue or chrome.

Manufacturing Dates: 1981 to date.

Stocks: plastic.

Rifling: 6R.

Weight, Unloaded: 36 oz. in 9mm and .38 Super, 40 oz. in .45 A.C.P.

Sights: fixed.

Serial Numbers: n/a.

Serial Number Location: right side of frame, forward to the trigger guard.

Major Variations: none.

Markings: left side of slide: Astra-Unceta y Cia., Guernica, Spain, Mod A-80

Price(s):
    very good—$275.00; excellent—$375.00

History: The Astra Model A-80 was designed to fill the need for a small, concealable, yet powerful double-action combat handgun. It features an enlarged magazine with capacities of 15 rounds in the 9mm Luger, 15 rounds
in the .38 Super, and 9 rounds in the .45 A.C.P. chamberings. Following
the current trend in pistol styling, the forward portion of the trigger
guard is concave to provide a firm grip with a two-hand combat hold. It
appears that the firearms industry has again turned around to become a
buyers' market instead of the sellers' market that it had been for years.
The Astra A-80 is a case in point. In the recent past it was left to small
vendors of custom pistol parts or to advanced gunsmiths to convert a
pistol from virtually any manufacturer into a gun that a left-hander
could use with comfort, or to revamp it for use as a combat pistol. The
Astra already has most of the custom combat features, and it also can be
purchased with a left-handed slide release for southpaws. The industry
has come a long way in a short time to try and cater to the prospective
purchaser's needs.

Mechanical Functioning: This is a recoil-operated, double-action, semiautomatic pistol featuring all-steel construction, simple takedown, and
the option of an ambidextrous takedown lever. In many respects this
pistol is similar to the Walther pistols. Like the PPk, there is a protrusion-
style loaded chamber indicator, and reminiscent of the Walther P.5, an

internal safety that holds the firing pin out of contact with the hammer until the trigger is fully depressed. This feature renders obsolete most manual safeties since the pistol cannot discharge unless the trigger is pulled, much in the same manner as a double-action revolver is safe. However, since there is the question of what to do when you want to safely lower the hammer over a loaded chamber, a special decocking mechanism has been incorporated to trip the sear and lower the hammer without pulling the trigger. This decocking lever also is a la Walther P.5, and is located just forward of the grip on the left side of the frame. On the last shot the slide remains open, and the choice of a right-handed or a left-handed slide release lever is the buyer's. As with many modern pistols, the enlarged magazine capacity is provided by staggering the cartridges. The Astra A-80 is a double-action pistol and features a surprisingly smooth double-action trigger pull. The extractor is positive and of the pivoting bar type backed by a spring to the rear of the pivot hole. It is mounted on the outside of the slide and is retained by a vertical pin.

Astra-Unceta y Cia., S.A.
Apartado 3
Guernica, (Vizcaya) Spain

Model: Constable

Action Type: semiautomatic, blowback.

Caliber(s): .22 L.R., .32 A.C.P., .380 A.C.P.

Barrel Lengths: 3½", 6".

Finish: blue or chrome.

Manufacturing Dates: 1965–1991.

Stocks: plastic.

Rifling: 6R.

Weight, Unloaded: 25 oz.

Sights: windage adjustable on pocket models, adjustable micrometer rear on sport and TS-22.

Serial Numbers: n/a.

Serial Number Location: right frame.

Major Variations: Pocket model with 3½" barrel, windage adjustable sights, .22, .32, .380.
Sport with 6" barrel, micrometer sights, .22.
TS-22 with redesigned heavy slide, target micrometer sights, .22.

Markings: left side of slide: Astra Unceta y Cia., Constable, Guernica, Spain, and caliber designation.

Price(s):
Constable Pocket, very good—$200.00
Constable Pocket, excellent—$275.00
Constable Sport, very good—$250.00
Constable Sport, excellent—$325.00
Constable Stainless, very good—$275.00
Constable Stainless, excellent—$350.00

History: Developed in the mid-sixties, the Constable was a radical departure from standard Astra design at the time. It is a streamlined pistol, rather than of tubular design, and is strongly reminiscent of the Walther PP. It is a double-action pistol with an exposed hammer except in the TS-22 variation, which is single action only. The "Sport" model is very similar to the Walther PP Sport, even down to the removal of the front sight for disassembly. The European designation for the Constable is the Model 5000.

Mechanical Functioning: Almost identical to the Walther PP, the Astra Constable is a double-action, blowback-operated, semiautomatic pistol. Like the Walther, the safety is slide-mounted and intercepts the floating firing pin and then drops the hammer when engaged. Unlike the Walther, takedown is accomplished by pulling down a slide located on the left side of the frame forward of the trigger, allowing the slide to be removed. The magazine is of detachable box type and holds 10 .22s, 8 .32s, or 7 .380s.

Astra-Unceta y Cia., S.A.
Apartado 3
Guernica, (Vizcaya) Spain

Model: 2000 Cub

Action Type: semiautomatic, blowback.

Caliber(s): .22 Short R.F., .25 A.C.P.

Barrel Lengths: 2¼", 4" (The 4" version is called "Camper" in the U.S.)

Finish: blue or chrome.

Manufacturing Dates: 1954 to date. U.S. importation ceased in 1968. "Camper" was produced during 1958–1966.

Stocks: plastic.

Rifling: 6L.

Weight, Unloaded: 11 oz.

Sights: fixed.

Serial Numbers: n/a.

Serial Number Location: right side of frame above trigger.

Major Variations: Cub—2¼" barrel.
Camper—4" barrel.
Conversion kit to change from or to .22 Short R.F. and .25 A.C.P. available.

Markings: left side of slide: Astra-Unceta Y Cia. S.A.-Guernica, Cal 6.35 .25 Made in Spain.
Grips have Astra trademark and are marked "Cub" or "Camper."

Price(s):
Cub .22, blue, very good—$150.00
Cub .22, blue, excellent—$175.00
Cub .22, chrome, very good—$175.00
Cub .22, chrome, excellent—$200.00
Cub .25, blue, very good—$175.00
Cub .25, blue, excellent—$200.00
Cub .25, chrome, very good—$200.00
Cub .25, chrome, excellent—$225.00
Camper .22 Short, blue, very good—$275.00
Camper .22 Short, blue, excellent—$300.00
Camper .22 Short, chrome, very good—$300.00
Camper .22 Short, chrome, excellent—$325.00
Conversion kit—$125.00

History: This model was introduced in 1954 and has been named "Cub" in the 2¼" version and "Camper" in the 4" version. A four-piece conversion kit was available for both .22 Short and .25 A.C.P. calibers. Between 1957 and 1968 about 67,000 pistols were manufactured for Colt and trade-named "Colt Junior." They are identical to the Cub, but may have checkered wood grips instead of the standard plastic. Engraved and silver-plated versions of the Model 2000 were also available.

Mechanical Functioning: This is a straight blowback, semiautomatic pistol that is almost identical internally to the Model 200 Astra with the following exceptions: This model has an external hammer, a side-mounted magazine release, and no grip safety. The exterior was redesigned also. The detachable box magazine holds six rounds. There is a manually operated side safety, and a magazine disconnector. The safety holds the slide to the rear for takedown.

Astra Cub .25 A.C.P.

Astra-Unceta y Cia., S.A.
Apartado 3
Guernica, (Vizcaya) Spain

Model: 200 Firecat

Action Type: semiautomatic, blowback.

Caliber(s): .25 A.C.P.

Barrel Lengths: 2⅕".

Finish: blue, nickel, or silver.

Manufacturing Dates: 1920–1968.

Stocks: plastic.

Rifling: 6L.

Weight, Unloaded: 11⅘ oz.

Sights: fixed.

Serial Numbers: n/a.

Serial Number Location: right side of frame above trigger.

Major Variations: most Model 200s have loaded chamber indicators.
the very early style was a small bar located in a concave cut in the top of the slide over the chamber.
the late style consists of an indicator pin protruding from the rear of the slide.
Model 200/1, 200/2, etc. refer to engraving, plating, or other decorative touches.

Markings: left side of slide: Astra-Unceta Y Cia. S.A.-Guernica, Cal 6.35 .25 Made in Spain.
Very early barrels were marked "Hope."
"Firecat" on grips of guns for U.S. consumption.

Price(s):
Model 200, blue, very good—$225.00
Model 200, blue, excellent—$250.00
Model 200, engraved, blue, very good—$250.00
Model 200, engraved, blue, excellent—$300.00
Firecat, blue, very good—$175.00
Firecat, blue, excellent—$200.00
Firecat, nickel, very good—$175.00
Firecat, nickel, excellent—$200.00
long magazine—add $10 to $15.

History: First made in 1920, and based on the Victoria and Astra Model 1911 .25, this pistol represents the epitome of Eibar style pistols, and its long production run proves the point. The Model 200 in the United States was called the "Firecat," and importation was halted in 1968 due to the Gun Control Act of 1968. It was available in a variety of styles including blued, chromed, nickel-plated, engraved, and gold-damascened. Production and European sales continue.

Mechanical Functioning: This is a straight blowback, semiautomatic pistol with a six-shot detachable box magazine of standard Eibar pattern, and with Browning 1906 takedown features. It features an internal hammer and a floating firing pin. There are three safeties: a magazine disconnector that prevents firing when the clip is removed, a grip safety that blocks the sear and prevents firing unless depressed at the time the trigger is pulled, and a side-mounted manual safety that blocks the firing train and can also lock the slide in the retracted position. Most pistols had a loaded chamber indicator as described above. Takedown is achieved by first making sure that the pistol is unloaded and then withdrawing the slide to the rear and locking it in place with the side-mounted safety. At this point the barrel can be rotated until its locking lugs are visible in the ejector port and are detached from the receiver. Hold the slide tightly, for it's under heavy spring tension from the recoil spring, and release the safety. The slide assembly can now be moved forward and off of the frame. Assembly is in the reverse order. This pistol is entirely made of steel.

Astra Model 200 with Extended Magazine

Astra-Unceta y Cia., S.A.
Apartado 3
Guernica, (Vizcaya) Spain

Model: 357

Action Type: revolver, double action.

Caliber(s): .357 Magnum.

Barrel Lengths: 3", 4", 6", or 8½".

Finish: blue or stainless steel.

Manufacturing Dates: 1972–1988.

Stocks: checkered wood.

Rifling: 6R.

Weight, Unloaded: with 6" barrel, 40 oz.

Sights: adjustable Smith & Wesson–style rear sight, ramp front.

Serial Numbers: n/a.

Serial Number Location: right side of frame below and forward of cylinder recess.

Major Variations: blue is available in all barrel lengths.
stainless steel is available only in the 4" barrel length.

Markings: left side of barrel: .357 Magnum Ctg.
right side of frame on sideplate: Astra trademark and address.

Price(s):
blue, 3" barrel—$225.00
blue, 4" barrel—$200.00
blue, 6" barrel—$200.00
blue, 8½" barrel—$250.00
stainless, 4" barrel—$275.00

History: This revolver is based on the earlier Astra "Cadix" series of revolvers and was developed as the market called for a heavier frame to handle the magnum calibers. As with the products of most foreign manufacturers the availability of arms depends to a great deal on what the importers believe will sell in the U.S. and on prior marketing agreements. Astra is no exception, and there have long been fine arms produced by the company that rarely ever see our shores. In the revolver field the medium-frame Cadix revolvers in .22 L.R.R.F., .22 W.R.F., .32 S&W Long, and .38 Special are still available in Europe, but are no longer imported. The stainless version of the Cadix is marketed in Europe as the "Inox," and the Astra version of the S&W Chief's Special is called the Model 250. They sell the large-frame revolvers that were made for the American market M357 in .357 Magnum, M41 in .41 Magnum, M44 in .44 Magnum, and M45 in .45 Colt, as they are here. A target revolver in .38 Special caliber on this frame, the "Model 960," is marketed in Europe. As with all Astra handguns, they can be had on special order in chrome- or silver-plated finish, and engraved or gold-damascened. Unlike its predecessor, the Cadix, the Model 357 holds six shots in .38/.357 caliber instead of five.

Mechanical Functioning: The Model .357 is a double-action revolver based on, and is a close copy of, the Smith & Wesson Hand Ejector design. Other than some cosmetic details, the major differences between the Astra and the Hand Ejector are recessed chambers for full cartridge case head support, a spring-loaded floating firing pin, and a four-position mainspring tension adjustment for variable trigger pull. Like the early Smith & Wessons, the sideplate is retained by four screws rather than S & W's current method of using a tongue and groove and three screws. The front sight is pin retained and can be removed. The action is locked via a center pin through the cylinder that locks the cylinder to the breechface and by a locking pin in the barrel shroud. The cylinder swings out to the left when the action is unlocked by pushing a catch on the left side of the frame, which in turn pushes the center pin out of engagement with the breechface, and that in turn forces the forward pin in the barrel shroud out of the hollow ejector rod. Ejection is manual and simultaneous and accomplished by pushing on the ejector rod when the cylinder has been opened. Available on this same frame are revolvers in .41 Magnum, .44 Magnum, and .45 Long Colt with adapters for .45 A.C.P. Various types of barrels are also available, all with sighting ribs. The long-barreled versions are equipped with oversize target grips, and a 4″ barreled stainless version can be had.

Astra-Unceta y Cia., S.A.
Apartado 3
Guernica, (Vizcaya) Spain

Model: 400 (1921)

Action Type: semiautomatic, blowback.

Caliber(s): 9mm Largo.

Barrel Lengths: 6″.

Finish: blue.

Manufacturing Dates: 1921–1946.

Stocks: checkered wood or plastic.

Rifling: 6R.

Weight, Unloaded: 35 oz.

Sights: fixed.

Serial Numbers: n/a, but 105,257 pistols were produced according to Astra, but other sources say 106,175 was the magic number.

Serial Number Location: right side of frame at extreme rear, and above that on the slide.

Major Variations: the civilian version is called the Model 400.
the military version is called the Model 1921.
two M1921s made without Astra markings and denied by Astra as their product are the "Ascaso" and the "RE."
while appearing identical, the rifling twist rate differs from the Astra product.

Markings: on the top of the slide behind the front sight: Astra trademark.

Price(s):
Model 400, very good—$250.00
Model 400, excellent—$300.00
Model Nazi, very good—$500.00
Model Nazi, excellent—$600.00
Model Navy, very good—$750.00
Model Navy, excellent—$900.00

History: A very interesting gun based on an improved Campo-Giro action, the Model 400 was the first of the Astra "tubular" pistols. Sturdy and well made, the 400 was accepted for military use by Spain, Germany, Columbia, France, Chile, Ecuador, and El Salvador. The civilian Model 400 usually had plastic grips, while the military Model 400 usually came with checkered wood. A very rare variant of this pistol is chambered for the .32 A.C.P. During the Spanish Revolution this pistol was copied, with two variations apparently used by the Republicans: The F. ASCASO, and the pistol with "RE" (Republica Espanola) on the grips.

Mechanical Functioning: This is a straight blowback, semiautomatic pistol, which is very unusual for heavy calibers. Its success derives from the heavy slide and the very strong recoil spring, plus the amount of energy necessary for the slide to overrun and cock the hammer. Another amazing feature of this arm when it is in good condition is its ability to feed and fire the following cartridges interchangeably: 9mm Largo, 9mm Steyr, 9mm Luger, 9mm Browning Long, .38 A.C.P., and the .380 A.C.P. These are fed through the magazine and caught and held by the extractor, obviating the headspace problem.

Astra Model 400
Photo courtesy of Interarms

Astra-Unceta y Cia., S.A.
Apartado 3
Guernica, (Vizcaya) Spain

Model: 900

Action Type: semiautomatic, recoil operated.

Caliber(s): 7.63mm Mauser.

Barrel Lengths: 5½".

Finish: blue.

Manufacturing Dates: 1928–1937.

Stocks: wood.

Rifling: 6R.

Weight, Unloaded: 40½ oz.

Sights: adjustable tangent.

Serial Numbers: n/a.

Serial Number Location: left frame above grip.

Major Variations: Model 900—7.63mm Mauser, fixed 10-shot magazine.
Model 902—7.63mm Mauser, fixed 20-shot magazine.
Model 903E—7.63 Mauser, detachable 10- or 20-shot magazine.

Markings: left side of frame: Astra Automatic Pistol Cal 7.63, Patented July 12, 1928, Unceta y Compania Guernica (Spain) - or - Astra Automatic Pistol Cal. 7.63.
on Chinese import models: Astra China Company

Price(s):
very good—$1,500.00
excellent—$1,750.00
early Bolo grip, very good—$2,250.00
early Bolo grip, excellent—$2,750.00
Japanese markings, very good—$1,750.00
Japanese markings, excellent—$2,000.00

History: During the 1920s, Mauser enjoyed an excellent export market for their C-96 "Broom Handle" and "Bolo" pistols, and aware of the potential sales, Astra developed the 900 Series pistols to compete with Mauser. Although similar in exterior appearance to the C-96, internally Astra designers opted for simplicity. About 35,000 Model 900s were said to have been produced, with 30,000 reportedly sold in China. This model was also produced in selective fire versions in both 7.63 Mauser and 9mm Largo.

Mechanical Functioning: This well-made and finely designed short recoil-operated, semiautomatic pistol differed internally from the Mauser in many aspects. The barrel was inserted into the barrel extension, rather than formed with it. Instead of removable lockwork, the Astra has a sliding sideplate to expose the action. The operation is also different in that as the barrel and bolt recoil back on firing, they are locked together until the bolt lock strikes a wedge in the frame, pushing it down to disconnect the trigger bar and unlock the bolt. Like the Mauser, loading on the 900 and 902 was accomplished with a stripper clip, loading from the top with the bolt locked in the rearward position. Astras will also be found with detachable box magazines, but these, invariably, are of the selective-fire type. Takedown of the Astra 900 series is accomplished by first being sure that the arm is unloaded. Then after cocking the hammer and lining the safety up with the groove in the sideplate, push the barrel back slightly to relieve spring tension and push the rearmost square crosspin through from right to left. The sideplate may now be removed by sliding it rearward. By placing the safety in the "fire" position and pushing rearward on the barrel again, the round head bolt in the center of the frame can be withdrawn, allowing the barrel extension to be lifted off of the frame. During this last operation be careful of the stop spring, which holds the whole unit under tension. To remove the bolt use a screwdriver to press in the firing pin and turn it 90 degrees clockwise and remove it from the bolt. Now the bolt-retaining cross pin may be removed from the side of the barrel extension, allowing the bolt assembly to be withdrawn to the rear and out. Assembly is in the reverse order.

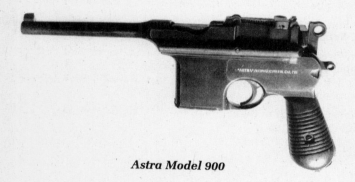

Astra Model 900

Astra-Unceta y Cia., S.A.
Apartado 3
Guernica, (Vizcaya) Spain

Model: 1911

Action Type: semiautomatic, blowback.

Caliber(s): .25 A.C.P., .32 A.C.P.

Barrel Lengths: 3¼".

Finish: blue.

Manufacturing Dates: 1911–1920.

Stocks: wood or hard rubber.

Rifling: 6R.

Weight, Unloaded: 21½ oz.

Sights: fixed.

Serial Numbers: n/a, but appear to have started at 1 and run to at least 22,000 in the 1911 style, and possibly to 35,000. In the 1915, 16 Series, 1–150,000.

Serial Number Location: right side of frame above trigger.

Major Variations: Model 1915—8-round magazine instead of 6 rounds, and slightly longer barrel and slide.
Model 1916—about the same as Model 1915, but with improved Eibar-type sear system.

Markings: left side of slide. 7.65mm 1911 Model Automatic Pistol, Astra Patent.

Price(s):
    M1911, very good—$150.00
    M1911, excellent—$250.00
    M1915, very good—$125.00
    M1915, excellent—$195.00
    M1916, very good—$135.00
    M1916, excellent—$200.00
    Victoria, very good—$140.00
    Victoria, excellent—$225.00

History: This model was the successor to the Unceta Victoria .32, which started production in 1908. In 1911, the name Astra was adopted, along with a new numbering system. In 1914, due to the pressures of the then current war, it was redesigned with a larger magazine capacity and redesignated the Model 1915, along with a new serial number range. In 1916 the name was changed to Model 1916. About 150,000 of this type were made, most of them going to France and Italy for military use. The entire model type was discontinued at the end of the war in favor of the Model 400.

Mechanical Functioning: This is a straight blowback operated, semiautomatic pistol with a six-shot detachable box magazine. The side safety on this concealed hammer pistol blocked the firing train and also locked the slide back for takedown. The firing pin is of the floating type. The left side of the lower rear gripframe had a lanyard loop mounted, and the magazine catch was at the bottom rear of the gripframe, and the recoil spring was mounted under the barrel. The takedown is of Browning M1903 style and is achieved by first being sure that the pistol is unloaded. Then remove the magazine and pull the slide to the rear and engage the safety to lock the slide in the rearward position. The barrel should now be able to be turned until the locking lugs are visible in the ejection port. The slide should now be firmly held and the safety released. The slide, under tension from the recoil spring, may now be removed forward and off of the frame. The recoil spring, recoil spring guide, and the barrel can now be removed from the bottom of the slide. Assembly is carried out in the reverse order. The pistol was of all steel construction and was solidly made.

Astra Model 1911 .32 A.C.P.

Auto Mag
Arcadia Machine & Tool (AMT)
Irwindale, CA 91702

Model: Auto Mag

Action Type: semiautomatic, recoil operated

Caliber(s): .44 A.M.P., .357 A.M.P.

Barrel Lengths: 6½", 8½", 10½".

Finish: stainless steel.

Manufacturing Dates: 1970–1977.

Stocks: plastic or laminated wood.

Rifling: 8L, 8G.

Weight, Unloaded: 44 oz.

Sights: adjustable.

Serial Numbers: various runs with prefixes H.S. (High Standard), L.E.J. (Jurras .357 A.M.P. Custom Run), A.O. (Post High Standard Production), X suffix on L.E.J. prefix (Jurras .44 A.M.P. Custom Run). Total production is less than 10,000.

Serial Number Location: bottom of gripframe.

Major Variations: detachable-shoulder-stock version.
4" and 12½" barrels.
.41 J.M.P. caliber.
barrels with and without ribs.

Markings: on left side of receiver: Automag, caliber, model, address.
on some pistols that will be preceded by the T.D.E. trademark, or have the High Standard name.

Price(s):
.44 A.M.P., very good—$2,000.00
.44 A.M.P., excellent—$2,500.00
.357 A.M.P., very good—$1,750.00
.357 A.M.P., excellent—$2,000.00
L.E.J. Custom Model 100 add 50%

History: Although founded in 1968 as the Auto Mag Corp. by Harry Sanford, the firm's first deliveries started in early 1971. In May 1971 the firm went bankrupt and was purchased by Thomas Oil Co. and renamed T.D.E. (Trust Deed Estates Corp.). Shortly after this, High Standard purchased trade-labeled Auto Mags, and finally in 1974, Lee Jurras Associates became the exclusive distributor. The factory began operations in Pasadena, California, and when T.D.E. took over the equipment, was moved to North Hollywood, California. A great many "Custom" variations will be found, with various wildcat calibers as well as many external and cosmetic changes.

Mechanical Functioning: This is a short-recoil, semiautomatic pistol with an external hammer and a detachable seven-shot box magazine. The breech lock is accomplished with a six-lug rotary bolt, and unlocking and cycling is accomplished with a camming protrusion unlocking the bolt and an accelerator, similar to the Browning .50 caliber heavy machine gun, assisting in pushing the bolt rearward. The safety disconnects the trigger, when engaged, as well as camming the hammer out of sear engagement and effectively locking the pistol. The hammer also has a safety notch cut.

Auto Mag

Auto Ordnance Corp.
West Hurley, NY 12491

Model: M1911A1

Action Type: semiautomatic, recoil operated.

Caliber(s): .45 A.C.P., 9mm Luger, .38 Super.

Barrel Lengths: 5″.

Finish: matte blue.

Manufacturing Dates: 1981 to date.

Stocks: plastic with medallion.

Rifling: n/a.

Weight, Unloaded: 39 oz.

Sights: fixed.

Serial Numbers: "E" prefix.

Serial Number Location: right frame over trigger.

Major Variations: n/a.

Markings: right frame: Auto-Ordnance Corp., West Hurley, N.Y., serial number
left slide: Thompson logo, Auto Ordnance Corp., and caliber

Price(s): very good—$275.00; excellent—$350.00

History: This is another in the series of U.S. M1911A1 pistols manufactured by several companies. This one is made to U.S. military specifications, and all parts are interchangeable with the military version. This model is made with the early-style long trigger.

Mechanical Functioning: This recoil-operated pistol is based on the Browning-designed Colt M1911A1. To disassemble this pistol, remove the magazine and check to make sure that the weapon is unloaded. Depress plug below the barrel in far enough to allow the barrel bushing to be turned to the right until the plug can be eased out to the front. Remember that this plug is under spring tension, so remove carefully. Pull the slide back until the rear edge of the smaller of the two cuts near the center of the slide on the left-hand side lines up with the rear end of the slide stock. Push the end of the slide stock in, right to left. This will push the slide stock out of the left-hand side far enough to be grabbed and pulled out entirely. When this is removed, the slide can be pulled directly forward off the receiver, taking the entire barrel assembly with it. The barrel bushing, recoil spring, recoil spring guide, and barrel may now be removed from the slide by turning the barrel bushing to the left as far as it will go, and withdrawing it to the front. Reassemble in the reverse order, making sure that the slide stop pin passes through the length at the bottom of the barrel, for this is the mechanism by which the pistol both locks and unlocks.

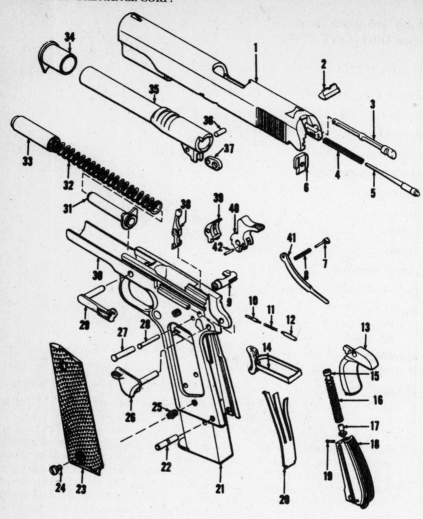

1	Slide	16	Mainspring	
2	Rear Sight	17	Mainspring Housing Pin Retainer	29 Slide Stop
3	Extractor	18	Mainspring Housing	30 Frame (Receiver)
4	Firing Pin Spring	19	Mainspring Cap Pin	31 Recoil Spring Guide
5	Firing Pin	20	Sear Spring	32 Recoil Spring
6	Firing Pin Stop Plate	21	Magazine	33 Plug
7	Magazine Catch Lock	22	Mainspring Housing Pin	34 Barrel Bushing
8	Magazine Catch Spring	23	Hand Grip with Medallion	35 Barrel
9	Magazine Catch		A. Left	36 Barrel Link Pin
10	Slide Stop Plunger		B. Right	37 Barrel Link
11	Plunger Spring	24	Grip Screw	38 Disconnector
12	Safety Catch Plunger	25	Stock Screw Bushing	39 Sear
13	Grip Safety	26	Safety Catch	40 Hammer
14	Trigger	27	Hammer Pin	41 Hammer Strut
15	Mainspring Cap	28	Sear and Disconnector Pin	42 Hammer Strut Pin

Auto Ordnance M1911A1 Thompson .45

Auto Ordnance Corp.
West Hurley, NY 12491

Model: 1927 A-5 (pistol/carbine)

Action Type: semiautomatic, blowback.

Caliber(s): .45 A.C.P.

Barrel Lengths: 13″.

Finish: blue.

Manufacturing Dates: 1977–1994.

Stocks: walnut wood.

Rifling: n/a.

Weight, Unloaded: 6¾ lbs.

Sights: adjustable rear sight, post front.

Serial Numbers: n/a.

Serial Number Location: right side of receiver.

Major Variations: magazine types: 5-, 15-, 20-, and 30-shot detachable box
magazines;
39- and 50-shot drum magazines.

Markings: original style Thompson and Auto Ordnance markings on right
side of receiver.

Price(s): very good—$375.00; excellent—$500.00.

History: The Thompson Model 1927 A-5 was introduced in 1977 to commemorate the Thompson Model 1928-A Submachine gun, the major differences being lighter weight, the absence of a detachable stock, and no
full-auto feature. The 1927 A-5 has the original 13″ finned barrel and the
vertical foregrip. It has an adjustable rear sight, and a fixed blade front
sight. There was some question as to the legal classification of this gun,
but Auto Ordnance was able to have it classified as a standard pistol. It
has a 13-inch barrel, and is made from the new style semiautomatic
frame that the Model 1927 A-1 uses, which prevents it from being converted to full automatic fire. There is no provision to attach a buttstock
as there was on the gun that this model commemorates. The drum magazine is standard equipment, but all of the Thompson clips and drums
can be used with it. This weapon is really too big to be called a true
pistol in the sense that a handgun should be operable with one hand.
This is a pistol in regard to its legal classification because it is just a
little too heavy to use any way other than with two hands. However, as
a perimeter defense weapon I don't think that it has an equal. It delivers
a very potent round and probably carries more shots than should be
needed in all but the most dire circumstances. The two-handed hold
yields excellent accuracy for point shooting, and the recoil with top
loads is surprisingly mild.

Mechanical Functioning: The Auto Ordnance Model 1927 A-5 Thompson is a blowback-operated semiautomatic pistol based on the Thompson Carbine Action and made safe by the strength of the receiver and weight of the bolt. This "handgun" was designed to be used with both hands. Takedown is accomplished by first making sure that the gun is unloaded and removing the magazine. Make sure the bolt is in the closed position and that the safety is in the off position. On the bottom rear of the frame there is a frame latch. Push up on this catch and slide the frame to the rear until it is caught by the sear. Press it in again with a small screwdriver so that the sear is cleared, and remove it the rest of the way off of the receiver. The frame is usually quite tight and sometimes it may be necessary to give it a few taps with a non-marring tool to get it started. The bolt is removed next by pushing forward on the small plate holding the two recoil springs at the rear. Then lift up slightly and pull the entire assembly out of the receiver. The firing pin spring and firing pin spring guide can now be removed through the hole in the rear of the receiver. Slide the bolt to the rear by raising the muzzle slightly. The hammer should now slide out through the hole in the rear of the receiver. The cocking handle can now be removed through the large hole in the top of the receiver. The bolt should now be able to be dropped out. Assembly is in the reverse order.

Thompson Model 1928 A-5 .45

B.R.F.
Pretoria, South Africa

Model: Junior

Action Type: semiautomatic, blowback.

Caliber(s): .25 A.C.P.

Barrel Lengths: 2¼".

Finish: blue or chrome.

Manufacturing Dates: 1957.

Stocks: black plastic, but other colors have been reported.

Rifling: 6L.

Weight, Unloaded: 13³/₈" oz.

Sights: none, aiming groove on top of slide.

Serial Numbers: interspersed throughout the P.A.F. Junior range.

Serial Number Location: rear grip strap.

Major Variations: a few pistols had cocking indicators.

Markings: on left slide; B.R.F.
U-SA
and P.A.F. mark on most parts.

Price(s):
blue, very good—$175.00
blue, excellent—$275.00
chrome, very good—$275.00
chrome, excellent—$325.00
blue with cocking indicator, very good—$250.00
blue with cocking indicator, excellent—$300.00
chrome with cocking indicator, very good—$275.00
chrome with cocking indicator, excellent—$400.00
blue with PAF logo on slide, very good—$200.00
blue with PAF logo on slide, excellent—$275.00
blue, rough ground slide, no mark, very good—$125.00
blue, rough ground slide, no mark, excellent—$175.00
blue, sight rib, very good—$200.00
blue, sight rib, excellent—$275.00
blue, low slide, very good—$175.00
blue, low slide, excellent—$225.00

History: The history of B.R.F. is shrouded in mystery, and even queries to South African collectors have not shed light on this firm. What is known is that B.R.F. purchased the remaining stocks and equipment when the Pretoria Arms Factory (P.A.F.) went out of business. B.R.F. attempted to overcome the "Junior's" poor reputation by removing the P.A.F. name from the gun. They were unsuccessful, and only about 200 pistols were assembled, about 50 of them in chrome. See also P.A.F.

Mechanical Functioning: The B.R.F. is a Browning Model 1906–type blow-back action, with the recoil spring mounted underneath the barrel. The safety located at the left rear of the frame intercepts the sear and in some pistols lifts a rod to lock the slide. The pistol is striker-fired. The barrel is retained by a single large lug fitting into a frame recess. The early production of the P.A.F. had a bad habit of shearing off the front face of the frame by the barrel lug upon firing during counterrecoil, with the embarrassing effect of letting the whole slide assembly fly off the front of the gun. By the time B.R.F. had purchased the parts from the bankrupt P.A.F., none of the early-style frames remained, and the B.R.F. frames are all of the late P.A.F. type with thick frame webs eliminating the chance of frame shear during counterrecoil. Takedown of the B.R.F. is accomplished by making sure that the pistol is unloaded, pulling the trigger, and then withdrawing the slide to the rear until the barrel lug lines up with the cut in the slide visible in the ejection port. Holding the slide in that position, rotate the barrel so the barrel lug disengages from the frame and turns into the slide. Thus unlocked, the slide assembly can be moved forward and off of the frame. The firing pin, firing pin spring, and firing pin spring guide can be withdrawn out of the rear of the slide, and the barrel and recoil spring and guide out from the bottom of the slide. Assembly is in the reverse order.

B.R.F. Junior, Chrome-plated

Bauer Firearms Corp.
Fraser, MI 48026

Model: 25-SS

Action Type: semiautomatic, blowback operated.

Caliber(s): 25 A.C.P.

Barrel Lengths: 2⅛″.

Finish: stainless steel.

Manufacturing Dates: 1972–1984.

Stocks: wood or plastic mother-of-pearl.

Rifling: 6R.

Weight, Unloaded: 10 oz.

Sights: fixed.

Serial Numbers: n/a.

Serial Number Location: left side of frame above trigger.

Major Variations: standard.
  Bicentennial Commemorative.

Markings: right side of slide: Bauer Automatic, .25 Caliber Automatic.
  left side of slide: Bauer Firearms Corp, Fraser Michigan USA.

Price(s):
  Bicentennial, very good—$150.00
  Bicentennial, excellent—$200.00
  Standard, very good—$100.00
  Standard, excellent—$125.00

History: They say that imitation is the sincerest form of flattery. However, in the firearms field, imitation of a successful product that is no longer available in a given geographical area is an almost assured formula for success. When Bauer Firearms Corporation was formed and started to manufacture this pistol in 1972, four years after the passage of the GCA-68, they knew they were going to have a winner. The Bauer .25 is a virtually identical copy of the Browning Baby model, even down to the point where you can interchange parts. However, the Bauer has something going for it that the European model, which was so long in production, does not have. Except for the grips, it is made entirely of stainless steel with all of the attendant virtues of that metal. It is small, light, compact, reliable, and safe. But of course, it is based on a design that dates back to the early 1920s which has certainly been proven by the test of time.

Mechanical Functioning: The SS-25 Bauer Automatic pistol is a straight blowback, striker-fired, semiautomatic pistol, with a six-round, detachable box magazine. It is crafted entirely of stainless steel, and it is an exact copy of the Browning Baby .25 automatic. The safety is manual and blocks the sear when engaged. There is also an automatic functioning magazine safety to prevent firing when the magazine is removed. The magazine catch is located at the bottom rear of the gripframe. Field stripping is accomplished by retracting the slide back slightly over ½ inch and locking it in place by swinging the manual safety upward. The barrel can now be rotated until the locking lugs are visible in the ejection port. While holding the slide in place, release the safety, and now the slide and barrel assembly can move forward just far enough to clear the striker base and then lift it upward. The slide assembly can now be dismounted. Assemble in reverse order, but always remember, before field stripping, remove the magazine and be sure that the chamber is cleared.

Bauer SS-25

Bayard
Anciens Etablissements Pieper
Herstal, Belgium

Model: 1908

Action Type: semiautomatic, blowback operated.

Caliber(s): 6.35mm, 7.65mm, 9mm K.

Barrel Lengths: 2¼".

Finish: blue or nickel.

Manufacturing Dates: 1909 to the mid-1920s.

Stocks: hard rubber.

Rifling: 6L.

Weight, Unloaded: 17 oz.

Sights: fixed.

Serial Numbers: starting point unknown, but the range of about 100,000 to about 200,000 show German Imperial military stamps indicating war-time make, and serials seem to run to almost 300,000.

Serial Number Location: right side of frame at rear and above it on the slide.

Major Variations: .25 A.C.P. (Model 1912).
.32 A.C.P. (Model 1910).
.380 A.C.P. (Model 1911).
.32 A.C.P. German Military.

Markings: left side of slide: (caliber), Modele Depose.
left side of frame: Anciens Etablissements Pieper, Herstal, Belgium.
right side of slide: Made in Belgium.

Price(s):
.25 A.C.P., blue, very good—$150.00
.25 A.C.P., blue, excellent—$225.00
.32 A.C.P., blue, very good—$145.00
.32 A.C.P., blue, excellent—$240.00
.380 A.C.P., blue, very good—$180.00
.380 A.C.P., blue, excellent—$325.00
.32 German Military, very good—$125.00
.32 German Military, excellent—$225.00

History: A fairly unique pistol, the Bayard 1908 was based on the designs of Bernard Clarus, developed between 1905 and 1907 and purchased by Anciens Etablissements Pieper. The first guns made under this patent were produced in 1908 but were not announced to the general public until late 1909 or early 1910; hence the confusion about the model name. The most accepted nomenclature for this pistol is the Bayard Model 1908; however, occasionally it is seen as the Model 1910 if it is in .32 A.C.P., the Model 1911 in .380 A.C.P., or the Model 1912 in .25 A.C.P.

These are very small pistols for the two larger calibers of .32 and .380 and in size are about the same as your ordinary .25 pistol. Unfortunately, due to its small size and light weight, the recoil is very uncomfortable, especially in .380 caliber, and a special buffer arrangement had to be used to cushion the shock. In all three calibers the magazine held six shots.

Mechanical Functioning: The Bayard Model 1908 and all of its variations are straight blowback, semiautomatic pistols with detachable box magazines, inserted through the gripframe and retained by a latch at the bottom of the gripframe. It has an internal hammer and floating firing pin. It has a mechanical thumb safety on the left rear of the frame, which when engaged inhibits the sear. An unusual feature of the Bayard 1908 is the location of the barrel, which is bored through the front of the frame rather than being mounted on the frame or attached to the slide, or being part of the slide group. In order to take this pistol down, it is necessary to push the front sight back and raise it slightly. This allows it to be unhooked and removed from the slide entirely. The slide may then be retracted fully, and lifted up out of its guide and then off the receiver.

Bayard Model 1908

Bayard
Anciens Etablissements Pieper
Herstal, Belgium

Model: 1923

Action Type: semiautomatic, blowback operated.

Caliber(s): .25 A.C.P., .380 A.C.P., .32 A.C.P.

Barrel Lengths: 3½″ in .32 and .380 and 2½″ in .25 A.C.P.

Finish: blue.

Manufacturing Dates: 1923–1940.

Stocks: hard rubber.

Rifling: 6L.

Weight, Unloaded: 20 oz. in .32 and .380, 12 oz. in .25 A.C.P.

Serial Numbers: n/a.

Serial Number Location: right side of frame to the rear of the grip.

Major Variations: .25 A.C.P. 1923 version, early types had a magazine safety.
.32 A.C.P., 1923 version, early types had a magazine safety.
.380 A.C.P., 1923 version, early types had a magazine safety.
.25 A.C.P., 1930 version, early types had a magazine safety.
.32 A.C.P., 1930 version, early types had a magazine safety.
.380 A.C.P., 1930 version, early types had a magazine safety.

Markings: left side of slide: Anciens Etablissements Pieper, Herstal, Belgium. right side of slide: (Caliber) Modele Depose.

Price(s):
.25 A.C.P., 1923, early, very good—$195.00
.25 A.C.P., 1923, early, excellent—$300.00
.32 A.C.P., 1923, early, very good—$225.00
.32 A.C.P., 1923, early, excellent—$350.00
.380 A.C.P., 1923, early, very good—$240.00
.380 A.C.P., 1923, early, excellent—$375.00
.25 A.C.P., 1923, standard, very good—$155.00
.25 A.C.P., 1923, standard, excellent—$275.00
.32 A.C.P., 1923, standard, very good—$180.00
.32 A.C.P., 1923, standard, excellent—$300.00
.380 A.C.P., 1923, standard, very good—$220.00
.380 A.C.P., 1923, standard, excellent—$350.00
.25 A.C.P., 1930, very good—$150.00
.25 A.C.P., 1930, excellent—$295.00
.32 A.C.P., 1930, very good—$200.00
.32 A.C.P., 1930, excellent—$325.00
.380 A.C.P., 1930, very good—$225.00
.380 A.C.P., 1930, excellent—$375.00

History: The Bayard 1923 was the logical development for Pieper after the complex manufacturing that the model of 1908 entailed. This pistol is very similar to the Browning design; however, it also incorporates a shock-absorbing device to aid in recoil reduction in .38 and .380 A.C.P. The early variation of the Model 1923 had incorporated a magazine safety. However, the factory, not long into the production of this model, issued a statement that automatic safeties might be broken or rendered inoperative and that condition might be more dangerous than not having a safety present at all. It further stated that if a cartridge had been inadvertently left in the chamber, and an empty magazine then inserted, the pistol might be fired. Whereas, if there was no magazine safety, then people would be more careful and more prone to use manual safety. In this author's opinion, there could be a great deal of argument that the factory was cost-conscious and wished to eliminate some of the mechanical features. In 1930 another change was adopted in this model. The magazine catch was altered to a two-pointed sliding design, rather than the hinged, Browning-style catch.

Mechanical Functioning: The Model 1923 is a simple blowback-operated, semiautomatic pistol with an internal hammer and floating firing pin. In exterior shape, it was very similar to the Browning 1910. After initial production runs, the magazine safety was eliminated, but the manual safety on the left side of the frame forward of the grip remained. The Model 1923 also retained the Model 1908's hammer and sear system, which had been designed by Bernard Clarus. The recoil spring is axially mounted around the barrel. The magazine is of detachable box style and in all calibers holds six rounds.

Manufacture D'Armes Automatiques Bayonne (MAB)
Bayonne, France

Model: B

Action Type: semiautomatic, blowback operated.

Caliber(s): 6.35mm

Barrel Lengths: 2".

Finish: blue.

Manufacturing Dates: 1932–mid-1960s.

Stocks: plastic or hard rubber.

Rifling: 6R.

Weight, Unloaded: 9½ oz.

Sights: fixed.

Serial Numbers: started at 79084. In 1949 reverted to 25001.

Serial Number Locations: right side of slide.

Major Variations: French model.
   U.S. export model.

Markings: left side of slide: Pistolet Automatique MAB Brevete Modele B.
   right side of slide: on French models: blank.
   right side of slide: on WAC models: Made in France for W.A.C.

Price(s):
   French Model B, very good—$175.00
   French Model B, excellent—$250.00
   W.A.C. Model B, very good—$125.00
   W.A.C. Model B, excellent—$200.00
   Nazi proofed Model B, very good—$300.00
   Nazi proofed Model B, excellent—$350.00

History: Manufacture D'Armes Automatiques Bayonne, of Bayonne, France, produced a wide range of pistols since their inception in 1921. When the Germans rolled through France in 1940, the plant naturally came under German supervision. Eventually, all of the output was destined for the Reich's military and police use. After the war, commercial production was resumed, and in the early 1950s Western Arms Corporation, an importer in California, took on the line; therefore, there will be several variations to be found. There are the early French models that have no markings other than "French," those made under German supervision that bear Nazi proofs, and those postwar U.S. export models that are plainly marked W.A.C. on both the right-hand side of the slide and usually on the grips. The MAB Model B was first made in 1932 and remained in production until the 1960s. It was a .25 automatic, hammerless pocket pistol of medium quality.

Mechanical Functioning: The MAB Model B is a straight blowback, semi-automatic pistol with a six-round detachable box magazine inserted through the gripframe and retained by a spring-loaded catch at the bottom rear of the butt. It is striker-fired, and its barrel is permanently fixed to the bottom of the frame. The slide is open-topped from the breech face forward, with the top of the barrel exposed. The recoil spring rides underneath the barrel, and the safety is manual and is located just above and slightly to the rear of the trigger.

MAB Model B

Manufacture D'Armes Automatiques Bayonne (MAB)
Bayonne, France

Model: D

Action Type: semiautomatic, blowback operated.

Caliber(s): 7.65mm, 9mm K.

Barrel Lengths: 4".

Finish: blue.

Manufacturing Dates: 1933 to date.

Stocks: plastic.

Rifling: 6R.

Weight, Unloaded: 25 oz.

Sights: fixed.

Serial Numbers: started at 10730 and ran to 114690 in 1945. It then went back and restarted at 50001.

Serial Number Location: right side of frame above trigger.

Major Variations: French Model.
U.S. Export Model.
Nazi proofed.
French Military.

Markings: left side of slide: Pistolet Automatique Cal. (caliber), MAB Brevete Modele D.
right side of slide: on French models: blank.
right side of slide: on W.A.C. models: made in France for W.A.C.

Price(s):
Model D, 7.65mm, very good—$100.00
Model D, 7.65mm, excellent—$175.00
Model D, 9mm K, very good—$125.00
Model D, 9mm K, excellent—$200.00
Model D, 7.65mm, W.A.C., very good—$100.00
Model D, 7.65mm, W.A.C., excellent—$150.00
Model D, 9mm K, W.A.C., very good—$100.00
Model D, 9mm K, W.A.C., excellent—$150.00
Model D, 7.65mm, Nazi, very good—$200.00
Model D, 7.65mm, Nazi, excellent—$300.00
Model D, 9mm K, Nazi, very good—$275.00
Model D, 9mm K, Nazi, excellent—$350.00
Model D, 7.65mm, French Military, very good—$250.00
Model D, 7.65mm, French Military, excellent—$325.00
Model D, 7.65mm, adj. sights, thumbrest grips, very good—$100.00
Model D, 7.65mm, adj. sights, thumbrest grips, excellent—$150.00

History: Manufacture D'Armes Automatiques Bayonne, of Bayonne, France, produced a wide range of pistols since their inception in 1921. When the Germans rolled through France in 1940, the plant naturally came under German supervision, and virtually all of the output was destined for the Reich's military and police use. After the war, commercial production was resumed and in the early 1950s Western Arms Corporation, an importer in California, took on the line; therefore there will be several variations to be found. There are the purely French models that have no markings other than "French," those made under German supervision that bear Nazi proofs, and those postwar U.S. export models that are plainly marked "W.A.C." on both the right-hand side of the slide and usually on the grips. The MAB Model D is a 7.65mm or 9mm K caliber pistol that was first made in 1933 and whose production continued until the mid-1970s. It is essentially the same pistol as the Model C but with a slightly longer barrel and longer grip. During this pistol's production life, it not only had commercial sales, but was also used by the Nazi military as well as the French military as secondary Marshall arms. These pistols will be found both with and without lanyard loops at the base of the butt.

Mechanical Functioning: The MAB Model D is a straight blowback, semiautomatic pistol with a nine-round detachable box magazine in 7.65mm, and an eight-round detachable box magazine in 9mm K. The magazine is inserted through the gripframe and is retained by a catch just to the rear of the trigger on the left side of the frame. This pistol had both grip safety as well as manually operated thumb safety. Similar to the Browning design, the recoil spring was wound axially around the barrel, and the entire assembly was retained by a sleeve with a bayonette-style catch in a manner similar to the Model 400 Astra. It is striker-fired, and disassembly is in the same manner as the Browning Model 1910.

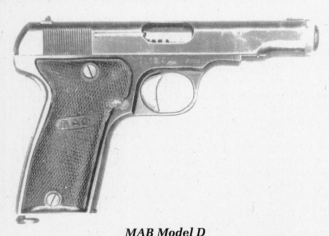

MAB Model D

Manufacture D'Armes Automatiques Bayonne (MAB)
Bayonne, France

Model: F

Action Type: semiautomatic, blowback operated.

Caliber(s): .22 L.R.

Barrel Lengths: 2½" to 7¼".

Finish: blue.

Manufacturing Dates: 1950–mid-1950s.

Stocks: plastic.

Rifling: 6R.

Weight, Unloaded: 29 oz.

Sights: fixed with high blade front.

Serial Numbers: started at 1 but may have run out of sequence.

Serial Number Location: right side of frame above trigger guard.

Major Variations: French Model.
　　U.S. Export Model.

Markings: left side of slide: Pistolet Automatique MAB Brevete Modele F.
　　right side of slide: French Model: blank.
　　right side of slide: W.A.C. Model: Made in France for W.A.C.

Price(s):
　　Model F, 2½" to 3½" barrel, very good—$125.00
　　Model F, 2½" to 3½" barrel, excellent—$200.00
　　Model F, 4" to 5½" barrel, very good—$150.00
　　Model F, 4" to 5½" barrel, excellent—$225.00
　　Model F, 6" to 7¼" barrel, very good—$175.00
　　Model F, 6" to 7¼" barrel, excellent—$275.00
　　Model F, W.A.C., 2½" to 3½" barrel, very good—$125.00
　　Model F, W.A.C., 2½" to 3½" barrel, excellent—$200.00
　　Model F, W.A.C., 4" to 5½" barrel, very good—$100.00
　　Model F, W.A.C., 4" to 5½" barrel, excellent—$200.00
　　Model F, W.A.C., 6" to 7¼" barrel, very good—$125.00
　　Model F, W.A.C., 6" to 7¼" barrel, excellent—$225.00

History: Manufacture D'Armes Automatiques Bayonne, of Bayonne, France, produced a wide range of pistols since their inception in 1921. When the Germans rolled through France in 1940 the plant naturally came under German supervision and virtually all of the output was destined for the Reich's military and police use. After the war, commercial production was resumed, and in the early 1950s, Western Arms Corporation, an importer in California, took on the line; therefore, there will be several variations to be found. There are the purely French models that have no markings other than "French," those made under German supervision that bear Nazi proofs, and those postwar U.S. export models that are plainly marked "W.A.C." on both the right-hand side of the slide and usually on the grips. The Model F was MAB's first venture into the field of .22 caliber pistols. Mechanically, it is rather awkward, and even though the grip is nicely angled to provide good point shooting, the pistol by no stretch of the imagination could be considered target quality. The sights were fitted with a high blade front similar to rifle sights, and with the shorter barrels it just did not provide enough sight radius for match competition. However, some of the longer-barreled models could be tuned to perform fairly well. There were perhaps as many as seven or eight barrel lengths available on this model, ranging from about 2½" to about 7¼". It appears that a great deal of modification was available on customer request.

Mechanical Functioning: The MAB Model F is a straight blowback-operated, semiautomatic pistol. It has a concealed internal hammer and a recoil spring mounted on a guide located below the barrel, which is fixed to the frame. The magazine is a ten-shot detachable box type inserted through the gripframe. Operation was single action only.

MAB Model F

Becker & Hollander Waffenbau
Suhl, Germany

Model: Beholla

Action Type: semiautomatic, blowback operated.

Caliber(s): 7.65mm.

Barrel Lengths: 2.9".

Finish: blue.

Manufacturing Dates: 1915 to about 1920.

Stocks: hard rubber or serrated wood.

Rifling: 6R.

Weight, Unloaded: 22 oz.

Sights: fixed.

Serial Numbers: 1 to about 45000.

Serial Number Location: left side of frame above trigger guard.

Major Variations: wood or hard rubber grips.
commercial or military markings.

Markings: left side of slide: Selbstade Pistole "Beholla" Ca. 7.65.
right side of slide: Becker U. Hollander Waffenbau.

Price(s):
military, hard rubber grips, very good—$275.00
military, hard rubber grips, excellent—$325.00
military, wood grips, very good—$300.00
military, wood grips, excellent—$350.00

History: The Beholla design was developed by Becker & Hollander Waffenbau at the beginning of World War I, and they must have had the war effort in mind, as virtually the entire production went to the German military. However, it appears that after the war the firm couldn't cope with peace, and in the middle of 1920 they apparently sold out. The new company, obviously using the same machinery, was named Stenda Werke GMBH Waffenbau, also of Suhl, Germany. Their early pistols were a continuation of the Beholla serial range, as some pistols even had Beholla marks on the left side of the slide. The same design during the war was also made by August Menz of Suhl, Germany, and for a short time after, and it was called the Menta. Later, H.M. Gering made this, his version named the Leon Hardt.

Mechanical Functioning: This is a straight blowback, semiautomatic pistol with a seven-shot detachable box magazine. It is striker-fired, and the thumb-operated safety intercepts the sear. The trigger is of pivoting type and is connected to the sear via a bar. There is no ejector per se; however, at maximum opening, the firing pin protrudes and it knocks out the case. Takedown of the Beholla is a serious job and best done on a regular workbench. Considering that this is a military pistol, it's a real wonder that the German military adopted it because the average soldier probably could not field-strip this weapon. In order to take the Beholla apart it is first necessary, as with all guns, to make sure that the pistol is unloaded. Then the barrel retaining pin, which can be seen through the hole in either side of the slide when it is at battery, must be removed. It is drifted out with a pin punch of the proper size through the openings in the slide sides. The slide is then pulled back to the rearward position and locked in place by engaging the safety. The barrel is tapped with a piece of wood, leather mallet, or soft brass hammer toward the rear until it disengages itself from the frame. The barrel can now be lifted out. Holding the slide, which is under tension from the recoil spring, release the safety and allow the slide to travel forward and off the frame. The firing pin can now be removed. Assembly is in the reverse order, but care must be exercised in reseating the barrel and resetting the barrel retaining pin. After the slide assembly has been placed on the receiver and pulled to the rearward position and locked in place, set the barrel in position and close the slide. Be careful to properly align the barrel stud, which is in the shape of a dovetail, with the dovetail slot machined into the frame. The metal is not exceptionally hard, and it's easy to cant the barrel very slightly and mar the slot, which could affect the tightness of the barrel mount. Sometimes a slight tap with a nonmarring mallet will be necessary to firmly set the barrel into the proper niche. At this time replace the barrel retaining pin, being sure that it is centered between the slide sides and not riding on either side and not binding the action. Like all of the pistols in this series, the Beholla is manufactured of all steel parts.

Beholla

Berdan Gunmakers Ltd.
Raban's Lane Industrial Estate
Aylesbury, Bucks, England

Model: Britarms 2000 Mark II

Action Type: semiautomatic, blowback.

Caliber(s): .22 L.R.

Barrel Lengths: 148mm.

Finish: combination of blue and satin chrome.

Manufacturing Dates: 1977–1980.

Stocks: oiled walnut adjustable grips, right hand or left hand, and large and small sizes.

Rifling: n/a.

Weight, Unloaded: 2.98 lbs. with steel barrel weight and empty magazine.

Sights: adjustable 3.4mm square notch rear and either 3.2mm, 3.6mm, or 4.0mm blade foresights.

Serial Numbers: Action Arms Ltd. imports start at BA92795.

Serial Number Location: left side of receiver above trigger guard.

Major Variations: Britarms 2000.
Britarms 2000 Mark II cocking has vertical finger grooves, and safety notch.
Britarms 2000 Mark III cocking lug is smooth with dished indents for grasping.

Markings: pre-Action Arms Ltd. Britarms have four (4) digit serial number. Action Arms Ltd. Imports have BA9 prefix and four (4) digit numbers. Action Arms Ltd. Imports have "Action Arms Ltd., Phila. Pa." markings.

Price(s): Action Arms Ltd. Imports had suggested retail price of $1,200.00 in 1978.

History: First manufactured January 1977, designed by Chris Valentine and Tom Redhead (a former British National Squad member). Imported into the U.S. by Action Arms, Ltd., P.O. Box 9573, Philadelphia, PA 19124.

Mechanical Functioning: Five-round magazine loads from above receiver with bolt held rearward. Releasing bolt chambers first round. Each pull of trigger fires one round. The bolt recoils rearward, extracting and ejecting spent case, then chambers fresh round in its travel forward. There is no automatic bolt hold-open after last shot is fired.

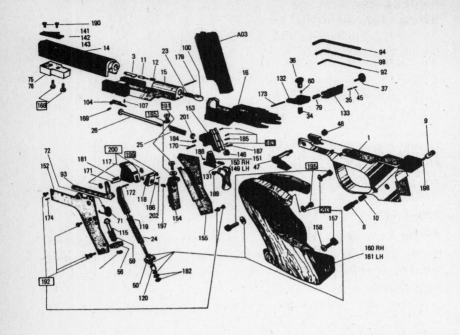

1	Frame	93	Disconnector Lever
3	Extractor Claw	94	Allen Key 4.0mm A/F
8	Magazine Release Button	98	Allen Key 1.5mm A/F
9	Magazine Release Connector	100	Firing Pin
10	Magazine Release Spring	104	Hold Open Lever
11	Extractor Plunger	107	Hold Open Lever Spring
12	Extractor Spring	115	Magazine Ejector Rod
14	Barrel	117	Hammer
15	Bolt	118	Sear
16	Bolt Cover	119	Hammer Shaft
23	Firing Pin Spring	120	Buffer
24	Hammer Spring	131	Trigger Weight Spring
25	Main Spring	132	Rear Sight Block
26	Guide Rod	133	Rear Sight Blade
34	Rear Sight Vertical Spring	141	Foresight 3.2mm
35	Rear Sight Spring (Index Pin)	142	Foresight 3.6mm
36	Sight Elevation Screw	143	Foresight 4.0mm
37	Sight Windage Screw	146	Trigger Adjustment Barrel
45	Windage Screw Plunger	149	Anatomical Trigger (L.H.)
47	Takedown Lever	150	Anatomical Trigger (R.H.)
48	Clamping Nut	151	Trigger Bar
50	Hammer Spring Stop	152	Trigger Side Plate
56	Magazine Ejector Block	153	Trigger Mounting Block
59	Magazine Ejector Rod Spring	154	Sear Block
60	Index Pin	155	Sear Cover
71	Spring Retainer Button	157	Grip Screw
72	Disconnector Lever Spring	158	Washer
75	Barrel Weight St.	160	Grips (R.H.)
76	Barrel Weight Al.	161	Grips (L.H.)
79	Rear Sight Lateral Spring	165	Washer
92	Allen Key 0.9mm A.F.		

166	Grip Nut
168	Barrel Weight Screw
169	Hold Open Lever Spindle
170	Trigger Bar Spindle
171	Hammer Spindle
172	Sear Spindle
173	Rear Sight Spindle
174	Trigger Unit Dowel
179	Firing Pin Dowel
181	Hammer Shaft Pivot
182	Lock Nuts
183	Adjustable Lock Screws
184	Forward Trigger Stop
185	Rear Trigger Stop
186	Sear Engagement Screw
187	Trigger Weight Screw
188	Trigger Barrel Lock Screw
189	Trigger Lock Screw
190	Foresight Screws
191	Trigger Unit Screw
192	Sideplate Screw
195	Grip Screw
197	Sear Spring
198	Magazine Connector Screw
199	Crinkle Washer
200	Crinkle Washer
201	Circlip
202	Sear Adjustment Lockscrew
203	Washer
A03	Magazine

Britarms Model 2000 Mark II

Pietro Beretta
Brescia, Italy

Model: Bantam (418)

Action Type: semiautomatic, blowback operated.

Caliber(s): 6.35mm.

Barrel Lengths: 2½".

Finish: blue.

Manufacturing Dates: 1946 through the 1950s.

Stocks: plastic.

Rifling: 6R.

Weight, Unloaded: 10 oz.

Sights: fixed.

Serial Numbers: started at 1A, but examples are known with a "C" suffix.

Serial Number Location: right side of frame above the trigger guard.

Major Variations: Model 418—blue.
　　Model 420—chrome plated and engraved.
　　Model 421—gold plated with fancy engraving.

Markings: left side of frame: P. Beretta, Cal. 6.35, Gardone, V.T.
　　right side of frame: Made in Italy.

Price(s):
　　Model 418, very good—$200.00
　　Model 418, excellent—$225.00
　　Model 420, very good—$300.00
　　Model 420, excellent—$350.00
　　Model 421, very good—$425.00
　　Model 421, excellent—$475.00

History: Beretta has long been well known for making quality pocket pistols. Before the war, they gained a good reputation with their Model 318. After World War II, they brought out the Model 418 which was known in the United States as the Bantam. It was introduced in 1946 and was different from the Model 318 in several respects. The grip was slightly more rounded for a better-feeling hold, and in order to pull the slide back more easily, the slide serrations were slanted, rather than vertical. As an added safety measure, the cocking indicator was added. The shape of the grip safety was also altered.

Mechanical Functioning: The Beretta Bantam is a straight blowback, striker-fired, semiautomatic pistol, with an eight-shot detachable box magazine. It is very closely based on the Model 1934 .25 A.C.P., and the Model 318 .25 A.C.P. pistols. While the external appearance appears original because of the design and shape of the grip and slide, the internal action is very reminiscent of the standard Eibar designs with a hinged trigger and hinged sear bar, which also incorporates the disconnector and runs along the left inside of the frame. The cocking indicator functions by a pin attached to the firing pin itself, around which the firing pin spring is loaded axially. To guide the indicator pin a hollow tube is utilized at the aft end of the striker spring. When it is cocked and held by the sear, the rear part of the firing pin protrudes through the frame at the rear of the slide, indicating that the firearm is cocked. The recoil spring is wound axially around a recoil spring guide and mounted under the barrel in a manner similar to the Colt. The manual safety is located on the left side of the pistol above the trigger, and when engaged, blocks the trigger. The grip safety is located in the rear gripstrap, and unless depressed, it inhibits the sear to prevent discharge. The magazine is of the detachable-box type and holds eight shots. It is retained by a spring-loaded catch located at the rear base of the butt. After making sure that the pistol is unloaded, pull the slide to the rear and lock it in place with the manual safety. Tap the barrel toward the rear to disengage it from the frame, and lift the rear end of the barrel up and out of the frame through the large opening in the forward top of the slide. Holding the slide firmly (since there is tension from the recoil spring acting on it), release the safety and slip the slide off of the front end of the pistol. The firing pin assembly can now be removed from the slide. The safety drifts out toward the left. Assemble in the reverse order. The frame is made of an aluminum alloy, and the grip safety is made of plastic.

Beretta Model 418 Bantam

Pietro Beretta
Brescia, Italy

Model: 1915/1919

Action Type: semiautomatic, blowback operated.

Caliber(s): 7.65mm.

Barrel Lengths: 3⅜".

Finish: blue.

Manufacturing Dates: 1919–1930.

Stocks: stamped metal.

Rifling: 6R.

Weight, Unloaded: 24 oz.

Sights: fixed.

Serial Numbers: n/a, but ran to at least the high 200,000s.

Serial Number Location: right side of the frame above trigger and above it on the slide.

Major Variations: commercial.
Italian Navy (RM).
Italian Air Force (RA).

Markings: left side of slide: Pistol Aut Beretta 7.35 Brev. 1915–1919.
grips: PB.

Price(s):
Commercial, very good—$250.00
Commercial, excellent—$300.00
Air Force, very good—$325.00
Air Force, excellent—$400.00
Navy, very good—$325.00
Navy, excellent—$400.00

History: Pietro Beretta, not being the type of manufacturer to be behind the times, developed a very workable automatic pistol during World War I, called the 1915. By the end of the war, using the lessons that he had learned, a greatly modified version of that pistol was issued and called the 1915/19. It differed from its predecessor in that the safety lever was altered, the barrel mounting was changed, and it had a concealed internal hammer. It had improved holding capabilities with a straight grip frame, and the wooden grips had been replaced by stained sheet metal. The magazine on the 1915/19 also had a finger extension to provide a better hold. The shape of the slide was altered, enlarging the port, extending it to the breech face. The front side was more rounded than the 1915, and the rear sight, instead of being drifted in a dovetail, was milled into the slide. Following the Beretta tradition, on the lower left side of the gripframe there was a lanyard loop mounted below the grip. This pistol was first introduced to the market in 1920 and stayed in production until about 1930 or 1931.

Mechanical Functioning: The Beretta 1915/19 is a straight blowback, semi-automatic pistol with an eight-shot detachable box magazine. It has an internal concealed hammer and a floating firing pin mounted in the slide. Ejection is vertical, and rather than a small port, the slide is milled from within ½-inch of the muzzle all the way back to the breech face, exposing the top half of the barrel. The recoil spring is mounted axially on a recoil spring guide and is inserted in the frame under the barrel. General functioning is very similar to Eibar concealed-hammer-type pistols. The barrel, unlike the Model 1915, is not mounted vertically; rather it is mounted in a slot horizontally milled into the frame. The safety is of the type that disengages the sear connector. Magazine retention is accomplished with a spring-loaded retainer mounted at the bottom rear of the gripframe. The pistol is of all steel construction including the grips.

Beretta Model 1915/19

Pietro Beretta
Brescia, Italy

Model: 1934 and 1935

Action Type: semiautomatic, blowback operated.

Caliber(s): 1934, 9mm K and 1935 7.65mm

Barrel Lengths: 3⅜".

Finish: blue.

Manufacturing Dates: 1934–1958.

Stocks: plastic or plastic with a metal sheath.

Rifling: 6R.

Weight, Unloaded: 25½ oz.

Sights: fixed.

Serial Numbers: n/a, but ran to at least 900,000.
Special serial groups with various prefixes or suffixes have been observed.

Serial Number Location: right side of frame above trigger guard.

Major Variations: commercial, prewar M1935.
commercial, prewar M1934.
commercial, postwar M1935.
military, Army (RE).
military, Navy (RM).
military, Air Force (RA or AM).
wartime, Police (PS).

Markings: prewar and wartime—left side of slide: P. Beretta - Cal 7.65 - M1935 (or M1934), Brevattato, Gardone, V.T. (date).
postwar—left side of barrel: Pietro Beretta, Gardone V.T. Cal. 7.65
postwar—right side of barrel: Made in Italy.

Price(s):
Model 1934, very good—$275.00
Model 1934, excellent—$325.00
Model 1935, very good—$250.00
Model 1935, excellent—$300.00
Air Force-RA, add—$75.00
Army-RE, add—$50.00
Navy-RM, add—$75.00
Police-PS, add—$25.00
German 4VT Proof, add—$50.00

History: The Beretta Model 1935 has often confused people as to what its exact nomenclature should be. When it was first developed and issued in 1935, it was marked "Model 1935." However, soon afterward because of its similarity to the Model 1934, the markings were changed to reflect Model 1934. After the war, the name again changed to Model 1935. It is identical to the Model 1934 except that it has been slightly reduced in size. Amazingly, even though this pistol was chambered for .32 A.C.P., a relatively weak cartridge, and the fact that the Model 1934 in .380 had already been developed, the Italian government adopted this weaker pistol for their air force, navy, army, and also for police use during World War II. It stayed in production until it was replaced by the Model 70 in 1958.

Mechanical Functioning: The Model 1935 Beretta is a straight blowback, semiautomatic pistol with an external hammer and a floating firing pin mounted within the slide. In other respects, it is very similar to the standard Eibar-pattern pistol. It has a pivoting trigger pinned at the top with a combination disconnector and sear bar attached to it under spring pressure running across the inside left portion of the frame, and utilizing the characteristic, long disconnector bar. Ejection is vertical, and rather than a small port, the slide is open from just behind the rear sight to just forward of the breech face as on the Model 1915/19. The magazine is an eight-shot, detachable-box type retained by a springloaded flange at the base of the gripframe. The recoil spring is axially mounted on a guide and mounted below the barrel. These guns are marked in Roman numerals designating their year of manufacture, using the Italian Fascist calendar, in which 1922 was year 1.

Beretta 1935
Photo courtesy of Orvel L. Reichert

Theodor Bergmann Waffenfabrik
Suhl, Germany

Model: Taschen

Action Type: semiautomatic, blowback operated.

Caliber(s): 6.35mm

Barrel Lengths: 2⅛".

Finish: blue.

Manufacturing Dates: early 1920s.

Stocks: wood with a medallion or hard rubber.

Rifling: 6R.

Weight, Unloaded: 13¼ oz.

Sights: fixed.

Serial Numbers: n/a.

Serial Number Location: right side of slide.

Major Variations: none.

Markings: left side of slide: Theodor Bergmann, Gaggenau, Waffenfabrik, Suhl, Germany.

Price(s):
    Model 2, very good—$250.00
    Model 2, excellent—$300.00
    Model 3, very good—$250.00
    Model 3, excellent—$300.00
    Model 2A, very good—$350.00
    Model 2A, excellent—$400.00
    Model 3A, very good—$350.00
    Model 3A, excellent—$400.00
    for extended clip for Model 2A, add 10%
    for original wood grips, add 5%

History: The Bergmann Model 2 was a late Bergmann pistol and was completely based on the Browning 1906 pattern. It can be found with both the Theodor Bergmann name and also with the Lignose name. Apparently the Lignose Powder Company formed the marketing organization called Aktien Gesellschaft Lignose Berlin and formed a division of that company in Suhl, Germany, primarily to market Bergmann pistols. There were two types of the Model 2 made: the Taschen and the Einhand. The Einhand is described elsewhere under "Lignose" in this book. The Taschen was exactly the same; however, it had a fixed trigger guard of standard style. They were well-made pistols, machined from steel and well fitted. At the rear of the receiver, just above the grip, there is a small indicator pin that projects when the internal hammer is cocked. The same pistol was also made with an extended frame to hold a longer clip. It was called a Model 3 in both the Bergmann series and the Lignose series.

Mechanical Functioning: The Bergmann Taschen series of pistols are straight blowback, semiautomatic pistols with detachable box magazines and a concealed internal hammer. They have a floating firing pin and a cartridge indicator that is floating and protrudes when struck by the cocked hammer. The internal design is almost of standard Browning 1906 pattern, and takedown is accomplished exactly the same as the 1906, whereby the slide is retracted until the barrel can be rotated 90 degrees and then the entire assembly slides off the front. Under the barrel there is a recoil spring, axially mounted on a guide. The trigger is pivoting, pinned at the top, and has a sear bar with a built-in elongated bar disconnector, and rides on the left side of the frame under the grip. The Model 2 has a six-shot magazine. The Model 3, with an elongated frame, has a nine-shot box magazine. All of the details of both guns are the same. As with the Lignose, the Bergmann was also available with the Chylewski Einhand device. This device is fully described in the "Lignose" section.

Bergmann Model 2 Taschen

Theodor Bergmann Waffenfabrik
Suhl, Germany

Model: 1896 #'s 2, 3, and 4

Action Type: semiautomatic, blowback operated.

Caliber(s): 6.5mm Bergmann.

Barrel Lengths: 4³/₈".

Finish: blue.

Manufacturing Dates: 1896–1897.

Stocks: wood or hard rubber.

Rifling: 4R.

Weight, Unloaded: 26¹/₂ oz.

Sights: fixed.

Serial Numbers: about 1 to 4400 for the 1896 numbers 3 and 4.

Serial Number Location: right side of frame below the breech and on barrel.

Major Variations: 1896 #2, 5mm: no extractor.
1896 #2, 5mm: with extractor.
1896 #3, 6.5mm: no extractor.
1896 #3, 6.5mm: with extractor.
1896 #4, 8mm.
target model with long barrel and set trigger.

Markings: left side of frame: Patent Breuete S.G.D.G.
right side of frame: Pistolet Bergmann (and trademark).

Price(s):
1896 #2, very good—$2,000.00
1896 #2, excellent—$2,500.00
1896 #3, very good—$2,500.00
1896 #3, excellent—$3,000.00
1896 #4, 8mm, very good—$4,000.00
1896 #4, 8mm, excellent—$4,500.00
Target 1896, very good—$7,500.00
Target 1896, excellent—$12,500.00

History: The Model 1896 is a refinement of Bergmann's Model 1894, which was designed by Louis Schmeisser, who later gained fame for his submachine guns. The year designation in the model name refers to the time when the pistol first reached production. The number following it refers to the caliber: Number 1 was a 5mm used in the 1894; number 2 was a 5mm used in the 1896; number 3 was the most popular caliber, 6.5mm, in the 1896; and number 4 was an 8mm that was used in the 1896. About the first 1,000 Model 1896 #3s utilized ammunition that was a rimless and grooveless cartridge, and the pistol itself had no provision for an extractor. This arrangement is quite common on blowback pistols, as the force of the cartridge case ramming the slide back is generally sufficient to bring the cartridge case out of the chamber, but two types of 6.5mm Bergmann ammunition will be found: those grooved for extractor and those without. Pistols made after the first thousand numbers generally have extractors. There were many modifications to the 1896 during its production life. The addition of the extractor, two different types of barrel mountings—one using a rotating lug in the later variety, the earlier variety using screw threads on the barrel. The later model had a larger and wider grip, had hard rubber grips rather than wooden ones, and also included a redesigned safety and safety spring. The bottom of the magazine sideplate was also redesigned, eliminating a flange that was on the earlier pistol. Any variation of the Bergmann 1896 is quite scarce and is very desirable for collectors.

Mechanical Functioning: The Bergmann Model 1896 is a straight blowback, semiautomatic pistol with an external hammer and a fixed magazine located forward of the trigger guard. Over the chamber on the right side there is a small hole that, according to many authors, served as a vent so that gasses would have a place to escape to in the event of a ruptured case. However, recent evidence indicates that Bergmann intended this hole to function primarily as a loaded-chamber indicator.

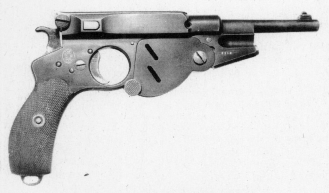

Bergmann Model 1896 #3

Bergmann/Bayard

Model: 1908, 1910, and 1910/21

Action Type: semiautomatic, recoil operated.

Calibers(s): 9mm Bergmann/Bayard.

Barrel Lengths: 4″.

Finish: blue.

Manufacturing Dates: 1908–1918.

Stocks: wood.

Rifling: 6L.

Weight, Unloaded: 35½ oz.

Sights: fixed.

Serial Numbers: 1 to about 14,000.

Serial Number Location: bottom of frame forward of magazine.

Major Variations: Model 1908—Commercial.
Model 1910—Danish Military.
Model 1910/21—Danish Military, large grips (manuf. by the Danish Royal Arsenal, Copenhagen).

Markings: right side of frame at rear: Danish Army acceptance number.

Price(s):
Model 1908, very good—$1,250.00
Model 1908, excellent—$1,500.00
Model 1910, very good—$1,000.00
Model 1910, excellent—$1,250.00
Model 1910/21, very good—$1,250.00
Model 1910/21, excellent—$1,500.00

History: The Bergmann/Bayard was the final in a series of military pistols designed by Louis Schmeisser and Theodor Bergmann, which began in 1894 and culminated with the Bergmann Marspistole in 1903. That pistol was the direct predecessor of the 1908, 1910, and 1910/21 variations and was made at the Bergmann Industrie Werke in Gaggenau, Germany. In 1907 Anciens Etablissements Pieper of Herstal, Belgium, purchased the manufacturing rights for all of the Bergmann pistols as well as their spare parts. Pieper then changed the designation on the pistols to the Bayard trademark and renamed them the 1908 series. After tests in 1910, the Danish government in 1911 adopted the Bayard Model 1908. They designated it the Model 1910 and ordered 4,840 pistols. These were numbered 1 to 4840 on the right side of the frame, and that number should not be confused with the serial number, which is located on the bottom of the frame forward of the magazine well. Pieper discontinued this pistol at the end of World War I. However, the Danish Ordnance Department still wanted more of them, so in 1922, they took over the manufacture of it, designating it the Model 1910/21. They were manufactured at two plants: the Royal Army Arsenal, from which pistols are marked "Haerens Tojhus," and the Army Storage Arsenal, marked "Haerens Rustkammer." These pistols start numbering at 1. The Danes continued to use these pistols up to 1940, when they adopted the FN/Browning High-Power.

Mechanical Functioning: The Bergmann/Bayard Model 1908 and its successors are recoil-operated semiautomatic pistols with an external hammer and a detachable box magazine inserted forward of the trigger guard. In cases of desperation, the pistols can also be loaded via a stripper slip from the top. There is a manual safety that locks the hammer in both the cocked and uncocked position and locks the action at the same time. The pistol was also supplied on order with a wooden shoulder stock holster. The clip holds six cartridges.

Bergmann/Bayard 1910/21

Browning Arms Co.
One Browning Place
Morgan, UT 84050

Model: Challenger

Action Type: semiautomatic, blowback.

Caliber(s): .22 L.R.

Barrel Lengths: 4½″ and 6¾″.

Finish: blue.

Manufacturing Dates: 1962–1975 by FN.

Stocks: checkered walnut.

Rifling: 6R.

Weight, Unloaded: 38 oz. with 6¾″ barrel.

Sights: adjustable target.

Serial Numbers: n/a.

Serial Number Location: front of gripstrap.

Major Variations: Standard model: gold Challenger, blue with gold inlays; Renaissance: chrome with engraving and carved stocks.

Markings: U.S. Model: left barrel flat; Browning Arms Company, St. Louis, Mo. and Montreal, P.Q.
right barrel flat; Made in Belgium.
.22 Long Rifle, European Model: left barrel flat; Fabrique Nationale D'Armes De Guerre, Herstal, Belgique.

Price(s):
    Standard Model, very good—$250.00;
    Standard Model, excellent—$300.00;
    Gold Challenger, very good—$600.00;
    Gold Challenger, excellent—$900.00;
    Renaissance, very good—$650.00;
    Renaissance, excellent—$950.00
    Target, very good—$225.00
    Target, excellent—$275.00
    Tir, very good—$250.00
    Tir, excellent—$300.00

History: Introduced in 1962 as the "Challenger" in the United States, and as the "Target" in Europe, this pistol was in the middle quality range of Browning .22 pistols between the Nomad (Standard) and the Medalist (Modele Concours, Match, or Modele 150 in Europe). The higher grades were introduced in 1971 and discontinued in 1974. The U.S. version was discontinued in 1975 due to the shrinking dollar at the time, but in Europe the production continued as the model "Tir."

Mechanical Functioning: This was a straight blowback-operated, semiautomatic pistol with a detachable ten-shot box magazine with a clip catch on the bottom of the gripframe. The trigger was adjustable with an overtravel screw on the trigger and a screw to vary the spring tension located on the rear of the frame above the gripframe. This model also had a slide stop to lock the slide open on the last shot. To disassemble, lock the slide back, remove the clip, unscrew the barrel-retaining screw on the bottom of the frame, and rotate the barrel up and off. Release the slide. Reassemble in reverse order.

Challenger Renaissance

Browning Arms Co.
One Browning Place
Morgan, UT 84050

Model: High Power

Action Type: semiautomatic, recoil operated.

Caliber(s): 9mm.

Barrel Lengths: 4^{21}/$_{32}$".

Finish: blue, nickel, chrome, black chrome, matte blue.

Manufacturing Dates: 1935 to date.

Stocks: checkered wood, plastic, pearl.

Rifling: 6R.

Weight, Unloaded: 32 oz.

Sights: fixed blade, adjustable target type, tangent (radial) sight.

Serial Numbers: n/a.

Serial Number Location: right side of frame above trigger.

Major Variations: two major types were produced by Fabrique Nationale: the "Ordinary" model with fixed sights, and the "Adjustable Sight" model with radial sights and provision for shoulder stock. Currently, Fabrique Nationale produces the Ordinary model and a model with target sights. But because of its widespread military use and long production history, enough variations have been produced to fill several books.

Markings: generally: for European market on left slide: Fabrique National D'Armes De Guerre, Herstal Belgique, Browning's Patent Depose for U.S. market;
Browning Arms Company, St. Louis, Mo., and Montreal P.Q., made in Belgium.

Price(s):
fixed sights—$400.50
adjustable sights add $100.00
nickel—$80.00
Model GP Competition—$550.00

History: Development in 1935 as the "Pistolet Automatique Browning Modele De Guerre Grande Puissance," though most people called it either the "GP," "HP," or "1935." It has become the most widely used military handgun in history, with each country using its own nomenclature, variations, and special markings. Experimental lightweight versions, as well as models with special sights, calibers, and selective fire devices have been produced. After World War II the factory renamed the pistol "High Power" for the civilian market and Model 1946 for the military. Other current names used in Europe are "Vigilante" for the fixed-sight model and "Capitan" for the adjustable-sight type. Capitan is also known as "High Power Sport," and with radial sights was known as the "Armee." During the 1970s some specifications were changed for ease of manufacture.

Mechanical Functioning: The Browning High Power operates on a locked breech semiautomatic system. While very closely related to the Browning/ Colt system, instead of using a barrel bushing, it uses a machined integral bushing at the face of the slide and on the rear of the barrel a forged barrel nose in place of the swinging link to cam the barrel down and up and to lock and unlock it into the slide operating on the slide pin. The overall design is much simpler than that of the Colt-Browning system. The disconnector, instead of being mounted within the frame, is mounted on the slide and also is used in conjunction with the magazine disconnect. The detachable box magazine holds 13 rounds in a staggered order. The clip release is mounted just below the trigger guard on the side of the gripframe.

Browning High Power
Photo courtesy of Orvel L. Reichert

Browning Arms Co.
One Browning Place
Morgan, UT 84050

Model: 1903
(Modele De Guerre;
Pistolet Automatique Browning
Grande Modele)

Action Type: semiautomatic, blowback.

Caliber(s): 9mm Browning Long, .380 A.C.P., 9mm Bergmann

Barrel Lengths: 5".

Finish: blue.

Manufacturing Dates: 1903–1940.

Stocks: hard rubber with Fabrique Nationale logo.

Rifling: 6R

Weight, Unloaded: 32 oz.

Sights: fixed.

Serial Numbers: n/a.

Serial Number Location: right frame, forward of slide lock.

Major Variations: standard model and three deluxe variations. A wood holster stock was also available as well as a 10-shot clip.

Markings: left slide: Fabrique Nationale D'Armes De Guerre, Herstal Belgique. Browning's Patent Depose.

Price(s):
    standard model, very good—$325.00
    standard model, excellent—$450.00
    standard model, light engraving, very good—$800.00
    standard model, light engraving, excellent—$1,100.00
    standard model, fancy engraving, very good—$2,000.00
    standard model, fancy engraving, excellent—$2,500.00
    military, very good—$250.00
    military, excellent—$350.00
    military cut for shoulder stock, very good—$300.00
    military cut for shoulder stock, excellent—$400.00
    military with stock, very good—$1,500.00
    military with stock, excellent—$2,000.00
    military 9mm Bergmann with stock, very good—$2,500
    military 9mm Bergmann with stock, excellent—$3,500

History: One of Browning's most successful designs, this pistol was adapted for military use by Belgium, Turkey, Czechoslovakia, Holland, and Russia, and was used by the Danish Police. Sweden adopted it in 1907 and manufactured this model as the Husqvarna M/07 from about 1923 until 1942. Reducing the size, Colt adopted the design in their 1903 pocket models.

Mechanical Functioning: This pistol has a seven-shot, detachable box magazine and is a recoil-operated blowback. The disconnector and trigger are standard Browning Pocket Pistol design. The manual safety locks both the mechanism and slide, and the automatic grip safety prevents firing until the gun is gripped. Mechanism is of the concealed-hammer type.

Browning Model 1903

Browning Arms Co.
One Browning Place
Morgan, UT 84050

Model: 1910

Action Type: semiautomatic, blowback.

Caliber(s): .32 A.C.P., .380 A.C.P.

Barrel Lengths: 3.42".

Finish: blue or nickel.

Manufacturing Dates: 1911–1980 (U.S. Import 1954–1960).

Stocks: plastic, hard rubber, mother-of-pearl.

Rifling: 6R.

Weight, Unloaded: 570 gm. in .32 A.C.P., 560 gm. in .380 A.C.P.

Sights: fixed.

Serial Numbers: n/a.

Serial Number Location: right side of frame over trigger.

Major Variations: engraved models as well as special order pistols were available, though the configuration remained constant.

Markings: on left side of slide: Fabrique Nationale D'Armes De Guerre, Herstal, Belgique;
Browning's Patent Depose on right side of barrel.
Exposed through the ejection port is the caliber designation.
The long production time has led to a great many special marks and stampings, and many have yet to be classified.

Price(s):
standard model, blue, .32 A.C.P., very good—$250.00
standard model, blue, .32 A.C.P. excellent—$300.00
standard model, blue, .380 A.C.P., very good—$275.00
standard model, blue, .380 A.C.P., excellent—$375.00
standard model, nickel, .32 A.C.P., very good—$275.00
standard model, nickel, .32 A.C.P., excellent—$325.00
standard model, nickel, .380 A.C.P., very good—$300.00
standard model, nickel, .380 A.C.P., excellent—$425.00
Renaissance (engraved) model, very good—$1,000.00
Renaissance (engraved) model, excellent—$1,500.00
.32 Japanese Military, very good—$375.00
.32 Japanese Military, excellent—$500.00
.32 Peruvian Military, very good—$500.00
.32 Peruvian Military, excellent—$650.00
.32 Military, very good—$350.00
.32 Military, excellent—$450.00
.32 Syrian Police, very good—$350.00
.32 Syrian Police, excellent—$425.00

History: Introduced in 1910 as the "Noveau Modele" to distinguish it from the M1900, at first produced only in .32 A.C.P. The .380 version was introduced in 1922 and called the Model 1910/22 (not to be confused with the Model 1922). Immensely popular and extensively copied, the M1910 remained in production (with a slight interruption during World War II) until it was slightly redesigned in 1955. The reissue was only in .380 A.C.P. and was produced until 1969. Another modification was made in 1971 for the U.S. market, enlarged and with adjustable sights in .380 A.C.P. It was discontinued in 1975 but remains in production in .32 A.C.P. in Europe as the FN Model 125.

Mechanical Functioning: Semiautomatic blowback-operated pistol with a grip safety, magazine safety, and manual safety. The recoil spring is wrapped around the barrel, reducing the necessary size of the slide. The pistol is striker-fired and has a six-shot detachable box magazine. Takedown is accomplished by removing the cup and making sure that the gun is unloaded, pulling the slide back and locking in position with the safety. Rotate the barrel to disengage it from the frame; release the safety and slowly slide off. Push in and rotate the recoil spring retainer 90 degrees, and remove it and the barrel. Assemble in reverse order.

1910 Renaissance .380

Browning Arms Co.
One Browning Place
Morgan, UT 84050

Model: 1922

Action Type: semiautomatic, blowback operated.

Caliber(s): .32 A.C.P., or .380 A.C.P.

Barrel Lengths: 4¹/₂".

Finish: blue.

Manufacturing Dates: 1912–1959 (Nazis 1940–1944).

Stocks: wood or plastic.

Rifling: 6R.

Weight, Unloaded: 25 oz.

Sights: fixed or adjustable.

Serial Number: not available; they apparently ran in many groups depending on contract.

Serial Number Location: right side of frame above trigger.

Major Variations: military and commercial models.

Markings: left side of slide: Fabrique Nationale D'Armes DeGuerre. Herstal-Belgique, Browning's Patent Depose.

Price(s):
   Model 1922, .32 Commercial, very good—$175.00
   Model 1922, .32 Commercial, excellent—$250.00
   Model 1922, .32 Nazi Military, very good—$250.00
   Model 1922, .32 Nazi Military, excellent—$350.00
   Model 1922, .32 Dutch Military, very good—$225.00
   Model 1922, .32 Dutch Military, excellent—$325.00
   Model 1922, .32 Belgian Military, very good—$200.00
   Model 1922, .32 Belgian Military, excellent—$300.00
   Model 1922, .380 Belgian Military, very good—$250.00
   Model 1922, .380 Belgian Military, excellent—$375.00
   Model 1922, .380 Czechoslovakian Military, very good—$300.00
   Model 1922, .380 Czechoslovakian Military, excellent—$425.00
   Model 1922, .380 French Military, very good—$250.00
   Model 1922, .380 French Military, excellent—$375.00
   Model 1922, .380 Swedish Military, very good—$250.00
   Model 1922, .380 Swedish Military, excellent—$375.00
   Model 1922, .380 Turkish Military, very good—$300.00
   Model 1922, .380 Turkish Military, excellent—$450.00
   Model 1922, .380 Yugoslavian Military, very good—$300.00
   Model 1922, .380 Yugoslavian Military, excellent—$450.00
   Model 1922, .380 adjustable sights, very good—$250.00
   Model 1922, .380 adjustable sights, excellent—$350.00
   Model 125, .32 A.C.P., very good—$225.00
   Model 125, .32 A.C.P., excellent—$325.00

History: Fabrique Nationale's entrance into the field of pocket pistols with extra magazine capacity was their Model 1922 and should not be confused with their Model 1910/22, which was just their Model 1910 in .380 A.C.P. caliber. The Model 1922 has a barrel about an inch longer than the 1910 and a gripframe that is also about an inch longer, in order to handle the increased magazine capacity. The long clip holds eight shots in .380 caliber, nine shots in .32 caliber. Although introduced in 1922, it has been in production almost steadily since then, and it has been known under various names. Its original name was Pistolet Automatique Browning Modele 1922 and was first offered in .32 A.C.P. During the German occupation from 1940 on, it was known as the Pistole 626 (p) and more than 350,000 were made in .32 A.C.P. The Dutch issue pistol was known as the Pistool M25 No. 1, and it was in service from 1925 through World War II. In .380 A.C.P. the pistol was adopted for military and police use in Belgium, France, Sweden, Czechoslovakia, Turkey, and Yugoslavia among others. After World War II, production was continued and has been called alternatively the Browning .380 after 1968 and came with adjustable sights. In Europe it was called the Model 125.

Mechanical Functioning: The Model 1922 Browning is a straight blowback-operated, striker-fired, semiautomatic pistol with a detachable box magazine inserted through the gripframe. The trigger is pivoted, and attached to it is a long sear bar, including the disconnector. The mainspring is mounted axially around the barrel. Takedown is accomplished in normal Browning fashion except that on this model there is a 1-inch-long shrouding at the end of the barrel, which must be given a half turn after first unlocking the spring catch. The working mechanism of this pistol is virtually identical to the Browning 1910. The reason for it is simple: there was no great change in the tooling to lengthen the grip nor to face off the end of the slide to allow the attachment of the extension. Thus Browning was able to get into the extra-magazine-capacity field of small military pistols without undue tooling expense or waste of time. Construction was all steel, except in later models after the war, which possessed some plastic parts. It is well made, and its long production life proves its durability.

Browning 1922

Budischowski
Mount Clemens, MI

Model: TP 70

Action Type: semiautomatic, blowback operated.

Caliber(s): .25 A.C.P., .22 L.R.

Barrel Lengths: 2⅝".

Finish: stainless steel.

Manufacturing Dates: 1973–1977.

Stocks: plastic.

Rifling: 6L.

Weight, Unloaded: 12⅜ oz.

Sights: fixed.

Serial Numbers: started at 1; about a dozen presentation guns with either "X" prefixes or with two or three letter "initial" prefixes.

Serial Number Location: left side of frame above the trigger.

Major Variations: none.

Markings: left side of slide: Budischowski TP 70, .25 Cal. Automatic Pistol, Norarmco, Mt. Clemens, Mich.

Prices:
    used: .22 L.R.R.F, very good—$350.00
    used: .22 L.R.R.F., excellent—$400.00
    used: .25 A.C.P., very good—$250.00
    used: .25 A.C.P., excellent—$350.00

History: The Budischowski TP 70 began life in Germany as a Korriphila, and because of the Gun Control Act of 1968 forbidding its importation, arrangements were made through Norarmco to manufacture the pistol here entirely of stainless steel. The pistol was manufactured from 1973 to 1977 by Norarmco, but because of production problems, only a few thousand pistols were manufactured, and eventually, Norarmco had to fold up its tent. A Miami company, American Arms and Ammunition, purchased the machinery and the rights to make the pistol, and they carried on production for a couple of years after 1978 under the Norton TP 70 name.

Mechanical Functioning: The Budischowski TP 70 is a straight blowback operated, semiautomatic pistol that is double action with an external hammer. It has a six-shot detachable box magazine inserted through the gripframe, as well as a magazine safety preventing firing after the magazine is withdrawn. It has a manually operated thumb safety on the left-hand top of the slide that is reminiscent of the Walther design, and it locks the floating firing pin to prevent the hammer from striking it. The hammer itself also has a half-cock notch, and like the Walther, the hammer can be safely lowered by engaging the manual safety which trips the sear and drops the hammer down onto a steel bar. Takedown is accomplished by first removing the magazine and making sure the chamber is empty. Then engage the manual safety. Retract the slide until the small notch cut into it on the right side just forward of the ejection port aligns with the takedown lever and hold the slide in place. Rotate the takedown lever from back to front and move the slide forward and off the frame. The recoil spring assembly can be lifted off the barrel, and then the barrel dropped out of the slide. Assembly is in reverse order.

Budischowski TP 70

Campo Giro
Esperania y Unceta
Guernica, Spain

Model: 1913–16

Action Type: semiautomatic, blowback operated.

Caliber(s): 9mm Largo.

Barrel Lengths: 6½".

Finish: blue.

Manufacturing Dates: 1916–1921.

Stocks: wood or hard rubber.

Rifling: 6R.

Weight, Unloaded: 33½ oz.

Sights: fixed.

Serial Numbers: started at 1.

Serial Number Location: left side of frame above trigger.

Major Variations: Model 1913.
　　Model 1913–16.
　　Model 1921.

Markings: left side of frame: Pista. Auta. Mod. 1913–16.

Price(s):
　　Model 1913, very good—$750.00
　　Model 1913, excellent—$1,000.00
　　Model 1913–16, very good—$400.00
　　Model 1913–16, excellent—$500.00
　　Model 1921, very good—$500.00
　　Model 1921, excellent—$650.00

History: The Campo Giro pistol was the invention of Colonel Don Venancio Lopez de Cedallos y Aguirre, who was the Count of Campo Giro in Spain. Around the year 1900 he invented a recoil operated, semiautomatic pistol which was finally developed in 1904 into prototype form and was then manufactured at Oviedo Arsenal in Spain. In 1910 he upgraded the pistol into the Model 1910 which was also adopted by the Spanish government. In 1913 he made his big transition. He developed a pistol that was straight blowback rather than recoil operated and yet could handle the heavy 9mm calibers. In addition to an exceptionally strong recoil spring, he also added a shock absorber to reduce the hammering that the slide would cause on recoil. The pistol was a successful one, and the Spanish Army sang great praises on it. In 1916 they modified it again and changed the location of the magazine release from behind the trigger guard to the bottom of the frame. In 1921 the model designation was changed in an attempt to become the official Spanish

Army pistol of that year; however, the manufacturer of that pistol, Esperanza y Unceta, decided to use the Campo Giro design as the basis for their Model 400 pistol, and it was that pistol that the Spanish Army finally decided upon and renamed the Model 1921.

Mechanical Functioning: The Campo Giro Model 1913 series is a straight blowback, semiautomatic pistol with an external hammer and a detachable seven-shot, box magazine that is inserted through the gripframe. The recoil spring is wound axially around the barrel, and is quite stiff so that it can absorb the shock from the 9mm Largo cartridge. Since this was an early automatic pistol, the makers were feeling their way with it and expected a series of problems. The major one encountered arose from the blowback method of operation. A point of diminishing returns was reached where if too stiff a recoil spring was used the pistol would not function, but if a spring that allowed functioning was used, the slide came back and hit the frame with sufficient force to cause deformation. The answer was a shock absorber that was installed in the frame to reduce the slide battering that was suffered in the prototype pistols. An unusual feature of this pistol is that the mainspring is of the "V" type leaf spring with one end supplying the power to the hammer, and the other end supplying force to the sear, with which to hold the hammer. The firing pin is of floating variety, and there is a mechanical safety at the rear left-hand side of the frame. This was the first of the tubular design pistols with the recoil spring fitted around the barrel, and the Astra 1921 is a very closely related successor to the Campo Giro.

Campo Giro Model 1913–16

Charter Arms
26 Beaver Street
Ansonia, CT 06401

Model: Bulldog

Action Type: Revolver, double action.

Caliber(s): .44 Special.

Barrel Lengths: 3″.

Finish: blue, nickel or stainless.

Manufacturing Dates: 1973–1991 and 1994 to date.

Stocks: checkered walnut or neoprene.

Rifling: 6R.

Weight, Unloaded: 19 oz.

Sights: fixed.

Serial Numbers: n/a.

Serial Number Location: right side of frame above and behind trigger.

Major Variations: square butt or Bulldog grips, standard, or with spurless hammer and neoprene grips.
milestone commemorative, engraved and silver plated.

Markings: left barrel: Bulldog .44 Special.
right barrel: Charter Arms Corp., Stratford Ct.

Price(s):
standard—$175.00
stainless—$250.00
neoprene grips and spurless hammer—$200.00

History: The Charter Arms Bulldog .44 Special was introduced in 1973 to meet the demand from law enforcement agencies and the public for a small, easily carried revolver that packs a more potent punch than a .38 Special. For several years prior to its release rumors had been floating around the industry that Charter was working on a 20-ounce .44 Magnum. This rumor was rightly not given much credence by the other gunmakers because of the high pressures of the magnum cartridge and the light weight of the revolver, both rendering a design that is virtually impossible to shoot. The announcement of a 19-ounce .44 Special caught the competition flatfooted, and to date there is still no real competitor in the big-bore small handgun field. About 1981 a commemorative Bulldog was issued, The Milestone, which was silver plated, engraved, and sold cased with accessories. Now an all stainless steel version is available. As a police undercover or off-duty weapon, or as a camp gun, this powerhouse, by virtue of size, weight, capacity, and ease of use, is in a class of its own. The .44 Special cartridge, although dwarfed by its big brother, the .44 Magnum, should be highly regarded.

A 240-grain bullet can be propelled out of the Bulldog with about 300 foot pounds of energy and terrific knockdown power. Most reloading manuals also have suggestions for optimum loads for the .44 Special cartridge for use in this revolver.

Mechanical Functioning: The Charter Arms Bulldog .44 Special is essentially a scaled-up "undercover." It is a five-shot, double-action revolver with a swing-out cylinder. The cylinder swings out to the left on a crane after the center pin is unlocked by a latch on the left side of the frame. Ejection is simultaneous and performed by pushing on the extractor rod in the center of the cylinder after the cylinder has been opened. The Bulldog has a hammer transfer block to prevent accidental discharge. It operates in conjunction with the trigger, and unless the trigger is pulled all of the way to the rear, thus lifting the transfer bar to alignment with the firing pin, the falling hammer cannot contact the firing pin. The firing pin is of the floating type and is mounted within the frame. The springs are all of the coil type for long life. The cylinder has clockwise rotation, and unlocks by pushing the cylinder latch forward, allowing the cylinder assembly to be pushed out toward the left. The cylinder lock is only at the rear through the ratchet. The sights are fixed, and consist of a square notch milled into the upper part of the frame. The front sight is of the ramp type. The Bulldog is made of either high-carbon steel or stainless steel.

Charter Arms .44 Bulldog

Charter Arms
26 Beaver Street
Ansonia, CT 06401

Model: Pathfinder

Action Type: revolver, double action.

Caliber(s): .22 L.R. or .22 W.M.R.

Barrel Lengths: 3″ or 6″.

Finish: blue or stainless steel.

Manufacturing Dates: 1970–1990.

Stocks: checkered walnut.

Rifling: 6R.

Weight, Unloaded: 3″ barrel is 18½ oz.

Sights: adjustable rear, ramp front.

Serial Numbers: n/a.

Serial Number Location: right side of frame.

Major Variations: round or square butt.
  stainless steel or blued steel.

Markings: left side of barrel: Pathfinder .22
  right side of barrel: Charter Arms Corp., Stratford CT.

Price(s):
  blue, .22 L.R.—$150.00
  blue, .22 W.M.R.—$150.00
  stainless .22 L.R.—$150.00
  Pocket Target Model, blue, .22 L.R., very good—$125.00; excellent—
  $175.00

History: The Pathfinder series was originally issued in 1970 as the "Pocket Target" model. The name was changed in 1971 to Pathfinder. This model was designed for the civilian market primarily as a hunter's "camp gun" or as a self-defense weapon for the home. It is available in two barrel lengths, 3-inch and 6-inch. The rear sight is adjustable for target work, and the front is a Patridge-type ramp sight. An optional choice on this model is uncheckered standard grips or checkered bulldog style grips.

Mechanical Functioning: The Charter Arms Pathfinder is essentially a modified Undercover. It is a six-shot, double-action revolver with a swing-out cylinder. The cylinder swings out to the left on a crane after the center pin is unlocked by a latch on the left side of the frame. Ejection is simultaneous and performed by pushing on the extractor rod in the center of the cylinder after the cylinder has been opened. The Bulldog has a hammer transfer block to prevent accidental discharge. It operates in conjunction with the trigger, and unless the trigger is pulled all the way to the rear, thus lifting the transfer bar to alignment with the firing pin, the falling hammer cannot contact the firing pin. The firing pin is of the floating type and is mounted within the frame. The springs are all of the coil type for long life. The cylinder has clockwise rotation, and unlocks by pushing the cylinder latch forward, allowing the cylinder assembly to be pushed out toward the left. The cylinder lock is only at the rear through the ratchet. The sights are fully adjustable, and consist of a target rear sight and a Patridge ramp front sight mounted on a pedestal base. The Pathfinder is made of either high-carbon steel or stainless steel.

Charter Arms Pathfinder, .22 L.R., Standard

Charter Arms Pathfinder, .22 W.M.R., Bulldog

Charter Arms
26 Beaver Street
Ansonia, CT 06401

Model: Target Bulldog

Action Type: revolver, double action.

Caliber(s): .357 Magnum, .44 Special.

Barrel Lengths: 4".

Finish: blue.

Manufacturing Dates: 1976–1988.

Stocks: checkered walnut.

Rifling: 6R.

Weight, Unloaded: 20½ oz.

Sights: adjustable rear, ramp front.

Serial Numbers: n/a.

Serial Number Location: right side of frame.

Major Variations: none.

Markings: left side of barrel: Target bulldog.
right side of barrel: Charter Arms Corp. Stratford, Ct.

Price(s):
.357 Magnum, very good—$125.00; excellent—$150.00
.44 Special, very good—$150.00; excellent—$175.00

History: Designed as a "target" revolver, and introduced in 1976, the Target Bulldog is essentially a fancier version of the Police Bulldog in .357 Magnum or in .44 Special and has fully adjustable target sights. The ejector rod is shrouded and pushes the empty cases out of the cylinder their full length. The .44 Special version was introduced in 1977.

Mechanical Functioning: The Charter Arms Target Bulldog is essentially a modified Undercover. It is a six-shot, double-action revolver with a swing-out cylinder. It is very similar to the Police Bulldog model, and most parts are interchangeable. However, the Police Bulldog is available only in .38 Special, whereas the Target Bulldog comes in either .357 Magnum or .44 Special. The cylinder swings out to the left on a crane after the center pin is unlocked by a latch on the left side of the frame. Ejection is simultaneous and performed by pushing on the extractor rod in the center of the cylinder after the cylinder has been opened. A convenient feature of this model is the full-length extraction of the fired cases, obviating the chance of case hang-up in a combat situation. The Target Bulldog has a hammer transfer block to prevent accidental discharge. It operates in conjunction with the trigger, and unless the trigger is pulled all of the way to the rear, thus lifting the transfer bar to alignment with the firing pin, the falling hammer cannot contact the firing pin. The firing pin is of the floating type and is mounted within the frame. The springs are all of the coil type for long life. The cylinder has clockwise rotation and unlocks by pushing the cylinder latch forward, allowing the cylinder assembly to be pushed out toward the left. The cylinder lock is only at the rear through the ratchet, and the forward end of the ejector rod is protected by a barrel shroud. The sights are fully adjustable, and consist of a target rear sight and a Patridge ramp front sight mounted on a pedestal base. The Target Bulldog is made of high-carbon steel.

Charter Arms Target Bulldog

Charter Arms Target Bulldog, Action Opened

Charter Arms
26 Beaver Street
Ansonia, CT 06401

Model: Undercover

Action Type: revolver, double action.

Caliber(s): .38 Special, .32 Smith & Wesson Long.

Barrel Lengths: 2" or 3".

Finish: nickel, blue or stainless.

Manufacturing Dates: 1965–1991.

Stocks: walnut, plain or checkered Bulldog.

Rifling: n/a.

Weight, Unloaded: 16 oz. with the 2" barrel.

Sights: fixed.

Serial Numbers: n/a.

Serial Number Location: right side of frame.

Major Variations: .38 Special is 5 shot.
.32 Smith & Wesson Long is 6 shot.
Available with spurless hammer.

Markings: left side of barrel: Undercover.
right side of barrel: Charter Arms Corp. Stratford, Ct. early models will
say "Bridgeport, Conn."

Price(s):
blue—$150.00
stainless—$175.00
blue spurless hammer, very good—$150.00; excellent—$175.00
stainless spurless hammer, very good—$175.00; excellent—$200.00

History: The Undercover was designed and developed by Douglas McClenahan
in 1964. He founded Charter Arms Corp. in Bridgeport, Connecticut, to
manufacture this revolver. It started out made of chrome-molybdenum
steel with an alloy gripframe, and now has a steel or stainless steel
frame. This revolver has won wide market acceptance for both police
work and self-defense. The current Charter Arms line is based on the
Undercover's mechanical design.

Mechanical Functioning: The Undercover is a five- or six-shot (depending
on caliber), double-action revolver with a swing-out cylinder and simultaneous ejection. It has a hammer transfer block to prevent accidental
discharge. The cylinder has clockwise rotation, and unlocks by pushing
the cylinder latch forward, allowing the cylinder assembly to be pushed
out toward the left.

Charter Arms Undercover

Witold Chylewski
Neuhausen, Switzerland

Model: Brevet

Action Type: semiautomatic, blowback operated.

Caliber(s): 6.35mm

Barrel Lengths: 2¼".

Finish: blue.

Manufacturing Dates: 1910–1920.

Stocks: checkered wood.

Rifling: 6R.

Weight, Unloaded: 13¼ oz.

Sights: fixed.

Serial Numbers: possibly started at 1.

Serial Number Location: left side of frame above trigger.

Major Variations: with or without screw locking cocking device in forward position.

Markings: on left side of cocking piece: Brevet Chylewski.

Price(s):
> no screw in cocking piece, very good—$650.00
> no screw in cocking piece, excellent—$800.00
> with locking screw, very good—$550.00
> with locking screw, excellent—$700.00

History: The Einhand pistol was the invention of Withold Chylewski, an Austrian citizen. Around 1910–1913 he contracted with Soc. Industrielle Suisse of Neuhausen, Switzerland, to build his prototype run of Einhand pistols. The exact number made is not known. Chylewski spent the years from around 1913 to around 1918 or 1919 in trying to interest some major company in purchasing his idea. He finally succeeded with Theodor Bergmann. Bergmann acquired the rights to the Einhand invention and manufactured it under the Bergmann name and also under the Lignose trademark.

Mechanical Functioning: The Chylewski is a .25 A.C.P., straight blowback, semiautomatic pistol with a six-shot detachable box magazine fitted through the gripframe. The primary thing of note about this small pistol is the fact that it could be operated with one hand. On the forward part of the trigger guard, it had a recurve that looked like a second trigger. This ran along a rail machined on the side of the frame, and impinged on a cut in the slide. When withdrawn to the rear, it hooked itself on the projection of the slide and then withdrew the slide at the same time it traveled rearward. When the slide was released, the cocking piece was pushed forward under the power of the recoil spring and back to the front of the trigger guard. In this manner, you had a hammerless, semi-automatic pistol that could be carried with a full magazine and no round in the chamber for absolute safety, and in an emergency, with only one hand you could put a round in the chamber and have it ready for firing while it was still in your pocket. When Bergmann manufactured the pistol under both the Bergmann and Lignose trade names, this idea was adopted with virtually no alteration.

Chylewski, Brevet

Charles PH. Clement
Liege, Belgium

Model: 1910

Action Type: semiautomatic, blowback operated.

Caliber(s): 6.35mm, or 7.65mm

Barrel Lengths: 2" to 4½".

Finish: blue.

Manufacturing Dates: 1909–1914.

Stocks: hard rubber.

Rifling: 6R.

Weight, Unloaded: 12³/₈ oz.

Sights: fixed.

Serial Numbers: continuation of numbers from the Models 1907 and 1908, generally ranging between the 6000s and the 30,000s.

Serial Number Location: left side of frame above trigger and above it on the barrel.

Major Variations: barrel lengths.

Markings: sometimes marked: Automatic Pistol Clement's Patent.

Price(s):
    Model 1910, 6.35mm, 2" barrel, very good—$300.00
    Model 1910, 6.35mm, 2" barrel, excellent—$425.00
    Model 1910, 6.35mm, 4½" barrel, very good—$375.00
    Model 1910, 6.35mm, 4½" barrel, excellent—$500.00
    Model 1910, 7.65mm, very good—$425.00
    Model 1910, 7.65mm, excellent—$550.00

History: Charles Ph. Clement was a fairly prolific arms maker in Liege, Belgium, between 1886 and 1914. From 1903 on, he manufactured a series of fairly unique little handguns. They were so widely received and appreciated that in the United States Smith & Wesson purchased rights to manufacture pistols under his patents, and in Belgium Pieper purchased rights for pistols to be marketed under the Bayard banner. Pieper later licensed Steyr to manufacture Clement-style pistols, and then Steyr subcontracted to Solothurn for them. His pistols can generally be recognized by the recoil spring being mounted above the barrel in a housing that is machined to resemble a barrel at first glance. The Model 1909 was one of the few pistols he made that was chambered for standard calibers. In 6.35mm it has been observed in barrel lengths from 2" to 4½", and was also significant because it was his first pistol that did not require the removal of screws in order to field-strip the pistol. The serial numbers of this model ran in series with the Models 1907 and 1908; therefore, production figures are not too accurate, and no one knows exactly how many of this model were made. All Clement pistols are considered to be scarce enough to rate them as highly collectible.

Mechanical Functioning: The Model 1909 Clement was a straight blow-back, semiautomatic pistol with a six-round detachable box magazine in both 6.35mm and 7.65mm models. The magazine was inserted through the gripframe and retained by a springloaded catch. Unusual for a Clement, there are no retaining screws to be removed in order to take it down. Instead, this pistol has a trigger guard that pivots on the front end by springing down the rear end of the trigger guard out of its recess and pushing down. The section containing the barrel, the recoil spring, and the recoil spring guide is unlocked and can be tipped up. The breech-block assembly can then be removed. There is a manual thumb safety on the rear left-hand side of the frame, and the magazine release is in the form of a push button located at the bottom right-hand side of the gripframe at the bottom rear of the grip. The entire backstrap assembly also pivots out and up, rotating on a pin through the rear of the frame. This section is unlocked by rotating a lever located on the bottom left-hand side of the gripframe to the rear of the grip. The grips are retained by a slightly beveled interior protruded portion that fits into a frame recess, and then the grip is locked down by a single screw at the bottom of the grip.

Clement Model 1910

Colt
150 Hoyshope Avenue
Hartford, CT 06102

Model: Ace

Action Type: semiautomatic, blowback operated.

Caliber(s): .22 L.R.

Barrel Lengths: 4³⁄₄″ Ace, 5″ Service Ace.

Finish: blue or nickel.

Manufacturing Dates: 1931–1941 with some assembled from parts in 1947; the Service Ace is 1935–1945; the Ace MK IV 1978 to 1982.

Stocks: checkered walnut.

Rifling: 6L.

Weight, Unloaded: 38 oz. Ace, 42 oz. Service Ace, 42 oz. Ace MK IV.

Sights: adjustable "Ace" type or Stevens type on Service Ace.

Serial Numbers: 1 to 10935; Service Model Ace: SM1 to about SM13803; SM14001 in 1978 to SM43830 in 1982.

Serial Number Location: right frame above trigger.

Major Variations: Ace.
　　　Service Ace.
　　　Ace MK IV.
　　　Signature Limited Edition.

Markings: left side of slide: Colt Ace .22 Long Rifle
　　　or: Colt Service Model Ace .22 Long Rifle.

Price(s):
　　　Post-War Ace, very good—$500.00
　　　Post-War Ace, excellent—$600.00
　　　Post-War Ace, nickel, very good—$350.00
　　　Post-War Ace, nickel, excellent—$650.00
　　　Post-War Ace Signature, very good—$750.00
　　　Post-War Ace Signature, excellent—$1,000.00
　　　Ace, very good—$1,000.00
　　　Ace, excellent—$1,500.00
　　　Service Ace, very good—$1,500.00
　　　Service Ace, excellent—$2,000.00

History: The Colt Ace was introduced in 1931 as a sub-caliber model of the Colt 1911A1 for practice use for target shooters. The standard Model Ace was quite pleasant to shoot. Recoil was light, and the accuracy was good. However, the army perceived the need for a good training pistol, and in 1935 Colt began experimenting with David M. (carbine) Williams's design for a floating chamber. This device quadrupled the recoil of the pistol, even in the minute .22 caliber, given the same perceived recoil as the full-sized .45. The army seemed to like such a device and purchased a good quantity of them. However, the general shooting public wasn't so sure, and therefore, from 1937, when the Service Model Ace was in general production, until it was discontinued, the Standard Ace sold right along with it. In 1978 Colt decided they had a good thing with the .22 on the .45 frame, and they reintroduced the Ace, this time with sights similar to the Gold Cup. Throughout the career of the Ace it was always given a little bit of special care to assure that the actions functioned smoothly, as Colt did with the rest of their target line. And finally, a special note about the last Standard Ace pistols, which were completed in 1947. Although they were officially discontinued in 1941, after the war, Colt found a few remaining receivers and slides, and they completed them as pistols in that year.

Mechanical Functioning: The original Ace .22 pistol is built on the same frame as the Model 1911A1 and differs mainly in that it is a blowback-operated pistol instead of being recoil-operated. The magazine is of a detachable box type and holds ten rounds. Like the National Match, it features an all hand-honed action and carefully fitted parts. The Service Model Ace is also identical with the National Match .45 except for caliber, operation, and magazine capacity. However, it was intended primarily to be a training arm for the army to help teach recruits and others how to fire the .45 automatic inexpensively. It utilized the "Carbine" Williams patented floating chamber, which quadrupled the recoil of the Ace, bringing it in line with the heavier .45 automatic. The more recent issue of the Ace in the MK IV series follows the "Carbine" Williams pattern of floating chamber. As a practice gun to get someone used to the recoil of the .45, this gun is great. However, as a target arm in .22 caliber, we wonder about the wisdom of such heavy recoil. Be that as it may, all three varieties of the Colt Ace are extremely fine guns and relatively accurate. All of them encompass the safety features of the original 1911, that is, grip safety, and positive-functioning, manual-hammer safety. They also feature the crisp trigger pull of the National Match generation of weapons.

Colt Ace
Photo courtesy of the T.W. Motter Collection

Colt
150 Hoyshope Avenue
Hartford, CT 06102

Model: Agent

Action Type: revolver, double action.

Caliber(s): .38 Special.

Barrel Lengths: 2″.

Finish: blue or Parkerized.

Manufacturing Dates: 1955–1986.

Stocks: checkered walnut.

Rifling: 6L.

Weight, Unloaded: 14½ oz. early style, 16 oz. current model.

Sights: fixed.

Serial Numbers: began at 33,900LW running concurrently with the Cobra, Aircrewman and Courier. In 1969 the prefix numbering began with "A," and used "B," "C," "F," "H," and "M." In 1976 this was switched to the suffix "M," then going to "R."

Serial Number Location: n/a.

Major Variations: from 1955 to 1973 the barrel was plain and tapered, and the ejector rod was exposed.
After 1973 the barrel had an integral shroud.

Markings: on left side of barrel: Agent, .38 Special CTG.
on right side of barrel: Colt's Mfg. Co., Hartford, Ct. USA.
left frame: Rampant Colt Trademark on sideplate.

Price(s):
blue, early, very good—$275.00
blue, early, excellent—$350.00
blue, late, very good—$225.00
blue, late, excellent—$300.00
nickel, early, very good—$250.00
nickel, early, excellent—$400.00
nickel, late, very good—$250.00
nickel, late, excellent—$350.00
matte finished, very good—$150.00
matte finished, excellent—$250.00

History: This model was introduced in 1955, essentially an aluminum alloy Cobra frame with the major difference being a shorter, stubbier grip. This was designed to be a very lightweight concealable revolver for police use. The finish was "Dual tone" with blued steel parts and black anodized frame. The weight due to the foreshortened gripframe was ½ oz. lighter than the Cobra, and the revolver initially was available only in blue with square butt stocks. The 1973 version has a heavier barrel with an integral shroud.

Mechanical Functioning: The functioning is of standard Colt double-action revolver style. The cylinder is six-shot with long flutes and peripheral locking notches and large cylinder stop grooves. Rotation of the cylinder is in the clockwise direction. The firing pin is fixed on the hammer, and when the hammer is in the full down position, the firing pin protrudes through a hole in the wall of the breech face. The cylinder lockup is on the rear only, with the locking bolt protruding through the breechface and engaging a circular cut in the center of the ratchet. The action is unlocked by pulling the cylinder release latch located on the left-hand side of the frame in a cut in the sideplate rearward and swinging the cylinder to the left. The ejection is manual and simultaneous and is accomplished by a reciprocating ejector rod. The hammer fall and trigger rebound are both powered by a single V-shaped leaf spring that rests on the trigger rebound bar on the lower end and engages a strut attached to the hammer on the upper side. There is an automatic internal safety feature that prevents the hammer from falling all the way and allowing the firing pin to strike the cartridge in the event that the revolver is dropped or if the sear releases without the trigger being pulled. If the trigger is not pulled all the way to the rear, then a hammer block that is attached to the trigger via a connector will not slide down the right inside of the frame far enough to allow the hammer to clear it. It works on the opposite principle, like the current Mark III and Mark V Colts, in that instead of providing a method of transferring the force of the falling hammer to the firing pin when the trigger is pulled, the "positive safety," as this is called, instead blocks the hammer, keeping it from allowing the firing pin to protrude through the breechface unless the trigger is pulled. The Agent is made of steel with an aluminum alloy frame.

Colt Agent
Photo courtesy of the T.W. Motter Collection

Colt
150 Hoyshope Avenue
Hartford, CT 06102

Model: Bankers' Special

Action Type: revolver, double action, Colt style.

Caliber(s): .22 L.R., .38 Colt New Police, .38 Smith & Wesson.

Barrel Lengths: 2".

Finish: blue.

Manufacturing Dates: 1926–1943.

Stocks: checkered walnut.

Rifling: 6L.

Weight, Unloaded: 19 oz. in .38, 23 oz. in .22.

Sights: fixed.

Serial Numbers: concurrent with the Police Positive, starting at 177,000 running to 185,000, then skipping to 329,000 and running to 406,726.

Serial Number Location: frame, in crane recess.

Major Variations: square or round butt frames.
Fitzgerald trigger guard cut.

Markings: left side of barrel: caliber and Bankers' Special.
right side of barrel: Colt name and address with 1884, 1905, and 1926 patent dates.
left side of frame on sideplate: Rampant Colt Trademark.

Price(s):
.22 round butt, very good—$1,000.00
.22 round butt, excellent—$1,500.00
.22 square butt, very good—$1,250.00
.22 square butt, excellent—$1,750.00
.38 round butt, very good—$750.00
.38 round butt, excellent—$1,000.00
.38 square butt, very good—$1,000.00
.38 square butt, excellent—$1,250.00
.22 with Fitzgerald cut, very good—add $400.00
.22 with Fitzgerald cut, excellent—add $500.00
.38 with Fitzgerald cut, very good—add $400.00
.38 with Fitzgerald cut, excellent—add $500.00

History: Introduced in 1926 in the .38 caliber, this revolver was based on the square-butt Police Positive frame and is very similar in appearance to the early Colt Detective Special. The primary difference is cylinder length. The Bankers' Special is 1¼" and the Detective Special has 1⅝" to accommodate a longer cartridge. The .22 L.R. version had a round butt, and the cylinder was rebated to accept the cartridge rim. This was introduced in 1933, and starting in 1934 both the .22 and the .38 were made with round butt frames.

Mechanical Functioning: The functioning is of standard Colt double-action revolver style. The cylinder is six-shot with long flutes and peripheral locking notches, and large cylinder stop grooves. The cylinder rotation is in the clockwise direction. The firing pin is fixed on the hammer and protrudes through the breechface upon firing. The cylinder is rear-locking only via a bolt that protrudes through the frame and engages a cut in the center on the ratchet. It is unlocked by pulling the cylinder release rearward and swinging the cylinder to the left. The extraction is manual and simultaneous and is accomplished by a reciprocating ejector rod. The hammer fall and trigger rebound are both powered by a single V-shaped leaf spring. There is an automatic internal safety feature that prevents the firing pin from contacting the cartridge without the trigger being pulled. If the trigger is not pulled all the way to the rear, then a hammer block that is attached to the trigger via a connector will not slide down the right inside of the frame far enough to allow the hammer to clear it. It works on the opposite principle, like the later Mark III and Mark V Colts, in that instead of providing a method of transferring the force of the falling hammer to the firing pin when the trigger is pulled, the "positive safety," as this is called, instead blocks the hammer, keeping it from allowing the firing pin to protrude through the breechface unless the trigger is pulled. The Bankers' Special is made of steel with an aluminum alloy frame.

Colt Bankers' Special .22 L.R.

Colt
150 Hoyshope Avenue
Hartford, CT 06102

Model: Bisley

Action Type: revolver, single action.

Caliber(s): .32 Colt, .32 Smith & Wesson, .32–44, .32–20, .38 Colt, .38 Smith & Wesson, .38 Special, .38–40, .38–44, .41 Colt, .44 Russian, .44 Smith & Wesson, .44–40, .45 Colt, .455 Eley.

Barrel Lengths: from 3" to 16" with 4¾", 5½", and 7½" standard.

Finish: blue or nickel.

Manufacturing Dates: 1894–1915 (44,350 manuf.).

Stocks: hard rubber.

Rifling: 6L.

Weight, Unloaded: about 37 oz.

Sights: fixed or adjustable.

Serial Numbers: 154000 to 325000 in the single action army range.

Serial Number Location: bottom of frame forward or trigger guard.

Major Variations: with or without rod ejector.
fixed sight or flat top target.

Markings: barrel top: Colt's Pat. F.A. Mfg. Co. Hartford Ct. USA.
Bisley Model, Caliber in left side of barrel.
Colt Patent dates on left side of frame under cylinder.

Price(s):
single action Bisley, standard model, very good—$2,000.00
single action Bisley, standard model, excellent—$3,500.00
single action Bisley, flattop target model, add 200%
single action Bisley, other than standard calibers, add 50% to 100%.
single action Bisley, nonstandard barrel lengths, add 20% to 30%.
single action Bisley, no ejector housing, adding 25% to 35%.

History: The Colt Bisley revolver was basically the same as the Colt Single Action Army, the primary differences being that the frame has a deeper flat on the rear surface where it abuts the gripstrap, to help provide the extra length to the Bisley grip. The hammer is of target style. It is wider and has a different curve than the single-action army; and instead of a roller bearing to ride on the mainspring, a stirrup is provided, with the mainspring having a curved, forked end. The Bisley trigger, internally the same as the Single Action Army, externally is more than double the width, offering a broad contact surface. But the most astounding style is in the grips. Trigger guard, gripstrap, and stock should be considered as a single unit with the trigger guard being larger, the grips extending down deeper than the Single Action Army and being curved in a different manner. Although the initial starting date is listed as 1894, only a couple dozen revolvers were made between 1894 and 1896 when normal production started, and most of them were shipped to England. This model was available in two frame variations: the flattop target with an adjustable rear sight for windage only, and the fixed sight model which is the milled groove.

Mechanical Functioning: Aside from the aforementioned differences, this is a standard pattern Single Action Army on the internal action. It is a single-action revolver with a side gate loading. The hammer has a half-cock notch that is not entirely safe for carrying purposes with a loaded chamber underneath the hammer. A loading notch, whereby the hammer on the second click releases the bolt from the cylinder, allowing it to spin freely, and the loading gate on the right side of the frame can be opened, and spent cartridges either ejected via the rod ejector or loaded. The hammer then goes to the third click, which is the full cock notch, turning the cylinder and locking it in place. The mainspring, rather than being flat at the top, is hooked in order to engage the stirrup and the hammer.

Colt Bisley

Colt
150 Hoyshope Avenue
Hartford, CT 06102

Model: Camp Perry

Action Type: double action, single shot.

Caliber(s): .22 L.R.

Barrel Lengths: 8″ or 10″.

Finish: blue.

Manufacturing Dates: 1926–1941 (2488 manuf.).

Stocks: checkered walnut.

Rifling: 6L.

Weight, Unloaded: 34½ oz.

Sights: rear adjustable for windage, front adjustable for elevation.

Serial Numbers: 1 to 63 were experimental preproduction pistols, from 1920 to 1926 with regular production numbers starting at 101 in 1926 and ending about 2525 in 1941.

Serial Number Location: inside crane recess on frame.

Major Variations: first type 10″ barrel, "Officers Model" lockwork. second type: 8″ barrel, short hammer fall.

Markings: left side of barrel: Cal .22 Long Rifle.
left side of chamber: Camp Perry Model.
on barrel top: Colt name and address.
on left frame on sideplate: Rampant Colt trademark.

Price(s):
first type, very good—$1,000.00
first type, excellent—$1,250.00
second type, very good—$1,250.00
second type, excellent—$1,500.00

History: The Camp Perry was built on the Officer's Model frame, with the top left portion under the top strap removed so that an integral barrel and chamber could be swung out on the crane. The Colt Camp Perry was developed experimentally in the early 1920s, and production began in 1926. In 1933 the second type was introduced with the 8″ barrel and modified lockwork for a shorter hammer fall. Only 2,488 Camp Perry models were produced, and only 440 of them were of the second type.

Mechanical Functioning: The functioning is of modified Colt double-action Officer's Model revolver style. The firing pin is fixed on the hammer, and protrudes through the breechface upon firing. The barrel assembly is rear-locking with a bolt that protrudes through the frame and engages a cut below the barrel. It is unlocked by pulling the release latch rearward and swinging the barrel assembly to the left. The extraction is manual and is accomplished by a reciprocating ejector rod. The hammer fall and trigger rebound are both powered by a single V-shaped leaf spring. There is an automatic internal safety feature that prevents the firing pin from contacting the cartridge without the trigger being pulled. If the trigger is not pulled all the way to the rear, then a hammer block that is attached to the trigger via a connector will not slide down the right inside of the frame far enough to allow the hammer to clear it. It works on the opposite principle, like the current Mark III and Mark V Colts, in that instead of providing a method of transferring the force of the falling hammer to the firing pin when the trigger is pulled, the "positive safety," as this is called, instead blocks the hammer, keeping it from allowing the firing pin to protrude through the breechface unless the trigger is pulled. The item that really makes the Camp Perry special, however, is the integral barrel/crane assembly. When Colt decided to make a single-shot target pistol, they rightly figured that an open cylinder gap could reduce bullet velocity, and if the timing isn't exactly perfect, could adversely affect the accuracy. Their solution was unique to say the least. They started with an Officer's Model frame and instead of a cylinder they attached the whole barrel assembly to the crane. But then came the problem: if you have a solid barrel extending all the way back to the breechface, how do you close the barrel? The answer was not so obvious. They removed the entire left forward side of the frame, leaving only the top strap and right forward side, and because of the contour milling on the side of the barrel assembly its opening style is not immediately obvious. The Camp Perry Model was of all steel construction.

Colt Camp Perry Model .22 L.R.

Colt
150 Hoyshope Avenue
Hartford, CT 06102

Model: Cobra

Action Type: revolver, double action.

Caliber(s): .38 Special, .38 New Police, .32 New Police, .22 LR.

Barrel Length: 2″, 3¼, 4″, 5″.

Finish: blue, nickel.

Manufacturing Dates: 1950–1973 (1st issue) and 1973–1981 (2nd issue).

Stocks: checkered walnut.

Rifling: 6L.

Weight, Unloaded: 15 oz.

Sights: fixed.

Serial Numbers: preproduction began at 1LW and ran concurrently with the Agent, which began at 33900LW running concurrently with the Aircrewman and Courier. In 1969 the prefix numbering began with A, and used B, C, F, H, and M. In 1976 this was switched to the suffix M, then going to R.

Serial Number Location: n/a

Major Variations: from 1950 to 1973 the barrel was plain and the ejector rod was exposed. After 1973 the barrel had an integral shroud. A hammer shroud was also available.

Markings: on left side of barrel: Cobra and caliber.
on right side of barrel: Colt's Mfg. Co., Hartford, Ct. USA.
left frame: Rampant Colt trademark on sideplate.

Price(s):
late, blue, very good—$250.00
late, blue, excellent—$400.00
late, nickel, very good—$300.00
late, nickel, excellent—$450.00
early, blue, 2″, very good—$275.00
early, blue, 2″, excellent—$425.00
early, blue, 3″, very good—$300.00
early, blue, 3″, excellent—$450.00
early, blue, 4″, very good—$325.00
early, blue, 4″, excellent—$500.00
early, blue, 5″, very good—$250.00
early, blue, 5″, excellent—$375.00
for hammer shroud, add $25.00 to $50.00

History: Developed in 1950 and marketed in 1951, this is essentially a lightweight Colt Detective Special. The frame was made of aluminum on a joint project between Colt and Alcoa, and the resultant material was called "Colt Alloy." After 1973 the design of the barrel was changed and the ejector rod was shrouded, adding 1½ oz. to the weight. "Bulldog" style grips were adopted at that time.

Mechanical Functioning: The functioning is of standard Colt double-action revolver style. The cylinder is six-shot with long flutes and peripheral locking notches and large cylinder stop grooves. The cylinder rotation is in the clockwise direction. The firing pin is fixed on the hammer and protrudes through the breechface upon firing. The cylinder is rear-locking only via a bolt that protrudes through the frame and engages a cut in the center on the ratchet. It is unlocked by pulling the cylinder release rearward and swinging the cylinder to the left. The extraction is manual and simultaneous and is accomplished by a reciprocating ejector rod. The hammer fall and trigger rebound are both powered by a single V-shaped leaf spring. There is an automatic internal safety feature that prevents the firing pin from contacting the cartridge without the trigger being pulled. If the trigger is not pulled all the way to the rear, then a hammer block that is attached to the trigger via a connector will not slide down the right inside of the frame far enough to allow the hammer to clear it. It works on the opposite principle, like the current Mark III and Mark V Colts, in that instead of providing a method of transferring the force of the falling hammer to the firing pin when the trigger is pulled, the "positive safety," as this is called, instead blocks the hammer, keeping it from allowing the firing pin to protrude through the breechface unless the trigger is pulled.

Colt Cobra .38

Colt
150 Hoyshope Avenue
Hartford, CT 06102

Model: Commando

Action Type: revolver, double action.

Caliber(s): .38 Special.

Barrel Lengths: 4″, 2″ (rare).

Finish: Parkerized.

Manufacturing Dates: 1942–1945.

Stocks: plastic.

Rifling: 6L.

Weight, Unloaded: 31 oz.

Sights: fixed.

Serial Numbers: 1 to 50,617.

Serial Number Location: n/a.

Major Variations: none.

Markings: on left side of barrel: Colt Commando, .38 Special.
on right side of barrel: Colt's Mfg. Co., Hartford, CT USA.
left frame: Rampant Colt trademark on sideplate.

Price(s):
very good—$400.00
excellent—$550.00

History: Based on the Official Police, and identical to it in all respects but finish, this revolver was produced under government contract during World War II for use by police agencies, factory guards, and other non-military users.

Mechanical Functioning: The functioning is of standard Colt double-action revolver style. The cylinder is six-shot with long flutes and peripheral locking notches, clockwise rotation, and large cylinder stop grooves. The firing pin is fixed on the hammer. The cylinder is rear-locking only and is unlocked by pulling the cylinder release rearward and swinging the cylinder to the left. The simultaneous ejection is manual and accomplished by a reciprocating rod. The hammer fall and trigger rebound are both powered by a single V-shaped leaf spring. The Colt Commando was of all steel construction.

Colt Commando

Colt
150 Hoyshope Avenue
Hartford, CT 06102

Model: Detective Special

Action Type: revolver, double action.

Caliber(s): .38 Special, .38 Smith & Wesson, .32 Colt, .32 Smith & Wesson.

Barrel Lengths: 2" or 3".

Finish: blue or nickel.

Manufacturing Dates: 1927–1946 (1st issue), 1947–1972 (2nd issue), and 1973–1986 (3rd issue).

Stocks: checkered walnut or plastic.

Rifling: 6L.

Weight, Unloaded: 21 oz.

Sights: fixed.

Serial Numbers: running with Police Positive Special starting at 331,000, going to 494,000 in 1948 and jumping to 510,001, and in 1949 jumping from 501,817 to 515,051, and jumping again from 519,410 to 525,001. In 1966 halting at 890,800 and starting again at D900,101. In 1969 beginning prefix A, in 1970 beginning prefix B, in 1972 beginning prefix C, in 1973 jumping to prefix F, and in 1974 prefix H, in 1975 prefix M, in 1976 suffix M, in 1977 suffix R, and in 1978 prefix S.

Serial Number Location: n/a.

Major Variations: round butt or square butt.
From 1927 to 1973 the barrel was plain and the ejector rod was exposed. After 1973 the barrel had an integral shroud. A detachable hammer shroud was also available.

Markings: on left side of barrel: caliber designation and Detective Special. on right side of barrel: Colt's Mfg. Co., Hartford, Ct. USA.
left frame: Rampant Colt Trademark on sideplate.

Price(s):
blue, 2" barrel—$375.00
blue, 3" barrel—$450.00
nickel, 2" barrel—$375.00
nickel, 3" barrel—$500.00
4" heavy barrel, very good—$250.00
4" heavy barrel, excellent—$300.00
early, .32 Colt, very good—$250.00
early, .32 Colt, excellent—$275.00
early, .38 Special, very good—$300.00
early, .38 Special, excellent—$375.00
hammer shroud—add $25.00 to $50.00

early square butt—add $75.00 to $150.00
Fitzgerald cuts—add 200% to 250%

History: This model started life in 1926 as the Police Positive Special with a 2″ barrel. In 1927 the name was changed to Detective Special. In 1934 the grip contour was changed to a round butt. In 1972 Bulldog style wrap around grips were adopted. In 1966 the frame designation became "D" rather than Police Positive Special.

Mechanical Functioning: The functioning is of standard Colt double-action revolver style. The cylinder is six-shot with long flutes and peripheral locking notches, clockwise rotation, and large cylinder stop grooves. The firing pin is fixed on the hammer. The cylinder is rear-locking only and is unlocked by pulling the cylinder release rearward and swinging the cylinder to the left. The simultaneous ejection is manual and accomplished by a reciprocating rod. The hammer fall and trigger rebound are both powered by a single V-shaped leaf spring. The Detective Special is of all steel construction.

Colt Detective Special
Photo courtesy of the T.W. Motter Collection

Colt
150 Hoyshope Avenue
Hartford, CT 06102

Model: Diamondback

Action Type: revolver, double action.

Caliber(s): .22 L.R. or .38 Special.

Barrel Lengths: 2½", 4", 6".

Finish: blue or nickel.

Manufacturing Dates: 1966–1986.

Stocks: wood.

Rifling: 6L.

Weight, Unloaded: 4" .22, 31¾ oz.; 4" .38, 27½ oz.

Sights: adjustable.

Serial Numbers: started at D1001, to D99,999. In 1976 started N01001, going to N15674 in 1977 and restarting at R01001.

Serial Number Location: inside crane recess.

Major Variations: barrel lengths, finish.

Markings: left side of barrel: Diamondback and caliber.
right side of barrel: Colt's Pat. F.A. Hartford, Ct. USA.
on sideplate: Rampant Colt trademark.

Price(s):
nickel, .22, 6", very good—$400.00
nickel, .22, 6", excellent—$500.00
nickel, .38, 4", very good—$325.00
nickel, .38, 4", excellent—$350.00
nickel, .38, 6", very good—$350.00
nickel, .38, 6", excellent—$375.00
nickel, .38, 2½", very good—$350.00
nickel, .38, 2½", excellent—$400.00
blue, .38 2½", very good—$325.00
blue, .38 2½", excellent—$350.00

History: The Colt Diamondback was first introduced in 1966, and it was based on the Detective Special frame with adjustable sights and provision for an oversize barrel and vent rib to match the frame. The ejector rod is shrouded and runs the full length of the barrel to provide a good barrel counterweight. The rear sight is of the Colt Accro type. The front sight is a quick-draw ramp. The grips are of checkered walnut with a Colt medallion, and this is considered to be a scaled-down Python of medium weight. The 2½" version is no longer available, and the current catalog only lists the 4" .22 in nickel.

Mechanical Functioning: This is a double-action revolver on the Colt pattern utilizing a rebound lever and a V-mainspring. One side of the leaf mainspring provides the impetus for the hammer fall, the opposite side provides pressure on the trigger for its return. The cylinder swings out toward the left, and ejection is manual and simultaneous, via an ejector rod.

Colt Diamondback
Photo courtesy of the T.W. Motter Collection

Colt
150 Hoyshope Avenue
Hartford, CT 06102

Model: Gold Cup National Match MK IV Series 70

Action Type: semiautomatic, recoil operated.

Caliber(s): .45 A.C.P.

Barrel Lengths: 5″.

Finish: blue.

Manufacturing Dates: 1970–1984.

Stocks: wood.

Rifling: 6L.

Weight, Unloaded: 38½ oz.

Sights: Eliason target rear, undercut front.

Serial Numbers: started in 1970 at 70N01001.

Serial Number Location: right side of frame above trigger.

Major Variations: The Colt Custom Shop has offered the pistol with ambi-dextrous safety, checkered flat mainspring housing, Pachmayr grips, wide grip safety, beveled magazine well, and checkered trigger guard.

Markings: on left side of slide: Colt's MK IV Series 70, Gold Cup National Match, .45 Automatic caliber, and the Rampant colt trademark.

Price(s):
Series 70—$750.00
.22 conversion unit, adjustable sights—$500.00
Gold Cup, D.E.A. Commemorative, very good—$800.00; excellent—$1,250.00
.22 conversion unit, fixed sights, very good—$250.00; excellent—$350.00

History: Introduced in 1970 as an improvement of the Gold Cup National Match, it differed from its predecessor primarily in the design of the barrel and bushing, now incorporating a "spring bushing" to always hold tension on the barrel, and a slight swelling on the end of the barrel to increase tension. The basic action is M1911, with improvements to increase accuracy and reliability, and with those improvements has laid to rest the myth that the .45 is inaccurate. This gun sets the standards by which others are judged.

Mechanical Functioning: This recoil-operated pistol is based on the Browning-designed Colt M1911A1. To disassemble this pistol, remove the magazine and check to make sure that the weapon is unloaded. Depress plug below the barrel far enough to allow the barrel bushing to be turned to the right until the plug can be eased out to the front. Remember that this plug is under spring tension, so remove carefully. Pull the slide back until the rear edge of the smaller of the two cuts near the center of the slide on the left hand side lines up with the rear end of the slide stock. Push the end of the slide stock in, right to left. This will push the slide stock out on the left-hand side far enough to be grabbed and pulled out entirely. When this is removed, the slide can be pulled directly forward off the receiver, taking the entire barrel assembly with it. The barrel bushing, recoil spring, recoil spring guide and barrel may now be removed from the slide by turning the barrel bushing to the left as far as it will go, and withdrawing it to the front. Reassemble in the reverse order, making sure that the slide stop pin passes through the length at the bottom of the barrel, for this is the mechanism by which the pistol both locks and unlocks.

Colt Gold Cup National Match
Photo courtesy of the T.W. Motter Collection

Colt
150 Hoyshope Avenue
Hartford, CT 06102

Model: Government MK IV Series 70

Action Type: semiautomatic, recoil operated.

Caliber(s): .45 A.C.P., 9mm Luger, .38 Super.

Barrel Lengths: 5".

Finish: blue, nickel, satin nickel.

Manufacturing Dates: 1970–1984.

Stocks: wood.

Rifling: 6L.

Weight, Unloaded: 38 oz. in the .45; 39 oz. in the 9mm and .38 Super.

Sights: fixed.

Serial Numbers: started at 70G-01001 in .45 A.C.P. to 70G-99,999 in 1976. Restarted at 01001G70, now into the 70B series. In .38 Super: 70S03801. In 9mm: 70L02601. In nickel: X70N20801. BB in the serial number indicates old style bushing.

Serial Number Location: right side of frame above trigger.

Major Variations: old style barrel bushing.
Combat Government.

Markings: left side of slide: Colt's MK IV Series 70, Government Model, Caliber.
right side of slide: Government Model.

Price(s):
.45 blue, very good—$450.00; excellent—$600.00
9mm blue, very good—$400.00; excellent—$550.00
.38 Super, blue, very good—$425.00; excellent—$575.00
Combat Government Model, very good—$525.00
Combat Government Model, excellent—$600.00
MK IV, BB serial number, very good—$600.00
MK IV, BB serial number, excellent—$750.00

History: The Colt Government MK IV Series 70 began production in 1970 and was a radical change from what preceded it. Although the guns looked exactly alike on the outside, the new Model Government incorporated something that forever put to rest the myth that the .45 was inaccurate. Instead of the standard barrel bushing that had been used for 60 years, Colt manufactured what they call the Accurizor barrel and bushing, consisting of a barrel with a slight swell at the end and a bushing with spring fingers on it to grab that swelling and hold it very tightly and rigidly in place when the gun is at battery. To commemorate this event, they added the MK IV Series 70 to the firearms designation.

However, right at the beginning of production, Colt decided to use up some of the old bushings and barrels that it had on hand. Therefore, a very rare find in the Series 70 is a firearm with a "BB" prefix to the serial number, indicating that this arm was made with the old-style barrel bushing. Besides the standard pistols that had been made previously to the Series 70, they did add one major variation called the "Colt Government Combat Model." This could be considered America's equivalent to the S.I.G. P.210-6, a refined and honed, fixed-sight military issue-style target pistol. The Combat features a Gold Cup front sight, a white outlined rear, the flat mainspring housing, and long trigger, as well as the beveled magazine well and front grip serrations and a wide ejection port. It is capable of Match accuracy.

Mechanical Functioning: The Colt Government MK IV Series 70 pistols are built on the Model 1911 Colt-Browning design. They are recoil-operated semiautomatic pistols, with, in .45 caliber, a seven-round, detachable box magazine. The primary difference between it and the standard Model 1911A1 is of course the bushing and barrel system. Aside from the bushing and barrel, all parts are interchangeable with the Standard Army issue.

Colt Government Model MK IV Series 70

Colt
150 Hoyshope Avenue
Hartford, CT 06102

Model: Junior

Action Type: semiautomatic, blowback operated.

Caliber(s): .22 short, or .25 A.C.P.

Barrel Lengths: 2¼".

Finish: blue.

Manufacturing Dates: 1958–1968 and again in 1971–1973.

Stocks: wood or plastic.

Rifling: 6L.

Weight, Unloaded: 12 oz.

Sights: fixed.

Serial Numbers: started at 10CC in 1958, and ran to 85082CC. Numbers were shared between the .22 and the .25. In 1971 the Colt Auto .25 started at OD10001 and ran to OD120471 in 1973.

Serial Number Location: right frame above trigger.

Major Variations: .22, .25 in Junior.
.25 in "Colt .25 Auto."

Markings: left side of slide: Junior Colt, Caliber.
right side of slide: Colt's Pt.F.A. Mfg. Co., Hartford Ct. USA.
right side of frame: made in Spain for Colt's U.S. version.
left side: Colt Automatic Caliber .25.

Price(s):
Junior, .22 short, nickel finish, very good—$300.00
Junior, .22 short, nickel finish, excellent—$375.00
Junior, .25 A.C.P., nickel finish, very good—$300.00
Junior, .25 A.C.P., nickel finish, excellent—$350.00
Junior, .22 short, blue finish, very good—$275.00
Junior, .22 short, blue finish, excellent—$325.00
Junior, .25 A.C.P., blue finish, very good—$250.00
Junior, .25 A.C.P., blue finish, excellent—$300.00
Colt .25 Auto, very good—$200.00
Colt .25 Auto, excellent—$275.00

History: The Colt Junior was born in 1958 and began life as the Astra Cub, made by Astra-Unceta of Guernica, Spain. They were manufactured for Colt, trade-labeled for them, and called the Junior Colts. Production lasted for 10 years until the Gun Control Act of 1968 curtailed importation. Grips were available in checkered walnut with the Colt medallion, or in checkered plastic with a molded Colt medallion. After 1968, because Colt did have a good market for the .25, they were wondering what they should do, so they purchased rights from Astra to bring the model back and manufacture it here in America under license. However, instead of calling it the Junior, they called it the Colt Automatic Caliber .25. By the end of 1973, Colt dropped the .25 from its production line, and the .25 hasn't been seen since.

Mechanical Functioning: The Colt Junior, or as it is known under the Astra name in Europe, the Cub or the Model 2000, was a blowback-operated, semiautomatic pistol with an external hammer and a seven-round detachable box magazine. Internally, the firearm is a standard Eibar pattern. It has a manual safety that also acts as a slide lock. An unusual feature of this pistol is the magazine catch, which operates as a button that passes through the left-hand grip. The pistol also possesses an automatic magazine safety preventing the gun from firing if the magazine is withdrawn.

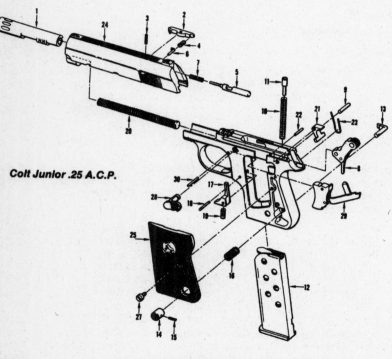

Colt Junior .25 A.C.P.

1	Barrel	11	Hammer Spring Guide	21	Sear
2	Extractor	12	Magazine	22	Sear Pin
3	Extractor Pin	13	Magazine Catch	23	Sear Spring
4	Extractor Spring	14	Magazine Catch Button	24	Slide
5	Firing Pin	15	Magazine Catch Button Pin	25	Stock
6	Firing Pin Retaining Pin	16	Magazine Catch Spring	27	Stock Screw
7	Firing Pin Spring	17	Magazine Safety	28	Thumb Safety
8	Hammer-with Strut and Pin	18	Magazine Safety Pin	29	Trigger with Disconnector
9	Hammer Pin	19	Magazine Safety Spring	30	Trigger Pin
10	Hammer Spring	20	Recoil Spring Assembly		

Colt Junior

Colt
150 Hoyshope Avenue
Hartford, CT 06102

Model: Lawman MK III

Action Type: revolver, double action.

Caliber(s): .357 Magnum.

Barrel Lengths: 2″, 4″.

Finish: blue or nickel.

Manufacturing Dates: 1969–1983.

Stocks: checkered walnut.

Rifling: 6L.

Weight, Unloaded: 35 oz. with 4″ barrel.

Sights: fixed.

Serial Numbers: starting in 1969 with J1001.
    in 1972 prefix "J" became suffix "J."
    in 1976 prefix "L" began with L1001.
    in 1978 prefix "L" became suffix "L."

Serial Number Location: crane recess in frame.

Major Variations: barrel has shrouded ejector rod only on 2″ model.
    4″ barrel is plain.

Markings: left side of barrel: Lawman MK III, .357 Magnum ctg.
    left side of frame on sideplate: Rampant Colt trademark.

Price(s):
    blue, 4″ barrel, very good—$200.00
    blue, 4″ barrel, excellent—$250.00
    blue, 2″ barrel, very good—$225.00
    blue, 2″ barrel, excellent—$300.00
    nickel, 4″ barrel, very good—$225.00
    nickel, 4″ barrel, excellent—$275.00
    nickel, 2″ barrel, very good—$250.00
    nickel, 2″ barrel, excellent—$325.00

History: Introduced as a new development in medium frame revolvers, the Mark III Series was a radical departure from the previous Colt designs. It was called the "J" Frame and is recognizable by the forward leaning, enlarged trigger guard. As the Colt "Positive" action revolvers were removed from the line, they were replaced by the Mark III Series, which included the Officer's Model, Match, Lawman, Trooper, Metropolitan, and Official Police. All have been either discontinued or reworked into the Mark V configuration.

Mechanical Functioning: This is a double-action, solid-frame revolver with a swing-out cylinder swinging out to the left. Cylinder latching is from the rear only in standard Colt design with the opening latch mounted on the sideplate and pulling to the rear to unlock the cylinder. Ejection is manual and simultaneous. Most internal parts are of stainless steel. The chambers are counterbored so that the cartridge rims fall into a rebated section. This provides an additional amount of security in the event of a cartridge case rupture by providing full case head support and an additional gas deflector to protect the shooter. A connector is used to transmit energy from the hammer to the inertial (floating) firing pin, which eliminates the chance of accidental discharge if the weapon is dropped. Following the principles used on most modern revolvers, this connector functions as a transfer bar and when the trigger is pulled all the way to the rear it rises to the level of the firing pin allowing the falling hammer to strike it and thus transmit the energy of the hammer to the firing pin, firing the cartridge. Unless the trigger is pulled all the way to the rear, the connector will not rise to engage the firing pin and the hammer top will contact the frame on falling, with a cut-out section of the hammer over the firing pin. There is also a cylinder-hammer interlock preventing the cylinder from being opened or closed if the hammer is cocked. In this new line of revolvers Colt decided to eliminate their standard practice of using a V-shaped leaf spring to power both the hammer and the trigger return bar. In the Mark III series of revolvers all of the springs are of the coil type. The mainspring rides on a guide and that guide engages the hammer with a ball joint in a manner similar to the Smith & Wesson Chief's Special. Like all Colt revolvers the sideplate is located on the left side of the frame, and the cylinder latch slides in a groove cut into the sideplate. The cylinder latch engages a bolt that protrudes through the frame and locks the cylinder in the closed position by resting in a circular cut in the center of the ratchet. The cylinder is unlocked by pulling the latch to the rear which withdraws the locking bolt allowing the cylinder to be pushed out to the left for loading and unloading.

Colt Lawman MK III
Photo courtesy of the T.W. Motter Collection

Colt
150 Hoyshope Avenue
Hartford, CT 06102

Model: Metropolitan MK III

Action Type: revolver, double action.

Caliber(s): .38 Special.

Barrel Lengths: 4".

Finish: blue or nickel.

Manufacturing Dates: 1969–1972.

Stocks: service or target.

Rifling: 6L.

Weight, Unloaded: 36 oz.

Sights: fixed.

Serial Numbers: in series with Lawman MK III, Official Police MK III, Officer's Model, Match MK III, and Trooper MK III. Started at J1001 and running to J72201.

Serial Number Location: inside crane recess.

Major Variations: service or target stocks.
blue or nickel finish.

Markings: left side of barrel: Metropolitan MK III, .38 Special Ctg.
right side of barrel: Colt address.

Price(s):
target stocks, blue, very good—$200.00
target stocks, blue, excellent—$225.00
service stocks, blue, very good—$175.00
service stocks, blue, excellent—$200.00

History: The Colt Metropolitan MK III was introduced in 1969 with the MK III series of revolvers. It was intended to be the quintessential revolver for large city police departments that restrict their officers to the .38 Special cartridge. The Metropolitan MK III and the Official Police MK III are essentially identical revolvers; however, the Metropolitan MK III was available only in the 4" barrel version. It was available in blue or nickel and with Service or Target grips. The serial number range ran with the rest of the MK III series, and the MK III frame was entitled the "J" frame by Colt. The MK IIIs can be instantly recognized when viewing Colts, by the forward slanting oval of the trigger guard.

Mechanical Functioning: The MK III series is a departure from the standard Colt double-action series of revolvers. In it Colt eliminated all leaf springs and instead substituted stainless steel coil springs. Also incorporated is a transfer bar, making it impossible to discharge the weapon unless the trigger is fully retracted in the firing position. As with most of the modern Colts, the firing pin is of the floating type. The cylinder swings outward to the left. Ejection is manual and simultaneous. The cylinder is counter-bored as an additional safety measure in case of case rupture.

Colt Metropolitan MK III

Colt
150 Hoyshope Avenue
Hartford, CT 06102

Model: National Match

Action Type: semiautomatic, recoil operated.

Caliber(s): .45 A.C.P.

Barrel Lengths: 5".

Finish: blue or nickel.

Manufacturing Dates: 1933–1941.

Stocks: checkered walnut or plastic.

Rifling: 6L.

Weight, Unloaded: 39 oz.

Sights: Stevens style adjustable rear, or fixed with Patridge front.

Serial Numbers: running with M1911 Commercial, starting at C164800 and running to C208799.

Serial Number Location: right side of frame above trigger.

Major Variations: none.

Markings: left side of slide: National Match Colt Automatic Calibre .45.

Price(s):
    blue, fixed sights, very good—$1,250.00
    blue, fixed sights, excellent—$1,500.00
    blue, adjustable sights, very good—$1,500.00
    blue, adjustable sights, excellent—$1,750.00

History: When it first began production in 1933, the National Match was identical to the Standard 1911A1 Commercial Model with one very big difference. Since the leading match shooters of the day demanded perfection, or at least as close as possible to it, the Colt factory set aside special frames, slides, barrels, and parts made a little bit oversize and then hand-fitted them. All parts were honed to fit precisely, and then a carefully targeted match barrel was used. Trigger pull was hand-adjusted, and although the standard arched mainspring housing was used instead of the standard serrations, it was carefully checkered. The first issue used Patridge-type front sights, and later, a ramp front with a Stevens type adjustable rear sight was used. The trigger was of the standard 1911A1 short style, and in its day it was a masterpiece.

Mechanical Functioning: The Colt .45 National Match pistol is a recoil-operated, semiautomatic pistol with an external hammer and a seven-shot detachable box magazine. It is of the standard Colt/Browning design, in the configuration of the 1911A1. On this particular pistol, however, the entire action is hand-fitted and hand-honed. Disassembly for this pistol is the same as for the standard government model; however, great care must be taken when removing the barrel bushing, for the barrel and bushing are very carefully and closely fitted. The safety devices on this pistol were the same as the 1911A1; that is, the grip safety and the manual safety locking the slide as well as the hammer.

Colt National Match with Adjustable Sights

Colt
150 Hoyshope Avenue
Hartford, CT 06102

Model: New Pocket

Action Type: revolver, double action.

Caliber(s): .32 Short and Long Colt.

Barrel Lengths: 2½″, 3½″, 5″, 6″.

Finish: blue or nickel.

Manufacturing Dates: 1893–1905.

Stocks: hard rubber.

Rifling: 6L.

Weight, Unloaded: 16 oz. with 3½″ barrel.

Sights: fixed.

Serial Numbers: 1 to about 30,000.

Serial Number Location: n/a.

Major Variations: none.

Markings: left side of barrel: Colt DA.32.
on left side of frame on sideplate: Rampant Colt trademark, which at first was encircled by the words "Colt's New Pocket"; later it was superimposed over a stylized "C," and finally was alone.

Price(s):
New Pocket .32 Colt, very good—$325.00
New Pocket .32 Colt, excellent—$400.00
New Pocket .32 Smith & Wesson, very good—$350.00
New Pocket .32 Smith & Wesson, excellent—$425.00
Add 25% for pre-1898 manufacture

History: This was the first swing-out cylinder, small-framed revolver made in the United States, and it replaced the Colt New Line revolvers. It preceded the Pocket Positive and differed only in mechanical design. The Pocket Positive continued in the same serial range starting where the New Pocket left off. This was a very small-framed revolver, very easy to conceal, and quite comfortable for those with small hands.

Mechanical Functioning: The functioning is of standard Colt double-action revolver style. The cylinder is six-shot with long flutes and peripheral locking notches, clockwise rotation, and large cylinder stop grooves. The firing pin is fixed on the hammer. The cylinder is rear-locking only and is unlocked by pulling the cylinder release rearward and swinging the cylinder to the left. The simultaneous ejection is manual and accomplished by a reciprocating rod. The hammer fall and trigger rebound are both powered by a single V-shaped leaf spring. The positive safety lock was not on this model but was on its successor, the Pocket Positive. The New Pocket was all steel.

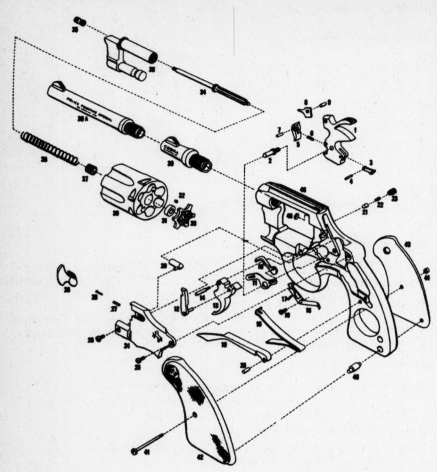

1	Hammer	17	Bolt Spring	33	Ratchet
2	Hammer Pin	18	Bolt Screw	34	Ejector Rod
3	Hammer Stirrup	19	Rebound Lever	35	Ejector Rod Head
4	Hammer Stirrup Pin	20	Rebound Lever Pin	36	Ejector Spring
5	Strut	21	Crane Lock Detent	37	Crane Bushing
6	Strut Spring	22	Crane Lock Spring	38	Crane
7	Strut Pin	23	Crane Lock Screw	39	Barrel
8	Firing Pin	24	Side Plate	40	Stock Pin
9	Firing Pin Rivet	25	Side Plate Screws (2)	41	Stock Screw
10	Safety	26	Latch	42	Stock - Left Hand
11	Safety Lever	27	Latch Spring	43	Stock - Right Hand
12	Hand	28	Latch Spring Guide	44	Stock Screw Nut
13	Trigger	29	Latch Pin	45	Recoil Plate
14	Trigger Pin	30	Cylinder	46	Main Frame
15	Main Spring	31	Cylinder Bushing		
16	Bolt	32	Cylinder Bushing Pin		

Colt New Pocket

Colt
150 Hoyshope Avenue
Hartford, CT 06102

Model: Police Positive

Action Type: revolver, double action.

Caliber(s): .32 Long Colt, .32 New Police, .38 New Police, .38 Smith & Wesson.

Barrel Lengths: 4", 5", 6".

Finish: blue or nickel.

Manufacturing Dates: 1905–1947, resumed in 1977 to 1978.

Stocks: hard rubber or checkered walnut.

Rifling: 6L.

Weight, Unloaded: early type, 20 oz. with a 2½" barrel; late type, 26½ oz. with a 4" barrel.

Sights: fixed.

Serial Numbers: started at 49500 in the New Police range in .32 caliber and with number 1 in the .38 Caliber. The .32 numbers ran with the Target model to number 253351 and the .38 ran to 406725 running with the Bankers' Special and later the .32! Don't confuse these numbers with the models G and C Police Positive Target Revolvers which had their own numbers. Late model Police Positives start at 19201M in the Detective Special range in 1977.

Serial Number Location: frame, in crane recess.

Major Variations: early style had light barrel and no ejector rod shroud and had two styles of gripframe, one slightly wider than the other. Late style has heavy barrel with shroud and Bulldog grips.

Markings: left side of barrel: Police Positive and caliber.
on right side of barrel: Colt's Mfg. Co., Hartford, Ct. USA.
left frame: Rampant Colt Trademark on sideplate.

Price(s):
    Police Positive .32 Long Colt, very good—$300.00
    Police Positive .32 Long Colt, excellent—$375.00
    Police Positive .32 Smith & Wesson, very good—$300.00
    Police Positive .32 Smith & Wesson, excellent—$375.00
    Police Positive .38 Smith & Wesson, very good—$300.00
    Police Positive .38 Smith & Wesson, excellent—$375.00
    Police Positive, late, .38 Special, very good—$300.00
    Police Positive, late, .38 Special, excellent—$375.00
    Police Positive, Detective Special, very good—$275.00
    Police Positive, Detective Special, excellent—$375.00
    Add 15% for nickel finish

History: The Police Positive evolved from the New Police and incorporated mechanical improvements such as the Colt Positive lock. The cylinder length on the Police Positive is 1¼", and this model should not be confused with the Police Positive special with a 1⅝" cylinder, and resultant longer frame. This was a service gun that went through few changes other than for cosmetic reasons from 1905 to 1943. In 1977 it was reintroduced in name only, as it was actually a Detective Special with a 4" barrel and oversized grips.

Mechanical Functioning: The functioning is of standard Colt double-action revolver style. The cylinder is six-shot with long flutes and peripheral locking notches, clockwise rotation, and large cylinder stop grooves. The firing pin is fixed on the hammer. The cylinder is rear-locking only and is unlocked by pulling the cylinder release rearward and swinging the cylinder to the left. The simultaneous ejection is manual and accomplished by a reciprocating rod. The hammer fall and trigger rebound are both powered by a single V-shaped leaf spring. The Police Positive is of all-steel construction.

Colt Police Positive

Colt
150 Hoyshope Avenue
Hartford, CT 06102

Model: Python

Action Type: revolver, double action.

Caliber(s): .357 Magnum.

Barrel Lengths: 2½", 3", 4", 6", 8".

Finish: blue, nickel, Colt Guard, stainless steel.

Manufacturing Dates: 1955 to date.

Stocks: target walnut or Pachmayr.

Rifling: 6L.

Weight, Unloaded: 4" barrel is 38 oz.

Sights: adjustable rear.

Serial Numbers: started at 1 in 1969 reaching 99,999 and restarting at E1001. In 1975 at E99,999 restarted at 1001E. At 99,999E in 1978 switched to 1001N and V01001.

Serial Number Location: inside crane recess.

Major Variations: barrel lengths.
finish.
grips.

Markings: left side of barrel: Python .357, .357 Mag. Ctg.
right side of barrel: Colt address.
on sideplate: Rampant Colt trademark.

Price(s):
blue, 2½"—$550.00
blue, 3"—$750.00
blue, 4"—$500.00
blue, 6"—$500.00
blue, 8"—$500.00
stainless, 4"—$600.00
stainless, 6"—$600.00
nickel, 4", very good—$400.00; excellent—$550.00
nickel, 6", very good—$400.00; excellent—$550.00
nickel, 8", very good—$425.00; excellent—$575.00

History: The Colt Python was introduced in 1955, and since then it has been the top of the line of the Colt revolvers. At first, it was intended to be primarily known as their target revolver, and it was the ultimate word in their Official Police–type action. The barrel features a ventilated rib and an ejector shroud that runs the full length of the barrel, which also provides a counterweight. The hammer is of the target type and has a wide, checkered spur. This revolver has earned as much of a reputation for target shooting as it has as a standard police service revolver. It is now available in all stainless steel, as well as blued or nickeled steel.

Mechanical Functioning: The Python is a double-action revolver based on the standard Colt action. It utilizes a leaf spring both to power the hammer and to operate the trigger rebound lever. The cylinder swings out to the left side, and ejection is manual and simultaneous via an ejector rod.

Colt Python
Photo courtesy of the T.W. Motter Collection

Colt
150 Hoyshope Avenue
Hartford, CT 06102

Model: Trooper MK III

Action Type: revolver, double action.

Caliber(s): .357 Magnum, .22 L.R., .22 MAG, .38 Special.

Barrel Lengths: 4″, 6″, or 8″.

Finish: blue, nickel.

Manufacturing Dates: introduced in 1969, superseded in 1982.

Stocks: checkered walnut.

Rifling: 6L.

Weight, Unloaded: 39 oz. with 4″ barrel.

Sights: adjustable target rear.

Serial Numbers: starting in 1969 with J1001.
  in 1972 prefix "J" became suffix "J."
  in 1976 prefix "L" began with L1001.
  in 1978 prefix "L" became suffix "L."

Serial Number Location: crane recess in frame.

Major Variations: none.

Markings: left side of barrel: Trooper MK III, .357 Magnum Ctg.
  left side of frame on sideplate: Rampant Colt trademark.

Price(s):
  .22 L.R., 4″ barrel, very good—$200.00
  .22 L.R., 4″ barrel, excellent—$275.00
  .22 L.R., 8″ barrel, very good—$250.00
  .22 L.R., 8″ barrel, excellent—$300.00
  .22 L.R., 6″ barrel, very good—$200.00
  .22 L.R., 6″ barrel, excellent—$275.00
  .357 Magnum, 4″ barrel, blue, very good—$175.00
  .357 Magnum, 4″ barrel, blue, excellent—$225.00
  .357 Magnum, 4″ barrel, nickel, very good—$200.00
  .357 Magnum, 4″ barrel, nickel, excellent—$250.00
  .357 Magnum, 6″ barrel, blue, very good—$175.00
  .357 Magnum, 6″ barrel, blue, excellent—$225.00
  .357 Magnum, 6″ barrel, nickel, very good—$200.00
  .357 Magnum, 6″ barrel, nickel, excellent—$250.00
  .357 Magnum, 8″ barrel, blue, very good—$225.00
  .357 Magnum, 8″ barrel, blue, excellent—$250.00
  .357 Magnum, 8″ barrel, nickel, very good—$250.00
  .357 Magnum, 8″ barrel, nickel, excellent—$275.00
  .22 W.M.R., 8″ barrel, nickel, very good—$200.00
  .22 W.M.R., 8″ barrel, nickel, excellent—$275.00

History: Introduced as a new development in medium-frame revolvers, the Mark III Series was a radical departure from the previous Colt designs. It was called the "J" Frame and is recognizable by the forward-leaning, enlarged trigger guard. As the Colt "Positive" action revolvers were removed from the line, they were replaced by the Mark III Series, which included the Officer's Model, Match, Lawman, Trooper, Metropolitan, and Official Police. All have been either discontinued or reworked into the Mark V configuration.

Mechanical Functioning: This is a double-action, solid-frame revolver with a swing-out cylinder swinging out to the left. Cylinder latching is from the rear only in standard Colt design with the opening latch mounted on the sideplate and pulling to the rear to unlock the cylinder. Ejection is manual and simultaneous. Most internal parts are of stainless steel. The chambers have counterbores for rebating the cartridge rims, and a connector is used to transmit energy from the hammer to the inertial firing pin. There is a cylinder-hammer interlock preventing the cylinder from being opened or closed if the hammer is cocked. The connector prevents firing if the trigger is not pulled or if the revolver is dropped.

Colt Trooper MK III
Photo courtesy of the T.W. Motter Collection

Colt
150 Hoyshope Avenue
Hartford, CT 06102

Model: Trooper MK V

Action Type: revolver, double action.

Caliber(s): .357 Magnum.

Barrel Lengths: 4″, 6″.

Finish: blue or nickel.

Manufacturing Dates: 1982–1986.

Stocks: checkered walnut.

Rifling: 6L.

Weight, Unloaded: 38 oz. with 4″ barrel .357 Magnum.

Sights: adjustable target rear.

Serial Number: n/a.

Serial Number Location: left frame in crane recess.

Major Variations: n/a.

Markings: left side of barrel: Trooper MK V, .357 Magnum Ctg.
  on left side of frame on sideplate: Rampant Colt trademark over "V."

Price(s):
.357 Magnum, 4″ blue—$300.00
.357 Magnum, 4″ nickel—$325.00
.357 Magnum, 6″ blue—$300.00
.357 Magnum, 6″ nickel—$325.00

History: Introduced as an improvement to the Mark III Series, the Mark V, Lawman, and Trooper have reconfigured gripframes for a more comfortable hold. Trigger to backstrap distance was reduced by 3/8″ as well as the depth to the bottom strap. The hammer fall has been shortened by 8 degrees, and a longer coil mainspring coupled with the reduced radial travel builds a fast cock time. The double action pull is smoother than the MK III, and is 15% lighter. Target trigger, target hammer, and oversize grips are standard.

Mechanical Functioning: This is a double-action, solid-frame revolver with a swing-out cylinder swinging out to the left. Cylinder latching is from the rear only in standard Colt design, with the opening latch mounted on the sideplate and pulling to the rear to unlock the cylinder. Ejection is manual and simultaneous. Most internal parts are of stainless steel. The chambers have counterbores for rebating the cartridge rims, and a connector is used to transmit energy from the hammer to the inertial firing pin. There is a cylinder-hammer interlock preventing the cylinder from being opened or closed if the hammer is cocked. The cylinder is counterbored so that the cartridge rims fall into a rebated section. This provides an additional amount of security in the event of a cartridge case rupture by providing full case head support and an additional gas deflector to protect the shooter. A connector is used to transmit energy from the hammer to the inertial (floating) firing pin, which eliminates the chance of accidental discharge if the weapon is dropped. Following the principles used on most modern revolvers, this connector functions as a transfer bar, and when the trigger is pulled all the way to the rear, it rises to the level of the firing pin allowing the falling hammer to strike it and thus transmit the energy of the hammer to the firing pin, firing the cartridge. Unless the trigger is pulled all the way to the rear, the connector will not rise to engage the firing pin and the hammer top will contact the frame on falling, with a cut-out section of the hammer over the firing pin. There is also a cylinder-hammer interlock preventing the cylinder from being opened or closed if the hammer is cocked. In this new line of revolvers Colt decided to continue their practice of using coil springs as on the Mark III series of revolvers. All of the springs are of stainless steel. The mainspring rides on a guide and that guide engages the hammer with a ball joint in a manner similar to the Smith & Wesson Chief's Special. As in all Colt revolvers the sideplate is located on the left side of the frame, and the cylinder latch slides in a groove cut into the sideplate. The cylinder latch engages a bolt that protrudes through the frame and locks the cylinder in the closed position by resting in a circular cut in the center of the ratchet. The cylinder is unlocked by pulling the latch to the rear, which withdraws the locking bolt allowing the cylinder to be pushed out to the left for loading and unloading.

Colt Trooper MK V
Photo courtesy of the T.W. Motter Collection

Colt
150 Hoyshope Avenue
Hartford, CT 06102

Model: Woodsman/Huntsman

Action Type: semiautomatic, blowback operated.

Caliber(s): .22 L.R.R.F.

Barrel Lengths: 4½" or 6".

Finish: blue.

Manufacturing Dates: 1955–1976.

Stocks: checkered plastic.

Rifling: 6L.

Weight, Unloaded: 31½ oz. in 6" barrel.

Sights: fixed.

Serial Numbers: started at 90001-C going to 194040C in 1969, then to 001001-S and running to 067801S, then to S100001S to S101335S. Thence to 300001S ending at 317736S.

Serial Number Location: right side of frame above trigger.

Major Variations: none.

Markings: left side of slide: Colt Automatic .22 Long Rifle.
left side of barrel: Colt address.
left side of frame: Rampant Colt and Huntsman.

Price(s):
very good—$200.00
excellent—$300.00

History: The Huntsman was significant when it started in 1955 as a continuation of the Challenger, in that Colt was still looking for the Plinkers market, and they chose a very fine weapon with which to attract that market. The Huntsman was essentially a stripped-down Colt Woodsman target pistol without benefit of the adjustable sights. It had a magazine catch on the butt as in the old Woodsman. It did not have a magazine disconnect, and the slide did not stay back on the last shot. It was available only in blue, and with plastic stocks. It was manufactured until 1976.

Mechanical Functioning: The Colt Huntsman is a straight blowback, semiautomatic pistol with a ten-shot detachable box magazine inserted through the gripframe, and retained with a catch at the bottom of the gripframe. It possesses an internal hammer and uses a floating firing pin. The safety is located at the left side of the frame and locks the slide as well as the hammer. The barrel is affixed to the frame, and the reciprocating slide abuts against the frame and barrel, one at battery.

Colt Woodsman
Photo courtesy of the T.W. Motter Collection

Colt
150 Hoyshope Avenue
Hartford, CT 06102

Model: 1902 Sporting and Military

Action Type: semiautomatic, recoil operated.

Caliber(s): .38 A.C.P.

Barrel Lengths: 6".

Finish: blue.

Manufacturing Dates: 1902–1929.

Stocks: hard rubber.

Rifling: 6L.

Weight, Unloaded: 35 oz. Sporting, 37 oz. Military.

Sights: fixed.

Serial Numbers: the Military started at 15001 in 1902 and ran to 15200, thereafter restarting at 15000 and running down to 11000 in 1907. In 1908 began at 30200 and ran to 47266 sharing serials with the 1903 from 39800 on. The 1902 Sporting started in 1903 at 3500 and ran to 10999 in 1907. In 1908 it went from 30000 to 30190.

Serial Number Location: right frame above trigger.

Major Variations: Sporting Model: no lanyard loop, round stub hammer, early slide grooves on front of slide, late on rear.
Military Model: lanyard loop on left side of gripframe, gripframe squared off at bottom, rounded hammer or spur hammer, forward or rear slide checkering or serrations.

Markings: right side of slide: Automatic Colt Calibre .38 Rimless, Smokeless. left side of slide: Patented Apr. 20, 1897, Sept 9, 1902 (Colt address).

Price(s):
> 1902 Sporting, forward serrations, very good—$2,500.00
> 1902 Sporting, forward serrations, excellent—$3,000.00
> 1902 Sporting, rearward serrations, very good—$2,000.00
> 1902 Sporting, rearward serrations, excellent—$2,500.00
> 1902 Military, forward serrations, very good—$1,750.00
> 1902 Military, forward serrations, excellent—$2,000.00
> 1902 Military, rearward serrations, very good—$1,750.00
> 1902 Military, rearward serrations, excellent—$2,500.00
> 1902 Military, U.S. Army, very good—$5,000.00
> 1902 Military, U.S. Army, excellent—$7,500.00

History: The Colt Model 1902 was another one of John Browning's designs. It had a modern look to it, and for its time it was one of the most reliable pistols in the world. It used a then-new .38 A.C.P. cartridge; in the Sporting Model, the magazine held seven shots, and in the Military

Model, the magazine held eight shots. To recognize this pistol and to tell it apart from the 1900, look for the following things: The 1900 had a combination rear sight and safety. It also came with wood grips. The 1902s had no safety and came with hard rubber grips. Also look for the patent dates. The difference between a Sporting 1902 and a Military 1902 is primarily in the shape of the gripframe. The 1902 Sporting had a rounded bottom rear edge, whereas the Military had a squared bottom rear edge of the gripframe.

Mechanical Functioning: The Model 1902 Colt was a recoil-operated, semi-automatic pistol with a detachable box magazine fitted through the gripframe. It utilized an outside hammer and a floating firing pin, but had no safety in the conventional sense; rather it had a half cock notch. The recoil system, a predecessor of the 1911 type, instead of using one strong link, used two smaller links in order to yank the barrel downward to unlock it from the breech as the slide traveled rearward upon firing. A word of warning to anyone who wishes to fire this pistol. While it may still be safe utilizing the .38 A.C.P. cartridge, do not under any circumstances use .38 Super or High Velocity .38 A.C.P. cartridges in this gun. This pistol was made for lower-pressure cartridges, and utilizing some of these modern cartridges could severely damage the pistol or injure the shooter.

Colt Model 1902 Military

Colt
150 Hoyshope Avenue
Hartford, CT 06102

Model: 1903 Pocket

Action Type: semiautomatic, recoil operated.

Caliber(s): .38 A.C.P.

Barrel Lengths: 4½".

Finish: blue.

Manufacturing Dates: 1903–1929 (26,000 manuf.).

Stocks: hard rubber.

Rifling: 6L.

Weight, Unloaded: 31 oz.

Sights: fixed.

Serial Numbers: started at 16001 in 1903 and ran to 37100 in 1917, thereafter running with the Model 1902 starting at 39800 and running to 47266 in 1929.

Serial Number Location: right or left side of frame above trigger.

Major Variations: rounded hammer on spur type
shallow or deep finger groove in slide.

Markings: right side of slide: Automatic Colt Calibre .38 Rimless Smokeless.
left side of slide: Patented Apr. 20, 1987, Sept. 9, 1902 (Colt address).

Price(s):
1903, round hammer, very good—$1,000.00
1903, round hammer, excellent—$1,250.00
1903, spur hammer, very good—$750.00
1903, spur hammer, excellent—$1,000.00

History: The model name of this pistol sometimes creates some confusion, as both it and the Model 1903 Pocket are essentially the same model year and are both called 1903s. The important distinction to remember is that this Model 1903 has an external hammer and is in .38 A.C.P. cartridge. The Model 1903 Pocket has an internal hammer and is in .32 or .380 A.C.P., and is more of a true pocket gun. This model was created primarily for the civilian market as an easier to handle Model 1902, and that is essentially what it is—just a chopped-down Model 1902. It is 1½" shorter and 6 ounces lighter and utilizes the 1902 Sporting frame. About 1908 the hammer was changed from the round-headed type to the spur type. This pistol was in production from 1903 until 1929.

Mechanical Functioning: The Model 1903 Colt was a recoil-operated, semiautomatic pistol with a detachable box magazine fitted through the gripframe. It utilized an outside hammer and a floating firing pin but had no safety in the conventional sense; rather it had a half-cock notch.

The recoil system, a predecessor of the 1911 type, instead of using one strong link utilized two smaller links in order to yank the barrel downward to unlock it from the breech as the slide traveled rearward upon firing. A word of warning to anyone who wishes to fire this pistol: While it may still be safe to use the .38 A.C.P. cartridge, do not under any circumstances use .38 Super or High-Velocity .38 A.C.P. cartridges in it. This pistol was made for lower-pressure cartridges, and utilizing some of these modern cartridges could severely damage the pistol or injure the shooter.

Colt Model 1903 Pocket

Colt
150 Hoyshope Avenue
Hartford, CT 06102

Model: 1903 Pocket Hammerless

Action Type: semiautomatic, blowback operated.

Caliber(s): .32 A.C.P.

Barrel Lengths: 4″ in first type, 3¾″ in second and third types.

Finish: blue or nickel; U.S. pistols were Parkerized.

Manufacturing Dates: 1903–1945 in .32 A.C.P.

Stocks: hard rubber, checkered walnut, ivory, pearl.

Rifling: 6L.

Weight, Unloaded: 23 oz.

Sights: fixed.

Serial Numbers: .32 A.C.P.: 1 to 572215.
Some after number 137400 with prefix "M."

Serial Number Location: left side of frame above trigger.

Major Variations: 1st type: This variation had a removable barrel bushing similar to the M1911 .45 A.C.P. The .32 caliber pistol, up to about number 72000, had a 4″ barrel. Thereafter, the barrel was 3¾″ in length. About serial number 95800 the extractor was enlarged to reduce a parts interchangeability problem between it and the .380 model. After serial number 95801, extractors between the two calibers could be interchanged.
2nd type: Around 1911 the forward end of the slide was simplified and the barrel bushing was eliminated. In .32 caliber this change occurred around serial number 105051. In .380 caliber the number is around 6252.
3rd type: In late 1926 or early 1927, the Tansley magazine safety was adopted. In .32 caliber the starting number was about 468097.

Markings: A great many variations in markings exist. On the left side of the slide to the rear of the slide serrations, on all variations, was the Rampant Colt insignia. Forward of the serrations, up to about number 10,000 was Browning's Patent, Apr. 20, 1897 and Colt's Pat. F.A. MFG. Co. Hartford Conn. U.S.A. After December, 1903, Dec. 22, 1903 was added to the patent date. About serial number 50,000 the patent legend was changed, eliminating Browning's name. On the right side of the slide: Automatic Colt, Calibre .32 rimless, smokeless. When the .380 was introduced the right side of the slide read: Automatic Colt, Calibre .380 hammerless. During the early 1920s the right side legends were changed from Automatic Colt to Colt Automatic. The left side markings were changed to: Colt Pt. F. A. Mfg. Co. Hartford. Ct. USA, Patented Apr. 20, 1897, Dec. 22, 1903.

Price(s):
Model 1903, .32 A.C.P., hammerless Pocket, 1st type, very good—$450.00; excellent—$650.00

Model 1903, .32 A.C.P., hammerless Pocket, 2nd type, very good—$350.00; excellent—$450.00

Model 1903, .32 A.C.P., hammerless Pocket, 3rd type, very good—$325.00; excellent—$400.00

Model 1903, .32 A.C.P., hammerless U.S., very good—$650.00; excellent—$1,000.00

History: The Model 1903 Pocket pistol is a Browning design, licensed to Colt and based on the FN Grande Modele. The proper nomenclature for the gun is Model 1903 Hammerless. In .380 caliber, it is the Model 1908. A very successful pistol, almost three-quarters of a million of them were sold since their first introduction in 1903 and their final end in 1945. During World War II, the U.S. government used about 17,000 .32 caliber pistols and around 3,000 .380 caliber pistols, most of these having the Parkerized finish. On both calibers, the stamp U.S. Property was marked on the right side of the frame above the trigger. These pistols were used by the army, navy, air force, the OSS, and also as a standard sidearm for general officers. Even though production ceased in 1945, distribution continued into 1946, utilizing parts that had been left over. The frame designation on these models was known as "M."

Mechanical Functioning: The .32 caliber Colt Model 1903 Pocket Hammerless Pistol was a blowback-operated, semiautomatic handgun, utilizing a concealed hammer.

Colt Model 1903 Pocket Hammerless
Photo courtesy of Butterfield and Butterfield

Colt
150 Hoyshope Avenue
Hartford, CT 06102

Model: 1908 Hammerless

Action Type: semiautomatic, blowback operated.

Caliber(s): .25 A.C.P.

Barrel Lengths: 2".

Finish: blue or nickel.

Manufacturing Dates: 1908–1946.

Stocks: hard rubber, walnut, ivory, pearl.

Rifling: 6L.

Weight, Unloaded: 12 oz.

Sights: fixed.

Serial Numbers: 1–409061.

Serial Number Location: left side of frame above trigger.

Major Variations: with or without magazine safety, military or civilian.

Markings: left side of slide: Colt's Pat. F.A. Mfg. Co. Hartford Conn. USA, Patented Aug. 25, 1896, Apr. 20, 1897, Dec. 22, 1903 (and later Jan. 25, 1910 and July 31, 1917 were added).

Price(s):
blue, no magazine disconnector, very good—$350.00
blue, no magazine disconnector, excellent—$450.00
blue, with magazine disconnector, very good—$325.00
blue, with magazine disconnector, excellent—$400.00
Military, very good—$1,000.00
Military, excellent—$1,250.00
nickel, no magazine disconnector, very good—$400.00
nickel, no magazine disconnector, excellent—$500.00
nickel, with magazine disconnector, very good—$375.00
nickel, with magazine disconnector, excellent—$450.00

History: The people at Colt are never ones to miss marketing opportunities, and when they saw the success in Europe of the Browning FN 1906, they knew they had something they needed to copy. Being friendly with Browning, of course, they were able to secure license to make this pistol and added just minor refinements to it. Like the Browning, this is a well-made little vest-pocket pistol, introduced in 1908. It stayed in production through World War II, and ended its life in about 1946 when the last of the spare parts were made into guns. During its 38-year history, it was available not only in blue and nickel, but also in a variety of high-grade finishes with accessory grips of rare materials. About serial number 141000 the Tansley magazine disconnector was added as an additional safety feature.

Mechanical Functioning: The Colt Model 1908 .25 automatic is a straight blowback-operated, semiautomatic pistol with a six-shot detachable box magazine. It is striker-fired and has three safeties: a grip safety to prevent firing unless the gun is actually held, a mechanical thumb safety on the left side of the receiver that locks the sear and also doubles as a slidelock, and after 1917 a magazine disconnector to prevent the pistol from firing when the magazine is removed. Takedown is accomplished in the same manner as the Browning 1906.

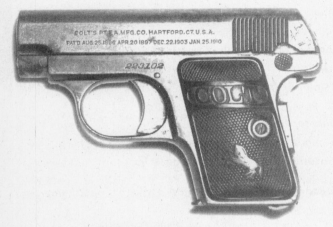

Colt Model 1908 Hammerless

Colt
150 Hoyshope Avenue
Hartford, CT 06102

Model: 1909 New Service (Army, Navy, and U.S.M.C.).

Action Type: revolver, double action.

Caliber(s): .45 Long Colt.

Barrel Lengths: 5½".

Finish: blue.

Manufacturing Dates: 1909–1910.

Stocks: plain walnut.

Rifling: 6L.

Weight, Unloaded: 40 oz.

Sights: fixed.

Serial Numbers: Colt numbers: 18000 to 49000.
military numbers on butt: Army: 1–18303.
military numbers on butt: Navy: 1–1000.
military numbers on butt: U.S.M.C.: 1–1200.

Serial Number Location: frame in crane recess, military number on bottom strap.

Major Variations: army, navy, and marine models.

Markings: top of barrel, Colt's Pat. F.A. Mfg. Co. Hartford, Ct. USA, Pt. Aug. 5, 1884, June 5, 1900, July 4, 1905.
left side of barrel: Colt D.A. .45.
base of butt: U.S. Army Model 1909.

Price(s):
1909 Army, very good—$850.00
1909 Army, excellent—$1,100.00
1909 Navy, very good—$1,250.00
1909 Navy, excellent—$1,500.00
1909 U.S.M.C., very good—$1,500.00
1909 U.S.M.C., excellent—$2,000.00

History: The Model 1909 Colt is basically a new service revolver in military dress. It fired the .45 Long Colt cartridge as did the single-action Army military; however, since this cartridge was filled with smokeless powder and was much more powerful than the earlier black-powder cartridge, the Army enlarged the rim slightly in order to prevent it from chambering in the old single-action Army. The revolver had plain walnut grips and a lanyard swivel-mounted in the center of the butt. The Marine Corps Model 1909 had a slightly smaller grip and a checkered walnut stock. There are two numbers on these guns. The Colt serial number running in the New Service series is found in the crane recess, and that is the actual serial number. The military number is on the bottom strap of the gripframe on either side of the lanyard loop.

Mechanical Functioning: The Colt Model 1909 is a double-action revolver based on the New Service frame and following the Colt pattern. It utilizes a leaf-shaped mainspring to provide both the driving energy for the hammer and the pressure on the trigger rebound lever in order to return the trigger. Cylinder rotation is clockwise, and as with all Colt double-action revolvers, locking is at the rear only. The cylinder swings out to the left, and ejection is manual and simultaneous via an ejection rod.

Colt Model 1909 Army

Coonan Arms, Inc.
326 Chester Street
St. Paul, MN 55107

Model: 357

Action Type: semiautomatic, recoil operated.

Caliber(s): .357 Magnum.

Barrel Lengths: 5″.

Finish: brushed stainless.

Manufacturing Dates: 1981–date.

Stocks: walnut.

Rifling: 6R.

Weight, Unloaded: 42 oz.

Sights: MMC windage rear.

Serial Numbers: preproduction run: 1 to under 1000.
production numbers start at 1000.

Serial Number Location: right side of frame above trigger guard.

Major Variations: early prototypes varied trigger guard contours.

Markings: right side of frame: Mfg. by Coonan Arms Inc., St. Paul Mn. USA.
left side of slide: Coonan .357 Magnum.

Price(s):
very good—$500.00
excellent—$650.00

History: This pistol was first designed by Don Coonan in 1978 while he was a student at Mancater State University. In 1980 Coonan Arms, Inc. was formed to develop this pistol, and first prototypes were completed in 1982. The design is based on the Colt M1911 pistol with several improvements necessary for this caliber. For instance, it has a specially designed clip to handle the rimmed cartridge. This pistol is one of the current entries into the field of .357 Magnum autos and it appears that Coonan has solved a myriad of problems without yielding to the temptation to create an overly complex design.

Mechanical Functioning: This is basically a Browning/Colt system pistol built on a modified Colt 1911 frame. It is a short recoil-operated, semiautomatic pistol with a seven-shot detachable box magazine. It has a thumb safety that intercepts the hammer at full cock and a grip safety that prevents firing unless depressed. It also has a true half-cock notch on the hammer that locks the sear and prevents it from slipping off or releasing the hammer if the trigger is pulled. The recoil spring, quite naturally, is extra heavy to compensate for this strong caliber. To prevent the rounds from stovepiping as they are stripped from the magazine, a short "hood" was added to the top of the barrel. When the rounds are pulled out of the magazine by the closing slide they have a natural tendency, since they are so long, of popping straight up and getting caught between the barrel and the breechface (stovepiping). On the Coonan the tip of the bullet instead hits the barrel hood ensuring that the round will be chambered. At battery this extension acts as a "mortise and tennon" to firmly align the rear of the barrel and face of the breech. This feature greatly diminishes motion in the rear of the slide at battery and assures a constant lockup position for enhanced accuracy. The magazine is quite interesting in that it had to be specially designed to accommodate the long .357 Magnum cartridge and feed it without a hangup on the cartridge rim. Coonan's answer was a clip made from a nickel-plated spring steel alloy for toughness, with an additional vertical crease for strength. It is composed of six parts and can be taken down easily for cleaning. Additionally, by using a small pin the follower can be pulled down for easier loading. Field-stripping the Coonan is done simply and without tools. After making sure that the gun is unloaded and removing the magazine, press the recoil spring plug in and turn the barrel bushing clockwise. BE CAREFUL. The recoil spring is very powerful and it can and will propel the plug across the room unless you maintain tension and control on the plug as you ease it out! Pull the slide back until the notch on the left-hand side lines up with the slide stop, and drift the slide stop out from right to left. The slide can now be pulled forward and off the gun. The recoil spring and guide can be removed, the barrel bushing can be rotated and pulled off, and the barrel removed. Assembly is in the reverse order. As you may have guessed, many parts are interchangeable with the Colt M1911.

Coonan Arms Model 357

CZ (Ceska Zbrojovka)
Brno, Czechoslovakia

Model: VZ 27

Action Type: semiautomatic, blowback.

Caliber(s): 7.65mm.

Barrel Lengths: 3³/₄".

Finish: blue.

Manufacturing Dates: 1927–1951.

Stocks: 1-piece Bakelite.

Rifling: 6R.

Weight, Unloaded: 25 oz.

Sights: fixed.

Serial Numbers: possibly starting at 1 and running at least to 570000.

Serial Number Location: left side of frame above grip.

Major Variations: military model of CZ pistols is prefixed VZ 27 rather than CZ-27.

Markings: left side of slide; Pistole Modell 27 Kal 7.65.
  top of slide, prewar: Ceska Zbrojovka A.B.V. Praze.
  top of slide, early war: Bohmische Waffenfabrik A.B. in Prag.
  top of slide, late war: fnh.
  top of slide, postwar: Ceska Zbrojovka A.B.V. Praze.
  top of slide, post-1948 (Communist): Ceska Zbrojovka Narodni Podnik.

Price(s):
  prewar: .32 A.C.P., very good—$275.00
  prewar: .32 A.C.P., excellent—$350.00
  early German: .32, very good—$400.00
  early German: .32, excellent—$450.00
  late German: .32, very good—$200.00
  late German: .32, excellent—$250.00
  German Police: .32, very good—$250.00
  German Police: .32, excellent—$300.00
  postwar: .32, very good—$150.00
  postwar: .32, excellent—$200.00
  Communist: .32, very good—$175.00
  Communist: .32, excellent—$225.00
  .32 A.C.P. adapted for silencer, very good—$450.00
  .32 A.C.P. adapted for silencer, excellent—$625.00

History: Designed in 1926 by Frantisek Myska, the Model 27 was based on the Model 24 but was a straight blowback rather than recoil operated with a rotating barrel lock. In 1939, after twelve years of use by the Czechoslovakian police, the German Occupation Army saw its potential and adopted it as a secondary military weapon and for police and Luftwaffe use. Two interesting variants the Germans developed were the .22 L.R.R.F. version for target practice and the long-barreled model modified for silencer. The early German pistols were made to prewar standards, but as the war progressed, quality declined greatly. By 1942 all production went to the Luftwaffe, and the pistols were marked only with the Code fnh and German proofs. At war's end, commercial production resumed, with prewar markings but starting at around serial number 480000. When the Communists took over Czechoslovakia in 1948 the factory was nationalized. It is estimated that nearly 600,000 of these pistols may have been made.

Mechanical Functioning: This is a straight blowback-operated, semiautomatic pistol with an exposed hammer. It fires as a single action only and has an eight-shot detachable box magazine.

CZ VZ 27

CZ (Ceska Zbrojovka)
Brno, Czechoslovakia

Model: VZ 38

Action Type: semiautomatic, blowback operated.

Caliber(s): 9mm K.

Barrel Lengths: 4⁵⁄₈".

Finish: blue.

Manufacturing Dates: 1938–1945.

Stocks: plastic wraparound.

Rifling: 6R.

Weight, Unloaded: 26 oz.

Sights: fixed.

Serial Numbers: started at 250,000.

Serial Number Location: left side of frame and slide.

Major Variations: early pistol had mechanical safety, standard version had no safety. Nazi 39(t).

Markings: on left slide: Ceska Zbrojovka AKC Spol V. Praze.

Price(s):
    VZ-38, with safety, very good—$450.00
    VZ-38, with safety, excellent—$650.00
    VZ-38, without safety, very good—$200.00
    VZ-38, without safety, excellent—$325.00
    Waffenampt Proofed, Add $750.00

History: The VZ-38 was designed in 1937 by Frantisek Myska and was designed specifically for the Czechoslovakian army and adopted as the Model VZ-38. The early examples of this pistol had a mechanical safety on the left side of the frame to lock the hammer. Very shortly after production began, that idea was rejected; since this was a double-action-only pistol, and the hammer was impossible to grab hold of to cock, it was felt with some justification that there was no reason to have a safety and so it was eliminated. When the Germans conquered Czechoslovakia in 1939, they naturally took over the factory in which these pistols were being made. The nomenclature was changed at that time to "Pistole 39(t)." Throughout the range of these pistols there have been minor variations.

Mechanical Functioning: The VZ-38 is a straight blowback-operated, semi-automatic pistol with an external hammer that operates as double action only. It uses a nine-shot detachable box-type magazine that loads through the gripframe and attaches via a clip at the bottom rear of the butt. Take-down is accomplished by first removing the magazine and making sure that the chamber is empty and then pushing a latch on the left side of the frame, which releases the slide and allows the barrel to hinge upward from the muzzle end. The slide can then be slipped rearward and out the barrel, leaving the barrel attached to the frame at the hinge. A sideplate on the left side of the pistol can then be slid upward and off the frame, exposing the working mechanism. The firing pin is of the floating variety, and a lanyard loop is provided at the base of the butt. The pistol has a natural contour for a two-handed hold in front of the trigger guard.

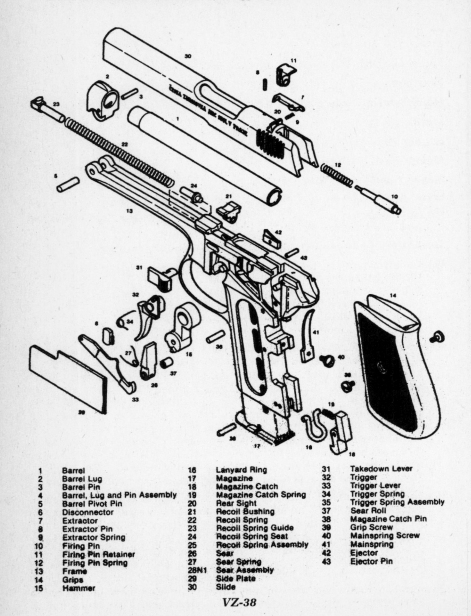

1	Barrel	16	Lanyard Ring	31	Takedown Lever
2	Barrel Lug	17	Magazine	32	Trigger
3	Barrel Pin	18	Magazine Catch	33	Trigger Lever
4	Barrel, Lug and Pin Assembly	19	Magazine Catch Spring	34	Trigger Spring
5	Barrel Pivot Pin	20	Rear Sight	35	Trigger Spring Assembly
6	Disconnector	21	Recoil Bushing	37	Sear Roll
7	Extractor	22	Recoil Spring	38	Magazine Catch Pin
8	Extractor Pin	23	Recoil Spring Guide	39	Grip Screw
9	Extractor Spring	24	Recoil Spring Seat	40	Mainspring Screw
10	Firing Pin	25	Recoil Spring Assembly	41	Mainspring
11	Firing Pin Retainer	26	Sear	42	Ejector
12	Firing Pin Spring	27	Sear Spring	43	Ejector Pin
13	Frame	28N1	Sear Assembly		
14	Grips	29	Side Plate		
15	Hammer	30	Slide		

VZ-38

DWM-Deutsche Waffen und Munitions Fabriken
Berlin, Germany

Model: Luger 1900

Action Type: semiautomatic, recoil operated.

Caliber(s): .30 Luger.

Barrel Lengths: 4³/₄″ standard, other lengths on special order.

Finish: blue.

Manufacturing Dates: 1900–1906.

Stocks: checkered walnut.

Rifling: 4R.

Weight, Unloaded: 29¹/₂ oz.

Sights: fixed.

Serial Numbers: 1 to about 22,000, and possibly into the 15,000s. On the Swiss Model, 1 to 5,000 and 5001A. U.S. test guns were about 6,151 to 7,150. British trials about 21–26.

Serial Number Location: front of frame forward of the trigger guard.

Major Variations: Commercial pistol.
USA Commercial pistol with eagle.
Swiss Commercial pistol.
Swiss Military.
Swiss Military with wide trigger.
U.S. test guns.
Bulgarian Military.
British trials.

Markings: on top of toggle: DWM monogram.
on top of barrel: national symbol for military guns.

Price(s):
Commercial, very good—$1,500.00
Commercial, excellent—$2,500.00
U.S. Commercial (eagle), very good—$2,500.00
U.S. Commercial (eagle), excellent—$3,500.00
Swiss Commercial, very good—$3,250.00
Swiss Commercial, excellent—$4,000.00
Swiss Military, very good—$2,500.00
Swiss Military, excellent—$4,500.00
Swiss Military, wide trigger, very good—$3,500.00
Swiss Military, wide trigger, excellent—$5,000.00
U.S. test, very good—$4,500.00
U.S. test, excellent—$6,000.00

History: The 1900 Luger was an outgrowth of the Borchardt-Luger, which utilized the operating characteristics of the Borchardt Toggleink but on a smaller, lighter frame. There is no question that this is perhaps the most beautiful pistol ever produced. It had excellent pointing characteristics and was comfortable to hold and fire. Compared to the Lugers that followed, the 1900 had a slightly longer frame. This pistol was adopted by both Switzerland and Bulgaria, with the Bulgarian pistols being extremely rare, on the order of 100 guns. Switzerland received a total of 5,100 of which 100 were reworks. The U.S. Army received 1,002 guns, and the British got about 6.

Mechanical Functioning: The Luger is a recoil-operated, striker-fired, semi-automatic pistol with a detachable, eight-shot box magazine. The lock at battery is provided by a toggle link which is not broken until the barrel-breechblock assembly recoils rearward with the toggle striking a camming surface and unlocking the assembly. The mainspring is of the Riband type. There is a magazine disconnector and a thumb-operated safety on the left side of the rear of the frame. The Model 1900 also features an anti-bounce lock on the right toggle to snap it down and prevent the toggle from unlocking. Another feature of the 1900 is the grip safety, which prevents firing unless it is depressed.

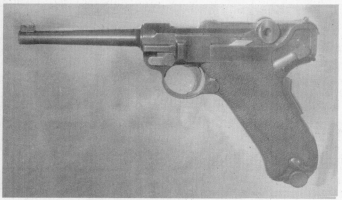

Luger Model 1900 U.S. Commercial

DWM-Deutsche Waffen und Munitions Fabriken
Berlin, Germany

Model: Luger 1904 Navy

Action Type: semiautomatic, recoil operated.

Caliber(s): 9mm Parabellum.

Barrel Lengths: 6".

Finish: blue.

Manufacturing Dates: 1905–1918.

Stocks: checkered walnut.

Rifling: 6R.

Weight, Unloaded: 35½ oz.

Sights: adjustable, barleycorn front, protected rocking rear.

Serial Numbers: 1905 type: 1 to possibly 1,250.
 1907 type: 1 to possibly 1,000B (Luger serials run 4 digits followed by a lower case letter to avoid duplication).
 1910 type: 1 to possibly 8,000B.
 1916 type: 1 to possibly 8,000 in 1916.
 1916 type: 7,750a in 1917.
 1916 type: 5,500 in 1918.
 Commercial serials unknown.

Serial Number Location: front of frame forward of the trigger guard.

Major Variations: 1905: had anti-bounce toggle, grip safety.
 1907: standard toggle, up safety, grip safety.
 1907: standard toggle, down safety, grip safety.
 1910: safety works on sear bar not grip safety.
 1916: no grip safety, used short frame.
 Commercial: no naval proofs.

Markings: on top of toggle: DWM monogram.
 on top of barrel: national symbol for military guns.

Price(s):
 1905 type, very good—$22,500.00
 1905 type, excellent—$30,000.00
 1907 early type, very good—$25,000.00
 1907 early type, excellent—$32,500.00
 1907 late type, very good—$5,000.00
 1907 late type, excellent—$7,500.00
 1910 type, very good—$4,500.00
 1910 type, excellent—$6,500.00
 1916 type, very good—$4,000.00
 1916 type, excellent—$5,500.00
 Commercial 1907, very good—$10,000.00
 Commercial 1907, excellent—$12,500.00

Commercial 1910, very good—$6,000.00
Commercial 1910, excellent—$8,500.00

History: This model was developed for the German Kriegsmarine (navy) and is fascinating in several respects. First, during its life it displays virtually all of the major mechanical changes to the Luger, while still maintaining its own model status. Second, it has unusual rear "ears" protecting the adjustable rear sight, which distinguishes the pistol from the rest of the pack. Estimates on the total production of the 1904 run from 80,000 to 100,000, with an unknown amount going for commercial sales. The nonmilitary Navys can be identified by the lack of naval acceptance marks.

Mechanical Functioning: The Luger is a recoil-operated, striker-fired, semi-automatic pistol with a detachable, eight-shot box magazine. The lock at battery is provided by a toggle link which is not broken until the barrel-breechblock assembly recoils rearward with the toggle striking a camming surface and unlocking the assembly. The mainspring is of the coil type from 1907 on. There is a magazine disconnector and a thumb-operated safety on the left side of the rear of the frame. The early Model 1904 also features an anti-bounce toggle to snap it down and prevent the toggle from unlocking. Another feature of the 1904 is the thumb safety, which intercepted the grip safety. Later types adopted the newer safety, and the final type had the army model style frame, safety, and hold-open.

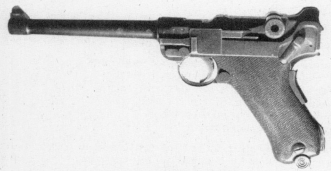

Luger Navy Model 1904

DWM-Deutsche Waffen und Munitions Fabriken
Berlin, Germany
and
Mauser Werke Oberndorf Am Neckar
Germany
and
Erfurt Arsenal
Erfurt, Germany

Model: Luger 1906

Action Type: semiautomatic, recoil operated.

Caliber(s): 9mm Parabellum or 7.65mm.

Barrel Lengths: 4″, 4¾″, 6″.

Finish: blue.

Manufacturing Dates: 1906–1935.

Stocks: checkered walnut.

Rifling: 6R.

Weight, Unloaded: 30 oz.

Sights: fixed.

Serial Numbers: Commercial: 25051 to about 69000.
    Military: 1 to about 1000B
    Mauser: 3635V–3780V; IS-999S; 1921V–2484V
    Swiss: 5001–15215 (DWM); 15216–27500 (Bern)
    Bulgarian: 1 to about 1250
    Brazil: 1 to about 5000
    Portugal: 1 to about 5000
    Portugal, Navy: 1 to about 1000
    Netherlands: 1 to about 4000.

Serial Number Location: front of frame forward of the trigger guard.

Major Variations: various military contracts.
    various barrel lengths.

Markings: on top of toggle: DWM monogram.
    on top of barrel: national symbol for military guns.

Price(s):
    1906 Commercial 7.65mm, very good—$900.00
    1906 Commercial 7.65mm, excellent—$1,800.00
    1906 Commercial 9mm Luger, very good—$1,250.00
    1906 Commercial 9mm Luger, excellent—$2,500.00
    1906 Commercial eagle, 7.65mm, very good—$1,750.00
    1906 Commercial eagle, 7.65mm, excellent—$2,500.00
    1906 Commercial eagle, 9mm Luger, very good—$2,250.00
    1906 Commercial eagle, 9mm Luger, excellent—$3,000.00

1906 Commercial Swiss, very good—$2,750.00
1906 Commercial Swiss, excellent—$3,650.00
1906 Brazilian, 7.65mm, very good—$2,000.00
1906 Brazilian, 7.65mm, excellent—$3,000.00
1906 Bulgarian, 7.65mm, very good—$2,500.00
1906 Bulgarian, 7.65mm, excellent—$3,500.00
1906 Bulgarian, 9mm Luger, very good—$2,250.00
1906 Bulgarian, 9mm Luger, excellent—$3,000.00
1906 Dutch, 9mm Luger, very good—$2,000.00
1906 Dutch, 9mm Luger, excellent—$2,500.00
1906 French, .30 Luger, very good—$2,500.00
1906 French, .30 Luger, excellent—$3,500.00
1906 Portuguese Army, 7.65mm, very good—$800.00
1906 Portuguese Army, 7.65mm, excellent—$1,500.00
1906 Portuguese Navy, 9mm, very good—$7,000.00
1906 Portuguese Navy, 9mm, excellent—$10,000.00
1906 Portuguese Navy Crown, very good—$9,000.00
1906 Portuguese Navy Crown, excellent—$13,000.00
1906 Russian 9mm Luger, very good—$8,500.00
1906 Russian 9mm Luger, excellent—$11,000.00
1906 Swiss Military, 7.65mm, very good—$2,250.00
1906 Swiss Military, 7.65mm, excellent—$3,000.00
1906 Swiss Police, 7.65mm, very good—$2,500.00
1906 Swiss Police, 7.65mm, excellent—$3,250.00

History: An outgrowth of the Model 1900, this pistol incorporated the lessons learned during the life of the 1900. Internally, the Riband mainspring was rejected in favor of the coil. Gone were the anti-bounce toggle locks and the dished toggles. The thumb safety on this model intercepted the sear instead of just locking the grip safety. DWM stopped making this model in 1914, but Waffenfabrik Bern in Switzerland continued it, and Mauser, when they acquired DWM in 1930, made some. Production nominally ceased in 1935, but Mauser has issued commemoratives since the 1970s.

Mechanical Functioning: The Luger is a recoil-operated, striker-fired, semi-automatic pistol with a detachable, eight-shot box magazine. The lock at battery is provided by a toggle link which is not broken until the barrel-breechblock assembly recoils rearward with the toggle striking a camming surface and unlocking the assembly. The mainspring is of the coil type. There is a magazine disconnector and a thumb-operated safety on the left side of the rear of the frame. The Model 1906 also features an anti-bounce lock on the right toggle to snap it down and prevent the toggle from unlocking. Another feature of the 1906 is the grip safety, which prevents firing unless it is depressed. This was the last Luger to incorporate the grip safety, and other than recent commemoratives, marked the change to the final frame type and toggle style.

DWM-Deutsche Waffen und Munitions Fabriken
Berlin, Germany
and
Mauser Werke Obendorf Am Neckar
Germany
and
Erfurt Arsenal
Erfurt, Germany

Model: Luger 1908 (P.08)

Action Type: semiautomatic, recoil operated.

Caliber(s): 7.65mm and 9mm Parabellum.

Barrel Lengths: 4″, 4³/₄″, 6″.

Finish: blue.

Manufacturing Dates: 1908–1945.

Stocks: checkered walnut.

Rifling: 6R.

Weight, Unloaded: 31¼ oz.

Sights: fixed rear, barleycorn front.

Serial Numbers: range from one to five digits, suffixes from A to Z.

Serial Number Location: front of frame forward of the trigger guard.

Major Variations: many variations depending on contract.

Markings: on top of toggle: DWM monogram.
on top of barrel: national symbol for military guns.

Price(s):
    1908 Bolivian, 9mm Luger, very good—$3,000.00
    1908 Bolivian, 9mm Luger, excellent—$4,500.00
    1908 Bulgarian, 9mm Luger, very good—$1,750.00
    1908 Bulgarian, 9mm Luger, excellent—$2,500.00
    1908 DWM Commercial, 9mm Luger, very good—$1,000.00
    1908 DWM Commercial, 9mm Luger, excellent—$1,500.00
    1908 Military, 9mm Luger, very good—$750.00
    1908 Military, 9mm Luger, excellent—$1,250.00
    1913 Commercial, 9mm Luger, very good—$1,500.00
    1913 Commercial, 9mm Luger, excellent—$2,000.00
    1914 Commercial, 9mm Luger, very good—$750.00
    1914 Commercial, 9mm Luger, excellent—$1,250.00
    1914 Artillery, 9mm Luger, very good—$1,500.00
    1914 Artillery, 9mm Luger, excellent—$2,000.00
    1914 Navy, 9mm Luger, very good—$2,500.00
    1914 Navy, 9mm Luger, excellent—$3,500.00
    1920 Artillery, 9mm Luger, very good—$1,000.00

1920 Artillery, 9mm Luger, excellent—$1,500.00
1920 Commercial, very good—$600.00
1920 Commercial, excellent—$850.00
1921 Krieghoff, very good—$1,500.00
1921 Krieghoff, excellent—$2,000.00
1923 Commercial Krieghoff, 9mm Luger, very good—$1,250.00
1923 Commercial Kreighoff, 9mm Luger, excellent—$1,750.00
1923 Dutch, 9mm Luger, very good—$1,750.00
1923 Dutch, 9mm Luger, excellent—$2,500.00
Simson Commercial, 9mm Luger, very good—$1,250.00
Simson Commercial, 9mm Luger, excellent—$3,000.00
Simson Military, 9mm Luger, very good—$2,500.00
Simson Military, 9mm Luger, excellent—$3,500.00
1933–35 Mauser Commercial, 9mm Luger, very good—$1,150.00
1933–35 Mauser Commercial, 9mm Luger, excellent—$2,200.00
1936 Persian, 9mm Luger, very good—$3,500.00
1936 Persian, 9mm Luger, excellent—$5,000.00
1936–9 S/42, 9mm Luger, very good—$700.00
1936–9 S/42, 9mm Luger, excellent—$950.00
1939–41-42, 9mm Luger, very good—$900.00
1939–41-42, 9mm Luger, excellent—$1,200.00
1940 42/42 BYF, 9mm Luger, very good—$1,500.00
1940 42/42 BYF, 9mm Luger, excellent—$2,200.00
1940–1 S/42, 9mm Luger, very good—$750.00
1940–1 S/42, 9mm Luger, excellent—$1,200.00
1941–2 BYF, 9mm Luger, very good—$525.00
1941–2 BYF, 9mm Luger, excellent—$800.00

History: The Model 1908 was the logical development after the Model 1906 and was virtually identical to it except for the lack of grip safety. The 1908 was made by DWM and Mauser commercially and for military use. Exclusively for military use were Model 1908s (P.08) made by Henrich Kreighoff Waffenfabrik, Suhl, Germany; Simson & Cie., Suhl, Germany; and Konigliche Gewehrfabrik, Erfurt, Germany. All told, about 2½ million P.08 Lugers were made.

Mechanical Functioning: The Luger is a recoil-operated, striker-fired, semi-automatic pistol with a detachable, eight-shot box magazine. The lock at battery is provided by a toggle link which is not broken until the barrel-breechblock assembly recoils rearward with the toggle striking a camming surface and unlocking the assembly. The mainspring is of the coil type. There is a magazine disconnector and a thumb-operated safety on the left side of the rear of the frame. The Model 1908 also features an anti-bounce lock on the right toggle to snap it down and prevent the toggle from unlocking. Another feature of the 1908 is the grip safety, which prevents firing unless it is depressed. On pistols made after 1914, a rising block was incorporated behind the magazine to act as a hold-open device. After 1913 a stock lug was added to the rear of the gripframe.

Luger, Artillery
Photo courtesy of Butterfield and Butterfield

Detonics Manufacturing Corp.
Bellevue, WA

Model: Mark I

Action Type: semiautomatic, recoil operated.

Caliber(s): .45 A.C.P.

Barrel Lengths: 3¼".

Finish: blue or nickel.

Manufacturing Dates: 1976–1980.

Stocks: walnut, checkered.

Rifling: 6L.

Weight, Unloaded: 29 oz.

Sights: fixed.

Serial Numbers: started at number 2,000.

Serial Number Location: right side of frame above trigger.

Major Variations: early models had a pin-retained recoil dampener and modified Colt Commander hammers.

Markings: left side of slide: Detonics, Patents Pending;
right side of frame over trigger: Detonics .45, Seattle, Wa., serial number

Price(s):
early style, blue, very good—$375.00
early style, blue, excellent—$500.00
early style, nickel, very good—$400.00
early style, nickel, excellent—$550.00
standard style, blue, very good—$350.00
standard style, blue, excellent—$475.00
standard style, nickel, very good—$325.00
standard style, nickel, excellent—$500.00

History: This is the first in the series of Detonics Combat Pistols, and early production was assembled from reworked government M1911A1 parts. About 1977, investment castings for Detonics Pistols came on line, and the use of government model parts ended. All pistols were of carbon steel until 1979, when the Mark V and Mark VI stainless pistols were introduced.

Mechanical Functioning: Recoil-operated semiautomatic pistol built along the lines of the U.S. Model 1911A1 with the following changes: elimination of barrel bushing and making the recoil mechanism into a single unit; configuring the external diameter of the barrel with a taper to tightly fit the muzzle to the mouth of the slide at battery, and a convex magazine follower in the six-shot clip.

Detonics Mark I

Detonics Manufacturing Corp.
Bellevue, WA

Model: Mark V, Mark VI, Mark VII, MC-1, MC-2

Action Type: semiautomatic, recoil operated.

Caliber(s): .45 A.C.P., 9mm Luger, .38 Special, .451 Magnum.

Barrel Lengths: 3¼".

Finish: stainless steel.

Manufacturing Dates: Mark V and Mark VI started in October, 1979; Mark VII and MC came on line in April of 1982. Production ended in 1988.

Stocks: checkered walnut or Pachmayr presentation.

Rifling: 6L.

Weight, Unloaded: Mark V is 20 oz.; Mark VII is 26 oz.

Sights: no sights on Mark VII;
fixed sights on Mark V and MC;
adjustable sights on Mark VI.

Serial Numbers: started at 10,000.

Serial Number Location: right side of frame over trigger.

Major Variations: Mark V has matte finish;
Mark VI is polished;
Mark VII is matte;
MC has dull, nonglare finish;
MC-2 is cased with accessories.

Markings: right side of frame over trigger: Detonics .45, Seattle, Wa., and serial number;
Detonics on left slide.

Price(s):
Mark V, .45 A.C.P.—$500.00
Mark V, 9mm and .38 Super—$600.00
Mark VI, .45 A.C.P.—$550.00
Mark VI, 9mm and .38 Super—$650.00
Mark VI, .451 Magnum—$850.00
Mark VII, .45 A.C.P.—$750.00
Mark VII, 9mm and .38 Super—$850.00
Mark VII, .451 Magnum—$1,000.00
MC-1, .45 A.C.P.—$600.00
MC-1, 9mm and .38 Super—$700.00

History: The Detonics pistol was designed in response to the need for a small, highly concealable weapon that was capable of handling the .45 A.C.P. round. First produced from reworked government .45 type parts in 1976, the Detonics were soon thereafter produced from the company's own investment castings. Production began with blued carbon steel units and in 1979 the Stainless Steel Mark V and Mark VI were added to the line. Because of the overwhelming popularity of the stainless steel models, the production facility was entirely dedicated to producing the stainless guns in August of 1981.

Mechanical Functioning: Recoil-operated semiautomatic pistol built along the lines of the U.S. Model 1911A1 with the following changes: elimination of barrel bushing and making the recoil mechanism into a single unit; configuring the external diameter of the barrel with a taper to tightly fit the muzzle to the mouth of the slide at battery, and a convex magazine follower in the six-shot clip. Beveled magazine well, throated feed ramp and barrel, relieved ejection port, and full clip indicator in the base of the magazine are included on these models.

Detonics MC-1

Detonics Manufacturing Corp.
Bellevue, WA

Model: Scoremaster

Action Type: semiautomatic, recoil operated.

Caliber(s): .45 A.C.P., .451 Magnum.

Barrel Lengths: 5″ or 6″.

Finish: polished stainless steel.

Manufacturing Dates: 1983–1992.

Stocks: Pachmayr presentation.

Rifling: 6L.

Weight, Unloaded: 41 oz.

Sights: low base Bomar rear, Millet front.

Serial Numbers: numbering starts at M2001.

Serial Number Location: right frame over trigger.

Major Variations: options available are interchangeable barrels and calibers, eight-round magazine, and target trigger.

Markings: right side of frame above trigger: Detonics .45, Seattle Wa. and serial number;
right side of slide: Scoremaster, Detonics Magnum.

Price(s):
.45 A.C.P., 5″ barrel—$850.00
.45 A.C.P., 6″ barrel—$900.00
.451 Mag., 6″ barrel—$1,000.00

History: Because of the growing interest in competitive shooting, the Scoremaster evolved to fill the need for an out-of-the-box, competition-ready firearm. Developed by Detonics' sister company, Technology Development Corporation, the Scoremaster incorporates the custom-type features the competitive shooter wants and needs, and at the same time it is also available in a more powerful .451 Detonics Magnum chambering for combat or hunting uses.

Mechanical Functioning: The Scoremaster is a semiautomatic recoil-operated pistol built along the lines of the U.S. Model 1911A1 with the following changes. The barrel bushing is eliminated, and the barrel is hand lapped into position in the slide end, and the configuring of the external diameter of the barrel with a taper to tightly fit the muzzle to the mouth of the slide at battery. The recoil mechanism is a single unit rather than separate recoil spring, recoil spring guide, and plunger. There is a convex magazine follower in the six-shot clip to help avoid magazine jams. This model also features an ambidextrous safety, which functions as the standard M1911 does and mechanically locks the sear. There is an extended grip safety that the factory labels "combat control grip safety." There is an extended magazine release, and Pachmayr grips are standard. The trigger system is of national match type, with a long wide trigger with an overtravel adjustment. The barrel is of extra weight, and the ejection port is over-sized (ported) to prevent ejection hang-ups. The rear sight is of the low base type and is fully adjustable for windage and elevation. The front sight can be easily interchanged to suit various shooting needs. The magazine well is beveled, and all parts are crafted from stainless steel. The receiver is of national match type and the entire gun is hand-fitted for maximum accuracy. The Scoremaster is advertised as an out-of-the-box match pistol with many custom features, which needs no additional customizing and is designed for I.P.S.C. competition.

Detonics Scoremaster

Dreyse
Rheinische Metallwaren u. Maschinenfabrik
Sommerda, Germany

Model: Vest Pocket Model 2

Action Type: semiautomatic, blowback operated.

Caliber(s): 6.35mm.

Barrel Lengths: 2".

Finish: blue.

Manufacturing Dates: 1909–1914.

Stocks: hard rubber.

Rifling: 4R.

Weight, Unloaded: 14 oz.

Sights: fixed.

Serial Numbers: possibly started at 1 to as high as 100,000.

Serial Number Location: right side of frame above trigger.

Major Variations: early model had 2 extractors.
late model had 1 extractor.

Markings: on left slide: Dreyse.

Price(s):
early model, very good—$175.00
early model, excellent—$250.00
late model, very good—$150.00
late model, excellent—$225.00

History: The .25-caliber Dreyse was another in the series of Louis Schmeisser designs and was first perfected in 1908; however, it probably was not in production until either late 1909 or perhaps 1910. On the exterior, the pistol resembles the Browning 1906; however, as with all Schmeisser pistol designs, the interior is not quite as simple. On the early side of the production, Schmeisser wanted to make sure that the pistol had positive extraction. Therefore, he had an extractor on both the left and right sides of the slide. But after about 1912, it was found that having two extractors was overkill, and they went to a single extractor. No one is quite sure just how many of these interesting little pistols were made; however, best estimate is just under 100,000 and they were sold into the 1920s. The nomenclature on these pistols is interesting. This was Louis Schmeisser's first .25 automatic pistol, and at the time of issue, its name was Vest Pocket. However, since it was the second type of Dreyse to come out, collectors naturally termed this model Number 2.

Mechanical Functioning: The Dreyse Model 2 Vest Pocket is a blowback-operated, semiautomatic pistol that is striker-fired. It utilizes a six-shot, detachable box magazine that is inserted through the gripframe and secured at the bottom of the butt by a spring-loaded catch. Although it resembles a standard Browning-style .25 in exterior appearance, looks are misleading. Disassembly is accomplished by gently lifting the rear sight and pulling backward to slide the entire sight rib off the gun. The pistol can now be held upside down by the butt, and with the slide withdrawn slightly to the rear, the barrel will drop out and the slide can be removed in the forward direction. Assembly in the reverse order.

Dreyse Vest Pocket Model 2

Dreyse
Rheinische Metallwaren u. Maschinenfabrik
Sommerda, Germany

Model: 1907

Action Type: semiautomatic, blowback operated.

Caliber(s): 7.65 mm.

Barrel Lengths: 3½".

Finish: blue.

Manufacturing Dates: 1907 to 1914.

Stocks: hard rubber.

Rifling: 4R.

Weight, Unloaded: 24 oz.

Sights: fixed.

Serial Numbers: started at 1 and ran to about 250,000.

Serial Number Location: right side above trigger.

Major Variations: grip screw on rear side of grip.
grip screw in center of grip.
early and late style finger grooves.

Markings: left side of frame: Dreyse, Rheinmetall ABT. Sommerda.

Price(s):
early model, side screw grips, very good—$225.00
early model, side screw grips, excellent—$325.00
standard model, center screw, sunken finger grooves, very good—$125.00
standard model, center screw, sunken finger grooves, excellent—$200.00
standard model, center screw, raised finger grooves, very good—$175.00
standard model, center screw, raised finger grooves, excellent—$250.00
WWI military, very good—$200.00
WWI military, excellent—$275.00
police marked, very good—$200.00
police marked, excellent—$275.00

History: The Dreyse 1907 was invented and designed by Louis Schmeisser, an engineer and designer with Rheinische Metallwaren u. Maschinenfabrik. This was his first design for a pistol using a standard cartridge, and it appears that it was developed in final form in about 1906 but not put into production until 1907. The reason for the Dreyse name on the pistol stems from the fact that the original name of the company was Waffen u. Munitionsfabrik von Dreyse. The name of the company had been changed in 1901, but the name Dreyse was very familiar to the Germans and was synonymous with fine weapons. In the about six or seven years that this firearm was produced, nearly a quarter million copies were made.

Mechanical Functioning: This is a blowback-operated, semiautomatic pistol which is striker-fired. It utilizes a detachable box-type magazine that holds eight rounds and incorporates a cocking indicator that projects from the rear of the slide. The pistol is of all-steel construction and is very well made. However, like many of Schmeisser's designs, it is unduly complicated and in turn, this causes great weaknesses. For one, retracting the slide in order to cock the pistol and load it requires a great deal of strength because of the very stiff recoil spring and a mechanical inefficiency in cocking it. It is also awkward to retract the slide for two reasons besides the stiffness: the slide serrations that are used to grip the slide for retraction are at the front by the muzzle, and as you are withdrawing the slide, projection from the frame midway down the pistol comes up and acts as a skirt around the slide. The trigger pull is rough because of the safety feature of the lockwork. When the slide has cocked, the striker pulling the trigger does not free the sear from engagement directly. Instead, it draws the striker back against the mainspring pressure until the striker can override the sear. This safety feature is reminiscent of a semi-double-action trigger pull.

Dreyse 1907

E.M.F.
(Early & Modern Firearms Co., Inc.)
Santa Ana, CA

Model: Dakota

Action Type: revolver, single action, Colt style.

Caliber(s): .22 L.R.R.F.; .22 W.M.R.; .357 Magnum; .44/40; .45 Long Colt; .30 M1 Carbine

Barrel Lengths: 3½"; 4⅝"; 5½"; 7½"; 12"; 16½".

Finish: blue with color-case-hardened frame, nickel, brass or steel backstrap and trigger guard.

Manufacturing Dates: about 1965 to 1987.

Stocks: walnut.

Rifling: n/a.

Weight, Unloaded: about 40 oz. with 5½" barrel in .357 Magnum.

Sights: fixed or adjustable.

Serial Numbers: n/a.

Serial Number Location: bottom of frame forward of trigger guard.

Major Variations: sights, barrel lengths, gripframe, and trigger guard metal.

Markings: left side of barrel: caliber.
left side of frame: E.M.F. address (Studio City, CA).
Italian Nitro proofs.

Price(s):
  Dakota .22 L.R.R.F.—$395.00
  Dakota, .30 M1 Carbine—$395.00
  Dakota, .357 Magnum—$395.00
  Dakota, .44/40—$395.00
  Dakota, .45 Long Colt—$395.00
  Dakota, Combo, .22 L.R.R.F.—$495.00
  Dakota, Combo, .22 Magnum—$495.00
  Dakota, .357 Magnum, nickel—$495.00
  Dakota, .45 Long Colt, nickel—$495.00
  Dakota, Target, .357 Magnum—$425.00
  Dakota, Target, .44/40—$425.00
  Dakota, Target, .45 Long Colt—$425.00
  Dakota, Buntline, .357 Magnum, 12" barrel—$450.00
  Dakota, Buntline, .44/40, 12" barrel—$450.00
  Dakota, Buntline, .45 Long Colt, 12" barrel—$450.00
  Dakota, Buckhorn, .357 Magnum, 16¼" barrel—$495.00
  Dakota, Buckhorn, .44/40, 16¼" barrel—$495.00
  Dakota, Buckhorn, .45 Long Colt, 16¼" barrel—$495.00
  Dakota, .357 Magnum, fully engraved—$550.00
  Dakota, .44/40, fully engraved—$550.00

Dakota, .45 Long Colt, fully engraved—$550.00
Dakota, .357 Magnum, engraved nickel—$600.00
Dakota, .44/40, engraved nickel—$600.00
Dakota, .45 Long Colt, engraved nickel—$600.00
Dakota, Sheriff, .357 Magnum—$425.00
Dakota, Sheriff, .44/40—$425.00
Dakota, Sheriff, .45 Long Colt—$425.00
Dakota, Bisley, various calibers—$570.00
Add for steel backstrap and trigger guard—$45.00

History: Dakota is the registered trade name on single-action, Colt-style revolvers manufactured for E.M.F. by Armi Jager of Luano, Italy. It is virtually an exact copy of the Colt Single Action Army and is well made. It comes in a profusion of styles, from short-barreled Sheriff models with fixed sights to super-long Buntlines with a 16½″ barrel and provision for a detachable shoulder stock as well as fancy target sights. It is also available in a variety of finishes and engraved. This is one of the overlooked future collectibles. It is available in so many styles at reasonable prices that in the odder variations it should become collectible in years to come.

Mechanical Functioning: The Dakota is essentially a Colt 1873 Single Action Army, and many parts are even interchangeable! It is a single-action revolver with a six-shot cylinder riding axially on a center pin, and it is indexed to the next chamber by a spring-loaded pawl attached to the hammer, engaging the ratchet. A cylinder bolt is unlocked by the bottom of the hammer as it rotates and then overrides the cam to again lock the cylinder. Loading is through a side port on half cock. There is a safety notch on the hammer, but it should not be relied on. Always keep an unloaded chamber under the hammer when carrying the E.M.F. Dakota and its variations.

E.M.F.
(Early & Modern Firearms Co., Inc.)
Box 1248
Santa Ana, CA

Model: 1875 Outlaw

Action Type: revolver, single-action Remington type.

Caliber(s): .357 Magnum, .45 Long Colt, .44/40.

Barrel Lengths: 7½".

Finish: blue and color case-hardened frame, brass trigger guard.

Manufacturing Dates: about 1955 to date.

Stocks: walnut.

Rifling: n/a.

Weight, Unloaded: 48 oz.

Serial Numbers: n/a.

Serial Number Location: bottom of frame forward of trigger guard.

Major Variations: custom engraved, case hardened or nickel plated frame.

Markings: n/a.

Price(s):
    Outlaw 1875, .357 Magnum—$425.00
    Outlaw 1875, .44/40—$425.00
    Outlaw 1875, .45 Long Colt—$425.00
    Outlaw 1875, .357 Magnum, engraved—$600.00
    Outlaw 1875, .44/40, engraved—$600.00
    Outlaw 1875, .45 Long Colt, engraved—$600.00

History: Outlaw is a registered trade name on revolvers imported by E.M.F. and made by Armi Jager of Luano, Italy. It is virtually an exact copy of the Remington 1875 revolver which was made from 1875 to 1889 in limited quantities. The engraved models of the Outlaw could become real "sleepers" for collectors because of this. As with the original Remington #3 Model 1875, the trigger guard is brass and screw detachable, and the rod ejector is fully protected by a long, bladed sheath. The grips are walnut, and the sights are fixed. The Outlaw can be considered to be an almost exact reproduction of the Remington #3 Model 1875, and most parts can be interchanged with the original.

Mechanical Functioning: It is a single-action revolver with a six-shot cylinder riding axially on a center pin, and it is indexed to the next chamber by a spring-loaded pawl attached to the hammer, engaging the ratchet. A cylinder bolt is unlocked by the bottom of the hammer as it rotates and then overrides the cam to again lock the cylinder. Loading is through a side port on half cock. There is a safety notch on the hammer, but it should not be relied on. Always keep an unloaded chamber under the hammer when carrying the E.M.F. Outlaw and its variations.

Collector's Note: This revolver is based on the Remington Model of 1875
Frontier revolver, which is quite scarce. It was also called the Remington New Model Army Revolver. The original was available in two
barrel lengths: 5½″ and 7½″, and was also chambered for either .44-40 or
.45 Colt. About 25,000 Remingtons were produced, of which about
10,000 were exported. With about 15,000 remaining in this country of
all types its scarcity is understandable. There is sometimes confusion
between this model and the Remington Model 1890 revolver, which was
known as the Improved Army Model. The most recognizable feature of
the Model 1890 is the reshaped ejector housing which was cut out and
squared off rather than angled up toward the front. Like the Model 1875,
the 1890 is rare, with only about 2,000 being made. Both of these guns
constitute a real "find" for collectors.

Echave & Arizmendi
Eibar, Spain

Model: Fast

Action Type: semiautomatic, blowback operated.

Caliber(s): .22 L.R., 6.35mm, 7.65mm, 9mm K.

Barrel Lengths: 3⅛".

Finish: blue or chrome.

Manufacturing Dates: mid-1950s.

Stocks: plastic or wood.

Rifling: 6R.

Weight, Unloaded: 25 oz.

Sights: fixed.

Serial Numbers: n/a.

Serial Number Location: left side of frame above trigger guard.

Major Variations: Model 221 (.22 L.R.).
    Model 631 (6.35mm).
    Model 761 (7.65mm).
    Model 901 (9mm K.).

Markings: left side of slide: Fast Eibar Spain, (caliber).
    on grips: Echasa.

Price(s):
    blue, Model 221, very good—$150.00
    blue, Model 221, excellent—$200.00
    blue, Model 631, very good—$125.00
    blue, Model 631, excellent—$175.00
    blue, Model 761, very good—$125.00
    blue, Model 761, excellent—$175.00
    blue, Model 901, very good—$150.00
    blue, Model 901, excellent—$200.00
    chrome, Model 221, very good—$150.00
    chrome, Model 221, excellent—$225.00
    chrome, Model 631, very good—$100.00
    chrome, Model 631, excellent—$200.00
    chrome, Model 761, very good—$100.00
    chrome, Model 761, excellent—$200.00
    chrome, Model 901, very good—$150.00
    chrome, Model 901, excellent—$225.00

History: The Fast was a series of pistols manufactured by Echave y Arizmendi of Eibar, Spain, under the trade name Echasa. As so often happens in many industries, this pistol was not only loosely based on another design, in this case the Walther PP, but was also made for others under a private label. Such was the case with the Echasa Fast pistol. It was trade-named for Mre. d'Armes de Bayonne in Bayonne, France, who marketed it as the Model GZ. From the number of pistols around it seems that most of the production was sent to the U.S. It will be found here either as the Fast, Echasa, or as the MAB GZ, and possibly with a combination of these names. It was available in a variety of calibers: .22 L.R., .25 A.C.P., .32 A.C.P., and .380 A.C.P., all built on the same frame and all approximately the same size and weight.

Mechanical Functioning: The Echasa Fast is a double-action, blowback-operated, semiautomatic pistol with an external hammer. The hammer has a very recognizable shape. Instead of following the usual pattern of having either a round-headed hammer or one with a spur, the Echasa hammer comes up and is flattened and squared off at the top on a plane with the slide top. It has a detachable box-type magazine which is inserted through the gripframe and retained by a catch located on the left side of the frame just to the rear of the trigger guard. The clip holds ten shots in .22, nine shots in .25, eight shots in .32, and seven shots in .380. This pistol is of steel construction, and although it was made to capture the market for inexpensive automatics, it does function rather well. It has fairly good balance and good pointing qualities, which is so important on a medium-frame pistol. Field stripping is accomplished by first clearing the action and making sure the firearm is unloaded, and then removing the magazine. Next pull down a small catch on the rear of the left side of the frame and pull the slide all the way to the rear, lifting up slightly on the rear of the slide and then moving the assembly forward and off the frame. Assembly is carried out in the reverse order.

Echave & Arizmendi Model Fast

French Government Arsenals

Model M1935A (Pistolet Automatique Modele 35A)

Action Type: semiautomatic, recoil operated.

Caliber(s): 7.65mm French Long.

Barrel Lengths: 4.3".

Finish: blue or black paint.

Manufacturing Dates: 1935 to 1942.

Stocks: black plastic.

Rifling: 4R.

Weight, Unloaded: 26 oz.

Sights: fixed.

Serial Numbers: four digit with letter prefix, presumably starting at A001.

Serial Number Location: left side of frame above trigger guard.

Major Variations: none.

Markings: on left side of frame: Mle. 1935A, S.A.C.M.

Price(s):
    1935-A, black paint, very good—$100.00
    1935-A, black paint, excellent—$150.00
    1935-A, blued, very good—$150.00
    1935-A, blued, excellent—$200.00
    1935-A, Nazi Proofs, very good—$175.00
    1935-A, Nazi Proofs, excellent—$250.00

History: This pistol was developed for Societe Alsacienne de Constructions Mecanique (S.A.C.M.), by an engineer named Charles Petter, and it formed the basis for the French 1935S, the 1950, and the S.I.G. P.210 series. It is based on the earlier designed Browning/Colt M1911 system to which it owes its lockup and swinging link, and the Russian Tokarev TT-30 pistol from which it derives its lockwork. The slide rail arrangement and safety system are Petter's own. It used the French 7.65mm Long cartridge which is nearly identical to the .30 Pederson round of World War I fame. Unfortunately, this cartridge, when considered for military use, is far too weak. The trials for the French military sidearm during the early 1930s was highlighted by the fact that although many European countries considered this cartridge, only France adopted it. Of course, the primary reason for the adoption of the Petter Pistol may have been the comfort of the pre–World War II French officers who rejected the Browning High Power as "too bulky." This pistol was also used by the occupying Germans as a secondary military pistol. During the early postwar years these pistols sold for as little as $7.50, and recently they have become a standard for pistol collectors, especially in central Europe. In fact, the pressure from collectors in Switzerland has contributed to the current price levels on this pistol. The reason for their interest is the direct lineal descent of the SIG P.210, their military pistol, from the "Petter."

Mechanical Functioning: This is a recoil-operated, semiautomatic pistol with an eight-shot detachable box magazine. Lockup is accomplished with a Browning/Colt-style swinging link system, which forces the barrel into its mating locking grooves in the slide, and on recoil allows the barrel and slide to move back a short distance before the barrel is yanked downward unlocking the breech. It is a single-action pistol with an exposed hammer and a floating firing pin located in the slide. It has a magazine disconnect to prevent firing if the magazine is removed. The manual safety is located on the left side of the slide, and rather than lock the sear it instead blocks the firing pin preventing the hammer from contacting it. Like the Tokarev TT-30 pistol, the firing unit (hammer, sear, and mainspring) comes out as a single unit retained by a compact housing on disassembly. The recoil spring is located below the barrel and rides on a guide.

French Model 1935A

French Government Arsenals

Model: 1935S

Action Type: semiautomatic, recoil operated.

Caliber(s): 7.65 French long.

Barrel Lengths: 4.1".

Finish: blue or black paint.

Manufacturing Dates: 1939–1949.

Stocks: black plastic.

Rifling: 4R.

Weight, Unloaded: 28 oz.

Sights: fixed.

Serial Numbers: generally four digit, possibly starting at A001.

Serial Number Location: right side of frame forward of the trigger guard.

Major Variations: SAGEM version known as 1935 SM-1 with redesigned safety.
MAC version known as 1935 SM-1 with redesigned safety.

Markings: left side of slide: M.A.S., M.A.C., M.A.T., SACM, or SA-GEM. right side of slide: Modele 1935S, Cal. 7.65L.

Price(s):
    MAC, very good—$100.00
    MAC, excellent—$175.00
    MAC, Nazi, very good—$125.00
    MAC, Nazi, excellent—$200.00
    MAS, very good—$100.00
    MAS, excellent—$175.00
    MAS, Nazi, very good—$150.00
    MAS, Nazi, excellent—$225.00
    MAT, very good—$100.00
    MAT, excellent—$175.00
    MAT, Nazi, very good—$150.00
    MAT, Nazi, excellent—$225.00
    SAGEM M-1, very good—$100.00
    SAGEM M-1, excellent—$175.00
    SAGEM Nazi, very good—$150.00
    SAGEM Nazi, excellent—$225.00
    SACM, very good—$100.00
    SACM, excellent—$175.00
    SACM Nazi, very good—$150.00
    SACM Nazi, excellent—$250.00
    MAC M-1, very good—$125.00
    MAC M-1, excellent—$175.00

History: Developed as a modification of the French 1935A, the 1935S was first made at Manufacture D'Armes de St. Etienne (M.A.S.) and was a stripped down version of the 1935A that could be made cheaply and quickly. Gone were the graceful curves that beautified the 1935A, and internally the barrel-locking lugs were replaced by a single step forward of the chamber to lock the pistol at battery. Aside from the looks and the weak cartridge, this was a successful military pistol and saw use throughout the world after the war in all the former French colonies. It was superseded by the Model 1950. It was made by MAS, MAC, SACM, MAT, and SAGEM.

Mechanical Functioning: This is a recoil-operated, semiautomatic pistol with an eight-shot detachable box magazine. Lockup is accomplished with a Browning/Colt-style swinging link system, which forces the barrel into its mating locking grooves in the slide, and on recoil allows the barrel and slide to move back a short distance before the barrel is yanked downward unlocking the breech. It is a single-action pistol with an exposed hammer and a floating firing pin located in the slide. It has a magazine disconnect to prevent firing if the magazine is removed. The manual safety is located on the left side of the slide, and rather than lock the sear it instead blocks the firing pin preventing the hammer from contacting it. Like the Tokarev TT-30 pistol, the firing unit (hammer, sear, and mainspring) comes out as a single unit retained by a compact housing on disassembly. The recoil spring is located below the barrel and rides on a guide.

French Model 1935S

French Government Arsenals

Model: 1950

Action Type: semiautomatic, recoil operated.

Caliber(s): 9mm Parabellum.

Barrel Lengths: 4.4″.

Finish: blue.

Manufacturing Dates: Begun in 1950.

Stocks: plastic.

Rifling: 4L.

Weight, Unloaded: 33 oz.

Sights: fixed.

Serial Numbers: n/a.

Serial Number Location: right side of frame forward of trigger guard.

Major Variations: none.

Markings: on left side of slide: MAS or MAC
on right side of slide: Type SE MAS 1950, Cal. 9mm.

Price(s):
MAS, very good—$325.00
MAS, excellent—$475.00
MAC, very good—$350.00
MAC, excellent—$500.00

History: The French Model 1950 is essentially a scaled-up Model 1935S
with few refinements. The Model 1950 answered the French need for
a pistol that not only met the N.A.T.O. caliber requirement but also
packed some punch. For twenty-five years prior to this pistol's adoption
the French had become used to the grossly underpowered 7.65mm
French Long cartridge and the small, light Model 1935A and Model
1935S pistols. These pistols were adopted primarily because they were
comfortable to carry, not because they were particularly effective. The
mistake of this policy was evident, and after World War II it was
decided that a change was necessary. A new pistol was first developed
in 1948 and was modified until it reached this final version. The Model
1950 has seen extensive combat use in Indo-China and in Algeria, and it
stood the test well. There were several advantages to the adoption of the
Model 1950. Like the Model 1935 it possessed the Tokarev TT-30 lockwork system and the Petter modifications and styling. This makes for
ease of care as well as inexpensive and rapid manufacture. It is a standard-
size military pistol by current standards, and it was both robust and
solid. Unlike the 1935S, the 1950 uses the 1935A twin lug locking system,
and as an additional departure from the 1935S, it has a nicely contoured
gripframe. It does, however, retain the 1935S's angular looks and slab
sides, as well as the simple blocking safety located on the slide.

Mechanical Functioning: This is a recoil-operated, semiautomatic pistol with a nine-shot detachable box magazine. Lockup is accomplished with a Browning/Colt-style swinging link system, which forces the barrel into its mating locking grooves in the slide, and on recoil allows the barrel and slide to move back a short distance before the barrel is yanked downward unlocking the breech. It is a single-action pistol with an exposed hammer and a floating firing pin located in the slide. It has a magazine disconnect to prevent firing if the magazine is removed. The manual safety is located on the left side of the slide, and rather than lock the sear it instead blocks the firing pin, preventing the hammer from contacting it. Like the Tokarev TT-30 pistol the firing unit (hammer, sear, and mainspring) comes out as a single unit retained by a compact housing on disassembly. The recoil spring is located below the barrel and rides on a guide.

French Model 1950

Frommer/Fegyvergyar
Budapest, Hungary

Model: Liliput

Action Type: semiautomatic, blowback operated.

Caliber(s): .22 L.R., 6.35mm

Barrel Lengths: 2⅛".

Finish: blue.

Manufacturing Dates: early 1920s.

Stocks: hard rubber.

Rifling: 4R.

Weight, Unloaded: 10½ oz.

Sights: fixed.

Serial Numbers: unknown, but generally in the 400,000s.

Serial Number Location: left side of frame above trigger guard.

Major Variations: none.

Markings: left side of slide: Fegyvergyar-Budapest Frommer Pat. Liliput cal. 6.35mm, U.S.A. Pats. A.F. Made in Hungary.

Price(s):
    .25 A.C.P., very good—$210.00
    .25 A.C.P., excellent—$300.00
    .22 L.R.R.F., very good—$325.00
    .22 L.R.R.F., excellent—$450.00

History: This model was designed after World War I had given enough experience with the earlier Frommer designs to point out their weaknesses. This pistol was manufactured as early as 1921, and it is not known just how many of this model were made. One thing, however, is certain. When the military began to look for a substitute for the Stop model, the experience that the Liliput provided proved to be the basis for the M29 .32 A.C.P. Military Pistol. That pistol is essentially just an enlarged Liliput. This is truly a small pocket pistol and was a radical departure from the standard Frommer style. It was the first pistol they made without a locked breech, and judging from their past performance that must have been tantamount to sacrilege. At the time this pistol was made the Frommer long recoil system had been used for twenty years. However, it was obvious from the few copies of this pistol that are around that it was an experiment to ascertain in miniature whether the blowback system could be relied upon using small calibers. The results are self-evident and the M29 is merely the Liliput scaled up. In its own right this is a fine little pistol. It is diminutive, yet it has a magazine safety, a grip safety, and a manual safety. The external hammer is a concession to the earlier Frommer designs. The Liliput itself is a scarce collector's item. It is to be found in both .25 A.C.P. and .22 L.R.

Mechanical Functioning: The Liliput is a single-action, blowback-operated, semiautomatic pistol. It has a six-shot detachable box magazine that is inserted through the gripframe and is retained by a spring-loaded catch located on the base of the butt. The external hammer has a half-cock notch for safety, and the pistol cannot be fired unless the magazine is inserted and the grip safety is depressed. The recoil spring is mounted on a guide under the barrel in Browning fashion, and there is a side safety in addition to the grip safety. The trigger pivots on a single pin, and the firing pin is of the floating type to prevent accidental discharge. This pistol replaced the Stop series but in different calibers. With its adoption the people at Fegyvergyar finally decided that a locked breech with low-power calibers was indeed overkill. Probably adding fuel to the fire was the high cost of machining and fitting their long recoil system. The Liliput also compares favorably in one other very important aspect—reliability. The Stop design was prone to jamming from a variety of sources. The lockwork had close tolerances and, because of the involved mechanism, thin sidewalls. The Liliput on the other hand had comparatively sloppy tolerances, could stand a beating, and functioned beautifully.

Frommer Liliput

Frommer/Fegyvergyar
Budapest, Hungary

Model: Stop Pocket Auto

Action Type: semiautomatic, recoil operated.

Caliber(s): 7.65mm, 9mm K

Barrel Lengths: 3⁷/₈" (Baby 2").

Finish: blue.

Manufacturing Dates: 1912 to possibly as late as the 1930s.

Stocks: hard rubber.

Rifling: 4R.

Weight, Unloaded: 21¹/₂ oz.

Sights: fixed.

Serial Numbers: possibly starting at 1 and running to over 250,000.

Serial Number Location: left side of frame below hammer.

Major Variations: Baby Stop with 2" barrel and weight of 17¹/₂ oz.

Markings: left side of slide: Fegyvergyar-Budapest-Frommer Pat. Stop Cal.
7.65mm, or
Fegyvergyar-Budapest-Frommer Pat. Stop Cal. 9mm
The Baby: left side of slide: Fegyvergyar-Budapest-Frommer Pat. Baby
Cal. 9mm or;
The Baby: left side of slide: Fegyvergyar-Budapest-Frommer Pat. Baby Cal.
7.65mm.

Price(s):
Stop, .32 A.C.P., Commercial, very good—$125.00
Stop, .32 A.C.P., Commercial, excellent—$200.00
Stop, .32 A.C.P., Military, World War I, very good—$150.00
Stop, .32 A.C.P., Military, World War I, excellent—$200.00
Stop, .32 A.C.P., Military M19, very good—$150.00
Stop, .32 A.C.P., Military M19, excellent—$200.00
Stop, .32 A.C.P., Police, very good—$175.00
Stop, .32 A.C.P., Police, excellent—$225.00
Stop, .380 A.C.P., Commercial, very good—$200.00
Stop, .380 A.C.P., Commercial, excellent—$250.00
Stop, .380 A.C.P., Military, very good—$250.00
Stop, .380 A.C.P., Military, excellent—$300.00
Baby Stop, .32 A.C.P., very good—$200.00
Baby Stop, .32 A.C.P., excellent—$250.00
Baby Stop, .380 A.C.P., very good—$200.00
Baby Stop, .380 A.C.P., excellent—$275.00

History: Developed in 1911 and first marketed in 1912, the Frommer Stop
became one of Austria-Hungary's most popular pistols. This pistol was

used in World War I by the Hungarian army (Honved) from 1914 to 1918, and adopted by the Independent Hungarian army after the war as the M19. It was also extensively used by Hungarian police agencies prior to World War II. All of this is quite surprising as the pistol used rather weak (by military standards) cartridges and was unduly complicated. Add to that a disconcerting habit of jamming and the propensity to be damaged when handled roughly, and it gives us pause as to just why the Hungarians were enamored of it.

Mechanical Functioning: This is a long, recoil-operated, external hammer, single-action, semiautomatic pistol. The lock up at battery is accomplished by means of a rotating bolt head, similar to the system used in the AR-15. The magazine is of detachable box variety and holds seven shots in .32 A.C.P., and six shots in .380 A.C.P. The Baby Stop holds six shots in the .32 A.C.P., and five shots in the .380 A.C.P. This design is very complicated for the calibers it uses, utilizing a locked breech when blowback would have been sufficient, and as a military sidearm it was not only prone to jamming, but due to its thin walls, it could be easily damaged.

Frommer Stop Pocket Auto

Frommer/Fergyvergyar
Budapest, Hungary

Model: 1910

Action Type: semiautomatic, recoil operated.

Caliber(s): 7.65mm Roth/Steyr

Barrel Lengths: 3⅞".

Finish: blue.

Manufacturing Dates: 1910–1914.

Stocks: grooved wood.

Rifling: 4R.

Weight, Unloaded: 22½ oz.

Sights: fixed.

Serial Numbers: n/a, but many appear to be in the 7000 range.

Serial Number Location: left side of frame beneath hammer.

Major Variations: Model 1901 in 8mm Roth Steyr, fixed magazine top loading with a charger.
Model 1906 in 7.65 Roth Sauer, fixed magazine top loading with a charger.
Model 1906 in 7.65 Roth Sauer, detachable box magazine.

Markings: on left side of frame: Fegyvergyar-Budapest Frommer Pat.

Price(s):
Model 1901 (1903) Commercial, very good—$1,250.00
Model 1901 (1903) Commercial, excellent—$1,850.00
Model 1901 (1903) Military test, very good—$1,600.00
Model 1901 (1903) Military test, excellent—$2,250.00
Model 1906 fixed magazine, very good—$875.00
Model 1906 fixed magazine, excellent—$1,500.00
Model 1906 removable clip, very good—$1,000.00
Model 1906 removable clip, excellent—$1,650.00
Model 1910 Commercial, very good—$1,000.00
Model 1910 Commercial, excellent—$1,450.00
Model 1910 Police, very good—$1,100.00
Model 1910 Police, excellent—$1,650.00

History: The Model 1910 was invented by Rudolph Frommer of Budapest, Hungary, around 1899 and was the final design of the series. The pistols, sometimes known as the "Roth Frommers" because the Roth Ammunition Company developed the first cartridge, started with the Model 1901 (1903) with no safety and a ten-shot fixed magazine. The 1906 was in 7.65 Roth Sauer and had a magazine capacity of nine rounds but still no safety. It did, however, recognize the potential of removable clips and was available both ways. In 1910 the pistol was again changed to try to capture some sales. It had a removable clip and was chambered for the popular .32 A.C.P. cartridge, and had a grip safety as well. It did not receive the success that was hoped for, but it did provide much of the basic mechanism for the well-received Frommer Stop which succeeded it in 1914.

Mechanical Functioning: The Model 1910 is a long recoil-operated, semi-automatic pistol that functions as a single action with an external hammer. It has an eight-shot detachable box magazine with clip bottom of the same pattern as the 1900 Luger, and like the Luger, it is fashioned from wood. The magazine is retained by a spring-loaded catch located on the left-hand side of the frame just to the rear of the trigger guard. This functions as a locked breech pistol, with the lockup functioning in a manner similar to the AR-15 with a rotary bolt face turning the lugs into a barrel extension. The only safety features are a half-cock notch on the hammer and a grip safety that disconnects the sear. The design is unique and was one of the first pistols made with the recoil spring mounted axially around the barrel with a thin, tubular jacket surrounding the assembly. As with many of the early automatic pistols it was quite awkward to hold and to shoot, and to boot had a very ungainly look. It was discontinued at the outbreak of World War I to free production space for more modern pistols.

Frommer Model 1910

Gabilondo y Cia.
Vitoria, Spain
and others

Model: Ruby

Action Type: semiautomatic, blowback operated.

Caliber(s): 7.65mm

Barrel Lengths: 3½".

Finish: blue.

Manufacturing Dates: 1914–1918.

Stocks: checkered wood, sometimes hard rubber.

Rifling: generally 6L or 6R.

Weight, Unloaded: 20 to 30 oz.

Sights: fixed.

Serial Numbers: n/a.

Serial Number Location: right side of frame above trigger.

Major Variations: 7- to 20-shot magazines with matching gripframe length. various names.

Markings: Gabilondo: 1915 Patent Ruby Cal. 7.65
Echeverria: Cal. 7.65 Hijos De Echeverria, Eibar.
Alkartasuna: Alkartasuna Fabrica De Armas, Guernica.
Esperanza: 7.65 1916 Model Automatic Pistol, Brunswig.
Retolaza: 7.65 1914 Automatic Pistol, Liberty.
Bolumburu: Regina.
Arizabalaga: Hijos De Arizabalaga 1916.
Zulaica: 1914 Automatic Pistol, M. Zulaica Y Cia. Eibar.
Gaztanaga: Destroyer.

Price(s):
Gabilondo, 7.65mm. Ruby, very good—$125.00
Gabilondo, 7.65mm. Ruby, excellent—$175.00
various makers, long gripframe, 12 shot, very good—$175.00
various makers, long gripframe, 12 shot, excellent—$250.00
Echeverria, very good—$125.00
Echeverria, excellent—$175.00
Alkartasuna, very good—$150.00
Alkartasuna, excellent—$175.00
Salaverria, very good—$125.00
Salaverria, excellent—$175.00
Esperanza, very good—$125.00
Esperanza, excellent—$175.00
Retolaza, very good—$125.00
Retolaza, excellent—$150.00
Beistigoi, very good—$125.00
Beistigoi, excellent—$175.00
Arizmendi, very good—$125.00

Arizmendi, excellent—$175.00
Zulaica, very good—$125.00
Zulaica, excellent—$175.00
Gaztanaga, very good—$125.00
Gaztanaga, excellent—$175.00

History: The term "Ruby," even though a trade name of Gabilondo y Cia., now denotes an entire class of pistols that was used by the French army during World War I. These pistols were first designed around 1910 and based on the design of Browning for his 1903. They featured concealed internal hammers, and straight blowback operation with recoil springs mounted under the barrel, with takedown done in much the same manner as the Browning 1903. As a class, they were fairly heavy pistols and designed to be rapidly and inexpensively made. At the outbreak of the war, when the French were caught napping and in dire need of a great many handguns, they turned to the Spanish firms to help them out of their plight. The primary contract went to the firm of Gabilondo, and by the middle of 1915 with orders already running at 30,000 pistols per month, the French decided that they needed even more. Not being able to keep up with the work, Gabilondo called on about a dozen other firms in Spain to help make pistols on their pattern, and thus as a class, Rubies can be found with a variety of names, and some differences of design, because they were made by so many different firms. It is possible, considering the commercial variants as well as the French military variants, to be able to have a hundred pistol collection of Rubies with no two pistols being alike.

Mechanical Functioning: The Ruby class of pistols was of standard Eibar based on the Browning 1906, and were blowback-operated, semiautomatic pistols with detachable box magazines. The average clip size was seven shots, although clips ranged up to 12 shots with the appropriate lengthening of the gripframe to cover the clip. Some postwar models held as many as 20 shots. For further variations, see also Astra Model 1915 and the Union pistol.

Ruby 7.65mm

Gabilondo y Cia.
Vitoria, Spain

Model: Ruby

Action Type: semiautomatic, recoil operated.

Caliber(s): .45 A.C.P.

Barrel Lengths: 4⁷/₈".

Finish: blue.

Manufacturing Dates: circa 1924.

Stocks: hard rubber.

Rifling: 6L.

Weight, Unloaded: 37½ oz.

Sights: fixed.

Serial Numbers: under 1,000.

Serial Number Location: right side of frame above trigger.

Major Variations: none.

Markings: left side of slide: Ruby Arms Co.

Price(s):
    Ruby .45 A.C.P., very good—$750.00
    Ruby .45 A.C.P., excellent—$1,250.00

History: After World War I, the firm of Gabilondo y Cia. decided to expand their line for commercial sales. They had done very well during the war selling Ruby pistols to the French army; so well, in fact, that they had to subcontract out much of the manufacture, because they could not keep up with the orders. This was the transitional period for this company. During World War I they had made an excellent reputation for themselves, as manufacturers of a rather durable, albeit plain, pistol called the Ruby. Unfortunately, after the war every shop in Eibar seemed to be turning out these pistols by the score, probably because they had already geared up to produce them for the French and decided to just keep making them because, given the state of the European countries at the time, any weapon would sell. Gabilondo must have noted that the Ruby was being considered in a worse light with each new pistol that was produced by their competitors and so they gradually gave up the trade name Ruby until the 1950s. During the mid-1920s they started to experiment with heavier calibers, and one of the early pistols they made was in .45 A.C.P. Externally it was an adaptation of the U.S. Model 1911, but internally it was still based on the Ruby design. Very few of these pistols were made, but they did accomplish the prototyping that was needed. This model become the direct precursor of the entire Llama series. The Llamas are all based on the M1911, and any relation to the Ruby has been eliminated. The Ruby .45 is very rare.

Mechanical Functioning: The Ruby .45 is a recoil-operated, semiautomatic pistol firing .45 A.C.P. and utilizing a detachable box magazine inserted through the gripframe with a spring-loaded catch retaining it located at the rear bottom of the butt. It has an external hammer, and internal sear connections are reminiscent of standard Eibar pattern. There is a mechanical safety located on the right rear side of the frame, which inhibits sear movement when engaged. There is no automatic slide lock on firing the last shot; however, for disassembly the slide can be retained in the locked position by withdrawing the slide and flipping the safety up until it engages in the second cut-out in the slide. Disassembly is accomplished much in the same way as on the U.S. Model 1911 since the pistol uses a barrel bushing system and a linked barrel with a cross pin which drifts out from right to left. There is an external hammer, and the pistol utilizes a floating firing pin. The extractor is mounted on the outside of the slide below the ejection port, and the ejector throws the spent cartridge upward and slightly to the right. This pistol is of medium quality but shows some thought had been put into it in order to function with the .45 cartridge.

Ruby .45 A.C.P.

Soc. Siderurgica Glisenti
Turin, Italy

Model: Glisenti

Action Type: semiautomatic, blowback operated.

Caliber(s): 9mm Glisenti or 7.65mm Glisenti.

Barrel Lengths: 4".

Finish: blue.

Manufacturing Dates: 1906 to the 1920s.

Stocks: hard rubber or wood.

Rifling: 6R.

Weight, Unloaded: 22 oz.

Sights: fixed.

Serial Numbers: n/a.

Serial Number Location: right side of frame toward the top rear.

Major Variations: M906: 7.65mm Parabellum.
M910: 9mm Glisenti wood grips.
M910: hard rubber grips.

Markings: trademark on right side of frame below serial number.

Price(s):
M906, very good—$350.00
M906, excellent—$600.00
M910, wood grips, very good—$300.00
M910, wood grips, excellent—$475.00
M910, hard rubber grips, very good—$295.00
M910, hard rubber grips, excellent—$425.00
Brixia, very good—$325.00
Brixia, excellent—$500.00

History: The Glisenti pistol is noteworthy primarily because it was one of
the early semiautomatic pistols adopted for military use. First developed in about 1905 and in production by 1906, the Italian army adopted
its as their M906 following Italian tradition of dropping the millennium
number. This first model was chambered for a 7.65mm bottlenecked cartridge, which appears to be identical to the Parabellum; however, because of the nature of the construction of the pistol, it is almost positive
that it was a much lighter load, and indeed, the DWM catalog lists it as a
7.65mm Glisenti, rather than 7.65mm Parabellum. In about 1909 it was
decided that the bullet was just too small for military use, and the caliber was increased to 9mm, once again, based on the Parabellum cartridge but with a much lighter load. This new pistol, of course, was the
M910. There was sometimes a great deal of confusion between the
Glisenti pistol and another pistol called the Brixia, which was intro-

duced around 1911. It was extremely similar to the Glisenti, and some people even think that the firm of Metallurgica Bresciana Gia Tempini of Brescia, Italy was just the reorganized name for Soc. Siderurgica Glisenti. It has also been said that the production of the M910 Glisenti was continued by this new firm, adding support to the belief that they were one and the same firm. The easiest way to tell the two pistols apart is by the method of grip attachment. On the Glisenti the method of removal of the grips is to first remove the sideplate, which is done by unscrewing a screw in the front, and rotating it up and off. This sideplate holds down the left grip. With the magazine removed, the right grip can be taken off by rotating a clip at the top 90 degrees on the inside of that grip. On the Brixia, however, the grips are removed by loosening a single screw at the bottom of each grip. It has been reported that the Glisenti pistol was used as late as World War II.

Mechanical Functioning: The Glisenti and the Brixia systems were both delayed blowback, semiautomatic pistols utilizing seven-shot detachable box magazines that were inserted through the gripframe. The blowback delay is actuated by a propping block which swings up on a mounting so its locking face passes through a cut in the barrel extension and engages a similar matching cut in the breechblock. During recoil, the block is carried back with the bolt until it rotates on its axis and finally unlocks itself from that bolt. The safety is manual and is located on the end of the breechblock. Only when it is cocked can it be engaged. This pistol is striker-fired, with the rear end of the firing pin protruding through the breechblock when cocked. Takedown is accomplished by unscrewing a small gnarled piece on the front of the firearm just above the trigger guard, and with the pistol lying on its right side, lifting the sideplate up and rotating it up toward the back and off the gun. At this point the grips and the rest of the moving parts that form the lockwork can be removed. The breechblock is removed by drifting out the wedgepin at the top of the frame, being careful of the very powerful mainspring.

Glisenti
Photo courtesy of Butterfield and Butterfield

Gustloff Werke Waffenfabrik
Suhl, Germany

Model: Gustloff

Action Type: semiautomatic, blowback.

Caliber(s): .32 A.C.P., a .380 A.C.P. is reported to exist.

Barrel Lengths: 3¾".

Finish: blue or none.

Manufacturing Dates: unknown, but thought to have been between 1939 and 1943.

Stocks: Bakelite or wood.

Rifling: 6R.

Weight, Unloaded: 26 oz.

Sights: fixed.

Serial Numbers: unknown, but serials observed range from 11 to over 1200.

Serial Number Location: bottom of butt to the rear of the magazine well.

Major Variations: double action.
single action.

Markings: on left side of slide: Gustloff-Werke Waffenfabrik, Suhl.
caliber designation on barrel chamber exposed by slide port.

Price(s):
.32 A.C.P., single action, *RARE*
.32 A.C.P., single action, *RARE*
.32 A.C.P., double action, *RARE*
.32 A.C.P., double action, *RARE*
.380 A.C.P., *RARE*
.380 A.C.P., *RARE*

History: The Gustloff is a mystery pistol. Developed in the early war years, it was in many ways well ahead of its time. It utilized forgings and stampings at a time when it was virtually unknown in the gun industry. Additionally, it used a pot metal frame. Most of these pistols were handmade, and all show traces of extensive hand fitting and not necessarily by craftsmen. It is rumored that these pistols were assembled by inmates from the Buchenwald concentration camp, and judging by the quality, this may be true. The Gustloff is one of the rarest of modern pistols, but because of its looks, may be sitting in a gun shop with a low price tag. This is truly a treasure hunter's pistol!

Mechanical Functioning: This pistol is a straight blowback, semiautomatic pistol that was designed to be manufactured cheaply. It utilizes forgings and stampings wherever possible. It has an internal hammer and no safety, but like the Sauer 38H can be uncocked by using the cocking lever on the left side behind and above the grip. Alternatively, the pistol can also be cocked in this manner. The firing pin is of the floating type to prevent accidental discharge with the hammer uncocked. Virtually the entire working action rides on a sheet metal plate under the left grip, and it is all retained either by rivets or spring tension.

Gustloff Pistol

C.G. Haenel
Waffen und Fahrradfabrik
Suhl, Germany

Model: Schmeisser Model I

Action Type: semiautomatic, blowback.

Caliber(s): 6.35mm.

Barrel Lengths: 2⅛".

Finish: blue.

Manufacturing Dates: 1922–1930.

Stocks: hard rubber.

Rifling: 4R.

Weight, Unloaded: 12⅜ oz.

Sights: fixed.

Serial Numbers: unknown, but have been observed from the mid-four digits to the mid-five digits.

Serial Number Location: right side of frame above trigger.

Major Variations: high sights.
    low sights.

Markings: on left side of slide: C.G. Haenel, Suhl, Schmeisser's Patent.

Price(s):
    high sight, very good—$200.00
    high sight, excellent—$250.00
    low sight, very good—$275.00
    low sight, excellent—$350.00

History: This pistol was the brainchild of Hugo Schmeisser and was first developed after World War I and was patented in 1920 and 1921. Hugo was the son of Louis Schmeisser, the designer of the first Bergmann automatics in the early 1890s. Like his father, Hugo worked at Bergmann's until he moved to C.G. Haenel in 1921 as chief engineer and firearms designer. This was the first of several guns to bear his name, the most famous of which were his submachine guns during World War II. This pistol was developed during a time that was probably the most creative point in the history of handguns, and the center of that creativity was Germany. There was a very good reason for this. During the post–World War I years Germany was in virtual state of terror. On one hand there were various political factions all vying for attention and using the most violent means at their disposal, and at the same time crime was running rampant. There was a great public need for a means with which to protect themselves, and the pocket pistols were the answer. Quite naturally all of the German gunmakers wanted to tap this huge domestic market, hence the wide variety of pistols available. This is a scarce pistol, and it is unknown just how many of this model were made.

Mechanical Functioning: This is a blowback-operated, semiautomatic pistol that is striker-fired. It has a six-shot, detachable box magazine that is retained by a spring-loaded catch located at the base of the butt. There is a protrusion-type cocking indicator. There is no ejection port, rather the face of the slide rests against the rear of the barrel at battery. One unique feature is that the magazine cannot be removed unless the safety is engaged, and once the clip is pulled out, the safety cannot be switched off. Reinsertion of the clip does not automatically disengage the safety. It must be done manually. Most magazine safeties operate automatically, and this was a not-too-welcome change of design. In the event that this pistol was needed in a combat situation, and there was a need for a rapid change of magazines, the delay in remembering to switch on the safety could be hazardous to your health! All is not negative, however. The lack of an ejection port kept the pistol clean and free of minor contaminants when carried in a pocket, and since Schmeisser was an outstanding designer this pistol was very reliable. In home use the safety was a very efficient teacher to always remember to engage the safety!

Haenel Schmeisser Model I

Hafdasa
Hispano Argentino Fabrica de Automoviles S.A.
Buenos Aires, Argentina

Model: Ballester-Molina

Action Type: semiautomatic, recoil operated.

Caliber(s): .45 A.C.P.

Barrel Lengths: 5".

Finish: blue.

Manufacturing Dates: mid-1930s through World War II.

Stocks: wood.

Rifling: 6R.

Weight, Unloaded: 39 oz.

Sights: fixed.

Serial Numbers: unknown quantity, but generally a four-digit number with a prefix letter.

Serial Number Location: right side of frame above trigger.

Major Variations: Ballester-Molina.
Ballester-Rigaud.

Markings: on left side of slide: Pistola Automatica Cal. .45 Fabricada Por 'HAFDASA' Patentes Internacionales Ballester-Molina (or Ballester-Rigaud) Industria Argentina.

Price(s):
Ballester-Molina, very good—$400.00
Ballester-Molina, excellent—$500.00
Ballester-Rigaud, very good—$450.00
Ballester-Rigaud, excellent—$550.00

History: The Ballester-Molina was developed by HAFDASA in Buenos Aires, Argentina, during the 1930s. It's a somewhat blatant copy of the Colt 1911A1 in exterior appearance, but the working action is quite different. The Colt 1911 and the .45 A.C.P. cartridge had long been accepted by the Argentinians, and the Colt had been manufactured in Argentina under license as the Model 1916 (1911) and the Model 1927 (1911A1). The Ballester was destined to be a less expensive replacement for the Colt but still had to embody its advantages. Early production was marked Ballester-Rigaud, and standard production models were called the Ballester-Molina. The Ballesters were produced in quantity through World War II, both for the Argentine military and paramilitary forces and also, according to some sources, for clandestine units of the British army. Some are still in use today by the Argentinians.

Mechanical Functioning: This pistol is a recoil-operated, semiautomatic pistol with a seven-shot detachable box magazine, and is loosely based on the Colt Model 1911 functioning system. Although very similar to the Colt, even in the general method of field stripping, there are several major differences. Unlike the Colt, the mainspring housing is an integral part of the gripframe, and since the depth on the mainspring is different, the hammer strut is shorter. There is no grip safety, and the manual safety is redesigned. The trigger is pinned and pivoting rather than of the sliding type, and the extension bar runs only on the right side to engage the disconnector and sear. Detail stripping is somewhat different in that tools are needed to drift out the trigger, hammer, and sear pins. While the clips are interchangeable with the Colt, and of necessity the magazine catch located in the same place, the catch is retained differently. The slide stop disassembly notch has been omitted.

Argentine Military Ballester-Molina

Argentine Military Ballester-Rigaud

Harrington & Richardson
Gardner, MA

Model: Self-Loading Pistol, .32 cal.

Action Type: semiautomatic.

Caliber(s): .32 A.C.P.

Barrel Lengths: 3½".

Finish: blue.

Manufacturing Dates: 1912–1920.

Stocks: hard rubber.

Rifling: 6R.

Weight, Unloaded: 20 oz.

Sights: fixed.

Serial Numbers: unknown.

Serial Number Location: left side of slide.

Major Variations: n/a.

Markings: right side of slide: Harrington & Richardson Arms. Co., Worcester, Massachusetts USA Pat. Aug. 20, 1907 Apr. 13, Nov. 9, 1909. left side of slide: H & R self-loading caliber .32

Price(s):
  very good—$250.00
  excellent—$300.00

History: The Harrington & Richardson .32 Automatic pistol is based on the Webley patents, primarily for the exterior design and the takedown. The H. & R. .32 Self-Loading pistol utilizes the Webley's positive aspects and then adds a few of its own. The design relies on the Webley Model 1906 and is very similar to the 1913 variation. Considering the production dates, it could be that H. & R. used the Webley shape, and then, when Webley looked over the American modifications, in turn adopted some of them on the Model 1906. This is a true hammerless pistol, vastly simplifying manufacturing over the Webley's hammer and concealed hammer pistols. But even so, it still retains the great inherent strength built into the Webley design. This is a rugged pistol. It is well designed for its purpose and seemingly lasts forever as a shooter. It is very comfortable to shoot, safe, and fairly accurate. Considering its lines, it is surprisingly easy to hold and has excellent pointing qualities. Although it was not expensive to produce, it could not compete with other, more established designs. It appears that part of the argument against the H. & R. .32 was its ungainly looks. Although that's a trait that the English seem to admire, the American market just didn't seem ready for it. H. & R. also made a similar, though reduced in size, .25 A.C.P. Self-Loading pistol. Both the .32 and especially the .25 pistols should make good investments for the collector. Neither has reached the rarefied price heights of other scarce pistols. It appears that the .32 A.C.P. pistol outnumbers the .25 A.C.P. by about two to one as an estimation of scarcity.

Mechanical Functioning: The Harrington & Richardson .32 A.C.P. Self-Loading pistol is a blowback-operated, semiautomatic pistol that is striker-fired. It has a detachable eight-shot box magazine that is inserted through the gripframe and retained by a springloaded catch. The magazine release is a button located on the bottom rear of the butt. There are two safeties: a grip safety that inhibits the sear unless depressed and a manual intercepting safety that locks the sear. It is located on the left side of the frame and overrides the slide. The sights are fixed and consist of a round front sight located on the barrel and a milled groove on the top of the slide. Takedown is very simple and is accomplished by pulling the spring steel trigger guard back and down, which pivots it on its forward end. This in turn releases a lug that engages the barrel and locks it in position. The barrel and slide are pushed forward and are removed as a unit and then broken down. The grips are retained by a single center screw on each side and are prevented from rotating by a small pin in the lower gripframe that protrudes into the grips. Removal of the grips gives access to the rest of the mechanism. Assemble in reverse order. As always, be sure the weapon is unloaded before dismounting!

Harrington & Richardson .32 Self-Loading Pistol

Hartford Arms and Equipment Co.
Hartford, CT

Model: Target Pistol (single shot, repeater, and 1925)

Action Type: semiautomatic, blowback operated.

Caliber(s): .22 L.R.

Barrel Lengths: 6¾".

Finish: blue.

Manufacturing Dates: 1925–1932.

Stocks: wood or hard rubber.

Rifling: 6R.

Weight, Unloaded: 31 oz.

Sights: fixed.

Serial Numbers: started at 1.

Major Variations: single shot.
 manual repeater.
 semiautomatic (1925).

Markings: left side of frame: Mfg'd By The Hartford Arms And Equipment Co., Hartford, Conn. Patented. .22 Cal. Long Rifle.

Price(s):
 semiautomatic, very good—$550.00
 semiautomatic, excellent—$650.00
 manual repeater, very good—$650.00
 manual repeater, excellent—$700.00
 single shot, very good—$650.00
 single shot, excellent—$750.00

History: Even though Hartford Arms and Equipment Co. was only in business for a relatively short time, from 1925 to 1932, when it was purchased by High Standard, their designs are significant. They looked very much like the Colt Woodman of the day, only they devised a simpler operation. They also set the style and design for a whole generation of High Standard pistols going up into the 1950s. Hartford produced three distinct models of their pistol: a semiautomatic pistol of standard design with a ten-shot removable box-type magazine fitted through the butt; a manual repeater, which is exactly like the semiautomatic, with the exception that in order to cock the arm you manually have to draw back the slide, manually push it forward because there is no recoil spring, and when you push it forward with the slide cocked, a side snap pops up, locking the slide in place so that it performs as a magazine-fed, locked breech weapon; and the single shot pistol, which in design and size was exactly like the semiautomatic and the manual repeater; however, instead of having a magazine, the entire gripframe was solid, and it possessed the locking slide of the manual repeater. The total production of Hartford Arms for all three models seems to be limited to about 4,000 pistols. All run within the same serial range starting at about 1. When High Standard took over the company, its first pistol, the Model A, was virtually identical to the Hartford Arms semiautomatic.

Mechanical Functioning: The Hartford Arms semiautomatic pistol is a blowback-operated weapon with a detachable ten-shot box magazine with the magazine catch located at the base of the gripframe. The barrel is solidly attached to the frame at a frame extension and the slide reciprocates along a milled track behind the barrel and extending backward. Takedown is achieved by cocking the weapon and then pulling the slide all the way to the rear, and pushing the small button on the slide that holds the recoil spring. Run the slide forward to battery again manually, and rotate the rear lever on the left side of the frame downward about 45 degrees, lowering the recoil block. The slide can now be removed by retracting backward. Takedown on the other two models of Hartford Arms are similar. When the grips are removed, a small sideplate covering the lockwork can be taken off, and the lockwork exposed. The internal action is of concealed hammer type with a long sear bar and disconnect connecting the trigger and the sear.

Hartford Arms Target Pistol

Heckler & Koch
D7238 Oberndorf/Neckar
Germany

Model: HK4

Action Type: semiautomatic, blowback operated.

Caliber(s): .22 L.R., .25 A.C.P., .32 A.C.P., .380 A.C.P.

Barrel Lengths: 3¹¹/₃₂″.

Finish: blue.

Manufacturing Dates: 1967–1984.

Stocks: plastic.

Rifling: polygonal.

Weight, Unloaded: 16½ oz.

Sights: fixed.

Serial Numbers: n/a.

Major Variations: different calibers, conversion kits.

Markings: left side of slide: Heckler & Koch GMBH, Obendorf/N, Made in Germany, Mod. HK-4.

Price(s):
  HK-4, .380 A.C.P., very good—$325.00; excellent—$450.00
  HK-4, .380 automatic with .22 LR conversion kit, very good—$425.00; excellent—$575.00
  HK-4, .380, 3 conversion kits in .22 LR, .25 & .32 Cal., very good—$625.00; excellent—$750.00
  HK-4, .22 LR conversion kit, very good—$125.00; excellent—$150.00
  HK-4, .25 cal. conversion kit, very good—$125.00; excellent—$150.00
  HK-4, .32 cal. conversion kit, very good—$125.00; excellent—$150.00

History: The Heckler & Koch HK4 is a double-action pistol based on the HSc Mauser design, and it was conceived primarily for its interchangeability of calibers. By simply interchanging the conversion kits, with one frame, you had four different guns: a .22, a .25 A.C.P., a .32 A.C.P., and a .380 A.C.P. in an excellent design. It was double action with an external hammer. At various times in this pistol's history, it has been imported by Imperato, Harrington & Richardson, S.A.C.O., and now, by Heckler & Koch, Inc.

Mechanical Functioning: The Heckler & Koch HK4 is a straight blowback, semiautomatic pistol with a shrouded external hammer. The most noteworthy thing about this pistol, other than the fact that it is an improvement on the Mauser HSc system, is the interchangeability of calibers made possible by the conversion system. With a single frame, .22 LR, .25 A.C.P., .32 A.C.P., and .380 A.C.P. can all be chambered. After making sure the firearm is unloaded, field stripping can be accomplished by first removing the magazine, making sure the hammer is cocked, and with the safety in the "on safe" position, push down on the takedown latch located on the inside front of the trigger guard. Move the slide assembly forward about a quarter of an inch, and then lift up and off the frame. Push the bottom of the barrel forward just enough to clear the extractor, and then pivot downward and back off and out the slide. Assembly is in the reverse order. The conversion kits for this pistol are quite simple and consist primarily of an extra barrel, recoil spring, and a magazine in the new caliber. To change calibers, make sure the weapon is unloaded and field-strip the pistol. Remove the unwanted barrel, insert the new barrel and recoil spring, and then change magazines to the new caliber. If converting from centerfire to rimfire, or rimfire to centerfire, then the front face of the breechblock must be changed. This is accomplished by removing it and turning it around so that the cartridge recess and firing pin hole matches the type of ammunition you wish to use. The procedure is as follows: Hold the front of the extractor outward until a small hole is visible, and insert a paperclip or small needle into this hole to hold it in this position. Using a screwdriver of the proper size, remove the screw retaining the faceplate and reverse it. Put the screw back in and then release the extractor. Insert the proper combination of barrel and recoil spring you wish to use, and reassemble the pistol utilizing the proper magazine. You are now ready to shoot in your new caliber. One note: one side of the breechblock is for rimfire; the other side is for centerfire. If you are changing from one centerfire caliber to another, you need not change the breechblock.

Heckler & Koch Model HK4

Heckler & Koch
D7238 Oberndorf/Neckar
Germany

Model: P9S

Action Type: semiautomatic, delayed blowback operated.

Caliber(s): 9mm Parabellum, .45 A.C.P.

Barrel Lengths: 4", 5¹/₂".

Finish: blue and plastic coating.

Manufacturing Dates: 1971 to 1984.

Stocks: plastic or wood.

Rifling: polygonal.

Weight, Unloaded: 32¹/₂ oz.

Sights: fixed or adjustable.

Serial Numbers: n/a.

Serial Number Location: left side of frame above trigger.

Major Variations: early models did not have recurved trigger guard.
    target models.
    combat models.

Markings: left side of slide: HK Mod. P9S Heckler & Koch GMBH Oberndorf/Neckar, made in Germany.

Price(s):
    P9S, Combat, very good—$450.00; excellent—$550.00
    P9S, Target, very good—$750.00; excellent—$900.00
    P9S, Competition, very good—$500.00; excellent—$700.00
    P9S, .45 Combat, very good—$475.00; excellent—$600.00
    P9S, .45 Target, very good—$800.00; excellent—$950.00
    P9S, 9mm with .30 Luger conversion kit—very good—$550.00; excellent—$650.00

History: The P9 series of pistols, first made around 1971, was the brainchild of Herbert Midel. It was available in several variations. The most noteworthy exterior variation on the frame was the absence of recurve on the forward part of the trigger guard on early models. On later models the arm was recurved at the front of the trigger guard and grooved for two-handed hold. It came with adjustable sights for the target models, and with fixed sights for the combat models. The Competition, however, used a 5" barrel and an extra barrel weight which was fitted to the protruding barrel, and as an accessory item it had a walnut target stock. The Competition kit included a standard 4-inch barrel, as well as the standard combat grips. Although nominally the gun was only available in two calibers, 9mm and .45 A.C.P., a conversion kit early on was available to allow the use of 7.65mm Parabellum. It included barrel, recoil spring, and magazine. The rifling on this pistol is polygonal, which means there are no lands and grooves as such, instead looking down the bore it looks like a slightly flattened circle which is said to increase bullet velocity, as well as giving improved barrel life.

Mechanical Functioning: The Heckler & Koch P9S is a delayed blowback, semiautomatic pistol with a detachable box magazine, holding nine shots in 9mm Parabellum, and 7.65mm Parabellum, and seven shots in .45 A.C.P. The pistol is double action and has a concealed internal hammer. The extractor acts as a loaded chamber indicator in the same manner as the Luger. The magazine is inserted through the gripframe and is secured by a catch at the bottom of the butt. The manual safety is located at the rear of the left side of the slide, and resembles a conventional Walther PP safety. An additional safety feature is a cocking and decocking device similar to the Sauer H-38, which is located on the left side of the frame forward of the grip. With this device, the internal hammer can be either lowered or cocked as the case may be, with complete safety. A striking feature of this pistol is the manner in which the delayed blowback is created. There is a two-part breechblock that locks into the rear of the barrel via rollers. These rollers are mounted on the front section of the block, which is lighter in weight than the rear side, and are forced outward when the pistol is at battery. On firing, the forward section with the rollers attempts to recoil. However, the inertia of the slide keeps the rollers forced out when in engagement with the barrel extension, preventing movement. These rollers are slowly forced inward, releasing the slide to travel backward and cycle the firearm. In many respects this slot could be said to be of inertia style, and relies on the interplay of forces between the barrel extension and the rollers, which can only be overcome by inertia, rather than by mechanical action as is found on most other pistols.

Heckler & Koch Model P9S

High Standard Manufacturing Corporation
New Haven, Hamden, and East Hartford, Connecticut

Model: Derringer

Action Type: manual repeater, superposed barrels.

Caliber(s): .22 L.R.R.F., .22 W.M.R., 22 Short and Long.

Barrel Lengths: 3½".

Finish: blue, nickel, gold, electroless nickel.

Manufacturing Dates: 1962–1984 (all operations ceased in 1984).

Stocks: plastic or walnut.

Rifling: 6R.

Weight, Unloaded: 11 oz.

Sights: fixed.

Serial Numbers: n/a.

Serial Number Location: right rear of barrel.

Major Variations: gold Derringer.
  Presidential Derringer.

Markings: left side of barrel: Derringer (caliber).
  right side of barrel: High Standard Mfg. Corp. (address).

Price(s):
  nickel, .22 L.R.R.F., very good—$150.00
  nickel, .22 L.R.R.F., excellent—$225.00
  nickel, .22 W.M.R., very good—$150.00
  nickel, .22 W.M.R., excellent—$225.00
  gold, .22 W.M.R., very good—$350.00
  gold, .22 W.M.R., excellent—$450.00
  Presidential, very good—$300.00
  Presidential, excellent—$500.00
  Model DM-100, .22 L.R.R.F., very good—$125.00
  Model DM-100, .22 L.R.R.F., excellent—$200.00
  Model DM-101, .22 W.R.F., very good—$125.00
  Model DM-101, .22 W.R.F., excellent—$200.00

History: The High Standard Derringer was introduced in 1965 to fill the need for a very flat, lightweight, and highly concealable handgun with an intended market in police sales. In its production life it had several variations. It was produced in only two calibers: .22 Long Rifle, and .22 Magnum. It only had one barrel length: 3½ inches. However, it was available in blue, nickel, and electroless nickel, and had one Commemorative issue, the Presidential Derringer, which was gold-plated and quite fancy. It came supplied with either plastic grips or as currently available on the nickeled gun, checkered walnut grips.

Mechanical Functioning: The High Standard Derringer is a double-action-only, hammerless handgun with superposed barrels. The barrels pivot at the center point through a hinge on the bottom of the barrel and are locked by a U-shaped top snap fitted over the rear of the frame. This lock itself is also pivoted at the top of the barrels, so that when grasped and pulled upward unlocking the barrels, it at the same time activates the ejector to push out the spent cartridges. The barrels and working parts are all steel, and the frame itself is formed of a light alloy. Rather than the barrels being joined as they are on many other over-under Derringers, in this case the barrels are formed from one solid billet and drilled through. The sights are grooved milled in the rear of the barrel and a raised lump forming the front sight. There are no safeties other than the fact that the trigger pull is somewhat hard. There is no front on the trigger guard; however, there is an anti-pinch extension coming out of the bottom of the frame to prevent someone from putting their finger behind the trigger upon firing and thus blocking the trigger, preventing it from moving backward. The grips are secured to the frame via a single screw per grip.

High Standard Derringer

High Standard Manufacturing Corporation
New Haven, Hamden, and East Hartford, Connecticut

Model: H-D Military

Action Type: semiautomatic, blowback operated.

Caliber(s): .22 L.R.

Barrel Lengths: 4½″, 6¾″.

Finish: blue.

Manufacturing Dates: 1939–1955.

Stocks: checkered walnut.

Rifling: 6R.

Weight, Unloaded: 40 oz.

Sights: adjustable rear.

Serial Numbers: n/a.

Serial Number Location: forestrap of frame.

Major Variations: H-D Automatic, no thumb safety.
   H-D Military Automatic, thumb safety.

Markings: left side of slide: High Standard H-D Military.
   left side of frame at barrel extension: Made in USA, The High Standard
   Mfg. Co., New Haven, Conn, Patented, .22 Long Rifle.

Price(s):
   H-D, very good—$750.00
   H-D, excellent—$1,250.00
   H-D Military, 4″ barrel, very good—$275.00
   H-D Military, 4″ barrel, excellent—$500.00
   H-D Military, 6¾″ barrel, very good—$300.00
   H-D Military, 6¾″ barrel, excellent—$550.00
   H-D Military, no slide stop, very good—$350.00
   H-D Military, no slide stop, excellent—$600.00
   U.S.A. H-D, very good—$475.00
   U.S.A. H-D, excellent—$600.00
   HD-MS with silencer, very good—$3,000.00
   HD-MS with silencer, excellent—$3,500.00

History: The roots of the H-D Military stem back to when High Standard
   purchased the Hartford Arms and Equipment Company. From 1932
   through 1951, all of the High Standard automatic pistols bore a very
   close resemblance to the Hartford pistols which is not unreasonable
   since High Standard purchased company, tools, and equipment when
   Hartford Arms went bankrupt. There were two styles of pistols that High
   Standard made in this early series, one having an exposed hammer, the
   other having a concealed hammer hidden within the frame and slide.
   All were essentially the same with minor differences. The H-D Military
   was based on the Model D; however, with an external hammer, and in

the Model H-D Military there were several variations. The first type to be made, the H-D, had no thumb safety. The Model H-DM, or as it is usually called, the H-D Military, did have a thumb safety. There was also a variation of the H-D that had no slide stop on the right-hand side of the frame to lock the slide back on the last shot. The final variation was the USA H-D which was made for the Army as a training pistol. The final major variation was a type of pistol made for the Office of Strategic Services during World War II. It consisted of an H-D Military with a barrel modified for permanent silencer mounting.

Mechanical Functioning: The High Standard H-D Military is a straight blowback-operated, semiautomatic pistol with a ten-shot detachable box magazine inserted through the grip frame and secured by a catch at the bottom of the butt. There is an external hammer with a provision for a half-cock notch. The firing pin is of the floating variety. On those models that have a thumb safety, it is located on the left-hand side of the frame and secures the sear and prevents the hammer from firing. On some models of this pistol, there is a slide stop on the right-hand side of the frame, which is actuated by the magazine button pushing up against it, thereby locking the slide in the rearward position upon the last shot. For takedown, remove the magazine and clear the chamber by pulling the slide back and making sure it is empty, thereby cocking the hammer. With the slide fully retracted, push the takedown button on the top of the slide to secure the recoil spring. Push the slide forward slightly and rotate the takedown latch located on the right side of the frame. Holding this latch down, pull the slide back and off the pistol. Assembly is in the reverse order.

High Standard Model H-D Military

High Standard Manufacturing Corporation
New Haven, Hamden, and East Hartford, Connecticut

Model: Olympic I.S.U. Military

Action Type: semiautomatic, blowback operated.

Caliber(s): .22 Short R.F.

Barrel Lengths: 6¾", 8".

Finish: blue.

Manufacturing Dates: 1965–1978.

Stocks: walnut.

Rifling: 6R.

Weight, Unloaded: 40½ oz.

Sights: adjustable target.

Serial Numbers: n/a.

Serial Number Location: right side of the slide.

Major Variations: frame mounted rear sight.
    slide mounted rear sight.
    military grip angle.
    standard grip angle.

Markings: left side of barrel: .22 Short
    left side of frame: Olympic.
    left side of slide: High Standard.
    right side of barrel: High Standard Mfg. Co. Hamden Conn. USA

Price(s):
    Olympic I.S.U., Military, frame mounted sight, very good—$700.00
    Olympic I.S.U., Military, frame mounted sight, excellent—$950.00
    Olympic I.S.U., standard, frame mounted sight, very good—$750.00
    Olympic I.S.U., standard, frame mounted sight, excellent—$1,000.00
    Olympic I.S.U., Military, slide mounted sight, very good—$650.00
    Olympic I.S.U., Military, slide mounted sight, excellent—$900.00
    Olympic I.S.U., standard, slide mounted sight, very good—$750.00
    Olympic I.S.U., standard, slide mounted sight, excellent—$850.00

History: For many years, the I.S.U. (International Shooter's Union) has been regulating all international match competitions. Of course, the major tournament is the Olympics, and for American shooters there are some very strange types of shooting done there, one of which is the "Rapid Fire Competition," whereby a silhouette target turns toward you, you have to lift the gun off a table and fire five shots at it as quickly as you possibly can before the target turns away from you again, which is in a matter of seconds. In such a competition, it is of absolute necessity to have as little recoil as possible to disturb your point of aim, and it was for this purpose in international shooting that the .22 short target pistol came into being. Not to be outdone by other companies, High Standard, who prided themselves on fine .22 match pistols, came out with the I.S.U. version called the "Olympic" and chambered for .22 short only. Target shooters being what they are, High Standard made several different versions of the pistol. They made a so-called military grip, which had the same angle and feel as the .45 automatic, for those shooters who use the .45 in centerfire competition and did not want to change grip angles. Then for the shooter who is comfortable with a standard design the standard grip angle is used as passed down from Hartford Arms. The early issue of the pistol came with 8″ or 6¾″ tapered barrels with a stabilizer and detachable weights. After 1964 only the 6¾″ barrel was available.

Mechanical Functioning: The High Standard I.S.U. Military and its variations are straight blowback, semiautomatic pistols with a ten-shot detachable box magazine secured by a catch at the bottom of the butt. They are of internal hammer variety and are equipped with adjustable triggers, adjustable target sights, and slide stops to hold the slide open on the last shot as well as a manual thumb safety. Takedown on these pistols is accomplished by making sure the firearm is empty, putting the empty magazine back in the gun, and pulling the slide to the rear, locking it in place. At this point a button on the front of the frame forward of the trigger guard and slightly above it can be depressed, and at the same time the barrel pulled forward and lifted upward and off the frame. Holding the slide tightly, the slide stop can be depressed, and the slide removed forward and off the frame. Assembly is in the reverse order.

High Standard Olympic I.S.U. Military

High Standard Manufacturing Corporation
New Haven, Hamden, and East Hartford, Connecticut

Model: Sentinel (series)

Action Type: revolver, double action.

Caliber(s): .22 W.M.R., .22 L.R.R.F., .357 Mag.

Barrel Lengths: 2½", 3", 4", and 6".

Finish: blue or nickel.

Manufacturing Dates: 1955–1976.

Stocks: walnut.

Rifling: 6R.

Weight, Unloaded: 27 oz. with 4" barrel.

Sights: adjustable rear.

Serial Numbers: n/a.

Serial Number Location: right side of frame.

Major Variations: fixed sights or adjustable sights, barrel length.

Markings: left side of barrel: Sentinel MK IV, caliber, .22 Magnum. right side of barrel: High Standard and address.

Price(s):
    Sentinel, .22 L.R.R.F., very good—$75.00
    Sentinel, .22 L.R.R.F., excellent—$125.00
    Sentinel, Deluxe .22 L.R.R.F., very good—$100.00
    Sentinel, Deluxe .22 L.R.R.F., excellent—$150.00
    Sentinel, Imperial .22 L.R.R.F., very good—$100.00
    Sentinel, Imperial .22 L.R.R.F., excellent—$150.00
    Sentinel, 1, .22 L.R.R.F., very good—$175.00
    Sentinel, 1, .22 L.R.R.F., excellent—$225.00
    Sentinel, 1, adjustable sights, very good—$200.00
    Sentinel, 1, adjustable sights, excellent—$250.00
    Sentinel, MK II, .357 Magnum, very good—$175.00
    Sentinel, MK II, .357 Magnum, excellent—$225.00
    Sentinel, MK III, very good—$200.00
    Sentinel, MK III, excellent—$250.00
    Sentinel, MK IV, .22 W.R.F. only, very good—$125.00
    Sentinel, MK IV, .22 W.R.F. only, excellent—$175.00
    Sentinel, Snub .22 L.R.R.F., very good—$200.00
    Sentinel, Snub .22 L.R.R.F., excellent—$225.00

History: High Standard was well known for making double-action Western-style revolvers, and in 1955 they decided to try their hand at making a regulation, swing-out cylinder style, double-action revolver of .38 Special size. The first in the series was simply called the "Sentinel," followed thereby by the "Sentinel Deluxe," the "Sentinel Imperial," and the different Marks of Sentinels. At each change of model, they were improved. The early models were made out of an aluminum alloy, and the later models were made out of steel. The actions were improved, and the trigger pull is now fairly good. The cylinder is a swing out and holds nine shots, except in .357 Magnum, which only holds six shots. They have been available in both fixed sights and adjustable sights. The only models in current production are the MK IV series which come in 2″, 4″ with adjustable sights, and a 6″ version called the "Camper" which does not have the ejector shroud the other two models have.

Mechanical Functioning: The High Standard Sentinel series are double-action revolvers with cylinders that swing out to the left side. The cylinders have simultaneous manual ejection. To open the cylinder, it requires pulling forward on the cylinder latch pin, which also doubles as the ejector rod when the cylinder is swung open. The current models of Sentinel also have a hammer block to prevent accidental firing in case the weapon is dropped. On the .22 calibers, cylinders are interchangeable between .22 Long Rifle and .22 Magnum. Interchange is accomplished by using a small pin punch and pushing in on the front of the frame in front of the trigger guard on the pin retaining the cylinder crane. The crane is then slipped out by pushing in on the pin, and a new crane and cylinder assembly can be inserted, being careful not to warp or bend the crane.

High Standard Manufacturing Corporation
New Haven, Hamden, and East Hartford, Connecticut

Model: Supermatic Citation (series)

Action Type: semiautomatic, blowback operated.

Caliber(s): .22 L.R.R.F.

Barrel Lengths: 5½″, 6¾″, 7¼″, 8″, 10″.

Finish: blue.

Manufacturing Dates: 1958–1984.

Stocks: walnut.

Rifling: 6R.

Weight, Unloaded: 45 oz.

Sights: adjustable.

Serial Numbers: n/a.

Serial Number Location: right side of frame.

Major Variations: slide or frame mounted rear sight.
barrel styles: bull, tapered, or fluted.
standard or military gripframe angle.

Markings: left side of barrel: .22 Long Rifle.
left side of frame: Supermatic Citation.
left side of slide: High Standard.
right side of barrel: High Standard address.

Price(s):
Supermatic Citation, early, tapered barrel, very good—$600.00
Supermatic Citation, early, tapered barrel, excellent—$850.00
Supermatic Citation, early, bull barrel, very good—$500.00
Supermatic Citation, early, bull barrel, excellent—$750.00
Supermatic Citation, late, fluted barrel, very good—$425.00
Supermatic Citation, late, fluted barrel, excellent—$550.00
Supermatic Citation, late, heavy barrel, very good—$425.00
Supermatic Citation, late, heavy barrel, excellent—$550.00
Supermatic Citation, late, military grip, very good—$400.00
Supermatic Citation, late, military grip, excellent—$500.00

History: The Supermatic Citation II is the latest in a long line of High Standard Supermatic Citations. They all featured interchangeable barrels, adjustable trigger pulls, trigger travel adjustments, adjustable target sights, slide stops, and fancy barrels. They came with the option of a standard frame angle, or a military frame angle to match the .45 Model 1911. The early pistols of the series had sights mounted on the slide. The later pistols of the series had the sights mounted to the gripframe.

Mechanical Functioning: The Citation series are blowback-operated, semiautomatic pistols with ten-shot detachable box magazines fitted through the gripstrap and retained by a catch at the bottom front of the butt. The triggers are large, serrated target types, with overtravel adjustments and pull adjustments. There is an internal hammer and a floating firing pin in the slide. The mechanical safety on the left side of the gun intercepts the sear, thus locking the hammer. Takedown and barrel interchange are accomplished by making sure the firearm is unloaded, reinserting the empty magazine, retracting the slide until it locks in the rear position via the slidelock and pushing the button in the front of the frame just above and forward of the trigger guard. This releases the barrel to be pulled slightly forward and up and off the frame. Now, either a new barrel may be put on, or holding the slide and releasing the slidelock, the slide may come off the frame at this point for cleaning. Assembly is in the reverse order.

High Standard Supermatic Citation

High Standard Manufacturing Corporation
New Haven, Hamden, and East Hartford, Connecticut

Model: Victor

Action Type: semiautomatic, blowback operated.

Caliber(s): .22 L.R.

Barrel Lengths: 4½", 5½".

Finish: blue.

Manufacturing Dates: 1972–1984.

Stocks: checkered walnut.

Rifling: 6R.

Weight, Unloaded: 47 oz. with 5½" barrel.

Sights: adjustable target.

Serial Numbers: n/a.

Serial Number Location: right side of frame.

Major Variations: 4½" solid rib barrel.
5½" vent rib barrel.
standard or military grip.

Markings: left side of barrel: The Victor .22 Long Rifle.
left side of slide: High Standard.
right side of barrel: High Standard and address.

Price(s):
Victor with 4½" solid rib barrel, military grip, very good—$500.00
Victor with 4½" solid rib barrel, military grip, excellent—$650.00
Victor with 4½" solid rib barrel, slant grip, very good—$2,000.00
Victor with 4½" solid rib barrel, slant grip, excellent—$2,500.00
Victor with 5½" vent rib barrel, slant grip, very good—$1,500.00
Victor with 5½" vent rib barrel, slant grip, excellent—$2,000.00

History: The High Standard Victor was first introduced in 1972 as the ultimate .22 target pistol, and for High Standard to say that was quite a statement considering how good their pistols were. On first issue it was available only in the military-style grip, and the weight and balance approximated that of the .45 Model 1911 automatic, and indeed the integral sight rib attached to the barrel was similar to the ribs that were put on Model 1911s as accessories during that time. From 1974 to 1975 a standard-style grip angle variation was available to those shooters who wanted the Victor and its inherent accuracy potential but disliked the Model 1911 gripframe. After 1975 only the military-style grip was available.

Mechanical Functioning: The High Standard Victor is a straight blowback-operated, semiautomatic pistol with a ten-shot detachable box magazine inserted through the gripframe and retained by a catch in the front of the bottom of the butt. It has an adjustable trigger pull, adjustable trigger stop, an internal hammer, and a thumb safety that locks the sear. It also has a slide stop that holds the slide open upon firing the last shot. The sights are mounted integrally to the barrel to provide a positive sighting plane with the barrel. Takedown is accomplished by making sure the pistol is unloaded, inserting an empty magazine, retracting the slide to the locked position, and pushing the takedown button on the front of the gripframe just above and forward of the trigger guard. This allows the barrel to be pulled forward slightly and up and off the pistol. The slide lock can now be released holding the slide, and the slide can be slid off the front of the frame. Assembly is in the reverse order.

High Standard Victor

Hispano-Argentine Fabricas de Automoviles S.A.
Buenos Aires, Argentina

Model: Hafdasa

Action Type: semiautomatic, blowback.

Caliber(s): .22 L.R.

Barrel Lengths: 2½".

Finish: blue.

Manufacturing Dates: circa 1935.

Stocks: black plastic.

Rifling: 6L.

Weight, Unloaded: 11 oz.

Sights: fixed.

Serial Numbers: seen in the high five digits.

Serial Number Location: left side of frame at rear.

Major Variations: Hafdasa.
  Zonda.

Markings: none other than the grip monogram: HA on Hafdasa.
  Zonda on Zonda.

Price(s):
  Hafdasa, very good—$275.00
  Hafdasa, excellent—$350.00
  Zonda, very good—$225.00
  Zonda, excellent—$300.00

History: This pistol was made by the same firm that made the Ballester Molina .45 pistols and the Criolla .22 pistols based on the Molina frame. The Hafdasa and the trade-named Zonda (which is identical) were obviously intended for the mass market as the inexpensive .22 pistol. The saving grace of the Hafdasa is that it is a hand-filling and comfortable pistol. Unfortunately, the safety, located at the top of the left grip, is circular in appearance with a ridge projection and can be quite difficult to rotate.

Mechanical Functioning: A simple blowback-operated, semiautomatic pistol with two ejection ports, one on either side. However, it functions not just as a port but as a means of cocking the action by grasping the forward end of the bolt, which has serrations, and pulling back. Not an easy task to master as the pressure needed to overcome the recoil spring, and cocking the hammer, can be quite a bit, as felt through two fingers! The pistol is inexpensively made and utilizes stampings wherever possible.

Hafdasa .22

Husqvarna Vapenfabrik
Husqvarna, Sweden

Model: Lahti, Swedish Model 40

Action Type: semiautomatic, recoil operated.

Caliber(s): 9mm Parabellum.

Barrel Lengths: 4³/₄".

Finish: blue.

Manufacturing Dates: 1940–1944.

Stocks: black plastic.

Rifling: 6R.

Weight, Unloaded: 46 oz.

Sights: fixed.

Serial Numbers: about 84,000 pistols made using four digit numbers with a letter prefix or up to a five digit number.

Serial Number Location: left side of frame above trigger.

Major Variations: none.

Markings: on right side of frame: unit markings at times.
on left side of slide: Husqvarna Vapenfabrik AB.

Price(s):
Lahti M40, very good—$250.00
Lahti M40, excellent—$400.00

History: The Lahti was adopted by Sweden in 1940 after that country had already adopted the Walther P.38 and could not get delivery on it due to Germany's war. Since the Swedish government was desperate for a powerful replacement for their Model 1907 pistol, they settled on their Finnish neighbor's Lahti. Believing that it performed well in the Russian-Finnish War of the winter of 1939, they purchased the rights to manufacture it. In 1940 the contract was given to Svenska Automat Vapen to produce the M40. Unfortunately, they were unable to fulfill the order, and the task was passed on to Husqvarna. The early guns experienced a high failure rate due to poor design and poor steel, and in the several years that it took to iron out the problems, the Swedes gave up. They now use the Lahti and the Walther P.1 (P.38).

Mechanical Functioning: The Lahti is a semiautomatic pistol based on the short recoil system. It has a concealed hammer, adjustable box magazine holding eight rounds, and a manual safety that intercepts the hammer and sear. To aid in unlocking, there is a little extra energy on its rearward travel. This one item probably saves the day for the Lahti, for it is one of the most reliable pistols in conditions of extreme cold.

Swedish Lahti M40

Husqvarna Vapenfabriks Aktiebolag
Husqvarna, Sweden

Model: 1907

Action Type: semiautomatic, blowback operated.

Caliber(s): 9mm Browning Long.

Barrel Lengths: 5".

Finish: matte blue.

Manufacturing Dates: 1907–1942.

Stocks: hard rubber.

Rifling: 6R.

Weight, Unloaded: 32 oz.

Sights: fixed.

Serial Numbers: n/a.

Serial Number Location: right side of slide above trigger.

Major Variations: none.

Markings: left side of slide: Husqvarna Vapenfabrik Aktiebolag.

Price(s):
    Military, Belgian, very good—$275.00
    Military, Belgian, excellent—$375.00
    Military, Swedish, very good—$225.00
    Military, Swedish, excellent—$325.00

History: The Husqvarna Model 1907 pistol was adopted by the Swedish government after trials lasting from 1903 through 1904. From 1907 until 1923 it was manufactured for the Swedish Military by its initial fabricator, Fabrique Nationale in Herstal, Belgium. It started life as the Browning Model 1903, and it set the standard for the world for medium-frame semiautomatic blowback-operated pistols. After this model was discontinued in about 1923 by Fabrique Nationale, the Swedish government decided to keep the pistol as their military standard and negotiated for the rights to produce it in original form but with their own markings. This was agreed to and production began on the Model 1907 at the Husqvarna plant. Although this pistol was superseded by the Lahti (Model 40) as the official military sidearm in Sweden in about 1940, according to some experts the production of the Model 1907 continued on into 1942. Specimens of the Husqvarna Model 1907 have been seen with the inscription ".380" etched into the left side of the slide below the ejection port. This designation should be treated with suspicion, and the chamber should be checked to see if the barrel has been changed to accommodate this different cartridge or if the mark has been applied just to aid sales. If converted deduct 50% from value.

Mechanical Functioning: The Husqvarna Model 1907 is a blowback-operated semiautomatic pistol utilizing an internal concealed hammer and a floating firing pin. It has a seven-shot, detachable box magazine that is inserted through the gripframe and retained by a spring-loaded catch located on the base of the butt at the rear. The manual safety is located on the left side of the frame at the rear and it intercepts the sear. The automatic grip safety located on the rear of the gripstrap prevents firing until it is depressed. On the last shot the slide will remain in the open position and will stay there until the magazine is removed or a loaded magazine is inserted, and then the slide can be withdrawn slightly to unlock and then close. The major innovative features of this pistol that were so widely copied were the concealed hammer, the recoil spring mounted on a guide and located beneath the barrel set into recesses in both the frame and the slide, and especially the interrupted grooved barrel lugs that engaged the frame and rotated into the slide for dismounting. To field-strip this pistol, first make sure that the weapon is unloaded. Remove the magazine and withdraw the slide until the safety can be engaged in the forward notch locking the slide back. The barrel can now be rotated so that the barrel lugs are visible in the ejection port and are level with the cut in the slide and are fully free of the frame. Holding the slide firmly because of the tension of the recoil spring, disengage the safety and run the slide forward and off of the frame. The recoil spring assembly and the barrel can now be removed from the slide. Assembly is in the reverse order. This pistol was crafted both in the Belgian and the Swedish variations from steel.

Husqvarna 1907

Interarms
10 Prince Street
Alexandria, VA 22313

Model: Virginian

Action Type: revolver, single action.

Caliber(s): .44 Magnum, .357 Magnum, .22 L.R.R.F., .22 W.R.M., .45 Colt.

Barrel Lengths: 5″, 5½″, 6″, 7½″, 8⅜″, 10½″, 12″.

Finish: blue with case hardened frame, or stainless steel.

Manufacturing Dates: 1977 to date.

Stocks: plain walnut or Pachmayr target grips.

Rifling: n/a.

Weight, Unloaded: 50 oz. with 6″ barrel.

Sights: adjustable rear, target rear, or fixed.

Serial Numbers: n/a.

Serial Number Location: bottom of frame.

Major Variations: Dragoon with adjustable sights.
Dragoon Deputy with fixed sights.
Dragoon Silhouette with target sights and long bull barrels.
Dragoon Convertible, small frame .22s.

Markings: left side of barrel: Virginian Dragoon (caliber).
left side of frame: Pat. No. 5803761, Date Apr. 16, 1974.

Price(s):
Virginian Dragoon, blue, very good—$175.00; excellent—$225.00
Virginian Dragoon, stainless, very good—$200.00; excellent—$250.00
Virginian Deputy, blue, very good—$175.00; excellent—$200.00
Virginian Deputy, stainless, very good—$175.00; excellent—$225.00
Virginian Silhouette, stainless, very good—$275.00; excellent—$325.00
Virginian Convertible, blue, very good—$125.00; excellent—$150.00
Virginian Convertible, stainless, very good—$150.00; excellent—$175.00

History: The Virginian Dragoon, which is now made by Interarms in Alexandria, Virginia, is a single-action revolver based on the Colt single-action Army frame for its external appearance and most of its interior design. However, it owes its true functioning and interior to the Virginian originally made by Hammerli of Lenzburg, Switzerland. Incorporated on the Interarms Virginian Dragoons is the Swiss safety system by which the center pin can be pushed back through the cylinder, and into the area where the hammer falls, preventing the hammer from striking the firing pin. This constitutes perhaps the first manual safety found on revolvers in the last sixty years. The Virginian series is available either with adjustable sights, fixed sights, or special target adjustable sights for the Virginian Dragoon Silhouette. It is also available in a wide variety of barrel lengths. The Silhouette style is available with 7½″, 8⅜″ and 10½″ barrels; the Deputy is available with 5″ or 6″ barrels; the Standard Dragoons are available with 5″, 6″, 7½″ or 8⅜″ barrels. All models are available in either blue with case-hardened frame or in stainless. The Convertible small-frame Virginian is available in the 5½″ barrel length.

Mechanical Functioning: The Virginian Dragoons are single-action revolvers built on the Western style and based on the Colt single-action Army. There are several frame styles. The large frame is slightly larger than the similar Colt product and is available made for fixed sights or milled for adjustable sights. The small-frame revolver is available only with adjustable sights. Both patterns are made in either carbon steel or stainless steel. The variation called the Silhouette is specifically made to comform to the match rules of the International Handgun Metallic Silhouette Association. These revolvers are available in a wide variety of calibers and are very well adapted to shooting the heavier calibers. The Western-style frame is better suited to high recoil than the double-action styles. The reason for this is that the double-action revolver is designed to keep the hand in the same place at all times in order to have a rapid second shot. Haste isn't a big issue with the single action. Hence on recoil the firearm uses some of the recoil energy to rotate upward, where the double action lets the hand absorb everything. The Virginians all have cylinders mounted axially on a center pin, which extends through the frame from front to rear and which can be removed by pushing the spring-loaded catch on the front of the frame inward and then pulling the pin out. Loading is carried out through a side gate located on the right side of the receiver, and ejection is carried out by means of a rod ejector located on the right side of the barrel in a housing. The Virginians are slightly larger in size than the original Colt single-action Armys and possess a manual safety by which the center pin can be pushed into the frame, preventing the hammer from contacting the firing pin.

Interarms Model Virginian
Photo courtesy of Interarms

Jager Waffenfabrik
Suhl, Germany

Model: Jager

Action Type: semiautomatic, blowback operated.

Caliber(s): 7.65mm.

Barrel Lengths: 3⅞".

Finish: blue.

Manufacturing Dates: 1914–1917.

Stocks: hard rubber.

Rifling: 4R.

Weight, Unloaded: 22½ oz.

Sights: fixed.

Serial Numbers: possibly starting at 1 and might run to the 12,000s.

Serial Number Location: left side of frame above trigger guard.

Major Variations: none.

Markings: left side of frame: Jager-Pistole D.R.P. Angem.

Price(s):
Commercial, very good—$200.00
Commercial, excellent—$350.00
Military, very good—$275.00
Military, excellent—$450.00

History: The Jager was obviously designed with potential government sales in mind. Unlike other pistols before and few since, the Jager was composed almost entirely of stampings or of easily machined pieces and could be made easily and cheaply in even the most basically equipped factory. This was a highly innovative idea; unfortunately, the firearms business is one of the most conservative markets possible. Unless a new firearm shows outstanding promise because of a radically new feature, it cannot hope to get away with a change of basic pattern. The Jager fell into this category. It was a very standard blowback pistol with ease of construction being its only saving grace. Had there been coupled with the cheapness some novelty in the mechanism that yielded an improvement there would have been a chance for success. Sadly for the makers, the German government, even at the height of World War I when they were procuring any gun that they could get their hands on, didn't think too much of the Jager, and they are said to have purchased less than 1,000 for military use even though they had a great need for weapons. Amazingly, this little pistol was said to have functioned fairly well, and has withstood the test of use. It seems that the primary problem with extant specimens is missing parts, with the most common lost piece being the magazine. Parts for the Jager are quite scarce, and missing parts can seriously affect the value of these guns. Be aware that a great many of these guns are not in functioning order, and when buying one for a collection don't bank on being able to find the missing part! Today the Jagers with Imperial Acceptance stamps are highly desirable collectors' items.

Mechanical Functioning: The Jager is a blowback-operated, semiautomatic pistol of unique design. It has a seven-shot, detachable box magazine, which is inserted through the gripframe and retained by a spring-loaded catch located at the base of the butt to the rear. This pistol is striker-fired. The safety is manual and mounted on the top left part of the back-strap. The frame is formed by two flat stampings, and the slide is a formed stamping. The forged barrel acts as a recoil spring guide and has protrusions that lock it in place on the frame stampings with an additional lug that acts as a slide guide. The front and rear straps hold the working mechanism and form the frame to which are attached the sides. The breechblock is a solid machined bar containing the striker and striker spring and is inserted into the hollow slide. Everything is held together by pins and screws into the front and rear gripstraps. If nothing else, this pistol points out the relative weakness of the 7.65mm cartridge. For all of the simplicity and the seeming weakness of the parts and their means of staying together, this refugee from a hardware store functions and holds up very well. For the purpose for which it was intended this pistol should be regarded as an engineering masterpiece.

Jager Pistol

Japanese Military

Model: Nambu, Type 14

Action Type: semiautomatic, recoil operated.

Caliber(s): 8mm Nambu.

Barrel Lengths: 4⅝″.

Finish: blue.

Manufacturing Dates: 1925–1945.

Stocks: serrated wood grips, late models plain.

Rifling: 6R.

Weight, Unloaded: 32 oz.

Sights: fixed.

Serial Numbers: Nagoya: 1 to about 7800.
   Tokyo: 1 to about 31900
   Kokura: 31900 to about 35500
   Nagoya Nambu, no clip retainer: 7800 to about 99999
   Nagoya Nambu with clip retainer: 1 to about 20500
   Toriimatsu: 50001 to 99999
   Toriimatsu starting at year 18.11: 1 to about 99000.

Serial Number Location: right side of frame, to the rear of the grip.

Major Variations: Standard (pre-1939) trigger guard.
   Winter trigger guard.
   many minor variations.

Markings: left side of frame by serial number: arsenal marks.

Price(s):
   small trigger guard, very good—$275.00
   small trigger guard, excellent—$450.00
   Winter trigger guard, very good—$225.00
   Winter trigger guard, excellent—$350.00

History: Adopted in 1925, the Type 14 Nambu was made by several different factories: Nagoya Army Arsenal, Tokyo Army Arsenal, Kokura Army Arsenal, Nambu Rifle Co. (Nagoya Nambu), and Nagoya Arsenal-Toriimatsu. All Nambu Type 14s also were marked to show month and year of manufacture, with 1926 being the first year. Thus, the stamp of 3.5 would mean 1928, May. This pistol went through several modifications. Starting in 1925 a high degree of workmanship was evident on these pistols, but as with most manufactured goods, as production wore on, a means of saving labor and money became more important. Add to this the exigencies of war and toward 1943 no one was even bothering to polish the guns. By 1945 they were becoming downright crude. However, these pistols can prove to be a fertile field for the collector, as they can be traced and there are many minor variations to look for.

Mechanical Functioning: The Type 14 Nambu is a semiautomatic pistol operating on a short recoil system. It uses an eight-shot detachable box magazine and has a manual thumb safety. To lock the pistol at battery it utilizes a separate locking block swinging up from the receiver and locking the bottom of the breechblock. Upon firing, the whole system moves rearward until the locking block is cammed open freeing the breechblock to continue its rearward travel. Be careful when dismounting this pistol that the locking block is reassembled properly—the pistol can be fired without it, but as a straight blowback which can be dangerous!

Japanese Nambu Type 14

Japanese Military

Model: Nambu, Papa, and Grandpa

Action Type: semiautomatic.

Caliber(s): 8mm Nambu.

Barrel Lengths: 4½″.

Finish: blue.

Manufacturing Dates: 1904–1928.

Stocks: wood.

Rifling: 6R.

Weight, Unloaded: 35 oz.

Sights: adjustable rear.

Serial Numbers: Tokyo Artillery Arsenal: 2450 to about 7050.
Tokyo Gas & Electric: 1 to about 5000, and from 8000 to about 9000.

Serial Number Location: right rear frame.

Major Variations: Tokyo Artillery Arsenal-Standard and Thailand Contract.
Tokyo Gas & Electric-Commercial, Tokyo Arsenal Contract, Navy Contract.
some models are slotted for shoulder stock.
Grandpa Nambu (Model 1902).

Markings: Acceptance stamps and arsenal marks at the rear on both left and
right side of frame. Tokyo Gas & Electric pistols have "TGE" on top of the
frame over the chamber.

Price(s):
Papa TGE Navy, very good—$1,000.00
Papa TGE Navy, excellent—$1,250.00
Papa TGE Commercial, very good—$1,000.00
Papa TGE Commercial, excellent—$1,500.00
Papa TGE Commercial, slotted for shoulder stock, very good—$1,250.00
Papa TGE Commercial, slotted for shoulder stock, excellent—$1,750.00
Papa TAA, very good—$750.00
Papa TAA, excellent—$1,000.00
Papa TAA, Thailand, very good—$2,000.00
Papa TAA, Thailand, excellent—$2,500.00
Grandpa, very good—$2,500.00
Grandpa, excellent—$3,500.00

History: The Papa Nambu was the invention of Kijiro Nambu. He started
work on this pistol in 1897, and it was first put into production in 1902.
Collectors refer to this type as "The Grandpa Nambu," since it was the
first in the series. There seems to be a great deal of confusion between
the Grandpa Nambu and the Papa Nambu. There are several visible differences between the two types, the most striking of which is the size
of the trigger guard. The small trigger guard belongs to the Grandpa
Nambu, the larger trigger guard belongs to the Papa Nambu and as for

the trigger, if it has a rounded edge, it belongs to the Grandpa Nambu, the squared edge is the Papa Nambu. Looking at the cocking knob, the convex was the Grandpa Nambu, and a concave knob was the Papa Nambu. A swivel lanyard loop was used on the Papa Nambu, whereas a fixed lanyard loop was used on the Grandpa Nambu. The Grandpa Nambu used a wooden magazine base, and the Papa Nambu used an aluminum magazine base. All of the Grandpa Nambu's were slotted for shoulder stocks. Very few of the Papa Nambus were, and they are very collectible. The Grandpa Nambu was introduced from 1903 to 1906 (# 1–2450). From 1906 until 1923 Tokyo Artillery Arsenal produced the Papa Nambus and from 1909 to 1928 they were produced by Tokyo Gas & Electric. The grips were of checkered walnut.

Mechanical Functioning: The Papa Nambu is a short recoil-operated, locked breech, semiautomatic pistol that is striker-fired. It has an eight-shot detachable box magazine that is inserted through the gripframe and retained by a catch located just to the rear of the trigger. There is a safety that blocks the trigger bar located on the front of the grip strap. Operation is single action.

Japanese Military Papa Nambu

J. Kimball Arms Co.
Detroit, Michigan

Model: Standard

Action Type: semiautomatic, delayed blowback.

Caliber(s): .30 M1 Carbine; .22 Hornet; .38 Special.

Barrel Lengths: 3″, 5″.

Finish: blue.

Manufacturing Dates: 1955 to 1958.

Stocks: black checkered plastic.

Rifling: 8R.

Weight, Unloaded: 1133 g. Standard; 822 g.

Sights: fixed on Standard, adjustable Micro sights on Target model.

Serial Number: 001 to about 238.

Serial Number Location: right side of frame under barrel.

Major Variations: Combat (Air Crewman)—fixed sights, 3½″ barrel.
Target—Micro sights, 5″ barrel.
late .30 M1 Carbine pistols had grooved chambers.

Markings: on left frame: J. Kimball Arms Co., Detroit, Mich. U.S.A.;
on left slide: caliber designation.

Price(s):
Standard Model, very good—$600.00
Standard Model, excellent—$900.00
Target Model, very good—$650.00
Target Model, excellent—$950.00
Combat Model, very good—$550.00
Combat Model, excellent—$850.00
for .38 Special, add 40%
for .22 Hornet, add 100%
for grooved chamber, add 15%

History: John W. Kimball designed this pistol for possible military consumption. However, the gun developed a disconcerting habit of cracking the frame lugs and possibly letting the recoiling slide travel unretarded toward the shooter. Grooving the chamber to provide greater friction on the cartridge case failed to help, and with only about 200 pistols marketed, the company went out of business in 1958.

Mechanical Functioning: Delayed blowback with unlocked breech, balance of mechanism and design similar to high Standard Model B. Retardation was accomplished by allowing the barrel to move slightly to the rear, until halted by a barrel recoil spring. Later production attempted to increase the delay by holding the cartridge with grooves inside the chamber.

Kimball Standard Model

Kimball Combat Model

Kimball Target Model

Korriphila GMBH
Ulm/Donau, Germany

Model: TP-70

Action Type: semiautomatic, blowback operated.

Caliber(s): .25 A.C.P.

Barrel Lengths: 2⅝".

Finish: blue.

Manufacturing Dates: 1970–1976.

Stocks: wood.

Rifling: 6L.

Weight, Unloaded: 12⅜ oz.

Sights: fixed.

Serial Numbers: n/a. but approved to start at 1 with suffix EBY. Serial ran to several thousand.

Serial Number Location: left side of frame.

Major Variations: half scale miniature TP-70 available with matching number.

Markings: left side of slide: Korriphila TP-70 Cal. 6.35mm Made in Germany.

Price(s):
    TP-70 .25, very good—$400.00
    TP-70 .25, excellent—$600.00
    TP-70 miniature, very good—$1,200.00
    TP-70 miniature, excellent—$1,800.00
    TP-70 matched set, very good—$1,800.00
    TP-70 matched set, excellent—$2,500.00

History: Korriphila was another excellent copy of the Walther PP design, only greatly reduced in size. It was a rare .25 A.C.P. pistol for it not only encompassed a double-action, exposed-hammer mechanism, but also had a magazine safety, a thumb safety that operated as the Walther and lowered the hammer safely besides blocking the firing pin, and a slide stop that held open the slide after the last shot. It was first developed around 1970 but was produced only in very limited numbers, apparently first in Heidelberg, Germany, then moving toward the end to Ulm/Donau, Germany. An intriguing feature of the Korriphila is that about 100 were available with a precision of miniature matching serial numbers in one-half scale. Toward the end of production, the HSP-70 was developed and marketed in very limited quantity. Rather than being a miniature of the Walther, this one was expanded in size to handle the 9mm Parabellum, and the action was changed to be recoil operated rather than blowback. Unfortunately for Korriphila the primary market for small handguns was closed to them because of the Gun Control Act of 1968, so in the early 1970s, they negotiated a contract with Norton Armaments Corporation of Mt. Clemens, Michigan, to manufacture the TP-70 in the United States under license. They did so under the trade name "Budischowski."

Mechanical Functioning: The Korriphila TP-70 is a straight blowback-operated, semiautomatic pistol, which is double action with an external hammer. It has a six-shot detachable box magazine inserted through the gripframe as well as a magazine safety preventing firing after the magazine is withdrawn. It has a manually operated thumb safety on the left-hand top of the slide that is reminiscent of the Walther design, and it locks the floating firing pin to prevent the hammer from striking it. The hammer itself also has a half-cock notch, and like the Walther, the hammer can be safely lowered by engaging the manual safety that trips the sear and drops the hammer down onto a steel bar. Takedown is accomplished by first removing the magazine and making sure the chamber is empty. Then engage the manual safety. Retract the slide until the small notch cut into it on the right side just forward of the ejection port aligns with the takedown lever and holds the slide in place. Rotate the takedown lever from back to front and move the slide forward and off the frame. The recoil spring assembly can be lifted off the barrel, and then the barrel dropped out of the slide. Assembly is in reverse order.

Korriphila TP-70

L.E.S., Inc.
Morton Grove, IL

Model: Rogak P-18

Action Type: double action semiautomatic, blowback.

Caliber(s): 9mm Parabellum.

Barrel Lengths: 5½".

Finish: stainless, matte or polished.

Manufacturing Dates: 1979.

Stocks: plastic.

Rifling: polygonal.

Weight, Unloaded: 36 oz.

Sights: fixed.

Serial Numbers: possibly starting at 2000.

Serial Number Location: left frame above trigger guard.

Major Variations: matte and polished frames.
.30 Luger or .45 A.C.P. announced by the factory.
double action or single action.

Markings: right side of slide: Rogak, Inc. Morton Grove, Ill.
left side of slide: L.E.S. P-18 9mm Para.

Price(s):
Standard matte, 9mm, very good—$250.00
Standard matte, 9mm, excellent—$345.00
Deluxe polished, 9mm, very good—$300.00
Deluxe polished, 9mm, excellent—$400.00

History: When this pistol was announced in 1978, the maker meant to capture the market with an oversize magazine capacity. Unfortunately, while L.E.S. was first with the most, production delays let the rest of the industry catch up, and today there is a plethora of large capacity 9mms on the market. Perhaps there is a lesson to be learned from the L.E.S. experience. In 1978 there was a tremendous publicity splash for this pistol, with its picture on the cover of several magazines. However, there was a long delay between the announcement and the gun writers testing the gun before the factory was ready to deliver in quantity to the dealers. Naturally this led to a great deal of loud comment from prospective purchasers. Add to this the normal gremlins that sneak into the production tooling process leading to the manufacture of some lemons before the complete process is resolved. What happens now is that the factory is under pressure to ship before they're really ready and some of the dogs get out. Of course they turn around and bite their creator in the form of vociferous complaints from customers. The moral of the story? If you're going to manufacture guns, don't tell anybody until you're ready to ship fully tested production pieces. Sadly, the L.E.S. story is not unique, and many fine guns and the firms that made them have suffered through this process. The P-18 is not a small gun, and it takes a good size hand to hold it comfortably. With the clip loaded, the P-18 weighs about 46 oz. There was a great deal of complaint with the early pistols about jamming. However, much of it could be traced to weak loads. This pistol, like some target .22s, lacks an extractor and relies on a swift blowback to be able to eject the case.

Mechanical Functioning: The L.E.S. Rogak P-18 is a blowback-operated, semiautomatic pistol that utilizes gas ports to retard the rapid recoil of the slide and a nylon buffer to take the shock. The direction the gas is vented is also said to help the buffer by providing an air cushion. The P-18 is double action with an external hammer and a slide-mounted safety that functions to block the hammer. There is no extractor on this pistol; rather with hot loads the gasses will hold the case against the breechblock on recoil, and then the ejector can kick the case out (as long as it is moving rearward rapidly!). The gun was offered in both single-action and double-action styles. It has an exposed hammer and a detachable box magazine that holds eighteen shots in a staggered row. It is inserted through the gripframe and retained by a spring-loaded catch located on the bottom of the butt. The safety is located on the slide and blocks the hammer.

Langenhan Gewehre v. Fahrradfabrik
Zella-Mehlis, Germany

Model: F.L. Model I

Action Type: semiautomatic, blowback operated.

Caliber(s): 7.65mm.

Barrel Lengths: 4³/₁₆″.

Finish: blue.

Manufacturing Dates: 1915–1918.

Stocks: checkered wood or hard rubber.

Rifling: 4R.

Weight, Unloaded: 20 oz.

Sights: fixed.

Serial Numbers: may have started at 1 to about 65,000.

Serial Number Location: right side of frame behind trigger.

Major Variations: early models had ejection port, later models did not. Prototypes had concealed trigger bar.

Markings: left side of barrel: D.R.P. Angem. F.L. Selbstlader Cal. 7.65; or F.L. Selbstlader DRGM 625263.
later models had F.L. Selbstlader DRGM 633251 on the left side of the slide.

Price(s):
early with ejector port, very good—$150.00
early with ejector port, excellent—$250.00
early with ejector port, and concealed trigger bar, very good—$200.00
early with ejector port, and concealed trigger bar, excellent—$300.00
late, no ejector port, very good—$150.00
late, no ejector port, excellent—$250.00

History: In 1915, Fritz Langenhan of Zella-Mehlis, Germany, began manufacturing a 7.65mm automatic pistol based on his original design. It had no markings other than the first marking described above, and thus early on the pistol was known as the F.L. During World War I, Germany, having a dire need for weapons, saw the 7.65mm Langenhan as if not an ideal handgun for the military, at least one that seemed to work, and virtually the entire production of almost 65,000 pistols was taken by the German Army. It is quite rare to find a Langenhan 7.65mm without Military Acceptance marks. The very early production had serrated wood grips and no ejector port. Some of them also had a concealed trigger bar. After the first thousand or two thousand models were made, the grips were changed to hard rubber type and the trigger bar was exposed as on the Walther pistols of the day. Production seems to have lasted throughout the war, but not afterward. During the 1920s, Langenhan reduced the design in size and called it the "Model II" in 6.35mm caliber. Thereafter, the 7.65mm F.L. became known to collectors as the "Model I," even though the factory never designated it as such.

Mechanical Functioning: The F.L. Selbstlader Model I is a straight blowback-operated, semiautomatic pistol with a detachable eight-shot box magazine. This design uses a concealed hammer with the firing pin located in a detached breechblock, which sits in the slide. Takedown is accomplished by loosening a screw at the rear of the slide and pushing the side stirrup located on the upper left-hand side of the slide upward. The entire assembly of slide and breechblock can slide off the weapon at this point. Unfortunately, this design is inherently dangerous because the retaining screw at any point could loosen or strip out its threads and if this does happen, then the breechblock would not be retained by anything solid and would blow out the rear end of the weapon on firing. Should you be using one of these pistols, always be sure that the retaining screw is tight.

Langenhan F.L. Model I

Le Francis Manufacture Francais D'Armes et Cycles Manufrance
Cedex, France

Model: Model 28 "Armee"

Action Type: semiautomatic, blowback operated.

Caliber(s): 9mm French Long.

Barrel Lengths: 5".

Finish: blue.

Manufacturing Dates: 1928–1938.

Stocks: wood.

Rifling: 6R.

Weight, Unloaded: 35 oz.

Sights: fixed.

Serial Numbers: seem to cover the 6000 to 8000 range although about 4000 were produced.

Serial Number Location: side of barrel lug.

Major Variations: none.

Markings: left side of slide: Manufacture Francais D'Armes et Cycles, St. Etienne, Cedex, France.

Price(s):
very good—$1,000.00
excellent—$1,250.00

History: The Le Francis Armee was initially developed to try and interest the French Army in purchasing it as their military pistol. Unfortunately, the French seemed to have made up their mind to adopt the Petter pistol after a long series of tests, and thus, the Le Francis Armee was made only from 1928 until 1938 with only around 4,000 pistols being produced. The design of the pistol is almost identical to the little .25 automatic pistols that Le Francis produced, the only exception being that of size. There is sometimes confusion about the name of the manufacturer. Le Francis is the trade name for Manufacture Francais D'Armes et Cycles; however, the name was also changed to the acronym "Manufrance," by which name it is currently known.

Mechanical Functioning: The Le Francis Model Armee is a straight blowback-operated, semiautomatic pistol utilizing a detachable box magazine that holds eight rounds. The mechanism is unusual in several respects. To load the pistol, you have to first remove the magazine, and load the magazine in the normal manner, and before reinserting the magazine, allow the barrel to pop open via the catch on the right side of the frame. That catch is spring loaded, and that spring is tensioned by the inserted magazine. It will generally pop open when the magazine is removed. When the barrel is open, a cartridge must be placed within it, the filled magazine replaced in the gun, and then the barrel snapped downward and locked with the catch. It is virtually impossible to draw the slide back by hand because of the enormous pressure of the recoil spring, and the mechanical advantage of the two pivoted arms that reach up from the spring and into the slide. The trigger action of this pistol is double action only, that is, even on firing, when the slide reciprocates, ejects the empty case and loads the new round, the striker is not cocked. Rather, on pulling the trigger, the trigger cocks the striker as it moves in its rearward journey, until hitting the stop and releasing the sear allowing the striker to jump forward and ignite the cartridge. In case of malfunction, the trigger bar can only contact the striker when the breech is closed.

Le Francis Model 28 "Armee"

Le Francis Manufacture Francais D'Armes et Cycles Manufrance
Cedex, France

Model: Pocket

Action Type: semiautomatic, blowback operated.

Caliber(s): 6.35mm, 7.65mm.

Barrel Lengths: 2½", 3½".

Finish: blue.

Manufacturing Dates: 1914–1960s.

Stocks: hard rubber.

Rifling: 6R.

Weight, Unloaded: 10½ oz.

Sights: fixed.

Serial Numbers: possibly 1 to about 275,000.

Serial Number Location: bottom right side of barrel at the rear.

Major Variations: Pocket model.
  Policeman model.
  Staff Officer's model.
  Champion model.

Markings: left side of slide: "Le Francais" type Pocket cal 6.35 Brevete S.G.O.G.
  right side of slide: Manufacture Francais D'Armes et Cycles De Saint Etienne.

Prices(s):
  Pocket model, very good—$150.00
  Pocket model, excellent—$250.00
  Policeman model, very good—$175.00
  Policeman model, excellent—$300.00
  Staff Officer's model, very good—$700.00
  Staff Officer's model, excellent—$950.00
  Champion model, very good—$300.00
  Champion model, excellent—$375.00

History: The Le Francis Pocket model was first developed in about 1913 and first manufactured in 1914, and for many years it was the leading 6.35mm pistol in France. It was manufactured on into the early 1960s, and it had several major variations. It was the weapon of choice for general officers in the French army to carry because it was lightweight and because of its concealability. Because of its popularity with other ranks of officers, it became known in the French army as "The Staff Officer's Model," and these pistols were regularly issued as such. The models are identifiable by the name of the model stamped on the side of the slide. However, for quick identification, the Pocket model has a 2⅜" barrel as does the Staff Officer. The Policeman has a 3⅜″ barrel length, and the Champion, which was supposedly the target pistol of the series, had a 5⅞″ barrel. Also unusual about the Le Francis Champion is that it had an adjustable rear sight and a very long striker housing at the rear of the slide. It also came with a grip extension to provide a better and longer grip. It was attached to the frame after the regular magazine was inserted. The Champion was only made for a couple of years around 1930. All of the Le Francis models were available with engraving. They are desirable finds for collectors and should double to triple the price the gun would ordinarily bring.

Mechanical Functioning: The Le Francis Model Pocket is a straight blowback-operated, semiautomatic pistol utilizing a detachable box magazine that holds eight rounds. The mechanism is unusual in several respects. To load the pistol, you have to first remove the magazine, and load the magazine in the normal manner, and before reinserting the magazine, allow the barrel to pop open via the catch on the right side of the frame. That catch is spring loaded, and that spring is tensioned by the inserted magazine. It will generally pop open when the magazine is removed. When the barrel is open, a cartridge must be placed within it, the filled magazine replaced in the gun, and then the barrel snapped downward and locked with the catch. It is virtually impossible to draw the slide back by hand because of the enormous pressure of the recoil spring and the mechanical advantage of the two pivoted arms, which reach up from the spring and into the slide. The trigger action of this pistol is double action only, that is, even upon firing, when the slide reciprocates, ejects the empty case, and loads the new round, the striker is not cocked. Rather, on pulling the trigger, the trigger cocks the striker as it moves in its rearward journey, until hitting the stop and releasing the sear, allowing the striker to jump forward and ignite the cartridge. In case of malfunction, the trigger bar can only contact the striker when the breech is closed.

Le Francis Pocket Model

Manufacture D'Armes LePage, S.A.
Liege, Belgium

Model: LePage Auto Pistol

Action Type: semiautomatic, blowback operated.

Caliber(s): 7.65mm, 9mm K, 9mm Browning Long.

Barrel Lengths: 3¾".

Finish: blue.

Manufacturing Dates: 1925.

Stocks: hard rubber.

Rifling: 6L.

Weight, Unloaded: 23½ oz.

Sights: fixed.

Serial Numbers: n/a.

Serial Number Location: left side of frame.

Major Variations: various calibers.

Markings: left side of slide: Manufacture D'Armes LePage, Liege, Belgique.

Price(s):
```
7.65mm, very good—$200.00
7.65mm, excellent—$300.00
7.65mm, very good—$300.00
7.65mm, excellent—$425.00
9mm K, very good—$325.00
9mm K, excellent—$450.00
9mm Browning Long, very good—$450.00
9mm Browning Long, excellent—$650.00
9mm Browning Long with detachable shoulder stock, very good—$700.00
9mm Browning Long with detachable shoulder stock, excellent—$975.00
```

History: Manufacture D'Armes LePage, S.A. of Liege, Belgium, was first established in 1790 and for a century and a half was producing fine firearms. In about 1925 it decided to get into the automatic pistol market. They marketed several different kinds of pistols: a .25 caliber pistol based on the Browning 1906 design; a .32 A.C.P.; a .380 A.C.P.; and a 9mm Browning Long pistol based on their own unique design. It is also rumored that they produced a .25 A.C.P. of their own design. Their pocket pistols were all of the fixed-sight design, while the 9mm Browning Long obviously was something to try to interest the military with, as it had an adjustable rear sight and could also be provided with a detachable shoulder stock.

Mechanical Functioning: The LePage is a straight blowback-operated, semi-automatic pistol with external hammer and detachable box magazine holding six shots in .25 A.C.P., eight shots in .32 A.C.P., eight shots in

.380 A.C.P., and twelve shots in 9mm Browning Long. It has an external hammer and a recoil spring mounted underneath the barrel. Disassembly is accomplished by making sure the pistol is unloaded, removing the magazine, cocking the hammer, applying the thumb safety, and withdrawing the slide to a point where the safety can be pulled out. The rear gripframe section containing the hammer can now be tilted back. The slide is pulled further back and the rear end raised to disengage it from the rails and then slide forward off the barrel. Assembly is in reverse order. There are three safeties on this pistol: the manual thumb safety blocking the sear, an automatic magazine safety to prevent firing when the magazine is removed, and a half-cock notch on the hammer. The gripframe is scalloped to provide a firm handhold and to prevent the fingers from slipping on the front gripstrap.

LePage Automatic Pistol

Akt. Ges. Lignose
(Bergman)
Berlin, Germany

Model: 2 and 2A

Action Type: semiautomatic, blowback.

Caliber(s): 6.35mm.

Barrel Lengths: 2⅛″.

Finish: blue.

Manufacturing Dates: about 1922 to the early 1930s.

Stocks: hard rubber or wood.

Rifling: 6R.

Weight, Unloaded: 13¼ oz.

Sights: fixed.

Serial Numbers: n/a.

Serial Number Location: right side of slide.

Major Variations: steel or brass cocking lever.
    wood or hard rubber grips.
    extended nine-shot magazine—solid trigger guard.

Price(s):
    Model 2, hard rubber grips, very good—$225.00
    Model 2, hard rubber grips, excellent—$300.00
    Model 2, wood grips, very good—$250.00
    Model 2, wood grips, excellent—$350.00
    Model 2A, hard rubber grips, steel cocking lever, very good—$200.00
    Model 2A, hard rubber grips, steel cocking lever, excellent—$275.00
    Model 2A, hard rubber grips, brass cocking lever, very good—$225.00
    Model 2A, hard rubber grips, brass cocking lever, excellent—$300.00
    Model 2A, wood grips, steel cocking lever, very good—$225.00
    Model 2A, wood grips, steel cocking lever, excellent—$325.00
    Model 2A, wood grips, brass cocking lever, very good—$250.00
    Model 2A, wood grips, brass cocking lever, excellent—$375.00
    add 10% for extended magazine.

History: This gun started life as the invention of Witwold Chylewski of Austria in 1913. The first run of it was made by S.I.G. in Neuhausen, Switzerland, in 1919, and in 1920 it was purchased by Bergman for the "Einhand" feature. This pistol may also be found with either brass or blued steel cocking levers, hard rubber or wood grips, or with a solid trigger guard of standard design. The Einhand was the "A" variation, the frame size was the "Model 2." It was built on a small frame with a six-shot detachable box magazine as standard. It had a nine-shot clip that protruded from the bottom. This scarce, well-made pistol is still functional in today's world.

Mechanical Functioning: This is a straight blowback-operated, semiautomatic pistol with a concealed hammer. Otherwise it is very similar to the Browning 1906 designs. It operates also under the Chylewski patent and is an "Einhand" or one-hand-operated pistol. Cocking is performed by retracting the curved attachment that serves as the forward part of the trigger guard. It rides on a groove cut into the frame below the slide and engages a cut in the slide. It retracts by pressure of the slide.

Lignose 2A

Akt. Ges. Lignose
(Bergman)
Berlin, Germany

Model: 3A

Action Type: semiautomatic, blowback.

Caliber(s): 6.35mm.

Barrel Lengths: 2⅛".

Finish: blue.

Manufacturing Dates: about 1922 to the early 1930s.

Stocks: hard rubber or wood.

Rifling: 6R.

Weight, Unloaded: 15 oz.

Sights: fixed.

Serial Numbers: n/a.

Serial Number Location: right side of slide.

Major Variations: steel or brass cocking lever.
wood or hard rubber grips.

Price(s):
Model 3A, hard rubber grips, steel cocking lever, very good—$200.00
Model 3A, hard rubber grips, steel cocking lever, excellent—$300.00
Model 3A, hard rubber grips, brass cocking lever, very good—$200.00
Model 3A, hard rubber grips, brass cocking lever, excellent—$325.00
Model 3A, wood grips, steel cocking lever, very good—$200.00
Model 3A, wood grips, steel cocking lever, excellent—$325.00
Model 3A, wood grips, brass cocking lever, very good—$225.00
Model 3A, wood grips, brass cocking lever, excellent—$350.00

History: This gun started life as the invention of Witwold Chylewski of Austria. The first run of it was made by S.I.G. in Neuhausen, Switzerland, in
1919, and in 1920 it was purchased by Bergman for the "Einhand" feature. This pistol may also be found with either brass or blued steel
cocking levers, hard rubber or wood grips, or with a solid trigger guard
of standard design. The Einhand was the "A" variation, the frame size
was the "Model 2." It was built on a long frame for the extended clip
magazine as standard. It had a nine-shot detachable box magazine. This
scarce, well-made pistol is still functional in today's world.

Mechanical Functioning: This is a straight blowback-operated, semiautomatic pistol with a concealed hammer. Otherwise it is very similar to
the Browning 1906 designs. It operates also under the Chylewski patent
and is an "Einhand" or one-hand-operated pistol. Cocking is performed
by retracting the curved attachment that serves as the forward part of the

trigger guard. It rides on a groove cut into the frame below the slide and engages a cut in the slide. It retracts by pressure of the slide.

Lignose 3A

Llama Gabilondo y Cia, SA
Vitoria, Spain

Model: Omni

Action Type: semiautomatic, recoil operated.

Caliber(s): 9mm Parabellum, .45 A.C.P.

Barrel Lengths: 4¼".

Finish: blue.

Manufacturing Dates: 1982–1986.

Stocks: black plastic.

Rifling: 6R, buttress style.

Weight, Unloaded: 40 oz.

Sights: fixed in 9mm, adjustable in .45.

Serial Numbers: production began at PA00028.

Serial Number Location: bottom of trigger guard.

Major Variations: none.

Markings: left side of slide: Llama Omni.

Price(s):
   9mm Parabellum—$375.00
   .45 A.C.P.—$350.00

History: This is a creation of the craftsmen at Gabilondo. They have achieved a good reputation through the years with the Colt-Browning-style pistols, and they now have entered the field of ultramodern combat handguns with the Omni. There are several interesting features. One is the redesigned rifling pattern that they call "Buttress Rifling." It differs from standard in that the trailing edge of the land is tapered at a shallow angle to the groove. This is said to reduce friction, thereby increasing velocity and in rapid fire possibly reducing bore temperature and friction. An additional side effect is the reduction of bullet deformation with one sharp cut followed by a gentle slope on the bullet's engraving. As with virtually all of the new crop of heavy-caliber autos to hit the market in recent years, the Omni has a recurved forward portion of the trigger guard for a nonslip two-handed hold for combat shooting. It also comes in both .45 A.C.P. and 9mm Parabellum, and is double action. If you're wondering why all of the major pistol makers have suddenly come out with such an interesting array of combat pistols, most of them chambered for both the .45 and the 9mm, it has to do with the Pentagon ruminating about switching from the seventy-year-old Colt M1911–style pistol. Contracts like that make gunmakers see more dollar signs than the normal civilian market can generate, and they all seem to feel that the possibility of adoption could be worth all of the expense to come up with a design for a good pistol. Hence, the Omni is born.

Mechanical Functioning: The Llama Omni is a double-action, recoil-operated, semiautomatic pistol with an external hammer and either fully adjustable sights, or a drift adjuster rear. It has a detachable box magazine with thirteen rounds in a dual column in 9mm Parabellum caliber and seven shots in .45 A.C.P. The magazine is inserted through the gripframe and retained by a spring-loaded catch located on the left side of the frame. The gripframe and leading edge of the trigger guard are grooved to provide a good two-hand combat hold. For ease of cocking, the hammer plunger is surrounded by ball bearings to reduce friction as the piece moves vertically. At the same time this feature helps to reduce the amount of force that it takes the recoiling slide to cock the hammer, or for that matter the amount of strength it takes to pull the slide back if the hammer is not cocked. There are two sear bars located on either side of the trigger and hammer. One is for double-action cocking, and the other is for single-action letoff. The firing pin is of two-piece construction with the philosophy that if a firing pin can break then pre-break it and design it to work with a ball joint. That way you can guarantee it won't break again. There are two automatic safeties and a manual safety.

Llama Omni

Luger

Model: "VOPO"

Action Type: semiautomatic, toggle link action.

Caliber(s): 9mm Luger, 7.65mm.

Barrel Lengths: generally 4".

Finish: blue.

Manufacturing Dates: postwar to about 1971.

Stocks: plastic.

Rifling: 6R.

Weight, Unloaded: 29½ oz., 4½" barrel.

Sights: fixed.

Serial Numbers: various—throughout the Luger range.

Serial Number Location: right side above trigger.

Major Variations: various models reworked to conform to standard P.08 dimensions.

Markings: East German Military proofs or Russian proof.
reddish brown plastic grips with concentric circles as a trademark.

Price(s):
very good—$375.00
excellent—$600.00

History: After World War II, there were great stocks of surplus and captured arms in Europe, many of them in Communist hands. Being frugal and needing weapons, they undertook the job of refurbishing old guns to their standards. We have come to know these reworks as VOPOs, an acronym for People's Police. Since they have been altered and refinished, the VOPOs are not well received by collectors . . . yet. They can still be had at a reasonable price, and although they are not "original," they do represent a true category of Luger.

Mechanical Functioning: The Luger is a recoil-operated, striker-fired, semiautomatic pistol with a detachable, eight-shot box magazine. The lock at battery is provided by a toggle link which is not broken until the barrel-breechblock assembly recoils rearward with the toggle striking a camming surface and unlocking the assembly. The mainspring is of the coil type. There is a magazine disconnector and a thumb-operated safety on the left side of the rear of the frame. The Model 1908 also features an anti-bounce lock on the right toggle to snap it down and prevent the toggle from unlocking. Another feature of the 1908 is the grip safety, which prevents firing unless it is depressed. On pistols made after 1914, a rising block was incorporated behind the magazine to act as a hold-open device. After 1913 a stock lug was added to the rear of the gripframe.

VOPO Luger

Magnum Research, Inc. (M.R.I.)
Minneapolis, MN 55418

Model: Desert Eagle

Action Type: semiautomatic, gas operated.

Caliber(s): .357 Magnum, .38 Special + P.

Barrel Lengths: 6" (standard), 8", 10", 14".

Finish: blue.

Manufacturing Dates: 1985 to date.

Stocks: black plastic.

Rifling: 6R.

Weight, Unloaded: steel frame: 60 oz.
aluminum frame: 52 oz.

Sights: combat blade rear, blade front, barrel grooved for scope mount.

Serial Numbers: start at 01.

Serial Number Location: right side of frame above grip.

Major Variations: there are several preproduction variations, major differences being in slide grooving, hammer design, sights, and locking system.

Markings: left side of slide: Eagle—.357 Magnum Pistol—I.M.I. Israel.
right side of frame: Magnum Research, Inc., Minneapolis, Minn.
Early prototypes had "Imported by Magnum Research, Inc., Minneapolis, Minnesota" on bottom of frame forward of trigger guard.

Price(s):
Desert Eagle, very good—$500.00
Desert Eagle, excellent—$950.00

History: The Eagle was developed and manufactured by Israeli Military Industries for the American market. This pistol was designed for hunting, target shooting, and law enforcement. It will be available with various options: replaceable sights, either fixed blade or adjustable rear; replaceable triggers, fixed one-stage, two-stage, or adjustable two-stage pull. It is advertised to use all .357 Magnum ammunition, as well as .38 Special + P loads. Collectors will want to watch for the several different styles of prototypes that have been made, for they will one day become very collectible. Some notable features are both wide and narrow slide serrations, and different types of locking bolts with either three or six lugs. Like most combat pistols, the Eagle has a recurved trigger guard for a two-handed hold, combat-style shooting. Various barrel lengths are available, ranging from the standard 6 inches up to 14 inches. A .44 Magnum kit will be offered after this pistol is in full production, and its clip will hold eight shots.

Mechanical Functioning: The Magnum Research Eagle pistol from Israel Military Industries is a semiautomatic gas-operated pistol with a rotary locking bolt and an external hammer. Prototype bolts have either six or three locking lugs. The detachable box magazine holds ten shots of .357 Magnum, and is retained by a spring-loaded catch located on the left side of the frame just to the rear of the trigger guard. Fixed sights are standard, but a whole range of combat and target sights are available. The standard trigger style is a fixed single stage, but optional fixed two stage or adjustable two stage triggers are available. The safety is located on the rear of the slide and is ambidextrous. It locks the floating firing pin and at the same time disconnects the trigger. There are two frame styles available, either steel or lightweight aluminum alloy. The center of gravity is just forward of the trigger for quick recovery during rapid fire. The factory advertising has claimed that this pistol can be taken down in 5 to 10 seconds, with assembly taking about 20 seconds. Field stripping is accomplished by depressing the magazine release, pressing the detent, rotating the barrel release forward, and pulling the bolt carrier rearward until it unlocks from the barrel. Pull the barrel assembly forward and off, slide bolt carrier forward and off. Assemble in reverse order.

M.R.I. Eagle

Mann-Werke AG
Suhl, Germany

Model: Pocket Pistol

Action Type: semiautomatic, blowback.

Caliber(s): 7.65mm, 9mm K

Barrel Lengths: 2³/₈″.

Finish: blue.

Manufacturing Dates: 1923 to about 1928.

Stocks: hard rubber.

Rifling: 4R.

Weight, Unloaded: 12⁵/₈ oz.

Sights: fixed.

Serial Numbers: observed in the 40,000 and 50,000 range.

Serial Number Location: right side of frame.

Major Variations: none.

Markings: left side of slide: Cal 7.65 Mann-Werke A.G. Suhl, Mann's patent.
on both grips at top: Mann

Price(s):
    7.65mm, very good—$150.00
    7.65mm, excellent—$275.00
    9mm K, very good—$300.00
    9mm K, excellent—$375.00

History: This pistol was developed by Fritz Mann in the early 1920s, and
appears to supersede his Vest Pocket 6.35mm pistol. The original name of
his firm when it started in late 1919 was Fritz Mann Werkzeug Fabrik, and
sometime around 1923 the name was changed to Mann Werke. The firm
appears to have gone out of business by 1928. Mann is typical of the gunmakers in post–World War I Germany. After the war there was such chaos
in Germany that most everyone felt the need to pack iron to defend themselves. It was a nation almost in anarchy, with the political parties all
vying to "control the streets," and what they didn't move in on the criminals did. In this atmosphere anyone who could assemble guns that worked
and could be priced in an affordable range was almost assured of success.
This gold rush lasted throughout the early 1920s. It has been said by several authorities that Mann developed a bottlenecked 6.35mm cartridge for
use in this pistol, and that it yielded improved ballistic performance over
the normal 6.35mm. However, this author has not seen this model with a
6.35mm barrel, nor heard of anybody having one. Should any still exist, it
would be an excellent find for a collector! Mann's first pistol, which was
produced only in 6.35mm, was of very unique design utilizing a solid
frame and a reciprocating bolt. The pistol, although flat, was quite awkward. Mann had intended to enlarge this model and sell it in 7.65mm

caliber, but somewhere along the way he saw the light and instead produced the Pocket Model. And in this pistol he created a very fine little weapon for self-defense. Although only slightly bulkier than a normal-sized 6.35mm pistol, it packs a much better wallop. It is somewhat based on the Browning designs, and as such presented a pistol with more eye appeal than his earlier model.

Mechanical Functioning: The Mann Pocket Pistol is a straight blowback, striker-fired, semiautomatic pistol and is loosely based on the Browning system. The magazine is of the detachable box type and holds five rounds in both the 7.65mm and the 9mm K calibers. The clip is inserted through the gripframe and is retained by a spring-loaded catch located on the bottom of the butt. The safety is located on the left side of the frame and inhibits the sear. The trigger pivots on a cross pin and uses the Browning style link to the sear. The recoil spring is mounted Browning style axially on the barrel. Field stripping can be accomplished without tools by first making sure that the pistol is unloaded and then removing the magazine, then pulling back on the slide until the barrel can be grasped and rotated. The slide is under spring tension and must be firmly held throughout this procedure. The barrel is unscrewed from the frame and withdrawn. The slide assembly can now be slid off the frame and the recoil spring, firing pin, striker spring, and striker spring guide removed. Assembly is in the reverse order.

Mann Pocket Pistol

Mauser
Oberndorf am Neckar, Germany

Model: 1896 "Broomhandle" Pistol

Action Type: semiautomatic, recoil operated.

Caliber(s): 7.63 Mauser and 9mm Parabellum.

Barrel Lengths: 4"–5½".

Finish: blue.

Manufacturing Dates: 1896–1939.

Stocks: walnut or hard rubber.

Rifling: 4R on early models.
6R on later models and military pistols.

Weight, Unloaded: nominal 45 oz.

Sights: adjustable.

Serial Numbers: started from 1, but in commercial production up to about 1903, Mauser "skipped" blocks of as much as 5,000 numbers, but sometimes went back and filled them. Also various military and police contracts had their own number blocks starting at 1.

Serial Number Location: on left barrel extension flat over chamber.

Major Variations: side milling on frame.
barrel length.
magazine type and size.
hammer and minor mechanical details.
style of gripframe: Broomhandle or Bolo.

Markings: top of barrel over chamber. Waffenfabrik Mauser or Mauser Werke.
side of frame: various military or police contract stamps.

Price(s):
M1896, 7.63 Mauser, 10 shot, Conehammer, very good—$1,100.00; excellent—$1,950.00
M1896, 7.63 Mauser, 10 shot, with Loading Lever, very good—$950.00; excellent—$1,650.00
M1896, 7.63 Mauser, Conehammer, with shoulder stock, very good—$1,650.00; excellent—$2,500.00
M1896, 7.63 Mauser, with loading lever, with shoulder stock, very good—$1,250.00; excellent—$2,000.00
M1896, 7.63 Mauser, with loading lever, transitional, very good—$950.00; excellent—$1,550.00
M1896, 7.63 Mauser, slabside, very good—$800.00; excellent—$1,250.00
M1896, 7.63 Mauser, early, small ring, very good—$800.00; excellent—$1,250.00
M1896, 7.63 Mauser, Italian, slabside, very good—$1,300.00; excellent—$1,850.00
M1896, 7.63 Mauser, Shallow Mill, with loading lever, very good—$975.00; excellent—$1,600.00

M1896, 7.63 Mauser, Turkish, Conehammer, very good—$1,700.00; excellent—$2,500.00

M1912, .45 A.C.P., clip fed, very good—$4,250.00; excellent—$5,500.00

M1921, .45 A.C.P., clip fed, very good—$2,250.00; excellent—$3,250.00

M1921, 9mm Luger, clip fed, very good—$3,400.00; excellent—$4,500.00

M1896, 7.63 Mauser, prewar, commercial, very good—$700.00; excellent—$1,100.00

M1896, 7.63 Mauser, Bolo, postwar, very good—$900.00; excellent—$1,450.00

M1896, 7.63 Mauser, Persian, very good—$1,500.00; excellent—$2,350.00

M1896, 7.63 Mauser, World War I, Military, very good—$600.00; excellent—$1,000.00

M1896, 9mm Luger, World War I, Military, very good—$650.00; excellent—$1,100.00

M1906/08, 7.65 Mauser, clip fed, very good—$2,550.00; excellent—$3,500.00

History: The C-96 or the Model 1896, Broomhandle, or Bolo, as it and its various models are generally known in the U.S., was first developed in 1895. The first production models were produced in 1896, but full production was not reached until 1897 and sales did not pick up until about 1899. During this time, the early "conehammer" mechanism was used. A large ring hammer was used from 1899 to 1902, and in 1902 the mechanism was altered. The safety swung up and locked the hammer with a projection. Before that time, the safety pivoted down. At this time, the firing pin–retaining plate was eliminated. About 1904 the small hammer was adopted, and around this time the 9mm was first made. It is estimated that as many as 1,200,000 C-96s and its variants have been made.

Mechanical Functioning: The C-96 is a recoil-operated, semiautomatic pistol utilizing both the detachable box-type magazine of various sizes and models with charger-loaded, fixed-magazine wells. These are located in front of the trigger guard. The hammer is external and is of various styles, as is the safety and its functioning. Slotting for shoulder stock was standard, and models after 1930 could be had with the "Schnellfever," or full auto selector.

Mauser 1896 Conehammer Broomhandle

Mauser
Oberndorf am Neckar, Germany

Model: HSc

Action Type: semiautomatic, blowback operated.

Caliber(s): 7.65mm, 9mm K

Barrel Lengths: 3½".

Finish: blue or nickel.

Manufacturing Dates: 1940–1945, 1968–1979.

Stocks: wood or plastic.

Rifling: 6R.

Weight, Unloaded: 23½ oz.

Sights: fixed.

Serial Numbers: began at 700,001. In 1946 the French occupied the Mauser plant and produced about 16,000 pistols from about number 952,000 to number 967,000. 1968 production had 00 previx on .32 A.C.P., 01 prefix on .380 A.C.P.

Serial Number Location: bottom front gripstrap.

Major Variations: commercial, prewar, and postwar.
Nazi police and military.
early models had gripscrew near bottom of grip.

Markings: left side of slide, wartime: Mauserwerke AG, Oberndorf aN Mod. HSc Kal. 7.65mm.
post-war: Mauserwerke AG, Oberndorf aN Modell HSc Made in Germany.

Price(s):
HSc, 7.65mm, commercial, prewar, very good—$1,750.00
HSc, 7.65mm, commercial, prewar, excellent—$2,500.00
HSc, 7.65mm, commercial, prewar, Nazi proofed, very good—$350.00
HSc, 7.65mm, commercial, prewar, Nazi proofed, excellent—$450.00
HSc, 7.65mm, blue, postwar, very good—$300.00
HSc, 7.65mm, blue, postwar, excellent—$350.00
HSc, 7.65mm, nickel, postwar, very good—$275.00
HSc, 7.65mm, nickel, postwar, excellent—$375.00
HSc, 9mm K, blue, postwar, very good—$325.00
HSc, 9mm K, blue, postwar, excellent—$375.00
HSc, 9mm K, nickel, postwar, very good—$300.00
HSc, 9mm K, nickel, postwar, excellent—$400.00
HSc, 9mm K, blue, cased, 1 of 5,000, very good—$250.00
HSc, 9mm K, blue, cased, 1 of 5,000, excellent—$400.00
HSc, 7.65mm, French, very good—$275.00
HSc, 7.65mm, French, excellent—$325.00
HSc, 7.65mm, Navy, very good—$600.00
HSc, 7.65mm, Navy, excellent—$750.00

HSc, 7.65mm, NSDAP SA, very good—$495.00
HSc, 7.65mm, NSDAP SA, excellent—$695.00
HSc, 7.65mm, Police, very good—$375.00
HSc, 7.65mm, Police, excellent—$500.00
HSc, 7.65mm, Swiss, very good—$1,250.00
HSc, 7.65mm, Swiss, excellent—$1,500.00

History: Around 1937, to compete with Walther in the field of double-action pistols, Mauser started designing what they call a Hahn Selbstpann which means "self-cocking," designating their pistols using it as the "HS" series. Walther quite naturally tried to inhibit the development of the HS pistol by claiming it was infringement on their patents. However, Mauser persisted, and in late 1937 produced a few sample pistols designating them the HSa. After comments were received from testing agencies, the HSb was created and once again sent to various people in agencies for testing. Finally, in 1939, the HSc was perfected and put into production, with the first models coming off the line in 1940; from 1940 until 1945 when the pistol was discontinued, about a quarter-million had been made. Right after the war the French, who were always short of fine handguns and having captured the Mauser factory, put the HSc back in production, making approximately 16,000 to 20,000 pistols for their police use as well as for use in Indo-China. In 1968 Mauser reintroduced the pistol with minor internal changes but using the same exterior, and it remained in production until the late 1970s.

Mechanical Functioning: The Mauser HSc is a double-action, straight blowback, semiautomatic pistol with an eight-shot detachable box magazine in .32 caliber, and seven shots in .380 caliber, which is inserted through the gripframe and retained by a spring-loaded catch at the bottom rear of the butt. The pistol utilizes a floating firing pin and semishrouded hammer. There is no sidelock per se, but the magazine follower holds the slide open when the last shot has been fired. Removal of the magazine closes the slide.

Mauser HSc
Photo courtesy of Orvel L. Reichert

Mauser
Oberndorf am Neckar, Germany

Model: 1910, 1914, 1934

Action Type: semiautomatic, blowback operated.

Caliber(s): 6.35mm, 7.65mm.

Barrel Lengths: 3".

Finish: blue.

Manufacturing Dates: 1910 to 1939.

Stocks: hard rubber or wood or black plastic.

Rifling: 6R.

Weight, Unloaded: 15 oz.

Sights: fixed.

Serial Numbers: started at 1 and ran to about 400,000 and then was changed to 1910/1934 variation. Serials picked up and ran to about 430,000.

Serial Number Location: forward left side of slide.

Major Variations: 1910 standard style, sidelatch.
1910/1914 style, no sidelatch.
1910/1934 style, contoured grip.

Markings: left side of slide: Waffenfabrik Mauser A.G. Oberndorf aN, Mauser's Patent.
1910/1934: Mauser-Werke A.G. Oberndorf aN, Cal. 6.35-D.R.P. u. A.P.

Price(s):
Mauser Model 1910, 6.35mm, very good—$350.00
Mauser Model 1910, 6.35mm, excellent—$450.00
Mauser Model 1914, 6.35mm, very good—$375.00
Mauser Model 1914, 6.35mm, excellent—$475.00
Mauser Model 1934, 7.65mm, very good—$375.00
Mauser Model 1934, 7.65mm, excellent—$500.00

History: Since 1907, Mauser had been trying to develop a good pocket blow-back pistol and tried out several designs, but in 1909 they finally perfected the design that was issued in 1910 for a .25 automatic pocket pistol. The early issues of this pistol are identifiable because of a small latch on the left side of the frame by the sideplate, which was used to take the sideplate off; hence the name "sidelatch," which is attributed to the first production run of these pistols. In 1914 the pistol was redesigned with the sidelatch removed and the sideplate instead was drifted up and off the pistol. In 1934 the pistol was once again redesigned, this time having a rounded back grip, rather than the straight grip. The model was finally discontinued in 1939.

Mechanical Functioning: This extremely well machined pistol is almost an engineering work of art. It is a straight blowback, semiautomatic pistol that holds nine shots in a detachable box magazine inserted through the gripframe and retained by a spring-loaded catch at the base of the butt. It is striker-operated and has two safeties: a manual safety on the left side of the frame just to the rear of the trigger, which blocks the sear, and a magazine disconnect that prevents firing when the clip is withdrawn. The recoil spring is mounted below the barrel and is mounted axially around the barrel holder guide. The barrel is removable from the frame, but it is locked to the receiver by a lug at the chamber end as well as one at the forward end, through which a barrel holder and guide passes. A slidelock holds the slide open on the last shot and goes forward automatically when a new magazine is inserted, stripping the first shot into the chamber.

Mauser 1910 .25 A.C.P.

Mauser
Oberdorf am Neckar, Germany

Model: 1914, 1934.

Action Type: semiautomatic, blowback operated.

Caliber(s): 7.65mm

Barrel Lengths: 4¼", 3½".

Finish: blue.

Manufacturing Dates: 1914–1934.

Stocks: wood, hard rubber or plastic.

Rifling: 6R.

Weight, Unloaded: 21 oz.

Sights: fixed.

Serial Numbers: 1–3000 on "Humpback."
3001 to around 525,000 on 1914 type.
525,000 to about 625,000 on 1934 type.

Serial Number Location: forward on left side of slide.

Major Variations: 1914-style grip contour.
1934-style grip contour.
Humpback and Humpback transitions.
many subvariations for various contracts.

Markings: left side of slide: Mauser address.
left side of frame: Mauser trademark.
right side of slide: caliber.

Price(s):
Mauser M1914, Humpback, very good—$2,000.00
Mauser M1914, Humpback, excellent—$2,500.00
Mauser M1914, Transition Humpback, very good—$1,500.00
Mauser M1914, Transition Humpback, excellent—$2,000.00
Mauser M1914, late Humpback, very good—$1,250.00
Mauser M1914, late Humpback, excellent—$1,750.00
Mauser M1914, War Commercial, very good—$350.00
Mauser M1914, War Commercial, excellent—$475.00
Mauser M1934, Army, very good—$400.00
Mauser M1934, Army, excellent—$500.00
Mauser M1934, Navy, very good—$650.00
Mauser M1934, Navy, excellent—$950.00
Mauser M1934, very good—$350.00
Mauser M1934, excellent—$475.00

History: Developed for police and military sales, the Model 1914 proved to be a popular and reliable gun. All told, between 1914 and 1942, when it was superseded by the HSc of the 1914 and its variants, over 600,000 pistols were sold. There are four readily identifiable types of 1914. The first made was the Humpback, which had serials in the 1–3000 range, and appears to be primarily a prototype weapon. In that range from around 1000 to 3000 are transitional Humpbacks. From 3001 to around 525,000 (1914 through 1934) are considered Model 1914s. After around 525,000, the grip design changed and a magazine disconnect was added. This variation is the Model 1934.

Mechanical Functioning: This is a straight, blowback-operated, semiautomatic pistol with an eight-shot detachable box magazine. It is striker-actuated, and the safety pivots a lever up to engage and lock the striker. The barrel is exposed and held in place, fixed to the frame by a pin running through the two lugs and the corresponding slots. This pistol is single action and is of all-steel construction with one-piece wraparound grips.

Mauser Model 1914

Mauser
Oberndorf am Neckar, Germany

Model: WTP Model 1 (Westentaschen Pistole)

Action Type: semiautomatic, blowback operated.

Caliber(s): 6.35mm.

Barrel Lengths: 2½".

Finish: blue or nickel.

Manufacturing Dates: 1921–1937.

Stocks: black plastic or hard rubber.

Rifling: 6R.

Weight, Unloaded: 9½ oz.

Sights: fixed.

Serial Numbers: 1 to about 50,000.

Serial Number Locations: on left side of slide, generally to the front and above the flat.

Major Variations: up to about number 25,000 the one-piece grips had a single rear retaining screw. After that there were two screws, one in each side. A rare variant was with the mark T-6.35 on the slide.

Markings: on left side of slide: Waffenfabrik Mauser A.G. Oberndorf A.N. late models also had: WTP-6.35-D.R.P. ua P.

Price(s):
    T-6.35, very good—$550.00
    T-6.35, excellent—$650.00
    1 screw grips, very good—$425.00
    1 screw grips, excellent—$550.00
    2 screw grips, very good—$375.00
    2 screw grips, excellent—$500.00
    nickel, engraved, very good—$1,250.00
    nickel, engraved, excellent—$2,500.00

History: The WTP was introduced in 1921 to offer some competition to the profusion of Colts and Brownings and their imitators on the market. It was also designed to cash in on the Mauser name during the firearms maker's gold rush in the early 1920s in Germany. There was an extremely good market for small, concealable pocket handguns, and since Mauser's smallest gun at the time the WTP was introduced was almost twice the size of the WTP, it fit right into a niche in the Mauser line. During this pistol's life, Germany, the intended market for this gun, was in a deplorable state. There was a virtual state of anarchy, and the average citizen felt the need for self-protection. Hence, the proliferation of a variety of pocket-size handguns. This was a very small, light, .25 automatic, but is overly complex compared to the Browning design. It did not sell well and in 1938 was replaced by the WTP II, which was more streamlined. During the life of this pistol, Mauser was also marketing the Model 1910 .25 A.C.P., which was larger and even more complex. Possibly less than 50,000 WTP Model Is were made, of which less than 25,000 of each major variant exist. Also less than 500 of the early pistols had the T-6.35 stamp. All in all, this is an excellent collector's handgun.

Mechanical Functioning: The WTP Model I is a straight blowback, semi-automatic pistol with a six-shot detachable box magazine that is inserted through the gripframe and retained by a spring-loaded catch located at the bottom rear of the butt. It is striker-fired and has an intercepting thumb-operated safety. There is also a magazine safety preventing discharge when the clip is removed. The back of the firing pin housing protrudes when cocked, acting as an indicator, and upon the last shot, a hold-open device locks the slide in rearward position. To disassemble this pistol check to make sure that it's unloaded. Pull the trigger and remove the magazine. Using the clip's floorplate, press and pull down on the takedown catch spring on the right-hand side of the frame. With this catch in the lowered position, push forward on the slide and run it off of the frame. To remove the barrel turn the slide upside down and push the barrel forward about ¼" and lift the rear end up and out of the slide. Reassemble in the reverse order. If the barrel is not seated properly during reassembly an additional safety feature prevents firing.

Mauser WTP Model I

Mauser
Oberndorf am Neckar, Germany

Model: 1878 ("Zig Zag")

Action Type: revolver, single action.

Caliber(s): 7.6mm revolver, 9mm revolver, 10.6mm revolver.

Barrel Lengths: 6½", 5⅛", 3⅛".

Finish: blue.

Manufacturing Dates: 1878.

Stocks: checkered wood or hard rubber.

Rifling: 5R.

Weight, Unloaded: 42 oz. in 10.6mm Model 1.

Sights: fixed.

Serial Numbers: n/a.

Serial Number Location: on frame below cylinder.

Major Variations: Model 1: various calibers, with solid frame.
Model 2: various calibers, with break-open action.

Markings: Model 1 on barrel: Waffenfabrik mauser, Oberndorf a/Neckar.
Model 2 on left side of frame: Gebr. Mauser & Cie., Oberndorf a/N.

Price(s):
Model 1, 9mm, very good—$1,500.00
Model 1, 9mm, excellent—$3,000.00
Model 2, 7.6mm, very good—$1,750.00
Model 2, 7.6mm, excellent—$2,750.00
Model 2, 9mm, very good—$1,500.00
Model 2, 9mm, excellent—$2,500.00
Model 2, 10.6mm, very good—$3,000.00
Model 2, 10.6mm, excellent—$4,500.00

History: The Mauser "Zig Zag" Model 1878 was developed by Peter Paul
Mauser for competition in the German Military Revolver Trials. It was
produced in two variations, the most noteworthy common feature of
them both being a series of angled grooves on the circumference of the
cylinder. A cylinder bolt rides in these grooves, and as the hammer is
cocked rotates the cylinder and also locks it in position to align it with
the barrel. It was produced in two models: Model 1 was a break-open
frame that was hinged at the top rear part and the break was located just
in front of the trigger guard. The latch consisted of a large ring forward
of the trigger guard, which was pulled forward, releasing the entire
barrel cylinder assembly to swing upward. The Model 2 is the same
cylinder system; however, it was built on a solid-frame revolver with
side gate loading. Both revolvers were considered too complex during
the German trials and therefore were never considered for adoption by

the German military. Mauser did market both of these models in the commercial version but in limited quantities.

Mechanical Functioning: The Mauser "Zig Zag" Model 1878s were six-shot single-action revolvers. Cylinder rotation was acutated by a stud that engaged one of the diagonal slots on the cylinder, causing the cylinder to rotate through ⅙ of its circumference as the hammer is pulled. On the solid frame, loading and ejection were carried out through a loading gate located on the left side of the frame on the flashguard. On the Model 1, ejection and extraction were carried out by opening the break action by pulling the large ring mounted just in front of the trigger guard forward and lifting the barrel cylinder assembly upward. On the Model 1 to prevent accidental opening on firing, a small metal pin is pivoted downward and through the catch whenever the trigger is pulled, thus locking the barrel catch.

Mauser Zig Zag Model 1

August Menz Waffenfabrik
Suhl, Germany

Model: Menta

Action Type: semiautomatic, blowback operated.

Caliber(s): 6.35mm, 7.65mm.

Barrel Lengths: 2.9".

Finish: blue.

Manufacturing Dates: 1916 to about 1920.

Stocks: hard rubber.

Rifling: 6R.

Weight, Unloaded: 22 oz.

Sights: fixed.

Serial Numbers: 7.65mm: 1 to about 15,000.
6.35mm: unknown to at least 6.000.

Serial Number Location: left side of frame above trigger.

Major Variations: 7.65mm which is identical to Beholla.
6.35mm which is identical to Beholla only scaled down.

Markings: left side of slide: Menta cal. 7.65 or Menta cal. 6.35.

Price(s):
7.65mm Commercial, very good—$200.00
7.65mm Commercial, excellent—$300.00
7.65mm Military, very good—$275.00
7.65mm Military, excellent—$350.00
6.35mm Commercial, very good—$500.00
6.35mm Commercial, excellent—$650.00

History: During World War I, Germany was in desperate need of weapons, and enterprising gun makers capitalized on this. The Menta is almost an identical copy of the Beholla pistol made by Becker & Hollander, also of Suhl, Germany. The pattern was already accepted by the Imperial forces. Menz tried to capitalize on this and obviously purchased rights to make this design. However, most of these have commercial marks, and military Mentas are quite scarce. After the war, Menz scaled down the design and created the Menta .25, which was identical but for size. It is not known how many .25s were made, but they are very seldom seen and constitute a "find" for collectors. The Beholla design was also manufactured by Becker & Hollander as the Beholla, by Stenda Werke as the Stenda, and by Gering as the Leon Hardt.

Mechanical Functioning: This is a straight blowback, semiautomatic pistol with a seven-shot detachable box magazine. It is striker-fired, and the thumb-operated safety intercepts the sear. The trigger is of pivoting type and is connected to the sear via a bar. There is no ejector per se; however, at maximum opening, the firing pin protrudes and it knocks out the case. Takedown is accomplished by drifting out a pin through the openings in the slide sides, which allows the removal of the barrel and slide.

Menta .765mm

Menta 6.35mm

Waffenfabrik August Menz
Suhl, Germany

Model: I and II

Action Type: semiautomatic, blowback operated.

Caliber(s): 7.65mm.

Barrel Lengths: 2⅝".

Finish: blue.

Manufacturing Dates: circa 1925.

Stocks: plastic.

Rifling: 6R.

Weight, Unloaded: 19 oz.

Sights: fixed.

Serial Numbers: n/a.

Serial Number Location: left side of frame on forward portion of trigger guard.

Major Variations: Model I has no markings and 10 flat-topped slide finger grooves.
Model II has markings and 10 sharp slide finger grooves.

Markings: Model I, only grip monograms.
Model II on left side of slide: Menz Kal. 7.65 Model II.

Price(s):
Model I, very good—$200.00
Model I, excellent—$325.00
Model II, very good—$275.00
Model II, excellent—$375.00

History: There has always been a great deal of confusion concerning the 7.65mm caliber Menz pistols. In the mid-1920s he brought out several pistols of interesting design. Pistols in 4.25mm and 6.35mm were both labeled Liliput. In the 7.65mm caliber he brought out one pistol with no markings other than the serial number and the monograms on the grip, and another model called the Menz Model II and the Menz Model PB Special, which was double action with an exposed hammer. He also produced the P & B Model III and IIIa in 7.65mm. However, all of the Menz pistols produced under the Menz trade name were marked save one. Because of this a great deal of confusion has come to pass. Writers at various times have described the Liliput as being the Model I; however, it appears from original research that Menz believed the Model I to be that first 7.65mm that he produced with no markings on it. It differed from the Model II in various minor respects. Externally, it had flat-topped finger grooves within the rear of the slide, whereas the Model II had pointed finger grooves for easier grabbing.

Mechanical Functioning: The Menz Model I and Menz Model II are blowback-operated, striker-fired, semiautomatic pistols with detachable box magazines containing six rounds. A mechanical safety is located on the left side of the frame, and a cocking indicator protrudes from the rear of the slide when the weapon is cocked. The barrel on this pistol is a one-piece forging with the frame and is partly exposed for the slide only comes up to the face of the breech, and thereafter covers only the bottom half of the barrel. The magazine is inserted through the gripframe and is retained by a spring-loaded catch located at the base of the butt to the rear. The recoil spring is located underneath the barrel and rides on a guide. The trigger is of the pivoting type connected to a sear bar riding across the magazine well. The disconnector is formed as an integral part of the sear bar and operates by falling into a slot cut into the slide at the battery position, allowing the sear bar to ride up and contact the sear. The extractor is mounted in the slide and comes to rest at the top of the chamber. Disassembly is accomplished by first making sure that the pistol is unloaded and then removing the magazine. Push in the firing pin block at the rear of the frame, which rests in the slide cutout, and then when pushed in about a quarter of inch, the slide may be lifted in the rear slightly and slid off of the front of the frame. The recoil spring, the recoil spring guide, the firing pin, the striker spring, and the striker spring guide may now be removed. Assembly is in the reverse order. The Menz Model II is very similar, and the above instructions apply to it as well as to the Model I.

Menz Model I

O.F. Mossberg & Sons, Inc.
7 Grasso Street
North Haven, CT 06473

Model: Brownie

Action Type: manual repeater.

Caliber(s): .22 R.F.

Barrel Lengths: 2½″.

Finish: blue.

Manufacturing Dates: 1921–1932.

Stocks: grooved wood.

Rifling: n/a.

Weight, Unloaded: about 15 oz.

Sights: fixed.

Serial Numbers: n/a.

Serial Number Location: bottom of butt.

Major Variations: none.

Markings: left side of barrel: O.F. Mossberg & Sons, New Haven Conn. USA.
left side of frame: Brownie.
right side of barrel: Pat. July 27, 1920.

Price(s):
Brownie, very good—$275.00
Brownie, excellent—$375.00

History: The Mossberg Brownie is a four-barreled, pepperbox type of derringer chambered for .22 rimfire. It was first made about 1921 and finally
discontinued in 1932. It somewhat resembles a small automatic in exterior design, until one looks at the thickness, which is about one inch.
Both the barrel block and barrel are of squarish design, and in the barrel
there are two sets of two parallel barrels, two above, two below. The
trigger guard is integral with the barrel group and breaks from the top
forward when released by a catch at the rear of the frame above the grip,
pivoting at the bottom of the grip frame. This is a double-action-only
pistol, and the pulling of the trigger also indexes the rotating firing pin
mounted in the breechblock, indexing it to each barrel in turn. While
Mossberg may not have sold a great many of these pistols, the design
has been well enough thought of to have been copied by other manufacturers from time to time. During the 1950s it was made by Tanfoglio
Fabbrica D'Armi and imported by E.I.G. More recently, it is being copied
by Advantage Arms of St. Paul, Minnesota, and by Armament Technolo-
gies, Inc. (Arm Tech.) of New Haven, Connecticut. The Mossberg and
the Advantage Arms pistols were made of all-steel construction and the
Arm Tech. product is made out of either carbon steel or stainless steel;

whereas the Tanfoglio product was made out of a nonferrous alloy. The Brownie was made to be a stripped-down, fairly plain pistol purely for personal defense, and to this end, it serves its purpose well. This pistol does have one predecessor, however, and it was also made by Mossberg. It was named the "Novelty" pistol and was first patented in December 1906. Both the patent and the manufacturing rights were sold to C.S. Shattuck in 1909.

Mechanical Functioning: The Brownie is a hinged-frame, double-action-only pistol with four fixed barrels, each fired sequentially by means of a rotating firing pin. The action is opened by depressing the rear sight, which pivots, raising the spring-loaded T-latch. The firing pin rotates in a clockwise direction. The overall length is 2½″. It has a thickness of about 1″. Ejection is manual, and there are no external parts other than the release lever to either get hung up or that would interfere with the functioning. There was no safety on this pistol, rather the heavy trigger pull gave it a safety of sorts as it would not discharge unless the trigger was pulled so as to impact sufficient force to the firing pin. The firing pin was set in the center of the standing breech and consisted of a rotating disc with a chisel-shaped firing pin protruding from about the center of the disc out to the edge. As the trigger was pulled, the firing pin would rotate and index to the next chamber in sequence for firing.

Mossberg Brownie

Fabrique D'Armes Nagant
Liege, Belgium

Model: 1878 and 1883

Action Type: revolver, double action.

Caliber(s): 9mm C.F., 7.62mm, 7.5mm, 9.4mm.

Barrel Lengths: 5½".

Finish: blue.

Manufacturing Dates: 1878–1886.

Stocks: checkered wood.

Rifling: 4L in 9mm CF, 3R in 7.62mm.

Weight, Unloaded: 29 oz.

Sights: fixed.

Serial Numbers: n/a, but appears to have started at 1 for the various contracts.

Serial Number Location: left side of frame forward of cylinder.

Major Variations: cylinders cannular or plain, extractors differing in shape, sizes and weights different, various military contracts.

Markings: left side of frame forward of cylinder: Brevet Nagant.

Price(s):
    Belgian Model, 1878 Officer's, very good—$225.00
    Belgian Model, 1878 Officer's, excellent—$325.00
    Belgian Model, 1883 Army, very good—$200.00
    Belgian Model, 1883 Army, excellent—$275.00
    Luxemburg Model, 1883 Officer's, very good—$225.00
    Luxemburg Model, 1883 Officer's, excellent—$325.00
    Luxemburg Model, 1884 Police, very good—$250.00
    Luxemburg Model, 1884 Police, excellent—$325.00
    Belgian Model, 1878/86 Officer's, very good—$200.00
    Belgian Model, 1878/86 Officer's, excellent—$300.00
    Swedish Model, 1887 Officer's, very good—$175.00
    Swedish Model, 1887 Officer's, excellent—$275.00
    Argentine Nagant, very good—$200.00
    Argentine Nagant, excellent—$275.00
    Brazilian Nagant, very good—$200.00
    Brazilian Nagant, excellent—$300.00

History: The Nagant revolvers were invented and manufactured by Emile and Leon Nagant and were manufactured by them in their plant in Liege, Belgium. They were among the early designers who were able to formulate a strong, solid-frame revolver, utilizing double action principles; and as revolver makers, they always stayed in the forefront years ahead of anything produced in the United States. At the time that Europeans were commonly using their revolvers for the military, with rapid-fire, double-action possibilities, America was still entrenched with the single-action Army Colt. The pattern 1878 revolver, first made for Belgium, formed the basis for the revolvers adopted by Luxemburg, Sweden, Argentina, and Brazil, but Nagant is probably best known for their development of the gas seal revolver that was used by the Russian army from 1895 through World War II. This series of revolvers, however, should be important to us for they formed the basic lockwork of the later Nagants, the only difference being that these are not gas seal.

Mechanical Functioning: The Nagant 1878 pattern revolver is a double-action, solid-frame revolver utilizing an exterior hammer and a fixed cylinder with a loading gate located on the right side of the frame. Ejection was carried out by means of a rod. It was available in several calibers, and rifling for each caliber varied, the most common pattern being 4 L in the 9mm, 3R in the 7mm.

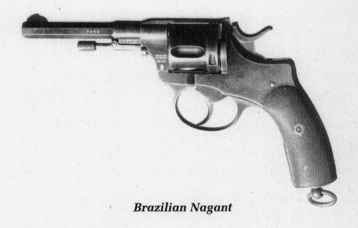

Brazilian Nagant

Nagant Freres
Liege, Belgium, and
Russian State Arsenals

Model: Russian M1895

Action Type: revolver, double action.

Caliber(s): 7.62mm Nagant.

Barrel Lengths: 4½″ or 3½″.

Finish: blue.

Manufacturing Dates: 1895–1944.

Stocks: checkered wood.

Rifling: 4R.

Weight, Unloaded: 27⅛ oz.

Sights: fixed.

Serial Numbers: n/a.

Serial Number Location: left side of frame forward of cylinder.

Major Variations: Russian Army, Imperial.
Russian Army, Soviet.
Russian Police.
Enlisted mens' revolvers were single action.
Officers' model was double action.

Markings: left side of frame: Imperial Russian or Soviet marks.

Price(s):
Imperial Army, Enlisted men's model, very good—$200.00
Imperial Army, Enlisted men's model, excellent—$300.00
Imperial Army, Belgian made, very good—$200.00
Imperial Army, Belgian made, excellent—$275.00
Imperial Army, very good—$175.00
Imperial Army, excellent—$225.00
Soviet Army, very good—$150.00
Soviet Army, excellent—$200.00
Russian Police, very good—$225.00
Russian Police, excellent—$325.00

History: The Russian Model 1895 Nagant revolver is noteworthy because it is the only military revolver adopted with what was called a gas check cylinder. This firearm was chambered for a cartridge called the 7.62mm Nagant, an interesting cartridge because the case extended beyond the nose of the bullet. When the revolver was fired the cylinder was firmly locked against the face of the barrel, and the cartridge case provided a gas seal, so that no gases could escape between the forward wall of the cylinder and the rear face of the barrel, thus improving velocity. Various versions of this interesting revolver were made for the Imperial Russian army, but apparently only officers were to be trusted with the double-action revolver. Enlisted men were only allowed single-action revolvers. The Soviet army apparently tried not to have such class distinctions, and it appears that all of their revolvers were double action. A very interesting variation is the model made for police. It features a shorter barrel as well as a shorter grip, and is the Nagant equivalent of a concealable pocket revolver. This gun is a rare find for collectors. The Model 1895 Nagant revolver was in continuous use with Russian forces from 1895 through the end of World War II.

Mechanical Functioning: The Model 1895 Nagant is a seven-shot, double- or single-action revolver, utilizing side gate loading and a rod ejector. Operation was normal for revolvers with one exception. The unique cartridge case which seated the bullet below the mouth of the cartridge actually protruded from the face of the cylinder when loaded. A recess in turn was cut into the front face of the cylinder matching the diameter of the rear base of the barrel, which protruded from the frame into the cylinder housing. At full cock, the cylinder was pushed forward by about ⅛" to engage the face of the barrel. At the same time, the protruding end of the cartridge case actually slipped inside the barrel leader. To compensate for changing head space, a small block at the rear wall of the frame behind the chamber also pivoted forward. Upon firing, the escaping gases would expand the cartridge case to seal the gap between the barrel and the cylinder, preventing the gases from escaping through that joint as in the normal revolver, and thus increasing velocity of the projectile. As the trigger returned after firing, the cylinder was brought back to its normal operating position.

Russian Imperial M1895 Nagant

Norwegian Military
Kongsberg Vapenfabrik
Kongsberg, Norway

Model: M1914

Action Type: semiautomatic, recoil operated.

Caliber(s): 11.25mm.

Barrel Lengths: 5".

Finish: blue.

Manufacturing Dates: 1917–1946.

Stocks: checkered wood.

Rifling: 6L.

Weight, Unloaded: 39 oz.

Sights: fixed.

Serial Numbers: from around C10000 to C10500 in Colt Commercial Range, and Kongsberg Vapenfabrik started at 1 and ran to 32900. 22001 to 32500 were Nazi Pistole 657(n).

Serial Number Location: left side of frame above trigger guard.

Major Variations: Colt Test Model.
Norwegian issue.
Nazi P.657.

Markings: left side of slide: 11.25mm Aut. Pistol M1914.
right side of slide: year of manufacture.

Price(s):
Colt Test Model, very good—$1,500.00
Colt Test Model, excellent—$2,000.00
Norwegian issue, very good—$1,250.00
Norwegian issue, excellent—$1,500.00
Nazi P.657, very good—$1,500.00
Nazi P.657, excellent—$1,750.00
Norwegian 1914, very good—$750.00
Norwegian 1914, excellent—$1,250.00

History: Just after the turn of the century the Norwegians were busily engaged in trying to find a new military pistol, as were most all major countries at the time. They held trials in 1907 and again in 1910, and in both trials the Colt .45 style came out very strong. In 1914 Norway ordered about 300 commercial pistols for the final test series, and the Browning/Colt design beat all other entries. Thus, a deal was negotiated with Colt for the Norwegians to manufacture their variation of the M1911 in their own plant at Kongsberg under license, and since they were adopted in the 1914 trials, that became the official designation. Aside from markings, they are virtually identical copies of the Colt

M1911 with the exception of an elongated slide stop that has a downward-curving edge. Following European tradition, all parts are numbered, inhibiting interchangeability. The pistol was manufactured from 1917 through 1930, and when the Germans marched in, they produced it again from 1940 to 1945 for their own use. The German nomenclature for the pistol was the Model 657(n). The pistol was produced in 1946 in very limited quantity for the Norwegian army.

Mechanical Functioning: The Norwegian M1914 is a recoil-operated, semi-automatic pistol with a seven-shot detachable box magazine inserted through the gripframe and retained by a catch located on the left side of the frame just behind the trigger. The functioning on this pistol is exactly the same as for a standard Model 1911 Colt.

Norwegian M1914

Cooperativa Obrera
Eibar, Spain

Model: Longines

Action Type: semiautomatic, blowback operated.

Caliber(s): 7.65mm.

Barrel Lengths: 3⁷/₈″.

Finish: blue.

Manufacturing Dates: circa 1920.

Stocks: hard rubber.

Rifling: 6L.

Weight, Unloaded: 21¼ oz.

Sights: fixed.

Serial Number: n/a.

Serial Number Location: right rear frame.

Major Variations: none.

Markings: left side of the slide: Cal 7.65 Model Automatic Pistol, Longines.

Price(s):
Longines, very good—$150.00
Longines, excellent—$225.00

History: The Longines pistol was produced by the Workers' Cooperative, Eibar, Spain, also known in Spanish as the Cooperativa Obrera. This was one of the many very small workshops located in Eibar, Spain, before the Spanish Civil War that turned out multitudes of inexpensive handguns. Not too much is known about this group other than they did not last past the Civil War. This is a shame because they were one of the few small shops that exhibited some originality, and they tried to produce a pistol that was fairly well finished and pretty nicely made compared to their compadres' products. Some authorities report that the Cooperativa Obrera also made guns under other names such as Omega or Rolex, but these reports are unconfirmed by this author. The Longines is noteworthy because of the exterior design. Somewhat resembling the Browning 1910 .32 without the grip safety, it appeared to be quite streamlined. However, upon disassembly, it turns out that this is just another pistol of standard Eibar design; that is, instead of having the recoil spring mounted axially around the barrel, it is mounted on a guide located beneath the barrel resting in the frame. However, Longines did an excellent job of disguising this, utilizing the streamlining effect. It does, probably because of the huge market for the Ruby, retain a certain Spanish flair by including a lanyard ring at the lower left hand side of the gripframe, and following standard Eibar pattern, the grip is cut for the loop. It appears that even with the exterior redesign they still don't want to risk losing the Ruby market.

Mechanical Functioning: The Longines is a straight blowback-operated, semiautomatic pistol based on the standard Eibar pattern. It utilizes a nine-shot detachable box magazine that is inserted through the grip-frame and is retained by a spring-loaded catch located at the base of the butt. Like most other Eibar pistols it has a concealed internal hammer. The disconnector rides in a slot machined on the side of the frame, protruding into the cutout of the rail area. When depressed, it pivots the trigger extension bar off of the sear. The safety is manual and is located on the left side of the frame just above the trigger and doubles as a slide-lock for takedown purposes. To disassemble this pistol, first make sure that the weapon is unloaded. Then remove the magazine and withdraw the slide to the rear until the safety can engage the cutout in the slide, locking it in the rear position. Rotate the barrel a quarter of a turn until the barrel lugs show themselves in the ejection port. Release the catch and slowly slide the slide off the front of the frame, being careful not to let the recoil spring jump loose. The recoil spring and its guide can now be removed and the barrel lifted out of the slide from the rear. Assembly is accomplished in the reverse order.

Longines .32 A.C.P.

Heinrich Ortgies & Co.
Erfurt, Germany, and
Deutsche Werke
Erfurt, Germany

Model: H.O. and D.

Action Type: semiautomatic, blowback operated.

Caliber(s): 6.35mm, 7.65mm, 9mm K.

Barrel Lengths: 2³/₄″ in 6.35mm, 3⁷/₈″ in 7.65mm and 9mm K.

Finish: blue.

Manufacturing Dates: 1920s.

Stocks: wood.

Rifling: 6R.

Weight, Unloaded: 13½ oz. in 6.35mm; 22 oz. in 7.65mm.

Sights: fixed.

Serial Numbers: thought to have started at 1 and ran to about 11,000 in 7.65mm for the H.O.
the D. may have started at 5,000 and ran to about 230,000.
the 6.35mm and 7.65mm may have run together.

Serial Number Location: bottom of frame forward of trigger guard.

Major Variations: None.

Markings: H.O., left side of slide. Deutsche Werke Aktiengesellschaft, Werk Erfurt, Ortgies Patent.
on barrel: caliber.
D., left side of slide: Deutsche Werke-Werk Erfurt.
right side of slide: Ortgies Patent.

Price(s):
H.O., 6.35mm, very good—$225.00
H.O., 6.35mm, excellent—$300.00
D., 7.65mm, very good—$250.00
D., 7.65mm, excellent—$325.00
D., 9mm K, very good—$375.00
D., 9mm K, excellent—$450.00

History: Heinrich Ortgies was an inventor said to have spent World War I in Liege, Belgium, and at the close of the war moved to Erfurt, Germany, where he started experimenting with this pocket pistol. He seems to have perfected his design about 1919 and began production in about 1920. In Germany, being what it was in those days, pocket pistols of good design sold like hotcakes because of the necessity of the average citizen to be able to defend himself due to the high crime rate and the anarchy prevalent at the time. Ortgies' pistol became so popular that the Deutschewerke decided to buy Ortgies' plant, and apparently made him an offer that he couldn't refuse. It appears that when Ortgies owned the plant, he manufactured around 11,000 pistols and when Deutschewerke took it over, they made perhaps as many as a quarter of a million pistols. The pistols were available in two calibers; 6.35mm, and 7.65mm, as well as a limited number in 9mm K.

Mechanical Functioning: Ortgies' pistol is a straight blowback, semiautomatic pistol utilizing a seven-round detachable box magazine in 6.35mm caliber, eight-round in 7.65mm caliber, and seven-round in 9mm K caliber. It utilizes an internal striker, and the only safety is the grip safety. The firearm could be fired whenever the grip safety was pushed in, for the grip safety locked in the in position. In order to make it safe once again, you had to push a button located on the left side of the frame just to the rear of the grip. However, because of the internal design of the firing pin, it still was not safe to carry. There have been instances recorded where the pistol could be in someone's pocket and jarred slightly, discharging, even with the safety in place. The reason for this is the design of the sear engagement lugs on the striker. Instead of being of solid construction, they were made in two prongs, which were easily broken, due to faulty heat treatment, or age embrittlement. Therefore, on this particular pistol, unless you intend to actually shoot it, do not put a round in the chamber.

Ortgies H.O.

P.A.F.
Pretoria Arms Factory
Pretoria, Republic of South Africa

Model: Junior

Action Type: semiautomatic, blowback.

Caliber(s): .25 A.C.P.

Barrel Lengths: 2¼".

Finish: blue.

Manufacturing Dates: 1950s.

Stocks: black plastic, but other colors have been reported.

Rifling: 6L.

Weight, Unloaded: 13⅜ oz.

Sights: none; groove on top of slide.

Serial Numbers: A-001 to A-11,000, although all do not seem to be used.

Serial Number Location: rear grip strap.

Major Variations: standard model had a slide height of ⅛" over barrel and sight groove, and may be found in either higher or lower slide heights. Early model had milled sight rib, late models had cocking indicator.

Markings: on left slide: Junior.
Vervaarding in Suid-Afrika.
Made in South Africa.
logo on both sides of forward slide.
early barrels were stamped: Cal. 6.35mm.
many parts marked P.A.F.

Price(s):
standard model, very good—$150.00
standard model, excellent—$200.00
thin web model, very good—$250.00
thin web model, excellent—$375.00
high slide model, very good—$175.00
high slide model, excellent—$225.00
low slide model, very good—$175.00
low slide model, excellent—$225.00
raised sight rib model, very good—$275.00
raised sight rib model, excellent—$350.00
cocking indicator—add 20%

History: This pistol began life as the first pistol manufactured in Africa and quickly earned a terrible reputation. The first pistols were made with a very thin web of steel forward of the barrel lug and had the disconcerting habit of shearing off on counter-recoil when the gun was fired, thus sending the barrel and slide toward the target. As a result of this unwholesome attribute, South African dealers dumped wholesale quantities of the Junior in the ocean. Pretoria Arms Factory corrected the problem but not in time to save the company, and only about 2,000 pistols are thought to have survived.

Mechanical Functioning: The P.A.F. is a Browning Model 1906 type blowback action, with the recoil spring mounted underneath the barrel. The safety located at the left rear of the frame intercepts the sear and in some pistols lifts a rod to lock the slide. The pistol is striker-fired. The barrel is retained by a single large lug fitting into a frame recess. The early production of the P.A.F. had a bad habit of shearing off the front face of the frame by the barrel lug upon firing during counterrecoil with the embarrassing effect of letting the whole slide assembly fly off the front of the gun. By the time the P.A.F. numbering had reached about 1000 none of the early style frames remained, and the following frames all seem to be of the late P.A.F. type with thick frame webs eliminating the chance of frame shear during counterrecoil. Takedown of the P.A.F. is accomplished by making sure that the pistol is unloaded, pulling the trigger, and then withdrawing the slide to the rear until the barrel lug lines up with the cut in the slide visible in the ejection port. Holding the slide in that position, rotate the barrel so the barrel lug disengages from the frame and turns into the slide. Thus unlocked, the slide assembly can be moved forward and off of the frame. The firing pin, firing pin spring, and firing pin spring guide can be withdrawn out of the rear of the slide, and the barrel and recoil spring and guide out from the bottom of the slide. Assembly is in the reverse order.

P.A.F. Junior, Standard Model

Anciens Etablissements Pieper
Herstal, Belgium

Model: Demontant and Basculant

Action Type: semiautomatic, blowback operated.

Caliber(s): 6.35mm, 7.65mm.

Barrel Lengths: 2″.

Finish: blue.

Manufacturing Dates: circa 1920.

Stocks: hard rubber.

Rifling: 6L.

Weight, Unloaded: 11 oz.

Sights: fixed

Serial Numbers: n/a.

Serial Number Location: right rear of frame.

Major Variations: Model 1919.
Model 1920.

Markings: left side of slide: Pistole Automatique.
right side of slide: N. Pieper patent.

Price(s):
Model 1919 Demontant, very good—$125.00
Model 1919 Demontant, excellent—$175.00
Model 1920 Basculant, very good—$125.00
Model 1920 Basculant, excellent—$150.00

History: Nicholas Pieper was not only a prolific arms maker at Anciens Etablissements Pieper, but he was also an inventor of some repute. On this
series of pistols he seems to have relied heavily on earlier work done by
Warnant, but still developed something that was fairly unique and was
used for a period of more than 20 years. There was some confusion on
some of his earlier pistols as to the nomenclature and model type. The
primary thing in identifying his pistols is to remember that even though
external appearances were very similar, there were two distinct types of
takedown. One was called the Demontant, the other Basculant. The
Demontant pistols and Basculant both had little levers on the left side of
the frame above the trigger. On the Demontant, flipping the lever down
would allow the removal of both barrel and slide assembly as a single
unit for takedown, and then both pieces would break down of their own
accord for further disassembly. The Basculant, on the other hand, had a
tip-up barrel which means that when you flipped the lever down, it
released the barrel to tip up, and at the same time, released the slide so
that it would move up and down of its own accord. However, for complete takedown of the Basculant variety, you needed a screwdriver in
order to remove the screw at the rear of the frame behind the safety. The

Model 1919 C is generally a Demontant pistol. The 1920 D is generally a Basculant type; however, there have been pistols with the 1920 stamping on the slide that are of the Demontant variety, so be very careful in identifying these. These pistols first began production in Steyr, Austria, as the Steyr Model 1909, being made under license from Nicholas Pieper. After World War I when Steyr's production seemed to be unsure, Pieper also began manufacturing this model, and seems to have made it throughout the 1920s.

Mechanical Functioning: The Pieper Model 1919 and Model 1920 are both blowback-operated, semiautomatic pistols with six-shot detachable box magazines. They both utilize internal hammers and have manual thumb safeties located on the left side of the frame behind the grip which locks the sear thus blocking the hammer. Takedown is accomplished on the Demontant variety by first making sure the weapon is unloaded, turning down the lever located just above the trigger on the left side of the frame, and tipping the mechanism out of the gun. The barrel and slide are then separated for cleaning. On the Basculant variety, turning down the same lever will pop the barrel upward, rotating it upon a screw located in a forward part of the frame. The screw at the rear part of the frame behind the safety can be removed in order to remove the slide assembly. Assembly is in the reverse order.

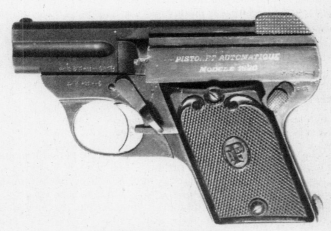

Pieper Demontant

Fabryka Broni w Radomiu
Radom, Poland

Model: Radom

Action Type: semiautomatic, recoil operated.

Caliber(s): 9mm Parabellum.

Barrel Lengths: 4⁹/₁₆″.

Finish: blue.

Manufacturing Dates: 1936–1944.

Stocks: plastic, black or brown.

Rifling: 6R.

Weight, Unloaded: 36½ oz.

Sights: fixed.

Serial Numbers: sequencing unknown.

Serial Number Location: right frame above trigger.

Major Variations: none.

Markings: left side of slide—F.B. Radom VIS Mod 35 Pat. Nr. 15567.
left side of slide—early models had the Polish eagle.
left side of slide—late war models just had German codes and proofs.

Price(s):
VIS-35, Polish, very good—$1,000.00
VIS-35, Polish, excellent—$1,250.00
VIS-35, early German, very good—$1,250.00
VIS-35, early German, excellent—$1,500.00
VIS-35, late German, very good—$350.00
VIS-35, late German, excellent—$500.00
VIS-35, German Navy, very good—$750.00
VIS-35, German Navy, excellent—$1,000.00

History: With war on the horizon, in 1930 Poland decided that it might be best to standardize their motley assortment of obsolete handguns and held a trial for submitted designs. The design submitted by Skrzypinski and Wilniewczyc, engineers for Skoda, won. Commencing in 1936, the Government Small Arms Factory manufactured the pistol under the name VIS-35. VIS was said to be the acronym for the inventors' initials W (V), I (and), S. It is also the Polish word for power, so you may draw your own conclusions. When the Germans captured Poland, they continued to produce this pistol for their growing needs, and as the war progressed and necessity grew, output became paramount. Thus the late pistols were quite crude.

Mechanical Functioning: This is a recoil-operated, semiautomatic pistol with an eight-shot detachable box magazine and external hammer. There is a grip safety but no conventional thumb safety. The switch at the top rear of the left side of the slide is actually a hammer block which trips the sear and safely lowers the hammer with a cartridge in the chamber. As this pistol has a floating firing pin, this is a safe way to carry it if loaded. The switch on the frame below it in the conventional place of a thumb safety is a hold-open device for dismounting. In the late war years, both were eliminated.

Radom, Polish

Radom, Early German

Radom, Late German

Randall Firearms Mfg. Corp.
Sun Valley, CA

Model: Service and Compact

Action Type: semiautomatic, recoil operated.

Caliber(s): 9mm Luger, .38 Super, .45 A.C.P.

Barrel Lengths: 5" or 4½".

Finish: stainless steel.

Manufacturing Dates: 1983–1984.

Stocks: Herritt checkered walnut.

Rifling: 10L.

Weight, Unloaded: 38 oz. Service Model, 36 oz. Compact Model.

Sights: fixed.

Serial Numbers: starts at 1.

Serial Number Location: right frame over trigger.

Major Variations: Service model.
  Service model with rib.
  Deluxe model.

Markings: left side of slide: Stainless Steel-Randall-Caliber

Price(s):
  Service Model, very good—$300.00; excellent—$400.00
  Compact Model, very good—$400.00; excellent—$500.00
  Service Model with rib, very good—$425.00; excellent—$550.00

History: The Randall Firearms Company just began manufacturing their Service and Compact Model pistols in 1983. They are entirely crafted from stainless steel, with the exception of the grips. The Service Models are virtually identical to the Colt Model 1911A1 and are available with either the long or short trigger with travel overstop. The safety is slightly longer to provide a better hold, and the hammer is slightly wider than the Target version of the Model 1911. The Service Model available is made to military specifications as well as made with an integral sighting rib. Two unusual features about this pistol are that it includes a full-length, stainless-steel recoil spring guide to prevent the recoil spring from kinking, and ported slide for positive ejection.

Mechanical Functioning: The Randall is a recoil-operated, semiautomatic pistol with a seven-shot detachable box magazine inserted through the gripframe and retained by a catch located on the left side of the frame just behind the trigger. The functioning on this pistol is exactly the same as for a standard Model 1911 Colt. It operates with a locked breech and upon firing the barrel and slide recoil together until a lug located at the bottom of the barrel hits the transverse pin attached to the slide stop and is yanked downward. The barrel is thus unlocked from the slide allowing the slide to continue in its rearward motion thus cycling the pistol. The firing pin is of the floating variety, and there are two safeties. A mechanical safety located on the left side of the frame locks the sear. A grip safety prevents firing until it is depressed. An additional safety is ground into the hammer in the form of a half-cock notch with a protruding lip which slides over the top of the sear. While it is fine to use the half-cock notch in case of hammer slippage, it is not a wise practice to carry the pistol in this condition. To field-strip the pistol, first make sure that it is unloaded and remove the magazine. Push the plug located on the front of the slide below the barrel and rotate the barrel bushing to the right until the plug can be eased out from the front. Be very careful because this plug is under spring tension and could fly out. Pull the slide back gradually until the rear edge of the center of the two recesses in the center of the slide on the left-hand side lines up with the rear end of the slide stop. Push the slide stop pin on the right side of the frame and pull the slide stop out the left-hand side. The slide assembly can now be taken off by sliding forward and off the frame. The barrel bushing can be rotated in the opposite direction as far as it will go, and then it and the barrel may be pulled straight out. Assemble in the reverse order.

Randall .45 Service Model

Remington Arms Co.
Bridgeport, CT 06602

Model: Double Derringer (Model 95)

Action Type: break open with superposed barrels.

Caliber(s): .41 R.F.

Barrel Lengths: 3".

Finish: blue or nickel.

Manufacturing Dates: 1866–1935.

Stocks: hard rubber or wood.

Rifling: 5L, but on the 6th type, the land is 50% wider than the groove.

Weight, Unloaded: 11 oz.

Sights: fixed.

Serial Numbers: 1st type: 1–1321.
2nd type: 1–2057.
3rd type: 1–4100.
4th type: 1–3022.
5th type: 1–L97257.
6th type: L75925–99941.

Serial Number Location: left side of frame under grip, on frame under barrel.

Major Variations: 1st type: no extractor.
2nd type: with extractor.
3rd type: with extractor.
4th type: with extractor.
5th type: with extractor.
6th type: with extractor.

Markings: 1st type: side of barrel, E. Remington & Sons.
2nd type: side of barrel, E. Remington & Sons.
3rd type: top of barrel, E. Remington & Sons.
4th type: top of barrel, Remington Arms Co.
5th type: top of barrel, Remington Arms UMC Co., side flutes on barrel.
6th type: Remington Arms UMC Co. plain sides on barrel.

Price(s):
1st type, very good—$1,250.00
1st type, excellent—$1,500.00
2nd type, very good—$1,500.00
2nd type, excellent—$1,750.00
3rd type, very good—$350.00
3rd type, excellent—$500.00
4th type, very good—$325.00
4th type, excellent—$375.00
5th type, very good—$350.00
5th type, excellent—$450.00

6th type, very good—$1,000.00
6th type, excellent—$1,250.00

History: The Remington Elliot Derringer, which was also known as the Double Derringer and the Remington Model #95, bridged the gap from earliest of cartridge arms on through to modern times. Invented by William H. Elliot in 1865 and first manufactured in 1866, this pistol has been one of the most popular in history. Remington continued to make this pistol until 1935, and since then, there has been a plethora of imitators. Unlike the Remington copies, which seem to come in every caliber under the rainbow, the original was only in .41 rimfire, and was made of steel. It is difficult to ascertain by serial number which model you have, as virtually all the models repeated earlier serial numbers. In order to identify your variety, look over the price list, which gives the individual characteristics of each type.

Mechanical Functioning: The Remington Elliot Double Derringer was a .41-caliber, two-shot pistol, utilizing superimposed barrels that were hinged to the frame at the top rear. A lever on the right side of the frame below the trigger latched the barrels in the down position via a cam at the bottom of the barrel. Swinging the lever unlatched the barrels, allowing them to swing upward. After 1869 the side of the barrel had an extractor to lift out the spent cases. The trigger is of the unprotected, sheath type, and the operation is single action with a hammer. When cocked, the firing pin oscillates, operating on a cam, for successive shots to fire each barrel in turn. The hammer has a safety notch for carrying it.

Remington Double Derringer

Remington Arms Co.
Bridgeport, CT 06602

Model: M51

Action Type: semiautomaic, blowback operated.

Caliber(s): .32 A.C.P., 380 A.C.P.

Barrel Lengths: 3½".

Finish: blue.

Manufacturing Dates: 1918–1934.

Stocks: hard rubber.

Rifling: 7R.

Weight, Unloaded: 21 oz.

Sights: fixed.

Serial Numbers: .32 A.C.P.: 60801 to 70280 and 90501 to 92627.
.380 A.C.P.: 1 to about 49000 and about 56000 to 60800.

Serial Number Location: left side of frame above trigger.

Major Variations: early models with plunge milled slide serrations; after 1920 had sharp-edged serrations.

Markings: right side of frame: Remington trademark.
early marking on rib: Remington Arms-Union Metallic Cartridge Co., Inc., Remington Ilion Wks., Ilion, N.Y. Pedersen's patents March 9, 20; Aug. 3, 20; Oct. 12, 20; June 14, 21.

Price(s):
.32 A.C.P., early, very good—$475.00
.32 A.C.P., early, excellent—$550.00
.32 A.C.P., late, very good—$425.00
.32 A.C.P., late, excellent—$500.00
.380 A.C.P., early, very good—$400.00
.380 A.C.P., early, excellent—$500.00
.380 A.C.P., late, very good—$350.00
.380 A.C.P., late, excellent—$450.00

History: The Remington Model 51 is a fairly unique pistol and is based on original designs of John D. Pedersen. This fame extends to the Pedersen device of World War I, and his genius was carried through on this pistol. Other features of the pistol were invented by Crawford C. Loomis. His pistol was designed to be a shooter. It is still very sought after by many policemen to carry off-duty because of its flatness, lightness, and because when you hold the gun it just seems to point itself. Though it was made in 1918, first shipments from the factory did not begin until 1919, with the .380 A.C.P. coming first. The .32 caliber pistol did not begin production until 1921. Both pistols appear to have ceased production in 1927, although the factory had good stocks of them and continued to sell the pistol until 1934. The caliber of the pistol is marked on the barrel over the chamber and can be viewed through the ejection port. Both the .32 and the .380 have the same exterior, and besides caliber, the only difference would be that the .32 magazine holds eight shots, while the .380 holds seven rounds. Although this pistol is quite collectible, it appears that its price is being held up more by people who wish to shoot it than collect it.

Mechanical Functioning: The Model 51 is a delayed blowback, semiautomatic pistol with a concealed hammer and a detachable box magazine. The delay in the operation of the pistol is the result of Pedersen's patented breechblock, which is a separate unit placed into the rear portion of the slide consisting of two parts: a lighter one that carries the breech face, and a heavy supporting block, which is in contact with the lighter portion at the moment of firing. The cartridge forces both of them rearward, but a projection catches the lighter breech face after it is moved a short way. The heavier section continues to move back until it strikes a release lever allowing the lighter section to then recoil backward. This hesitation causes a noticeable reduction in felt recoil. There are three safeties on the gun: a grip safety which prevents firing unless the gun is held in firing position; a magazine safety that prevents firing with the magazine removed; and a thumb safety that locks the internal hammer. One point that should be mentioned: when taking the gun down, many times people break the grips, since they are held in place in what is, for firearms, a unique way. There is a pin at the bottom of the gripframe to the rear of the grips that has to be drifted in. The grip is then pushed down toward the base of the gripframe, and when it is snapping down, it can then be lifted straight off. These grips are held in place by a thin, metal plate on the back of the grip, held in place by two rivets and fitted to the gripframe via an impingement fit.

Remington Model 51
Photo courtesy of Butterfield and Butterfield

Retolaza Hermanos
Eibar, Spain

Model: 1924 Liberty

Action Type: semiautomatic, blowback operated.

Caliber(s): .25 A.C.P., 6.35mm, 7.65mm.

Barrel Lengths: 2½″.

Finish: blue.

Manufacturing Dates: circa 1920s.

Stocks: hard rubber.

Rifling: 6R.

Weight, Unloaded: 13 oz.

Sights: fixed.

Serial Numbers: n/a.

Serial Number Location: right side of frame.

Major Variations: 6.35mm Model 1924.
7.65mm Model 1914.
6.35mm Grand Precision.

Markings: left side of slide. Cal. 6.35 Automatic Pistol-Eibar.

Price(s):
Liberty Model 1924, 6.35mm, very good—$100.00
Liberty Model 1924, 6.35mm, excellent—$150.00
Liberty Model 1914, 7.65mm, very good—$100.00
Liberty Model 1914, 7.65mm, excellent—$175.00
Liberty 6.35mm Grand Precision, very good—$125.00
Liberty 6.35mm Grand Precision, excellent—$175.00

History: The Liberty was a trade-name of Retolaza Hermanos of Eibar, Spain. The Retolaza brothers began their business in the 1890s manufacturing cheap pocket revolvers and Velo Dog revolvers. Early on they caught the habit of adopting a myriad of names. Apparently not bothering to let people know who made the guns, they were happy to allow dealers and distributors the luxury of choosing their own names to put on the firearms. During World War I, they saw which direction to turn as far as making money was concerned, and joined the rush to make cheap 7.65mm automatics for use by the French and other forces during the war. One of the trade names that was widely used was "Liberty." Their 7.65mm was called the "Model 1914" although it was first started around 1915, and it was used as a secondary marshall pistol by the French, who were desperate and would take anything. After the war and seeing a decreasing market for their 7.65mm automatics, they decided this was the time for personal defense and started manufacturing 6.35mm automatics. The Liberty Model 1924 is essentially a reduced version of the Model 1914 7.65mm. Around the same time, a Liberty with the markings "Grand Precision" was also made and appears to be a virtual duplicate of the Browning 1906 including the grip safety. This pistol was said to have been made under contract to Etxezagarra and Apitua of Eibar, Spain, a large distributing company.

Mechanical Functioning: The standard Liberty models 1914 and 1924 are of standard Eibar design. They are straight blowback, semiautomatic pistols with a detachable box magazine and a concealed internal hammer. They lack grip safety, but they do have a manual thumb safety. The 6.35mm Grand Precision, however, is very much like the Browning 1906 and includes magazine safety and grip safety, as well as a manual thumb safety located at the rear of the left side of the frame. Disassembly on all of these pistols is accomplished by first being sure that they are unloaded, removing the magazine, flipping the safety to the "on" position and withdrawing the slide, thus locking it in the rearward position, then rotating the barrel about a quarter of a turn to expose the barrel locking grooves in the ejection port. At this point the safety can be unlocked and the slide slid out the front end, taking care to watch out for the spring pressure of the recoil spring. Reassembly can be accomplished in the reverse order.

Liberty Model 1924

Rheinische Metallwaren u. Maschinenfabrik
Sommerda, Germany

Model: Rheinmetall

Action Type: semiautomatic, blowback operated.

Caliber(s): 7.65mm.

Barrel Lengths: 3⅝".

Finish: blue.

Manufacturing Dates: 1922 to 1927.

Stocks: wood or hard rubber.

Rifling: 4R.

Weight, Unloaded: 23½ oz.

Sights: fixed.

Serial Numbers: started at about 250,000.

Serial Number Location: n/a.

Major Variations: none.

Markings: left side of slide: Rheinmetall ABT. Sommerda.

Price(s):
     Rheinmetall with wood grips, very good—$225.00
     Rheinmetall with wood grips, excellent—$325.00
     Rheinmetall with hard rubber grips, very good—$250.00
     Rheinmetall with hard rubber grips, excellent—$350.00

History: This is a marked departure from Rheinische Metallwaren's previous pistols—the Dreyse series. In this pistol, they eliminated a great many moving parts and simplified the exterior design to make a more appealing pistol. The early pictures and diagrams of the Rheinmetall show a milled, matted rib with raised sights. However, the production pistols appear to have just a sighting groove. It appears that the numbering was a continuation of the Dreyse series and started at around 250,000. It is not known just how many Rheinmetalls were produced, but production quantities are thought to be low. It is a rarely encountered pistol and is quite a collectible one.

Mechanical Functioning: This pistol is based on the Browning 1910 design but lacks a grip safety. It is a simple, blowback-operated pistol, with an eight-shot detachable box magazine. It is striker-fired and the recoil spring runs axially around the barrel. The magazine is located at the bottom of the gripframe, and the pivoting trigger uses a Browning-style connector.

Rheinmetall

Romerwerke
Suhl, Germany

Model: Romer

Action Type: semiautomatic, blowback operated.

Caliber(s): .22 L.R.

Barrel Lengths: 2½" to 3", 6½".

Finish: blue.

Manufacturing Dates: 1925–1926.

Stocks: hard rubber.

Rifling: 6R.

Weight, Unloaded: 13¼ oz. with 2½" barrel.

Sights: fixed.

Serial Numbers: starting point unknown, running to less than 3000.

Serial Number Location: left side of frame behind trigger.

Major Variations: interchangeable barrels.

Markings: .22 Long Rifle on left side of barrel over chamber.

Price(s):
    Romer, short barrel only, very good—$525.00
    Romer, short barrel only, excellent—$650.00
    Romer, long barrel only, very good—$575.00
    Romer, long barrel only, excellent—$700.00
    Romer, combination, very good—$750.00
    Romer, combination, excellent—$950.00
    long barrel with adjustable front sight—add 10%.

History: In Germany during the post–World War I years the populace felt desperate for self-protection against the roving political mobs and marauding criminals. Because of this everybody who could make firearms tried to cash in on the boom. One beneficial side effect of this dark period in Germany's history was that the automatic pistol came of age. A great many different styles and actions were tried, as everyone tried a new twist to avoid patent litigation. Therefore, interesting new actions and ideas came into being and were given the test of the marketplace. The successful designs are still in production today. The Romer pistol entered the frantic firearms market of the early 1920s and immediately ran into stiff competition. Its primary claim to fame was the interchangeability of barrels, but it made the gun neither fish nor fowl. Though it is not large, there were much smaller pocket pistols packing more punch on the market. Although advertised as a "target pistol" with the 6½" barrel, it was really much too small and light for that kind of work. It did have some excellent features, however. The magazine was split so the follower could be held down on either side for fast loading. The barrels could be interchanged rapidly, and an effective gas seal was used in the event of case rupture. The pistol was finely made and finished, but it was a case of a good idea in the wrong time and the wrong place.

Mechanical Functioning: The Romer employed a simple blowback action and was striker-fired. The pistol used a seven-shot detachable box magazine that was inserted through the gripframe and retained by a spring-loaded catch at the base of the butt. Barrels are interchanged by forward pressure on the projecting lug at the front of the trigger guard. This unlocks the barrel, and it can then slide off. The rear of the barrel and face of the breechblock are unique in that the barrel is recessed about 1/2" to accept the breech extension. The telescoping barrel has an eliptical cut-out on the right side for ejection, but only on the inside. The outside mates with the breechblock step for a solid fit. This provides an added measure of safety in the event of a case rupture since all of the escaping gasses are trapped in the recess between breech and barrel, and with steel surrounding it the gasses are safely vented away from the shooter. There is a manual safety located on the left-hand side of the frame at the rear. When engaged, it intercepts the sear. Field stripping is accomplished by first making sure that the pistol is unloaded and then removing the magazine. The barrel is then removed and the slide withdrawn to the rear and lifted slightly to disengage it from the frame and then run forward and off the pistol. Assembly is in the reverse order. The Romer was finely made of high carbon steel.

Romer .22

Roth-Steyr
Austria-Hungary

Model: 1907

Action Type: semi-automatic, recoil operated.

Caliber(s): 8mm Roth-Steyr.

Barrel Lengths: 5″.

Finish: blue.

Manufacturing Dates: 1907 to the mid-1920s, with some samples dated into the early 1930s.

Stocks: grooved wood, sometimes with a brass regimental disc inlaid.

Rifling: 4R.

Weight, Unloaded: 36¼ oz.

Sights: fixed.

Serial Numbers: starting from 1 and running to at least 32,000 on Budapest manufacture, and at least to 52,000 on the Austrian Pistol. Ranges extend 10,000 numbers higher.

Serial Number Location: right side of frame above grip.

Major Variations: none.

Markings: on top of barrel rig: Waffenfabrik Steyr, for pistols manufactured in Austria, and;
Fegyvergyar Budapest, for pistols made in Hungary.

Price(s):
　　Austrian, very good—$300.00
　　Austrian, excellent—$475.00
　　Hungarian, very good—$350.00
　　Hungarian, excellent—$525.00
　　rare unit markings add 10%
　　Italian marks add 15%
　　German marks add 25%

History: This is strictly a military pistol and was never made for commercial sale. These pistols were said to have been manufactured in Steyr from 1908 to 1913 and from 1911 until 1914 in Budapest, with experts opining that later date stamps indicate pistols assembled from leftover parts or are reworks. The Model 1907 was designed by G. Roth and Karel Krnka, and first developed in prototype in 1904 in 7.65mm, 8mm, and 10mm variations. After testing the final form, the Roth Steyr was adopted by the Austro-Hungarian army in 1907 and saw use through late World War II by the Italians and Germans.

Mechanical Functioning: This is a long, recoil-locked breech, semiautomatic pistol that operates as double action only, that is, there is no provision for cocking the pistol other than by pulling the trigger when firing. This was the "Automatic" safety device since unless you were pulling the trigger, this gun would not discharge. Excellent as a safety, but unfortunately poor for marksmanship. The ten-shot magazine was fixed and loaded from the top via a stripper clip.

Austrian Roth-Steyr Model 1907

Russian State Arsenal

Model: Makarov

Action Type: semiautomatic, blowback operated.

Caliber(s): 9mm Makarov.

Barrel Lengths: 3³/₄".

Finish: blue.

Manufacturing Dates: from the late 1950s to date.

Stocks: 1-piece plastic.

Rifling: 4R.

Weight, Unloaded: 28¹/₈ oz.

Sights: fixed.

Serial Number: n/a.

Serial Number Location: left side of slide.

Major Variations: Russian Model DM.
   Chinese Model 59.
   East German Model M.
   Polish Model 64.

Markings: on left side of frame are proofs and year marks.

Price(s):
   Russian Model DM, very good—$250.00
   Russian Model DM, excellent—$500.00
   Chinese Model 59, very good—$450.00
   Chinese Model 59, excellent—$650.00
   East German Model M, very good—$200.00
   East German Model M, excellent—$250.00
   Polish Model 64, very good—$250.00
   Polish Model 64, excellent—$450.00

History: After the Russians consolidated their European gains following World War II and formed the Warsaw Pact, which forced their new allies to use the Tokarev pistol, they then decided to change to the Markarov. Like all Soviet equipment, it used ammunition that cannot be interchanged with anything! The 9mm Makarov round is slightly shorter than the 9mm Parabellum, and slightly wider—it has a .358-diameter bullet as opposed to a .355 for the normal 9mm. The closest we have to it would be the .38 A.M.U. cut down. It is about as powerful as you can go and still retain a blowback action. In many respects, the Makarov is a virtual copy of the Walther PP and is made without license from Walther. The primary differences between it and the PP are the lack of a loaded chamber indicator, an externally mounted slide stop, and a spring-type magazine catch on the bottom of the gripframe.

Mechanical Functioning: This is a blowback-operated, double-action pistol with an external hammer and detachable eight-round box magazine. It uses a floating firing pin and slide-mounted safety and hammer block. The pistol is dismounted after removing the clip and making sure the gun is unloaded, by pulling the trigger guard down and wrapping it gently to one side to rest on the frame. The slide can then be pulled to the rear and the back end included upward and then slide forward and off. Assemble in reverse order.

Soviet DM Makarov

SIG
(Schweizerische Industrie Gesellschaft)
Neuhausen, Switzerland

Model: P 210

Action Type: semiautomatic, recoil operated.

Caliber(s): 7.65mm, 9mm.

Barrel Lengths: 120mm—6″.

Finish: bright blue.

Manufacturing Dates: 1948 to date.

Stocks: plastic or walnut.

Rifling: 6R.

Weight, Unloaded: 960 gm.

Sights: fixed on 210-1, P.210-2, P.210-6
adjustable micrometer on 210-5.

Serial Numbers: prefix "P" on civilian models, "A" prefix on Swiss Military
pistols, and "D" prefix on German Border Police models. Commercial
numbers start at 50,001, Danish Military (M1949) start at 1.

Serial Number Location: left side of frame and slide.

Major Variations: 210-1 is the standard model with high polish blue finish
and wood grips;
210-2 has matte blue finish and plastic grips;
210-5 is the target model with extended barrel and micrometer sights; and
210-6 is the target model with standard barrel.
Luxus model has engraving and gold inlays.

Markings: Swiss proofs and the model designation.

Price(s):
P 210 Luxus, $3,000.00–$6,000.00
P 210-1 9mm, very good—$1,250.00
P 210-1 9mm, excellent—$1,750.00
P 210-1 .22 Conversion Unit only, very good—$500.00
P 210-1 .22 Conversion Unit only, excellent—$625.00
P 210-1 with 3 Conversion Units, very good—$1,750.00
P 210-1 with 3 Conversion Units, excellent—$2,750.00
P 210-2 7.65mm, very good—$1,000.00
P 210-2 7.65mm, excellent—$1,500.00
P 210-2 9mm Luger, very good—$1,500.00
P 210-2 9mm Luger, excellent—$1,750.00
P 210-5 7.65mm, very good—$1,000.00
P 210-5 7.65mm, excellent—$1,500.00
P 210-5 9mm Luger, very good—$1,500.00
P 210-5 9mm Luger, excellent—$2,000.00
P 210-6 9mm Luger, fixed sight, very good—$1,500.00

P 210-6 9mm Luger, fixed sight, excellent—$1,750.00
P 210-6 9mm Luger, adjustable sight, very good—$1,750.00
P 210-6 9mm Luger, adjustable sight, excellent—$2,000.00
S 47/8, German Border Patrol, very good—$2,500.00
S 47/8, German Border Patrol, excellent—$3,000.00
S 47/8, Swiss Military, very good—$3,000.00
S 47/8, Swiss Military, excellent—$3,500.00

History: This model's antecedents start with the Petter-designed French M1935A, for which S.I.G. secured the rights to manufacture in 1937. The pistol was redesigned to handle 9mm Luger and after experimentation was released as the Model SP 47/8, the name changing to P.210 in the early 1950s.

Mechanical Functioning: This is a Petter-patented locked-breech, recoil-operated, semiautomatic pistol with exposed hammer and eight-shot removable box magazine.

SIG P 210-6

J. P. Sauer & Sohn
Suhl, Germany

Model: M1913 Pocket Automatic

Action Type: semiautomatic, blowback operated.

Caliber(s): 7.65mm.

Barrel Lengths: 3".

Finish: blue.

Manufacturing Dates: 1913–1930.

Stocks: hard rubber.

Rifling: 6R.

Weight, Unloaded: 22 oz.

Sights: fixed.

Serial Numbers: possibly 1 to 175,000.

Serial Number Location: left side of frame above grip.

Major Variations: early model had groove on the top of cocking knob.
later models had fixed rear sight.

Markings: left side of slide: J P Sauer & Sohn, Suhl.
top of slide; patent.
early completely checkered grip.
late "S&S" in oval at top of grip.
very late grip: "Sauer," "Cal. 7.65" impressed.

Price(s):
early, no sight, very good—$225.00
early, no sight, excellent—$300.00
late, with sight, very good—$225.00
late, with sight, excellent—$275.00
very late, "7.65" grips, very good—$200.00
very late, "7.65" grips, excellent—$250.00

History: The Model 1913 Sauer, also known as the "old model Sauer," was the first Sauer to be introduced using that company's name. Prior to this time, the only reference to the company had been their trademark on the firearm. This pistol was introduced in 1913, and the production continued on into late 1929–early 1930 just after it was superseded by the Behorden. This was a very well made pistol, even if it was slightly complex. In future years, there should be an excellent collector market for this model.

Mechanical Functioning: The Model 1913 is a straight blowback, semiautomatic pistol that is striker-activated. It has a seven-shot, detachable box magazine with a magazine catch at the bottom rear of the gripframe. The recoil spring is axially mounted around the barrel, and the safety is thumb operated, and intercepts the trigger. Takedown is somewhat similar to the Savage, in that the entire breechblock unit is removable from the rear and thus releases the slide to move forward. Takedown is accomplished by pulling the slide all the way to the rear, and above the trigger and within the trigger guard is a small lever, which is pushed upward, locking the slide in the rear position. On early models, the rear cap unscrews. On later models, the rear sight is depressed to unlock the cap so it may unscrew. The cap is then pulled out with the entire breechblock assembly. When the slide is released by pulling back slightly, it can slide off the forward end of the frame. Almost an exact copy of this pistol, but slightly reduced, was made in .25 A.C.P. and it was also known as the Model 1913.

Sauer 1913 7.65mm.

J. P. Sauer & Sohn
Suhl, Germany

Model: Roth-Sauer

Action Type: semiautomatic, recoil operated.

Caliber(s): 7.65 Roth Sauer.

Barrel Lengths: 4″.

Finish: blue.

Manufacturing Dates: 1905.

Stocks: hard rubber.

Rifling: 6R.

Weight, Unloaded: 23 oz.

Sights: fixed.

Serial Numbers: unknown.

Serial Number Location: left side of the receiver.

Major Variations: none.

Markings: none other than the Sauer trademark on the grips.

Price(s):
    Roth-Sauer, very good—$750.00
    Roth-Sauer, excellent—$1,100.00

History: The Roth Sauer was first marketed in 1905 by the firm of J. P. Sauer & Sohn, in Suhl, Germany, with the inventor of note being Georg Roth of Vienna, Austria. This pistol is based on Roth's patents from 1898 but also has features found in earlier patents designed by Karel Krnka. Since Roth was a cartridge maker, this may have been one of the pistols that he and Krnka put together, simply so he could sell another cartridge. The caliber, known as 7.65 Roth Sauer, is essentially a shortened .32 A.C.P. of lighter power. This is an interesting pistol in several respects. First, it is a very finely finished pistol made from machined steel. With all of the compound radius cuts and the intricate detail this pistol is almost a work of art. Second, it is hard to deduce its exact use. The low-powered cartridge places the gun in the pocket pistol category, but its size almost demands a holster, so what function was it designed to fulfill? No one knows exactly how many Roth Sauer pistols were made, and in the United States they are very scarce. While the pistol was discontinued just before World War I, ammunition for it was made until the late 1930s in Europe, and from that one might deduce that quite a few pistols exist in Europe or that at any rate somebody was doing a lot of shooting with them. Although they were widely marketed in the years prior to World War I, very few are seen today, making them very collectible.

Mechanical Functioning: The Roth Sauer is a semiautomatic pistol, utilizing a locked breech and recoil operation. It has a seven-shot, fixed magazine, which is loaded through the top via a stripper clip. The magazine can be unloaded with a little difficulty in two different ways. Either you can cycle all of the cartridges through the action by repeatedly reciprocating the bolt, or you can press a magazine release button located on the left side of the frame. Unfortunately, with a full magazine the cartridges tend to jump out and bounce away, so be prepared to catch them. Functioning was quite complicated. Upon firing, it utilized Krnka's long recoil system, in which the barrel and breechblock both recoiled to the rear until the bolt hit a cam to rotate it in order to unlock it. The bolt traveled a slight bit further back, while the barrel moved forward, ejecting the empty case. As the barrel came to rest, it tripped a lock, allowing the bolt to fly forward and strip a fresh cartridge into the chamber. The force of closing rotated the bolt, locking it again. The trigger mechanism was also unusual. After the bolt had been cycled, the striker was held back engaged by the sear. Pulling the trigger compressed the striker spring to a degree where it would impart sufficient force in order to fire the pistol and then, as the trigger continued on its backward motion, it tripped the sear. Since there was not enough spring tension on the striker to fire the cartridge until the trigger was pulled, it was considered unnecessary to have any safeties at all on this pistol. This mechanism should not be confused with double action, as is found on another Roth design, the Roth-Steyr. In that pistol, pulling the trigger actually cocks the striker. On this pistol the manual operation of the bolt is necessary to cock the striker, and the trigger merely imparts additional compression to the spring.

Sauer Roth-Sauer 7.65mm

J. P. Sauer & Sohn GMBH
D-2330
Eckernforde, West Germany

Model: 38 H

Action Type: semiautomatic, blowback operated, double action.

Caliber(s): .22LR, 7.65mm, 9mm K.

Barrel Lengths: 3¼".

Finish: blue.

Manufacturing Dates: 1938–1945.

Stocks: plastic or wood.

Rifling: 4R.

Weight, Unloaded: 25¼ oz.

Sights: fixed.

Serial Numbers: started around 175,000 and ran to over 500,000.

Serial Number Location: left or right side of frame to the rear of the grip.

Major Variations: Commercial.
Military.
Military, no safety.
Military, lightweight.

Markings: early, left side of frame: J.P. Sauer & Sohn, Suhl, Cal. 7.65.
late, left side of frame: cal. 7.65.

Price(s):
9mm K, very good—$1,750.00
9mm K, excellent—$2,500.00
.22LR, very good—$2,250.00
.22LR, excellent—$3,000.00
7.65mm, very good—$275.00
7.65mm, excellent—$375.00
Military, 7.65mm, very good—$350.00
Military, 7.65mm, excellent—$450.00
Military, no safety, very good—$325.00
Military, no safety, excellent—$425.00
lightweight, very good—$500.00
lightweight, excellent—$675.00
Nazi Police, very good—$375.00
Nazi Police, excellent—$500.00

History: The venerable firm of J.P. Sauer & Sohn, realizing that the market could use a good double-action pistol, began experimenting in the early 1930s to come up with a better design, and several models and styles were tried, finally developing in 1938 the Model H (standing for Hahn). This was perhaps the most advanced pistol of its day, and had there not been a war, this pistol would have been the standard for the industry. It had a mechanical safety located on the slide that blocked the floating firing pin, but the most noteworthy feature was the internal concealed hammer, and the cocking and decocking lever located on the left side of the frame. This was a double-action pistol in which you could use a lever either to cock the hammer if you wished or to uncock it if there was a round in the chamber, allowing the hammer down safely, and the pistol to be carried. Unfortunately, as the war progressed, shortcuts had to be taken in the manufacturing of pistols, and one of the first items to go after the fine finish was the mechanical safety located on the slide. During the war, Sauer experimented with a lightweight model having a duralumin receiver. These pistols can also be found in .25 A.C.P. and in .380 A.C.P.

Mechanical Functioning: The Sauer .38H is a straight blowback-operated, semiautomatic pistol with an eight-shot detachable box magazine inserted through the gripframe with a spring-loaded catch retaining it on the left side of the receiver behind the trigger. The mechanism is double action, using a concealed hammer. On the left side of the frame is a cocking lever that will cock the hammer when it is in the down position or in the cocked position, will safely lower the hammer. A similar feature was also found on the Gustloff Werke pistol. Disassembly is quite simple. After making sure that the firearm is unloaded, and removing the magazine, pull the slide lock catch, which is located inside the trigger guard just forward of the trigger, downward, and while holding it down, withdraw the slide all the way to the rear and lift. The slide can now be removed forward and off the barrel. Assemble in the reverse order.

Sauer 38 H

Savage Arms Corp.
Utica, NY

Model: 1907

Action Type: semiautomatic, blowback operated.

Caliber(s): .32 A.C.P., .380 A.C.P.

Barrel Lengths: 3³/₄″, 4¹/₄″.

Finish: blue or nickel.

Manufacturing Dates: 1907–1920.

Stocks: hard rubber or steel.

Rifling: 6R.

Weight, Unloaded: 19 oz.

Sights: fixed.

Serial Numbers: .32 A.C.P. starting point is unsure, but ran to about 230,000.
.380 A.C.P. lowest is about 2000B, but some early pistols seemed to start at 5000B indicating lack of sequencing.
B suffix is .380 caliber,
A suffix is for special runs.

Serial Number Location: facing the front of frame below the slide.

Major Variations: 1908 type: burr cocking piece.
1909 type: burr cocking piece.
1912 type: burr cocking piece.
1913 type: burr cocking piece.
1914 type: spur cocking piece.
1918 type: burr cocking piece, no cartridge indicator.
1918 type: spur cocking piece.
Military type: burr cocking piece.
Military type: burr cocking piece.

Markings: various lettering styles of the Savage address.

Price(s):
Model 1908 type, .32 A.C.P., very good—$350.00
Model 1980 type, .32 A.C.P., excellent—$450.00
Model 1909 type, .32 A.C.P., very good—$325.00
Model 1909 type, .32 A.C.P., excellent—$425.00
Model 1912 type, .32 A.C.P., very good—$275.00
Model 1912 type, .32 A.C.P., excellent—$400.00
Model 1913 type, .380 A.C.P., very good—$375.00
Model 1913 type, .380 A.C.P., excellent—$450.00
Model 1914 type, .32 A.C.P., very good—$300.00
Model 1914 type, .32 A.C.P., excellent—$375.00
Model 1914 type, .380 A.C.P., very good—$325.00
Model 1914 type, .380 A.C.P., excellent—$425.00
Model 1918 type, .32 A.C.P., no cartridge indicator, very good—$275.00
Model 1918 type, .32 A.C.P., no cartridge indicator, excellent—$350.00
Model 1918 type, .32 A.C.P., very good—$275.00

Model 1918 type, .32 A.C.P., excellent—$400.00
Model 1918 type, .380 A.C.P., very good—$350.00
Model 1918 type, .380 A.C.P., excellent—$475.00
Military type, .32 A.C.P., very good—$250.00
Military type, .32 A.C.P., excellent—$350.00
Military type, .32 A.C.P., Portugese contract, very good—$400.00
Military type, .32 A.C.P., Portugese contract, excellent—$550.00

History: The Savage Model 1907 has long been the subject of controversy over just what should be the proper nomenclature of the pistol, with many people calling it the 1905, others calling it the Savage Automatic. It appears that the proper nomenclature is the Model 1907. The confusion probably stems from two sources. This pistol was invented by William Condit and Albert H. Searle, and in 1905 they patented their pistol. By the end of 1905 the designs had been sold to Savage Arms Company. In 1906, Savage decided to try to enter the U.S. competition for the army pistol, for which tests were to be held in 1907, and for this they utilized the design of a .45 caliber. By the middle of 1906, they decided to resume tooling up for the production of the .32 caliber pistol, which was finally introduced in August of 1907 with the official factory designation: Savage Automatic Pistol, Pocket Model, Caliber .32. In later years, the factory was to call it just the Model 1907. It does, however, appear that the first pistols were not on the market until early 1908.

Mechanical Functioning: The Savage Model 1907 is a straight blowback-operated, semiautomatic pistol with a ten-shot detachable box magazine in .32 caliber, and nine-shot detachable box magazine in .380 caliber. Although it appears to have a hammer, the projection scene at the rear of the slide is actually the tail end of the striker assembly, and it acts as an exposed cocking piece. Because of the nature of the beast, and since this is not a hammer in the usual sense, when it is lowered, the firing pin projects far enough to set off a cartridge. This pistol is absolutely unsafe to carry with a round in the chamber and the cocking piece lowered.

Savage 1907

Savage Arms Corp.
Utica, NY

Model: M1917

Action Type: semiautomatic, blowback operated.

Caliber(s): .32 A.C.P., .380 A.C.P.

Barrel Lengths: 3″.

Finish: blue.

Manufacturing Dates: 1920–1928.

Stocks: hard rubber.

Rifling: 6R.

Weight, Unloaded: 21⁷⁄₈ oz.

Sights: fixed.

Serial Numbers: .32 A.C.P. started at about 229,777 and ran to about 259,475.
.380 A.C.P. started at about 15750B and ran to about 29670B.

Serial Number Location: front of frame below barrel.

Major Variations: none.

Markings: left side of frame: Savage 1917 Model.

Price(s):
Model 1917, .32 A.C.P., very good—$150.00
Model 1917, .32 A.C.P., excellent—$225.00
Model 1917, .380 A.C.P., very good—$275.00
Model 1917, .380 A.C.P., excellent—$375.00

History: The Savage Model 1917 was the successor to the Model 1907 and all of its variants, and even continued in the same serial number range as those pistols. It had several differences from the 1907, the most striking of which was the shape of the grip—very wide and flared at the bottom, and then tapering toward the top on the backside, while the forward gripstrap was virtually straight up and down. The grips were unusual also for the Savage series. Instead of being the snap-in grips, they were held in place by grip screws. Like the 1907, it has a striker with a spur on it, so that at first glance it resembles a hammer. Though it is called the Model 1917, production of the Model 1907 continued until 1920, at which time the 1917 went into production. By the start of the depression in 1929, sales had already dropped to a point where production had been discontinued. About 28,000 .32 A.C.P. Model 1917s and about 13,000 .380 A.C.P. Model 1917s were made, making them both rather collectible.

Mechanical Functioning: The Savage Model 1917 in both calibers is a delayed blowback, semiautomatic pistol with a ten-shot detachable box magazine in .32 caliber, inserted through the gripframe and retained by a spring catch located on the forward part of the gripstrap. It has an exposed striker, allowing recocking without having to recycle the slide, and a side-mounted safety that inhibits the sear. Please note on these pistols it is very dangerous to attempt to lower the striker with a round in the chamber, as the firing pin will protrude through the breech face, and there may be enough force to discharge the cartridge. Takedown is accomplished by clearing the weapon and making sure it is unloaded. Remove the magazine, draw the slide back as far as it will go, and engage the thumb safety until it locks the slide. Grasp the breechblock and striker spur and turn 90 degrees to the right. The assembly may now be withdrawn out of the slide. While holding the slide firmly, release the safety and allow the slide to come off of the front of the frame. The barrel can now be lifted straight out of the frame. Assembly is in the reverse order.

Savage Model 1917 .32 A.C.P.

August Schueler
Suhl, Germany

Model: Reform

Action Type: manual repeater.

Caliber(s): 6mm RF., 6.35mm.

Barrel Lengths: 3″, 7″.

Finish: blue.

Manufacturing Dates: circa 1907–1914.

Stocks: hard rubber.

Rifling: 4R.

Weight, Unloaded: 12 oz.

Sights: fixed.

Serial Numbers: n/a.

Serial Number Location: on barrel.

Major Variations: 4 barreled 6.35mm.
single shot 6mm RF.

Markings: left side of barrels: Brevete D.M.P. 177023.
on grips: Reform Pistole.

Price(s):
Reform, 4 barrel, .25 A.C.P., very good—$425.00
Reform, 4 barrel, .25 A.C.P., excellent—$550.00
Reform, 1 barrel, 6mm RF, very good—$450.00
Reform, 1 barrel, 6mm RF, excellent—$575.00
Reform, both barrels, very good—$600.00
Reform, both barrels, excellent—$750.00

History: The Reform is an unusual pocket pistol manufactured by August Schueler of Suhl, Germany. The exact dates of manufacture are not known, nor is the quantity produced. It is assumed that production, judging by contemporary catalogs, was carried out from about 1907 until the beginning of World War I. The handgun that he developed was a multibarreled repeater of unique design, and was available in two variations. It could be had with a four-barreled insert chambered for .25 A.C.P., or for a single-barrel insert with a long barrel chambered for 6mm rimfire. During its day, the Reform and other pistols similar to it were extremely popular due to their light weight and thinness, leading to the ease of carrying it concealed.

Mechanical Functioning: The Reform pistol is a double-action, multibarreled, manually operated repeating arm. It has an external hammer and when cocked, the manual safety located on the left side of the frame effectively blocks the hammer and prevents it from dropping. A highly unusual system incorporated a rising block that was raised by the trigger lever, which in turn pushed each barrel up and in line with the firing pin to be fired. When using the four-barrel insert, upon each shot the barrels moved up one click aligning the next chamber with the firing pin. An unusual feature is that within about ⅛″ of the end of the barrel, there was an angled hole drilled from each barrel to the one above it. And as the block rose, bringing each chamber in sequential line, the last fired chamber was exposed. Upon firing, gases would enter the hole and flow through the already fired barrel knocking the spent cartridge case out; therefore, the only barrel that had to have manual extraction of the cartridge case was the fourth barrel, which was the last one fired. The barrels were inserted and replaced simply by pulling up on them while pushing down on them with the hammer in the forward position.

Reform Pistol with Three .25 A.C.P. Barrels

A.W. Schwarzlose GMBH
Berlin, Germany

Model: M1908

Action Type: semiautomatic, blowforward operated.

Caliber(s): .32 A.C.P.

Barrel Lengths: 4⅛".

Finish: blue.

Manufacturing Dates: 1908–1911, parts assembled in U.S. until 1913.

Stocks: hard rubber.

Weight, Unloaded: 18¾ oz.

Sights: front sight only.

Serial Numbers: may have started at 1, ran to over 6,000.

Serial Number Location: right side of frame.

Major Variations: early model had checkered finger grooves on slide. late model had grooved slide.

Markings: right side of frame: Schwarzlose trademark.
left side of frame: A. W. Schwarzlose GMBH, Berlin.
Warner Arms Corp. Overprints: Patent Dates on left side of slide.
Warner Arms Corporation, Brooklyn, N.Y. U.S.A. on right frame.
W.A.C. monogram on grips.

Price(s):
Model 1908, early, very good—$325.00
Model 1908, early, excellent—$475.00
Model 1908, early, W.A.C., very good—$300.00
Model 1908, early, W.A.C., excellent—$425.00
Model 1908, late, plain top grips, very good—$300.00
Model 1908, late, plain top grips, excellent—$425.00
Model 1908, late, full checkered grips, very good—$300.00
Model 1908, late, full checkered grips, excellent—$400.00
Model 1908, late, W.A.C., very good—$340.00
Model 1908, late, W.A.C., excellent—$495.00

History: Although made in very limited quantities, the Schwarzlose Model 1908 was significant enough that it should be listed in any compilation of collectible handguns. Andreas Wilhelm Schwarzlose was another of the prolific firearms inventors of the turn of the century, his first pistol being developed in 1893, and gaining fame primarily through his fully automatic weapons. Starting in about 1906, Schwarzlose began work on a pocket model pistol that finally went into production in 1908. In the public mind it stands alone as being a blowforward pistol rather than a blowback pistol, and in truth there was only one other, the Mannlicher 1894. Unfortunately, the pistol was an uncomfortable one to shoot, as even with the small caliber of .32 A.C.P., it packed quite a wallop, since there is no moving breechblock to take up some of the recoil energy. That and the faults of frequent jamming and extraction and ejection problems spelled the death for this pistol. It was discontinued in Germany in 1911, but its American distributor, Warner Arms Corporation of Brooklyn, New York, purchased the remaining stocks of parts and assembled and sold them in the United States until about 1913.

Mechanical Functioning: The Schwarzlose Model 1908 was a blowforward-operated, semiautomatic pistol with a detachable seven-shot box magazine inserted through the gripframe and retained by a spring catch at the base of the butt. It utilized a concealed hammer, powered by a long leaf spring and mounted behind the standing breech. It has a grip safety located in the forward part of the gripstrap. Upon firing, the barrel assembly is pushed forward, while the cartridge case remains held against the standing breechface. On the barrel's return, it strips a round out of the magazine and pops it back up against that breech face and into the chamber.

Schwarzlose Model 1908

Waffenfabriken Simson & Co.
Suhl, Germany

Model: Vest Pocket

Action Type: semiautomatic, blowback operated.

Caliber(s): 6.35mm.

Barrel Lengths: 2⅛″.

Finish: blue.

Manufacturing Dates: 1922 to early 1930s.

Stocks: hard rubber.

Rifling: 6R.

Weight, Unloaded: 13⅛ oz.

Sights: fixed.

Serial Numbers: n/a, but observed from 20,000s to 60,000s.

Serial Number Location: on frame forward of grip.

Major Variations: 1922 style: rounded frame bottom from trigger forward. 1927 style: flat frame sides.

Markings: right side of slide: Selbstladepistole Simson D.R.P. left side of frame: Waffenfabriken Simson & Co. Suhl.

Price(s):
    1922 style, very good—$300.00
    1922 style, excellent—$450.00
    1927 style, very good—$350.00
    1927 style, excellent—$500.00

History: The firm Waffenfabriken Simson & Company of Suhl, Germany, came out of World War I in a lucky position. According to the terms of the Versailles Treaty, they were the only plant in Germany allowed to manufacture military rifles. With this assurance of profit, in 1922 the people of Simson undertook the manufacture of a small handgun which they properly surmised would be well accepted in Germany, where anarchy was the rule rather than the exception and where the average citizen needed a small concealable firearm just for his own protection. They made what they called the Selbstladepistole Simson, a small 6.35mm caliber vest-pocket-size pistol, unusual because it has the ejection port located on the top of the semitubular slide, with the ejection being straight up. The original style issued in 1922 had a frame that was slightly rounded from the trigger on forward. In 1927 they decided to modify the frame slightly and change the contour so that it was flat for its entire length, eliminating the radius. In the early 1930s this pistol was discontinued.

Mechanical Functioning: The Simson Vest Pocket's style of 1922 and 1927 are striker fired, blowback-operated, semiautomatic pistols with six-shot detachable box magazines inserted through the gripframe and retained by a spring-loaded catch at the base of the butt. The safety is manually operated with the lever located on the rear left-hand portion of the frame, which engages the sear. To disassemble the pistol, first make sure that it is unloaded, and then pull the trigger. Remove the magazine and at the same time, push forward with your thumb on the rear of the slide, and with your other thumb, press forward on the catch located on the inside, forward end of the trigger guard. This will allow the slide to be removed in the forward direction. The striker and striker spring can now be removed. The recoil spring, which is axially wound around the recoil spring guide and the barrel, can be removed by pushing the recoil spring guide through the barrel lug towards the rear. The spring can then be lifted from the barrel lug, and the slide and the barrel lifted out. Assembly is in the reverse order.

Simson Vest Pocket .25 A.C.P.

Smith & Wesson
2100 Roosevelt Ave.
Springfield, MA 01101

Model: 10; M & P

Action Type: revolver, double action.

Caliber(s): .38 Special.

Barrel Lengths: 2″, 3″, 4″, 5″, 6″.

Finish: blue or nickel.

Manufacturing Dates: 1899 to date.

Stocks: checkered walnut.

Rifling: 5R.

Weight, Unloaded: 30½ oz. 4″ standard barrel.
34 oz. 4″ heavy barrel.

Sights: fixed.

Serial Numbers: starting at 1 and going to 20,975 for the first model (1899–1902); 20,976–33,803 (1902–1903) for the second Model 1902; 33,804–64,499 for the 1902 second type (1903–1905); 62,450–73,250 for the 1905 Model; 73,251–146,899 for the second and third types (1906–1909); 146,900–241,703 for the fourth type (1909–1915); 241,704–1,000,000 for the fifth type (1915–1942); in 1942 the Victory Series started at V1; at V769,000 a new hammer block was incorporated and the prefix changed to VS and ran to VS811,119; some converted revolvers have SV prefix; in 1945 commercial sales started at S811,120 and went to S1,000,000; in 1948 the numbers again started, this time at C1 to C1,000,000 in 1967; in 1967 the numbers started at D1.

Serial Number Location: bottom of butt.

Major Variations: barrel configurations: standard tapered barrel or straight heavy barrel in 3″ and 4″ lengths, round or square butt frame, many internal changes.

Markings: left side of barrel: Smith & Wesson.
right side of barrel: caliber designation.
right side of frame: on sideplate, S & W trademark.
right side of frame, forward of trigger guard: address stamp.
(These are general markings—there are many variations!)

Price(s):
Model 1899, army, very good—$850.00, excellent—$1,250.00
Model 1899, target, very good—$600.00, excellent—$1,000.00
Model 1899, civilian, very good—$400.00, excellent—$600.00
Model 1899, second type, very good—$350.00, excellent—$450.00.
Model 1899, second type, navy, very good—$750.00, excellent—$1,250.00
Model 1902, very good—$300.00, excellent—$425.00
Model 1902, target, very good—$650.00, excellent—$800.00
Model 1905, very good—$300.00, excellent—$400.00

Model 1905, target, very good—$550.00, excellent—$750.00
Model 1905, second type, very good—$300.00, excellent—$400.00
Model 1905, third type, very good—$300.00, excellent—$375.00
Model 1905, fourth type, very good—$300.00, excellent—$375.00
Model 1905, fifth type, very good—$275.00, excellent—$350.00
Victory, very good—$200.00, excellent—$250.00
Victory S, very good—$225.00, excellent—$275.00
Model 10 "S," very good—$225.00, excellent—$325.00
Model 10, very good—$225.00, excellent—$300.00
Model 10 heavy barrel, very good—$250.00, excellent—$325.00
for nickel plating add 5% (disc. 1991)

History: Introduced in 1899 as the Model 1899, this was to become one of Smith & Wesson's most successful models. The official title for this revolver was ".38 Hand Ejector Military & Police Model." It was also known as the "Military & Police," or just as the "M & P." In the first issue it was also called the Model 1899 Army & Navy Revolver. Production of this model is now approaching the 4,000,000 mark. Serial-numbered in series with the Model 10 are the Models 45, 12, 13, 64, and 65. Since February 1948 there have been no major mechanical changes in the lockwork of the Model 10. The wartime (1942–1945) Model 10 was called the Victory model.

Mechanical Functioning: This is a double-action, solid-frame revolver with a swing-out cylinder with simultaneous manual ejection. The Model 10 is built on the "K" frame, a medium-size frame incorporating a cylinder center pin with fore and aft locks to provide positive locking and alignment. The cylinder is unlocked by means of a thumbpiece, and when opened, the internal thumbpiece latch prevents the action from being cocked, or if cocked, prevents the cylinder from opening. Two automatic hammer blocks are incorporated; one operating as a physical block riding in a groove cut into the sideplate; the other by means of protrusions on the top of the rebound block and the bottom of the hammer. Both prevent accidental firing when dropped. The mainspring is of leaf design, and trigger overtravel is controlled by an insert at the inside rear of the trigger guard. This revolver is made of high-carbon steel.

Smith & Wesson Model 10 M & P, 4" Barrel

Smith & Wesson
2100 Roosevelt Ave.
Springfield, MA 01101

Model: 19; .357 Combat Magnum.

Action Type: revolver, double action.

Caliber(s): .357 Magnum.

Barrel Lengths: 2½", 4", 6" (4" only since 1991).

Finish: blue or nickel.

Manufacturing Dates: 1955 to date.

Stocks: checkered Goncaco Alves.

Rifling: 5R.

Weight, Unloaded: 35 oz. with 4" barrel.

Sights: micrometer click rear, quick draw front; various other combinations available.

Serial Numbers: started at K260,001. Texas Ranger ran from TR1 to TR10,000.

Serial Number Location: on bottom of butt.

Major Variations: square butt on 4" and 6" barrels, round butt on 2½" barrel Texas Ranger Commemorative. Target hammer, target or combat triggers available. In 1961 cylinder stop spring screw in front of trigger guard was eliminated.

Markings: left side of barrel: Smith & Wesson.
right side of barrel: caliber designation.
right side of frame: on sideplate, S & W trademark.
right side of frame, forward of trigger guard: address stamp.

Price(s):
2½" blue, standard, excellent—$300.00
2½" nickel, standard, excellent—$325.00
2½" blue, fancy sights, excellent—$325.00
2½" nickel, fancy sights, excellent—$350.00
4" or 6" blue, standard, excellent—$275.00
4" or 6" nickel, standard, excellent—$300.00
4" or 6" blue, fancy sights, excellent—$300.00
4" or 6" nickel, fancy sights, excellent—$325.00
4" or 6" target hammer, target trigger, blue standard, excellent—$350.00
4" or 6" target hammer, target trigger, nickel standard, excellent—$375.00
4" or 6" target hammer, target trigger, blue, fancy sights, excellent—$375.00
4" or 6" target hammer, target trigger, nickel, fancy sights, excellent—$400.00
Texas Ranger with knife, excellent—$750.00
Texas Ranger without knife, excellent—$500.00
early model with cylinder stop spring screw, blue, very good—$225.00; excellent—$300.00

early model with cylinder stop spring screw, nickel, very good—
$250.00; excellent—$325.00

2½" barrel, serial numbers K544672 to K544721, blue, very good—$275.00;
excellent—$350.00

2½" barrel, serial numbers K544672 to K544721, nickel, very good—
$275.00; excellent—$375.00

3" barrel, blue, very good—$375.00; excellent—$450.00

3" barrel, nickel, very good—$300.00; excellent—$475.00

History: The Model 19 Combat Magnum was developed after the Border
Patrol's famous agent Bill Jordan asked Smith & Wesson for a lightweight
.357 Revolver. Smith & Wesson's answer was the Model 19, built on the K
target frame. The first gun in the series was presented to Bill Jordan. In
1972 the Texas Ranger Commemorative was made, and sold encased with
a matching numbered Bowie knife. Ten thousand were made, with 50
being Class A engraved. The first 8,000 Texas Rangers were sold with the
knife as a set; the remaining knives and revolvers were sold separately.

Mechanical Functioning: This is a double-action, solid-frame revolver with a
swing-out cylinder with simultaneous manual ejection. The Model 19 is
built on the "K" frame, a medium-size frame incorporating a cylinder
center pin with fore and aft locks to provide positive locking and alignment. The cylinder is unlocked by means of a thumbpiece, and when
opened, the internal thumbpiece latch prevents the action from being
cocked, or if cocked, prevents the cylinder from opening. Two automatic
hammer blocks are incorporated; one operating as a physical block riding
in a groove cut into the sideplate; the other by means of protrusions on
the top of the rebound block and the bottom of the hammer. Both prevent
accidental firing when dropped. The mainspring is of leaf design, and
trigger overtravel is controlled by an insert at the inside rear of the trigger
guard. This revolver is made of high-carbon steel.

Smith & Wesson Model 19 2½" Barrel
Photo courtesy of Smith & Wesson

Smith & Wesson
2100 Roosevelt Ave.
Springfield, MA 01101

Model: 29

Action Type: revolver, double action.

Caliber(s): .44 Magnum.

Barrel Lengths: 4" (disc. 1992), 5" (500 manuf.), 6", 8⅜", 10⅝" (silhouette).

Finish: blue or nickel.

Manufacturing Dates: 1955 to date.

Stocks: checkered Goncaco Alves.

Rifling: 5R.

Weight, Unloaded: 47 oz. with 6" barrel.

Sights: adjustable white outline rear, red ramp front.

Serial Numbers: started at S130,927 numbered with the N frame series to S333,454 in 1969, then restarting at N1. Prototypes were S121,636-9.

Serial Number Location: on bottom of butt.

Major Variations: 4 screw sideplate variety prior to 1957 (Model 29).
no cylinder stop spring screw after 1961 (Model 29-2)
left-hand threaded extractor rod after 1959 (Model 29-1)

Markings: on left side of barrel: Smith & Wesson.
on right side of barrel: caliber designation
on right side of frame: on sideplate, S & W trademark.
on right side of frame, forward of trigger guard: address stamp.
(These are general markings—there are many variations!)

Price(s):
4" blue, excellent—$650.00
4" nickel, excellent—$675.00
8⅜" blue, excellent—$675.00
8⅜" nickel, excellent—$700.00
early, 4-screw sideplate, hardened center pin bushing, blue, very good—
$600.00; excellent—$850.00
early, 4-screw sideplate, hardened center pin bushing, nickel, very
good—$650.00; excellent—$900.00
early, 4-screw sideplate, no bushing, blue, very good—$500.00; excel-
lent—$750.00
early, 4-screw sideplate, no bushing, nickel, very good—$500.00; excel-
lent—$775.00
3-screw sideplate, cylinder stop spring screw, blue, very good—$450.00;
excellent—$550.00
3-screw sideplate, cylinder stop spring screw, nickel, very good—
$450.00; excellent—$575.00
5" barrel, blue, very good—$750.00

5" barrel, blue, excellent—$950.00
5" barrel, nickel, very good—$500.00
5" barrel, nickel, excellent—$1,000.00

History: Developed in 1954 and 1955, and based on the .44 hand ejector frame, this revolver is the brainchild of Elmer Keith and the collaboration of Remington Arms (developer of the cartridge) and Smith & Wesson. For many years this model held the distinction of being the world's most powerful handgun. The very early models had a replacement center pin bushing, for which no special stamping was noted and the three major changes of four- to three-screw sideplate, elimination of the cylinder stop spring screw, and the threading change on the extractor rod to prevent jamming. A new style is the 10⅝" barreled Model 29 Silhouette with an adjustable front sight.

Mechanical Functioning: This is a double-action, solid-frame revolver with a swing-out cylinder with simultaneous manual ejection. The Model 29 is built on the "NT" frame, a medium-size frame incorporating a cylinder center pin with fore and aft locks to provide positive locking and alignment. The cylinder is unlocked by means of a thumbpiece, and when opened, the internal thumbpiece latch prevents the action from being cocked, or if cocked, prevents the cylinder from opening. Two automatic hammer blocks are incorporated; one operating as a physical block riding in a groove cut into the sideplate; the other by means of protrusions on the top of the rebound block and the bottom of the hammer. Both prevent accidental firing when dropped. The mainspring is of leaf design, and trigger overtravel is controlled by a rod in the rebound block. This revolver is made of high-carbon steel.

Smith & Wesson Model 29 4" Barrel

Smith & Wesson
2100 Roosevelt Avenue
Springfield, MA 01101

Model: 34; 1953 .22/.32 Kit Gun, and 1935 .22/.32 Kit Gun

Action Type: revolver, double action.

Caliber(s): .22 L.R.

Barrel Lengths: 2″, 4″.

Finish: blue or nickel (disc. in 1986).

Manufacturing Dates: 1936–1942, 1950–1991.

Stocks: checkered walnut.

Rifling: 6R.

Weight, Unloaded: 24½ oz. with 4″ barrel.

Sights: adjustable rear.

Serial Numbers: 1935 type started at 530,003 in 1936 and ran to 534,636 in the .32 Hand Ejector Series in 1942. Production resumed in 1950 at 551,123. In 1953 the model was redesigned and incorporated the "I" frame. Numbers started at 101 and ran with the Model 35. In 1968 at number 135,465 the "M" prefix began at M1.

Serial Number Location: bottom of butt.

Major Variations: round or square butt; after World War II new style hammer block was used; 1953 model has new I frame with coil mainspring; changed from 4- to 3-screw sideplate in 1955 at number 11,000; changed from I frame to J frame in 1960 at number 70,000 (Model 34-1).

Markings: on left side of barrel: Smith & Wesson.
on right side of barrel: caliber designation.
on right side of frame: on sideplate, S & W trademark.
on right side of frame, forward of trigger guard: address stamp.
(These are general markings—there are many variations!)

Price(s):
Model 1935, prewar, blue, very good—$300.00
Model 1935, prewar, blue, excellent—$400.00
Model 1935, prewar, nickel, very good—$250.00
Model 1935, prewar, nickel, excellent—$450.00
Model 1935, postwar, blue, very good—$275.00
Model 1935, postwar, blue, excellent—$350.00
Model 1935, postwar, nickel, very good—$300.00
Model 1935, postwar, nickel, excellent—$375.00
Model 1953, 4-screw sideplate, blue, very good—$250.00
Model 1953, 4-screw sideplate, blue, excellent—$325.00
Model 1953, 4-screw sideplate, nickel, very good—$250.00
Model 1953, 4-screw sideplate, nickel, excellent—$350.00
Model 1953, I frame, blue, very good—$250.00

Model 1953, I frame, blue, excellent—$300.00
Model 1953, I frame, nickel, very good—$220.00
Model 1953, I frame, nickel, excellent—$325.00

History: Developed in 1935 in response to market demands for a lightweight .22 revolver to be carried in a fisherman's or hunter's "kit" (hence the name), this model was originally the 4"-barreled version of the .22/.32 target model. After 1953, when the frame was improved and the model designation changed to 34, the target version became the Model 35 and was merely the 34 with a 6" barrel. The serials for both ran together in the same range. The Model 35 was discontinued in 1973.

Mechanical Functioning: This is a double-action, solid-frame revolver with a swing-out cylinder with simultaneous manual ejection. The Model 34 is built on the "JT" frame, a medium-size frame incorporating a cylinder center pin with fore and aft locks to provide positive locking and alignment. The cylinder is unlocked by means of a thumbpiece, and when opened, the internal thumbpiece latch prevents the action from being cocked, or if cocked, prevents the cylinder from opening. Two automatic hammer blocks are incorporated; one operating as a physical block riding in a groove cut into the sideplate; the other by means of protrusions on the top of the rebound block and the bottom of the hammer. Both prevent accidental firing when dropped. The mainspring is of coil type, and the cylinder holds six shots.

Smith & Wesson Model 34, 4" Barrel

Smith & Wesson
2100 Roosevelt Ave.
Springfield, MA 01101

Model: 36; .38 Chief's Special

Action Type: revolver, double action.

Caliber(s): .38 Special.

Barrel Lengths: 2″, 3″, 3″ heavy barrel (disc. 1994).

Finish: blue or nickel (disc. 1994).

Manufacturing Dates: 1950 to date.

Stocks: checkered walnut.

Rifling: 5R.

Weight, Unloaded: 19 oz. with 2″ barrel.

Sights: fixed.

Serial Numbers: started at 1 and ran to 786,544. In 1969 started at J1 and went to J99,999. In 1970 started at 1J1 and ran to 994J94. In 1972 began at J100,000.

Serial Number Location: bottom of butt.

Major Variations: prior to 1953 had cylinder stop spring screw.
prior to 1955 had 4-screw sideplate.
prior to 1962 had ball-ended mainspring guide.
prior to 1966 had flat thumbpiece.
round and square butt available.
36-1 is the 3″ heavy barrel.
Chief Special Target with adjustable sights.

Markings: on left side of barrel: Smith & Wesson.
on right side of barrel: caliber designation.
on right side of frame: on sideplate, S & W trademark.
on right side of frame, forward of trigger guard: address stamp.
(These are general markings—there are many variations!)

Price(s):
2″ blue, excellent—$250.00
2″ nickel—$275.00
3″ heavy barrel, blue—$300.00
3″ heavy barrel, nickel—$325.00
Chief's Special with cylinder stop spring screw, blue, very good—$275.00, excellent—$350.00
Chief's Special with cylinder stop spring screw, nickel, very good—$275.00, excellent—$375.00
Chief's Special with 4-screw sideplate, blue, very good—$250.00, excellent—$325.00
Chief's Special with 4-screw sideplate, nickel, very good—$250.00, excellent—$350.00
Chief's Special with flat thumbpiece, blue, very good—$250.00, excellent—$325.00

Chief's Special with flat thumbpiece, nickel, very good—$250.00, excellent—$350.00

Chief's Special target, round butt, blue, very good—$700.00, excellent—$950.00

Chief's Special target, round butt, nickel, very good—$900.00, excellent—$1,200.00

Chief's Special target, square butt, blue, very good—$700.00, excellent—$850.00

Chief's Special target, square butt, nickel, very good—$750.00, excellent—$1,000.00

Chief's Special target, 3" heavy barrel, blue, very good—$850.00, excellent—$1,000.00

History: Introduced in 1950 on the new J frame, this small revolver was designed primarily with plainclothes detectives in mind. Originally intended to be available only in the 2" barrel length with a round butt, requests from police officers made feasible the 3" standard barreled version by the end of 1950. In October 1952 the square butt was started. In 1967 the heavy-barreled version began life. The model designation "36" began in 1957. Starting in 1955 a very small number of Model 36s with adjustable sights have been made, some being called the Model 50, and running in the same serial number series as the Model 36. The official name for the adjustable sight model is "The Chief's Special Target."

Mechanical Functioning: This is a double-action, solid-frame revolver with a swing-out cylinder with simultaneous manual ejection. The Model 36 is built on the "J" frame, a medium-size frame incorporating a cylinder center pin with fore and aft locks to provide positive locking and alignment. The cylinder is unlocked by means of a thumbpiece, and when opened, the internal thumbpiece latch prevents the action from being cocked, or if cocked, prevents the cylinder from opening. Two automatic hammer blocks are incorporated; one operating as a physical block riding in a groove cut into the sideplate; the other by means of protrusions on the top of the rebound block and the bottom of the hammer. Both prevent accidental firing when dropped. The mainspring is of coil type, and it has a five-shot cylinder. This revolver is made of high-carbon steel.

Smith & Wesson Model 36 2" Barrel
Photo courtesy of Smith & Wesson

Smith & Wesson
2100 Roosevelt Ave.
Springfield, MA 01101

Model: 38; Bodyguard Airweight

Action Type: revolver, double action.

Caliber(s): .38 Special.

Barrel Lengths: 2″, 3″ (low production).

Finish: blue or nickel.

Manufacturing Dates: 1955 to date.

Stocks: checkered walnut.

Rifling: 5R.

Weight, Unloaded: 14½ oz.

Sights: fixed.

Serial Numbers: started at 66,000 in the J frame series, and ran to 786,544. J1 started in 1969, 2J1 started in 1970, and ran to 994J94. J100,000 began in 1972.

Serial Number Location: bottom of butt.

Major Variations: four screw sideplate before 1956.
    flat thumbpiece before 1966.

Markings: on left side of barrel: Smith & Wesson.
    on right side of barrel: caliber designation.
    on right side of frame: on sideplate, S & W trademark.
    on right side of frame, forward of trigger guard: address stamp.
    (These are general markings—there are many variations!)

Price(s):
    blue, excellent—$250.00
    nickel, excellent—$275.00
    4-screw sideplate, blue, very good—$375.00
    4-screw sideplate, blue, excellent—$450.00
    4-screw sideplate, nickel, very good—$350.00
    4-screw sideplate, nickel, excellent—$475.00
    3″ barrel, blue, very good—$300.00
    3″ barrel, blue, excellent—$350.00
    3″ barrel nickel, very good—$300.00
    3″ barrel nickel, excellent—$375.00
    flat thumbpiece, blue, very good—$275.00
    flat thumbpiece, blue, excellent—$325.00
    flat thumbpiece, nickel, very good—$275.00
    flat thumbpiece, nickel, excellent—$350.00

History: The Model 38 was introduced in 1955 to meet the need for a small, lightweight .38 revolver that can be carried in the pocket and not snag on the hammer. The Model 38 incorporates a redesigned shrouded hammer that has but a small spur projecting over the extended frame to facilitate cocking. Identical to the Model 38 is the Model 49, which has a steel frame and was first made at the request of the Massachusetts State Police in 1959. The Model 38 has an aluminum frame, with a carbon steel barrel and cylinder.

Mechanical Functioning: This is a double-action, solid-frame revolver with a swing-out cylinder with simultaneous manual ejection. The Model 38 is built on the "JAC" frame, a medium-size frame incorporating a cylinder center pin with fore and aft locks to provide positive locking and alignment. The cylinder is unlocked by means of a thumbpiece, and when opened, the internal thumbpiece latch prevents the action from being cocked, or if cocked, prevents the cylinder from opening. Two automatic hammer blocks are incorporated; one operating as a physical block riding in a groove cut into the sideplate; the other by means of protrusions on the top of the rebound block and the bottom of the hammer. Both prevent accidental firing when dropped. The mainspring is of coil design and has a five-shot cylinder. This revolver has an aluminum alloy frame.

Smith & Wesson Model 38 Bodyguard Airweight

Smith & Wesson
2100 Roosevelt Ave.
Springfield, MA 01101

Model: 41

Action Type: semiautomatic, blowback.

Caliber(s): .22 L.R., .22 Short R.F.

Barrel Lengths: 5″, 5½″, 7⅜″.

Finish: blue.

Manufacturing Dates: 1957 to date.

Stocks: checkered walnut.

Rifling: 6R.

Weight, Unloaded: 42 oz. with 5½″ barrel.

Sights: adjustable target rear, Patridge front.

Serial Numbers: started at 1401.

Serial Number Location: left side of frame above trigger guard.

Major Variations: 5″ lightweight barrel.
5½″ heavy barrel.
5½″ heavy barrel with extendable front sight.
5″ light barrel.
Model 41-1, .22 Short R.F. variation.

Markings: left side of barrel: Smith & Wesson.
left side of slide: Smith & Wesson trademark.
right side of barrel: caliber
right side of slide: address stamp.

Price(s):
7⅜″ barrel, excellent—$600.00
5½″ barrel, excellent—$550.00
Model 41, 5½″ barrel with extendable sights, very good—$450.00
Model 41, 5½″ barrel with extendable sights, excellent—$600.00
Model 41, 5″ lightweight barrel, very good—$400.00
Model 41, 5″ lightweight barrel, excellent—$550.00
Model 41, 41-1 .22 Short, very good—$800.00
Model 41, 41-1 .22 Short, excellent—$950.00

History: The Model 41 was introduced in 1957 after a long developmental period. It was originally made with a 7⅜″ barrel with detachable muzzle brake. In 1959 the lightweight 5″ barrel was introduced, and in 1963 the 5½″ heavy barrel was introduced. In 1965 the extended front sight was offered on the 5½″ barrel. In 1960 the 41-1 variation was produced in .22 Short with an aluminum slide and was called the Rapid Fire Pistol. Fewer than 1,000 41-1 pistols were made. Currently available accessories for the Model 41 include barrel weights, extended trigger guard, and barrels.

Mechanical Functioning: The Smith & Wesson Model 41 is a semiautomatic, blowback-operated, concealed-hammer pistol using a ten-round detachable box magazine. The trigger had an adjustable stop. To dismount the pistol or change barrels, after making sure the pistol is unloaded:

1. Lock slide back.
2. Remove clip.
3. Pull trigger guard down, being careful not to let barrel assembly fall off.
4. Lift off barrel assembly.
5. Pull slide back and lift the rear slightly upward.
6. Slice forward and off.
7. Reassemble in the reverse order.

Smith & Wesson 41 with 7⅜" Barrel

Smith & Wesson 41 with 5½" Barrel

Smith & Wesson
2100 Roosevelt Ave.
Springfield, MA 01101

Model: 49; Bodyguard

Action Type: revolver, double action.

Caliber(s): .38 Special.

Barrel Lengths: 2″, 3″ (special order).

Finish: blue or nickel (disc.).

Manufacturing Dates: 1959 to date.

Stocks: checkered walnut.

Rifling: 5R.

Weight, Unloaded: 20½ oz.

Sights: fixed.

Serial Numbers: started at 163051 of the J series in 1959 and ran to 786544. J1 started in 1969, 1J1 in 1970, and ran to 994J94. J100000 started in 1972.

Serial Number Location: bottom of butt.

Major Variations: flat thumbpiece prior to 1966.
stainless steel cylinder.
3″ barrel on special order.

Markings: on left side of barrel: Smith & Wesson.
on right side of barrel: caliber designation.
on right side of frame: on sideplate, S & W trademark.
on right side of frame, forward of trigger guard: address stamp.
(These are general markings—there are many variations!)

Price(s):
blue, excellent—$275.00
nickel, excellent—$300.00
3″ barrel, blue, very good—$300.00
3″ barrel, blue, excellent—$350.00
3″ barrel, nickel, very good—$300.00
3″ barrel, nickel, excellent—$375.00
stainless cylinder, very good—$350.00
stainless cylinder, excellent—$500.00
flat thumbpiece, blue, very good—$275.00
flat thumbpiece, blue, excellent—$325.00
flat thumbpiece, nickel, very good—$275.00
flat thumbpiece, nickel, excellent—$350.00

History: The Model 49 was developed in 1959 at the request of the Massachusetts State Police for a steel-framed pocket .38. Built exactly the same as the Model 38, save for the fact that it is steel and not an aluminum alloy, the Model 49 incorporates the same extended frame to provide the hammer shroud necessary to prevent the hammer from snagging cloth when carried in a pocket. The redesigned hammer also allows enough purchase so the shooter may use the single-action mode of firing. All Model 49s manufactured after the fall of 1982 have a smooth combat trigger as standard equipment, rather than the thin grooved trigger.

Mechanical Functioning: This is a double-action, solid-frame revolver with a swing-out cylinder with simultaneous manual ejection. The Model 49 is built on the "JC" frame, a medium-size frame incorporating a cylinder center pin with fore and aft locks to provide positive locking and alignment. The cylinder is unlocked by means of a thumbpiece, and when opened, the internal thumbpiece latch prevents the action from being cocked, or if cocked, prevents the cylinder from opening. Two automatic hammer blocks are incorporated; one operating as a physical block riding in a groove cut into the sideplate; the other by means of protrusions on the top of the rebound block and the bottom of the hammer. Both prevent accidental firing when dropped. The mainspring is of coil design and has a five-shot cylinder. This revolver is made of high-carbon steel.

Smith & Wesson Model 49, 2" Barrel
Photo courtesy of Smith & Wesson

Smith & Wesson
2100 Roosevelt Ave.
Springfield, MA 01101

Model: 52; .38 Master

Action Type: revolver, double action.

Caliber(s): .38 Special Wadcutter, .38 A.M.U.

Barrel Lengths: 5″.

Finish: blue.

Manufacturing Dates: 1961–1993.

Stocks: checkered walnut.

Rifling: 6R.

Weight, Unloaded: 41 oz.

Sights: Micrometer click rear, Patridge front.

Serial Numbers: began at 50,000 in the Model 39 range. This ran to 115,000 in 1970 and at that time the "A" prefix was added. The 52-A was in the range of 35,850 to 35,927.

Serial Number Location: left side of frame above trigger guard.

Major Variations: Model 52-A—alloy frame, .38 A.M.U. (87 manuf.).
Model 52—double action with a set screw to convert it to single action.
Model 52-1—single action only.
Model 52-2—coil spring extractor adopted.

Markings: left side of slide: Smith & Wesson address.
left side of frame under serial number: model designation.
on barrel over chamber: caliber designation.

Price(s):
Model 52-A, very good—$2,250.00
Model 52-A, excellent—$2,500.00
Model 52, very good—$650.00
Model 52, excellent—$800.00
Model 52-1, very good—$375.00
Model 52-1, excellent—$450.00

History: The Model 52 was developed in 1961 at the behest of the Army Marksmanship Training Unit in Fort Benning, Georgia, to use the semi-rimless, .38 A.M.U. cartridge that the A.M.T.U. had designed. It was originally designated as the Model 39-1; but afraid of confusion, Smith & Wesson renamed it the Model 52-A, when in 1963 the few surplus pistols they had were released to distributors. The first model 52s were based on the Model 39, but had a set screw to prevent full trigger travel and maintain a single-action mode. The 52-1 change to single-action lockwork was made in 1963, and in 1971 the extractor was improved and the model designation changed to 52-2.

Mechanical Functioning: This is a semiautomatic pistol utilizing a recoil operating system and is designed to fire the rimmed .38 Special and range wadcutter cartridge, with the bullet seated flush with the case mouth. It is single action only and has a five-round detachable box magazine. It has an adjustable trigger stop to prevent overtravel. The Model 52 is designed to be an extremely accurate target pistol, and is hand-fitted and well tested for accuracy. It is of all-steel construction, and an accessory counterweight is available.

Smith & Wesson Model 52
Photo courtesy of Smith & Wesson

Smith & Wesson
2100 Roosevelt Ave.
Springfield, MA 01101

Model: 58; .41 Military and Police

Action Type: revolver, double action.

Caliber(s): .41 Magnum.

Barrel Lengths: 4".

Finish: blue or nickel.

Manufacturing Dates: 1964–1979.

Stocks: checkered walnut.

Rifling: 5R.

Weight, Unloaded: 41 oz.

Sights: fixed.

Serial Numbers: production serial numbers started at S258,032.

Serial Number Location: bottom of butt.

Major Variations: none.

Markings: on left side of barrel: Smith & Wesson.
on right side of barrel: caliber designation.
on right side of frame: on sideplate, S & W trademark.
on right side of frame, forward of trigger guard: address stamp.
logo over sideplate, right side.
(These are general markings—there are many variations!)

Price(s):
blue, very good—$325.00
blue, excellent—$400.00
nickel, very good—$300.00
nickel, excellent—$425.00

History: Introduced in 1964 to take the place of the then discontinued .44 Special Military Model of 1950, this gun was touted by all and sundry to be the ideal sidearm for police officers. It did have two major advantages: low cost and a very underrated cartridge, the .41 Magnum, which could easily stop anything on four wheels without the punishing recoil of the .44 Magnum. And for all normal duty uses, the fixed sights were very sufficient. Unfortunately, the Model 58 did not live up to expectations though Smith & Wesson gave it every chance.

Mechanical Functioning: This is a double-action, solid-frame revolver with a swing-out cylinder with simultaneous manual ejection. The Model 58 is built on the "N" frame, a medium-size frame incorporating a cylinder center pin with fore and aft locks to provide positive locking and alignment. The cylinder is unlocked by means of a thumbpiece, and when opened, the internal thumbpiece latch prevents the action from being cocked, or if cocked, prevents the cylinder from opening. Two automatic hammer blocks are incorporated; one operating as a physical block riding in a groove cut into the sideplate; the other by means of protrusions on the top of the rebound block and the bottom of the hammer. Both prevent accidental firing when dropped. The mainspring is of leaf design, and trigger overtravel is controlled by a bar in the trigger rebound block. This revolver is made of high-carbon steel.

Smith & Wesson Model 58 .41 Military and Police

Smith & Wesson
2100 Roosevelt Ave.
Springfield, MA 01101

Model: 59

Action Type: semiautomatic, recoil operated.

Caliber(s): 9mm Parabellum.

Barrel Lengths: 4″.

Finish: blue or nickel.

Manufacturing Dates: commercial production 1971–1982.

Stocks: plastic.

Rifling: 6R.

Weight, Unloaded: 27½ oz.

Sights: adjustable rear, ramp front.

Serial Numbers: commercial production began at A170,000 and ran with the automatic numbers.

Serial Number Location: left side of frame above trigger guard.

Major Variations: smooth front strap and smooth back strap.
smooth front strap and serrated back strap.
serrated front and back strap are standard.

Markings: left side of slide: Smith & Wesson and address.
left side of frame: model designation.
barrel over chamber: caliber designation.

Price(s):
blue, very good—$275.00; excellent—$350.00
nickel, very good—$275.00; excellent—$375.00
early, smooth front and back strap, very good—$400.00; excellent—$550.00
early, smooth front and serrated back strap, very good—$350.00; excellent—$450.00

History: First experimented with in 1964 and first produced at the behest of the Navy in 1969, the Model 59 is essentially a Model 39 with an enlarged grip to accommodate a 14-shot magazine. The very early production of the Model 59 was significant in two respects. First is that when the 59 was initially released, it was made without serrations on the gripstrap. The factory tried to alter these to standard style, but about 100 got out—a very rare find for the collector. Second, the enlarged magazine coupled with the double-action mechanism spurred the rest of the arms industry to attempt to duplicate the Model 59, leading to the plethora of double-action pistols on today's market.

Mechanical Functioning: The Model 59 is a double-action, recoil-operated semiautomatic pistol with a 14-shot detachable box magazine. The frame is made of aluminum alloy; the balance of the parts are of steel. The grips are made of a tough nylon because of the necessary thinness due to the bulk of the grip. Similar in most all respects to the Model 39, with the exception of the magazine size, the Model 59 also has a straight back strap rather than the Model 39's curved one.

5107	Rear Sight Windage Nut
6001	Barrel
6005	Barrel Bushing
6011	Trigger Plunger Pin
6013	Ejector-depressor Plunger
6014	Ejector-depressed Plunger Spring
6015	Ejector Magazine Depresser
6017	Ejector Spring
6019	Firing Pin
6022	Firing Pin Spring
6041	Magazine Catch Plunger
6042	Magazine Catch Plunger Spring
6049	Manual Safety
6054	Manual Safety Plunger
6056	Rear Sight Leaf
6057	Rear Sight Assembly
6059	Recoil Spring
6076	Rear Sight Slide
6078	Extractor Pin
6079	Manual Safety Plunger Spring
6079	Extractor Spring
6083	Slide Stop Plunger
6084	Slide Stop Plunger Spring
6088	Slide
6095	Rear Sight Windage Screw
6103	Sear Release Lever
6107	Disconnector
6108	Disconnector Pin
6110	Drawbar Plunger
6111	Drawbar Plunger Spring
6121	Trigger Plunger
6122	Trigger Plunger Spring
6126	Trigger Play Spring Rivet
6127	Trigger Play Spring
6144	Hammer
6149	Mainspring
6151	Stirrup
6152	Stirrup Pin
6153	Trigger
6217	Mainspring Plunger
6252	Drawbar
6253	Frame (factory exchange only)
6254	Frame Stud
6256	Insert
6257	Insert Pin
6257	Trigger Pin
6258	Magazine Assembly
6259	Magazine Follower
6260	Magazine Butt Plate
6262	Magazine Catch
6264	Stock Screw

6265	Magazine Spring
6266	Magazine Tube
6267	Sear Pin
6269	Slide Stop
6272	Stock, Left
6272	Stock, Right
6288	Sideplate
6304	Sear Spring Retaining Pin
6308	Extractor
6319	Slide Stop Plunger Rivet
6320	Sear

6323	Recoil Spring Guide Assembly
6325	Magazine Butt Plate Catch
6339	Magazine Catch Nut
6350	Sear Spring
6352	Slide Stop Button
7158	Rear Sight Windage Screw Plunger
7159	Rear Sight Windage Screw Plunger Screw

Smith & Wesson Model 59

Smith & Wesson
2100 Roosevelt Ave.
Springfield, MA 01101

Model: 60; Stainless Chief's Special

Action Type: revolver, double action.

Caliber(s): .38 Special.

Barrel Lengths: 2″ (disc. 1995), 3″.

Finish: satin finished stainless.

Manufacturing Dates: 1965 to date.

Stocks: checkered walnut.

Rifling: 5R.

Weight, Unloaded: 19 oz.

Sights: fixed.

Serial Numbers: starting at 401,754 and running to 712,250. In 1969 changing to "R" prefix starting at R1.

Serial Number Location: bottom of butt.

Major Variations: bright polished with polished hammer and trigger, under serial number 410,698.
bright polished but with dark case-hardened hammer and trigger under serial number 480,000.
satin finish, hammer and trigger case-hardened and flash-plated over number 490,001.
adjustable sights.

Markings: on left side of barrel: Smith & Wesson.
on right side of barrel: caliber designation.
on right side of frame: on sideplate, S & W trademark.
on right side of frame, forward of trigger guard: address stamp.
Smith & Wesson logo on left frame.
(These are general markings—there are many variations!)

Price(s):
excellent—$300.00
bright, polished, number under 410,698, very good—$350.00; excellent—$450.00
bright polished, number under 480,000, very good—$275.00; excellent—$350.00
early adjustable sights model, very good—$600.00; excellent—$850.00
late adjustable sights model, very good—$350.00; excellent—$450.00

History: The Model 60 was designed with police use in mind and is made entirely from stainless steel. The very early Model 60s were made of highly polished stainless including the hammer and trigger. However, Smith & Wesson found that the hammer and triggers were too soft for continuous use, so in 1966 they were case-hardened to a dark finish. In late 1966 the combination of police requests for a satin finish, plus the obvious savings to the factory in time and ease of manufacture, resulted in the current finish of the Model 60: brushed stainless, flash chrome-plated hammer and trigger.

Mechanical Functioning: This is a double-action, solid-frame revolver with a swing-out cylinder with simultaneous manual ejection. The Model 60 is built on the "E" frame, a small stainless "J" frame incorporating a cylinder center pin with fore and aft locks to provide positive locking and alignment. The cylinder is unlocked by means of a thumbpiece, and when opened, the internal thumbpiece latch prevents the action from being cocked, or if cocked, prevents the cylinder from opening. Two automatic hammer blocks are incorporated; one operating as a physical block riding in a groove cut into the sideplate; the other by means of protrusions on the top of the rebound block and the bottom of the hammer. Both prevent accidental firing when dropped. The mainspring is of coil design and has a five-shot cylinder. This revolver is made of stainless steel.

Smith & Wesson Model 60 Stainless Steel Chief's Special

Smith & Wesson
2100 Roosevelt Ave.
Springfield, MA 01101

Model: 65; Stainless .357 Military and Police

Action Type: revolver, double action.

Caliber(s): .357 Magnum.

Barrel Lengths: 3", 4".

Finish: satin stainless steel.

Manufacturing Dates: 1974 to date.

Stocks: checkered walnut.

Rifling: 5R.

Weight, Unloaded: 34 oz.

Sights: fixed.

Serial Numbers: starting with the "D" prefix, numbered in series with the Model 10.

Serial Number Location: bottom of butt.

Major Variations: none.

Markings: on left side of barrel: Smith & Wesson.
on right side of barrel: caliber designation.
on right side of frame: on sideplate, S & W trademark.
on right side of frame, forward of trigger guard: address stamp.
(These are general markings—there are many variations!)

Price(s):
4" barrel, excellent—$275.00
3" barrel, excellent—$300.00

History: The Model 65 was developed originally for the Oklahoma Highway Patrol and was built as the Model 64-1 .357 Magnum. For regular sale and to avoid confusion, it was redesignated the Model 65. In all other particulars, it is exactly the same as the Model 10 Heavy Barrel, only in stainless and in caliber .357 Magnum. This is an excellent police sidearm for urban utilization where shooting distances of over 50 yards are extremely rare.

Mechanical Functioning: This is a double-action, solid-frame revolver with a swing-out cylinder with simultaneous manual ejection. The Model 65 is built on the "F357" frame, a medium-size frame incorporating a cylinder center pin with fore and aft locks to provide positive locking and alignment. The cylinder is unlocked by means of a thumbpiece, and when opened, the internal thumbpiece latch prevents the action from being cocked, or if cocked, prevents the cylinder from opening. Two automatic hammer blocks are incorporated; one operating as a physical block riding in a groove cut into the sideplate; the other by means of protrusions on the top of the rebound block and the bottom of the hammer. Both prevent accidental firing when dropped. The mainspring is of leaf design and has a six-shot cylinder. This revolver is made of stainless steel.

Smith & Wesson Model 65—4″ Barrel
Photo courtesy of Smith & Wesson

Smith & Wesson
2100 Roosevelt Ave.
Springfield, MA 01101

Model: 66; .357 Combat Magnum Stainless

Action Type: revolver, double action.

Caliber(s): .357 Magnum.

Barrel Lengths: 2½″, 3″ (limited production), 4″, 6″.

Finish: satin stainless.

Manufacturing Dates: 1971 to date.

Stocks: checkered Goncaco Alves.

Rifling: 5R.

Weight, Unloaded: 35 oz. in 4″ barrel.

Sights: block micrometer rear, ramp front.

Serial Numbers: started at K949,100 and then ran with the K frame numbers which after K999,999 ran to 5 digit with a prefix digit preceding the "K."

Serial Number Location: bottom of butt.

Major Variations: round butt in 2½″ barrel.
square butt in 4″ and 6″ barrel.

Markings: on left side of barrel: Smith & Wesson.
on right side of barrel: caliber designation.
on right side of frame: on sideplate, S & W trademark.
on right side of frame, forward of trigger guard: address stamp.
logo on left side of frame.
(These are general markings—there are many variations!)

Price(s):
2½″ barrel, standard, excellent—$300.00
3″ barrel, standard, excellent—$400.00
4″ barrel, standard, excellent—$275.00
6″ barrel, standard, excellent—$300.00
target trigger, target hammer, 4″, excellent—$325.00
target trigger, target hammer, 6″, excellent—$350.00

History: The Model 66 was developed and first made in 1970, though actual release to the public was delayed until 1971, hence the mid-1970 starting serial number. This model is identical to the Model 19 .357 Combat Magnum with the exception that it is entirely made from stainless steel (except for the rear sight). The frame designation "F" stands for medium frame, stainless, and the "T" means target sights. The F frame is identical to the K frame in all dimensions.

Mechanical Functioning: This is a double-action, solid-frame revolver with a swing-out cylinder with simultaneous manual ejection. The Model 66 is built on the "FT357" frame (the "KT" frame in stainless), a medium-size

frame incorporating a cylinder center pin with fore and aft locks to provide positive locking and alignment. The cylinder is unlocked by means
of a thumbpiece, and when opened, the internal thumbpiece latch prevents the action from being cocked, or if cocked, prevents the cylinder
from opening. This is accomplished by a long bar sliding in a milled
groove in the inside left side of the frame and which is attached through a
milled section to the thumbpiece. On the forward end of this bar there is a
standing portion with a cylindrical protrusion. When pushed forward
by the thumbpiece, it in turn pushes the center pin out of the frame to
unlock the cylinder. At the rear of this bar is another standing portion that
blocks the underside of the hammer when in the forward position, and
when in the rearward position the hammer can block it from going forward to open the cylinder. Two automatic hammer blocks are incorporated. One operates as a physical block riding in a groove cut into the
sideplate, and it in turn rides on the rebound block by means of a raised
pin on the block fitting into a cut-out on the safety bar. The other is more
subtle and operates by means of protrusions on the top of the rebound
block and the bottom of the hammer. When they are in line they prevent
forward motion of the hammer beyond a point where the firing pin does
not protrude through the breechface. Both prevent accidental firing when
dropped. The mainspring is of leaf design, and trigger overtravel is controlled by an insert at the inside rear of the trigger guard. This revolver is
made of stainless steel.

Smith & Wesson Model 66 4" Barrel
Photo courtesy of Smith & Wesson

Smith & Wesson
2100 Roosevelt Ave.
Springfield, MA 01101

Model: 547; 9mm Military and Police

Action Type: revolver, double action.

Caliber(s): 9mm Parabellum.

Barrel Lengths: 3″, 4″ heavy barrel.

Finish: blue.

Manufacturing Dates: 1981–1985.

Stocks: checkered walnut.

Rifling: R5.

Weight, Unloaded: 34 oz. with 4″ barrel.

Sights: fixed.

Serial Numbers: started about 6D57700 and runs in the Model 10 range.

Serial Number Location: bottom of butt.

Major Variations: 3″ heavy barrel, round butt.
4″ heavy barrel, square butt.

Markings: on left side of barrel: Smith & Wesson.
on right side of barrel: caliber designation.
on right side of frame: on sideplate, S & W trademark.
on right side of frame, forward of trigger guard: address stamp.
logo on left side.
(These are general markings—there are many variations!)

Price(s):
3″ round butt, very good—$250.00; excellent—$300.00
4″ square butt, very good—$175.00; excellent—$250.00

History: The Model 547 9mm Military and Police was developed in 1981 to meet the demand for a high-quality revolver chambered for 9mm Parabellum by foreign police agencies. The Model 547 fits the bill. Based on the Model 10 Military & Police revolver, the 547 differs in several aspects. For one, since the 9mm Luger case is of the rimless variety, many revolver makers resorted to half-moon clips for extraction. Not so with the 547. Instead, the extractor uses retractable leaf springs that engage the cartridge when the extractor rod is pushed out. This model has a special short spur combat extractor groove hammer, and on the 3″ version has a grip cut-out for speed loaders.

Mechanical Functioning: This is a double-action, solid-frame revolver with a swing-out cylinder with simultaneous manual ejection. The Model 547 is built on the "K" frame, a medium-size frame incorporating a cylinder center pin with fore and aft locks to provide positive locking and alignment. The cylinder is unlocked by means of a thumbpiece, and when opened, the internal thumbpiece latch prevents the action from being cocked, or if cocked, prevents the cylinder from opening. Two automatic hammer blocks are incorporated; one operating as a physical block riding in a groove cut into the sideplate; the other by means of protrusions on the top of the rebound block and the bottom of the hammer. Both prevent accidental firing when dropped. The mainspring is of leaf design, and trigger overtravel is controlled by an insert at the inside rear of the trigger guard. This revolver is made of high-carbon steel.

Smith & Wesson Model 547 9mm Military and Police

Smith & Wesson
2100 Roosevelt Ave.
Springfield, MA 01101

Model: 559

Action Type: semiautomatic, recoil operated.

Caliber(s): 9mm Parabellum.

Barrel Lengths: 4".

Finish: blue or nickel.

Manufacturing Dates: 1982–1983.

Stocks: plastic.

Rifling: 6R.

Weight, Unloaded: 40 oz.

Sights: adjustable rear.

Serial Numbers: in the A series running with other automatic pistols.

Serial Number Location: left side of frame above trigger.

Major Variations: Model 459 has alloy frame.
Model 559 has steel frame.
ambidextrous safety.

Markings: left side of slide: Smith & Wesson and address stamp.
left side of frame: model designation.

Price(s):
Model 559, blue, excellent—$425.00
Model 559, nickel, excellent—$450.00
Model 459, nickel, excellent—$375.00
Model 459, blue, excellent—$350.00

History: The Model 559 is an improved version of the Model 59. Some of the differences between it and the Model 59 include a rear sight that is fully adjustable for windage and elevation and has vertical ears to protect it from damage. It also has three safeties: the manual safety and magazine safety from the Model 59, and a new firing pin safety that locks the firing pin until the trigger is pulled completely to the rear, which means that the gun cannot discharge accidentally. Also available is an ambidextrous manual safety. Like the Model 59 it has a 14-round magazine. The Model 559 and the Model 459 are identical but for the fact that the Model 559 is of all-steel construction, including the frame, while the Model 459 has a lightweight alloy frame.

Mechanical Functioning: The Model 559 is a double-action, recoil-operated semiautomatic pistol with a 14-shot detachable box magazine. The magazine is inserted through the gripframe and is retained by a spring-loaded catch located on the left side of the frame just aft of the trigger guard. The frame is made of steel on the Model 559, and of aluminum on the Model 459, and the balance of the parts are of steel. The grips are made of a tough nylon because of the necessary thinness due to the bulk of the grip. Similar in most all respects to the Model 539, with the exception of the magazine size, the Model 559 also has a straight back strap rather than the Model 539's curved one. Field stripping is accomplished by first making sure the pistol is unloaded and removing the magazine. Set the safety to "fire." Pull slide back and align the notch on the left side of the slide with the slide stop and drift the slide stop out from right to left. Pull slide forward and off frame. Turn the slide upside down and remove the recoil spring assembly by compressing it slightly and then lifting out; then rotate the barrel bushing and pull forward to remove it. Now the barrel can be removed by lifting the rear end up and out of the slide. Assembly is in the reverse order.

Smith & Wesson Model 559

Smith & Wesson
2100 Roosevelt Ave.
Springfield, MA 01101

Model: 586; Distinguished Combat Magnum

Action Type: revolver, double action.

Caliber(s): .357 Magnum.

Barrel Lengths: 4″, 6″, 8³⁄₈″ (disc. 1991).

Finish: blue or nickel (disc. 1991).

Manufacturing Dates: 1981 to date.

Stocks: checkered Goncaco Alves.

Rifling: R5.

Weight, Unloaded: 42 oz. with 4″ barrel.

Sights: adjustable rear, ramp front.

Serial Numbers: started at AAA0001.

Serial Number Location: bottom of bolt.

Major Variations: standard or fancy sights.
   standard, combat or target triggers.
   standard of fancy grips.

Markings: on left side of barrel: Smith & Wesson.
   on right side of barrel: caliber designation.
   on right side of frame: on sideplate, S & W trademark.
   on right side of frame, forward of trigger guard: address stamp.
   on sideplate: Smith & Wesson logo.
   (These are general markings—there are many variations!)

Price(s):
   4″ barrel, blue, excellent—$325.00
   4″ barrel, nickel, excellent—$350.00
   6″ barrel, blue, excellent—$325.00
   6″ barrel, nickel, excellent—$350.00

History: The Model 586 is built on the new Smith & Wesson "L" frame, which in size is in between the "N" and the "K." It has a larger cylinder than the "K" frame with provision to rebate the cartridge head for safety. For better balance in target shooting and combat target shooting, it has a heavyweight barrel with a full-length extractor shroud. Standard equipment is a wide, semitarget hammer and a smooth combat trigger. The normal choices of front and rear sights are available; however, the rear Smith & Wesson micrometer sight is of blackened stainless rather than the normal blued steel.

Mechanical Functioning: This is a double-action, solid-frame revolver with a swing-out cylinder with simultaneous manual ejection. The Model 586 is built on the "L" frame, a medium-size frame incorporating a cylinder center pin with fore and aft locks to provide positive locking and alignment. The cylinder is unlocked by means of a thumbpiece, and when opened, the internal thumbpiece latch prevents the action from being cocked, or if cocked, prevents the cylinder from opening. Two automatic hammer blocks are incorporated; one operating as a physical block riding in a groove cut into the sideplate; the other by means of protrusions on the top of the rebound block and the bottom of the hammer. Both prevent accidental firing when dropped. The mainspring is of leaf design, and trigger overtravel is controlled by an insert at the inside rear of the trigger guard. This revolver holds six shots and is made of high-carbon steel.

Smith & Wesson 586 Distinguished Combat Magnum

Smith & Wesson
2100 Roosevelt Ave.
Springfield, MA 01101

Model: 629

Action Type: revolver, double action.

Caliber(s): .44 Magnum.

Barrel Lengths: 4″, 6″, 8⅜″.

Finish: satin stainless.

Manufacturing Dates: 1979 to date.

Stocks: checkered Goncaco Alves.

Rifling: R5.

Weight, Unloaded: 47 oz. with 6″ barrel.

Sights: adjustable white outline rear, red ramp front.

Serial Numbers: started about N629062 in the NT frame range.

Serial Number Location: bottom of butt.

Major Variations: type of trigger.
    grip type.

Markings: on left side of barrel: Smith & Wesson.
    on right side of barrel: .44 Magnum caliber.
    on right side of frame: on sideplate, S & W trademark.
    on right side of frame, forward of trigger guard: address stamp.
    (These are general markings—there are many variations!)

Price(s):
    4″ barrel, excellent—$375.00
    6″ barrel, excellent—$375.00
    8⅜″ barrel, excellent—$400.00

History: The Smith & Wesson Model 629 has got to be the hunter's delight. It is an all stainless steel .44 Magnum revolver that comes standard with blackened stainless steel rear sights, target hammer, and smooth combat trigger, which on this model is the wide trigger with no serrations. It comes with accessories in a presentation case.

Mechanical Functioning: This is a double-action, solid-frame revolver with a swing-out cylinder with simultaneous manual ejection. The Model 629 is built on the "N Target" frame, a medium-size frame incorporating a cylinder center pin with fore and aft locks to provide positive locking and alignment. The cylinder is unlocked by means of a thumbpiece, and when opened, the internal thumbpiece latch prevents the action from being cocked, or if cocked, prevents the cylinder from opening. Two automatic hammer blocks are incorporated; one operating as a physical block riding in a groove cut into the sideplate; the other by means of protrusions on the top of the rebound block and the bottom of the hammer. Both prevent accidental firing when dropped. The mainspring is of leaf design, and trigger overtravel is controlled by an insert at the inside rear of the trigger guard. This revolver holds six shots and is made of stainless steel.

Smith & Wesson Model 629 .44 Magnum 4" Barrel

Smith & Wesson
2100 Roosevelt Ave.
Springfield, MA 01101

Model: .35 Automatic Pistol (1913)

Action Type: semiautomatic, blowback operated.

Caliber(s): .35 Smith & Wesson automatic.

Barrel Lengths: 3½″.

Finish: blue or nickel.

Manufacturing Dates: 1913–1921.

Stocks: wood.

Rifling: 6R.

Weight, Unloaded: 25 oz.

Sights: fixed.

Serial Numbers: 1-8350.

Serial Number Location: forward gripframe.

Major Variations: 1st type: numbers 1 to about 200, original safety.
2nd type: numbers from about 200 to about 1000, left rear safety.
3rd type: numbers from about 1000 to 3100, rear pressure safety.
4th type: numbers from about 3100 to 3800, front to back magazine catch.
5th type: numbers from about 3900 to 5900, recoil spring guide above tunnel.
6th type: numbers from about 3900–5400, square recoil spring guide tunnel.
7th type: numbers from about 5900–7200, no trademark on left frame.
8th type: numbers from about 7200–8350, "Smith & Wesson" on left barrel, ".35 S & W Auto Ctg." on right side.
Some early models had a slotted recoil spring guide on the forward end.

Markings: late type: Smith & Wesson on left barrel.
late type: .35 S & W Auto Ctg on right barrel.
early type: .35 S & W Auto Ctg. on left barrel.
early type: S & W Trademark on left frame flat.

Price(s):
1st type, very good—$675.00
1st type, excellent—$825.00
2nd type, very good—$525.00
2nd type, excellent—$675.00
3rd type, very good—$500.00
3rd type, excellent—$625.00
4th type, very good—$525.00
4th type, excellent—$675.00
5th type, very good—$475.00
5th type, excellent—$575.00

6th type, very good—$475.00
6th type, excellent—$575.00
7th type, very good—$475.00
7th type, excellent—$550.00
8th type, very good—$475.00
8th type, excellent—$550.00
for nickel add $50.00 to $90.00
slotted recoil spring guide rod add 15%.

History: The Smith & Wesson .35 Auto is essentially a Clement pistol, a variation of Clement's Model 1909 which Smith & Wesson purchased the rights to make. Unfortunately, Smith & Wesson made several mistakes with regard to this pistol. First of all, it was designed around an odd caliber, the .35 automatic, which was slightly weaker than the .32 A.C.P., and had a slightly different-size cartridge case. A .35 automatic cartridge would fit in, but it would be very dangerous to shoot. The second drawback was its design. It was awkward for the standard American taste of the day. The safety was located in a odd place, and it was of light construction. Assembly and disassembly were not simple. All of this led to very slow sales, and after World War I it was decided to discontinue the pistol.

Mechanical Functioning: The Smith & Wesson .35 Automatic is a straight blowback-operated, semiautomatic pistol with an internal concealed hammer. Instead of the normal heavy slide, this had a light cut-out breechblock, which necessitated a very strong recoil spring. In order to cock this pistol and to chamber a cartridge, a breechblock disconnector had to be used to allow the breechblock to be operated only against the force of the hammer spring.

Smith and Wesson Model .35 Automatic Pistol
Photo courtesy of Orvel L. Reichert

Smith & Wesson
2100 Roosevelt Ave.
Springfield, MA 01101

Model: Straight Line Target

Action Type: single shot, side swing barrel.

Caliber(s): .22 L.R.

Barrel Lengths: 10".

Finish: blue.

Manufacturing Dates: 1925–1936.

Stocks: wood.

Rifling: 6R.

Weight, Unloaded: 34 oz.

Sights: adjustable target rear.

Serial Numbers: started at 1 and ran to 1870.

Major Variations: adjustable trigger.
rebounding hammer.

Markings: left side of barrel: Smith & Wesson.
right side of barrel: .22 Long Rifle Ctg.

Price(s):
Straight Line, standard trigger, very good—$550.00
Straight Line, standard trigger, excellent—$850.00
Straight Line, adjustable trigger, very good—$600.00
Straight Line, adjustable trigger, excellent—$925.00
Straight Line, adjustable trigger, rebounding hammer, very good—$575.00
Straight Line, adjustable trigger, rebounding hammer, excellent—$875.00
Straight Line, adjustable trigger, nonrebounding hammer, very good—
$550.00
Straight Line, adjustable trigger, nonrebounding hammer, excellent—
$850.00
cased with accessories add $250.00 to $400.00.

History: The Straight Line is a very rare target pistol that was made by Smith & Wesson from 1925 to 1936 in limited quantities. It was a single-shot pistol, with a frame style of a semiautomatic. The Straight Line was never well accepted by target shooters for several reasons. The primary reason was that the trigger pull was absolutely inconsistent. Although it came in two different trigger styles, adjustable trigger and nonadjustable trigger, the problem was with the sear engagement in the hammer. Because of the design of the mainspring and the tunnel in which the hammer traveled, there was a very close fit with the plunge-type extension of the hammer; there was a chance of a high degree of frictional grabbing either if the temperature was low or if there was too much oil, or dirt, or not enough oil, or even excess humidity. This caused a very inconsistent hammer fall, which led to a very inconsistent sear break. To try to correct this situation, they reduced the size of the hammer slightly, so that it would be loose in its guide tunnel. Unfortunately, this allowed some radial movement of the rear of the hammer and since the hammer was moving, the notch might not be in perfect alignment in relation to the sear point. Once again, this led to an inconsistent trigger pull.

Mechanical Functioning: The Smith & Wesson Straight Line .22 single-shot pistol resembles in appearance a semiautomatic pistol with an external hammer. However, loading is accomplished by using the latch to unlock the side swing feature and swinging the barrel clockwise to open it. Extraction and reloading can then be carried out. The hammer could be called a modified striker, as it works on a plunger system and thus reciprocates rather than moving radially. This is one of the major causes of the problems cited under "History." For safety, this was one of the first handguns to utilize a rebate for the chamber to protect against blown cartridge cases. Before firing, the pistol had to be manually cocked.

Smith & Wesson Straight Line

Smith & Wesson
2100 Roosevelt Ave.
Springfield, MA 01101

Model: .32 Safety Hammerless ("Lemon Squeezer")

Action Type: revolver, double action.

Caliber(s): .32 Smith & Wesson.

Barrel Lengths: 2", 3", 3½", 6".

Finish: blue or nickel.

Manufacturing Dates: 1888–1937.

Stocks: hard rubber.

Rifling: 5R.

Weight, Unloaded: 14¼ oz. with 3" barrel.

Sights: fixed.

Serial Numbers: 1 to 242981.

Serial Number Location: bottom of butt.

Major Variations: 1st model: push button latch (to number 91417).
2nd model: T-latch (to about number 170,000).
3rd model: no patent dates on barrel (to end of production).

Markings: Smith & Wesson on left side of barrel.
patent dates on top of barrel on early models.

Price(s):
1st model, blue, very good—$400.00
1st model, blue, excellent—$450.00
1st model, nickel, very good—$375.00
1st model, nickel, excellent—$450.00
2nd model, blue, very good—$350.00
2nd model, blue, excellent—$400.00
2nd model, nickel, very good—$350.00
2nd model, nickel, excellent—$400.00
2nd model, blue, 6" barrel, very good—$400.00
2nd model, blue, 6" barrel, excellent—$450.00
2nd model, nickel, 6" barrel, very good—$400.00
2nd model, nickel, 6" barrel, excellent—$450.00
3rd model, blue, very good—$350.00
3rd model, blue, excellent—$400.00
3rd model, nickel, very good—$325.00
3rd model, nickel, excellent—$400.00

History: The Smith & Wesson "New Departure" Hammerless .32 was developed in 1888 to fill the need for a reliable, safe revolver that could be carried in a pocket and that could be drawn quickly without having to worry about it snagging on cloth. It accomplished this well, and indeed it was extremely safe. It was double action only and possessed a rear grip safety that prevented the rebounding hammer from cocking unless the trigger was actually pulled and the gun held in the hand. During its production life, there were three distinct variations. The first type was made from about 1888 to around 1902, and therefore serial numbers under about 70,000 are antique under U.S. law. This model can be recognized quickly by the fact that in order to swing the barrel and cylinder up, you unlatch it by pushing down a button at the top of the frame at the rear of the barrel extension. The second model was made from 1902 to 1909, and the latch was changed from the push button to a "T" type, with an external hook that you pulled upward on. It was also within this model group that the 6"-barrel variation was made, which is more of a curiosity than anything else, because it is just too long to have functioned well as a pocket pistol. The third model was made from 1909 until the production ended in 1937. Most of the changes on this model were internal, but it can be recognized by the variation in stamping. Instead of the patent dates on the top of the barrel, it simply had "Smith & Wesson Springfield, Mass."

Mechanical Functioning: The Smith & Wesson .32 New Departure Hammerless had a concealed internal hammer and was double action only. It was a top-break five-shot revolver with simultaneous, automatic ejection. The grip safety acted to prevent the hammer from cocking by placing a mechanical block on it unless the safety was depressed. On firing, when pulling through on the trigger, just before letup, there was a slight hesitation so that you would be able to aim and then continue pulling in order to fire. So although this is a double-action revolver, the slight hesitation gave you a chance to aim and follow through as though you were firing in single action.

Smith & Wesson .32 Safety Hammerless

Smith & Wesson
2100 Roosevelt Ave.
Springfield, MA 01101

Model: 61; Escort

Action Type: semiautomatic, blowback operated.

Caliber(s): .22 L.R.

Barrel Lengths: 2⅛″.

Finish: blue or nickel.

Manufacturing Dates: 1970–1974.

Stocks: plastic.

Rifling: 6R.

Weight, Unloaded: 14 oz.

Sights: fixed.

Serial Numbers: starting in March 1970 at B1001 to B7800, the magazine safety was added at B7801 and ran to B9850. The barrel nut was added at B9851 and this ran until B40,000 when the frame became forged aluminum. That went until B65,438 when it was discontinued. B1 to B500 were presentation numbers and were made in late 1970 on the 61-1 variation.

Serial Number Location: n/a.

Major Variations: Model 61: standard type.
Model 61-1: magazine safety added.
Model 61-2: barrel nut added.
Model 61-3: aluminum frame.

Markings: on left side of slide: Smith & Wesson.
on left side of frame: address
on right side of slide: .22 Long Rifle Ctg.
on right side of frame: Smith & Wesson trademark.

Price(s):
Model 61, blue, very good—$150.00
Model 61, blue, excellent—$225.00
Model 61, nickel, very good—$175.00
Model 61, nickel, excellent—$250.00
Model 61-1, blue, very good—$175.00
Model 61-1, blue, excellent—$250.00
Model 61-1, nickel, very good—$200.00
Model 61-1, nickel, excellent—$275.00
Model 61-1 Presentation, blue, very good—$250.00
Model 61-1 Presentation, blue, excellent—$350.00
Model 61-1 Presentation, nickel, very good—$300.00
Model 61-1 Presentation, nickel, excellent—$400.00
Model 61-2, blue, very good—$150.00

Model 61-2, blue, excellent—$225.00
Model 61-2, nickel, very good—$175.00
Model 61-2, nickel, excellent—$250.00
Model 61-3, blue, very good—$150.00
Model 61-3, blue, excellent—$225.00
Model 61-3, nickel, very good—$175.00
Model 61-3, nickel, excellent—$250.00

History: First produced in March 1970, the Model 61 Escort was Smith & Wesson's first attempt at making a small pocket pistol, and at the time of issue was not well received. Early pistols had a disconcerting habit of jamming, which, since marketing was directed toward police, diminished sales. The problem was corrected, and the pistol went through several design changes after that to try to enhance marketability. Smith & Wesson dropped the Model 61 in 1973, though part guns were sold into 1974. The excuse was that the small automatic did not fit Smith & Wesson's image.

Mechanical Functioning: This is a straight blowback pistol with the recoil spring mounted above the barrel. For takedown, simply depress the recoil spring guide and lift out the front sight, which allows the removal of the slide. The barrel is fixed to the frame, and the magazine is of detachable box type and holds five rounds.

Smith & Wesson 61 Escort

Bonifacio Echeverria Star SA
Eibar, Spain
Importer: Interarms
Alexandria, VA

Model: BM

Action Type: semiautomatic, recoil operated.

Caliber(s): 9mm Parabellum.

Barrel Lengths: 4″.

Finish: blue or chrome.

Manufacturing Dates: 1976 to date.

Stocks: plastic.

Rifling: 6R.

Weight, Unloaded: 25 oz.

Sights: fixed.

Serial Numbers: n/a.

Serial Number Location: right side of frame above trigger.

Major Variations: BM is all steel.
BKM has a lightweight frame.

Markings: left side of slide: Star Echeverria S.A. Eibar, Spain, Caliber 9mm.

Price(s):
BM, blue, excellent—$600.00
BM, chrome, excellent—$625.00
BKM, blue, excellent—$600.00

History: Bonafacio Echeverria began operations about 1908, and throughout its history has always been making automatic pistols. Hence they have accumulated a little bit of experience in the field. Virtually their entire production, which falls under the trade name "Star," have been copies of the Colt/Browning system used in the Model 1911, usually with minor modifications. The series BM and BKM pistols are no different. Introduced in 1976 and made to date, the only difference between the two models is the fact that the BKM has a lightweight, duraluminum alloy frame. The BKM is available only in blue, while the BM, being made of all steel, can be had in either blue or chrome. They were designed with the personal protection market in mind, and as a concealable pistol that packs some punch for the law enforcement field. And in that end they do what they set out to accomplish. The BM and BKM are quite comfortable to carry, and the recurved backstrap has a good feel and lets the gun point well for snap shooting. Since it's based on the Colt .45, its functioning is generally familiar to most pistol users.

Mechanical Functioning: The Star Models BM and BKM are alike internally. They are based on the Colt/Browning Model 1911 system and are recoil-operated, semiautomatic pistols with eight-round detachable box magazines that are fitted through the gripframe and retained by a spring-loaded catch just below and behind the trigger on the left side of the frame. Unlike the Model 1911, however, the backstrap is solid, and there is no grip safety. There is, however, a half-cock notch on the external hammer and a manual safety which locks the sear, thus locking the hammer. Takedown is accomplished by first making sure the weapon is unloaded, then removing the magazine. Pull the slide back until an angled notch just forward of the finger grooves lines up with the safety. Flip the safety up, locking the slide in the rearward position. At this point, the slide stop latch can be pushed out from the right to the left. Holding the slide tightly because of the tension of the recoil spring, let it ride forward and off the frame. Lift the rear end of the recoil spring guide and remove the guide and spring assembly toward the rear of the slide. The barrel bushing can now be removed by turning counterclockwise until the lug aligns with the open track in the slide and then pull it out towards the front. Tip the barrel link to the front, and then pull the barrel straight out. The pistol is now field stripped. Assembly is in the reverse order.

Bonifacio Echeverria Star SA
Eibar, Spain
Importer: Interarms
Alexandria, VA

Model: PD

Action Type: semiautomatic, recoil operated.

Caliber(s): .45 A.C.P.

Barrel Lengths: 4".

Finish: blue.

Manufacturing Dates: 1975 to date (U.S. importation disc. 1991).

Stocks: checkered walnut.

Rifling: 6R.

Weight, Unloaded: 25 oz. (alloy frame).

Sights: adjustable rear, ramp front.

Serial Numbers: n/a.

Serial Number Location: right side of frame above trigger.

Major Variations: none.

Markings: left side of slide: Star Echeverria S.A. Eibar, Spain, Caliber .45.

Price(s):
    Star Model PD, excellent—$300.00

History: The Star PD was first announced in 1975 and is a very compact .45 A.C.P. pistol. The frame is made of duraluminum, which accounts for its very light weight, which is 25 ounces. And like the rest of the Star line, it generally follows the precepts laid down by the Colt/Browning 1911 style. It has a fully adjustable rear sight and a solid backstrap, eliminating the grip safety. The forward strap is grooved for more positive hand holds. The magazine is of box type and is detachable and holds six rounds of .45 A.C.P. All in all, the Star Model BM is probably one of the smallest and lightest .45 caliber pistols in the world. This pistol was designed with the police market in mind, and it is a very concealable powerhouse that's easy to carry because of its light weight. Its grip is nicely angled for rapid point shooting, and the front strap is serrated for a nonslip holding surface. The rear sight is fully adjustable, and the front sight is of the quick-draw ramp variety. Mechanically it's like the Colt .45 Auto, so most users would be familiar with its mechanisms. As a hideout gun the Star PD is tough to beat. However, since it weighs only 25 ounces and it fires ammunition with a heavy bullet, Mr. Newton gets to throw in his two cents. The recoil is heavy. The best bet is to start with target ammo to get used to the pistol and work up to full-bore loads gradually. In this way you will not only get used to the recoil but you'll also retain your accuracy.

Mechanical Functioning: The Star Model PD is based on the Colt/Browning Model 1911 system and is a recoil-operated, semiautomatic pistol with a six-round detachable box magazine that is fitted through the gripframe and retained by a spring-loaded catch just below and behind the trigger on the left side of the frame. Unlike the Model 1911, however, the backstrap is solid, and there is no grip safety. There is, however, a half-cock notch on the external hammer and a manual safety which locks the sear, thus locking the hammer. Takedown is accomplished by first making sure the weapon is unloaded, then removing the magazine. Pull the slide back until an angled notch just forward of the finger grooves lines up with the safety. Flip the safety up, locking the slide in the rearward position. At this point, the slide stop latch can be pushed out from the right to the left. Holding the slide tightly because of the tension of the recoil spring, let it ride forward and off the frame. Lift the rear end of the recoil spring guide and remove the guide and spring assembly towards the rear of the slide. The barrel bushing can now be removed by turning counterclockwise until the lug aligns with the open track in the slide and then pull it out towards the front. Tip the barrel link to the front, and then pull the barrel straight out. The pistol is now field stripped. Assembly is in the reverse order.

Star Model PD

Bonifacio Echeverria Star SA
Eibar, Spain

Model: I

Action Type: semiautomatic, blowback operated.

Caliber(s): 6.35mm, 7.65mm, 9mm K.

Barrel Lengths: varies from 3″ to 6″.

Finish: blue.

Manufacturing Dates: 1919–1929.

Stocks: wood or hard rubber.

Rifling: 6R.

Weight, Unloaded: about 32 oz.

Sights: fixed.

Serial Numbers: unknown, but seems to be a continuation of the Model 1914 series with all three calibers running together from about the 30,000 range through the 120,000 range.

Serial Number Location: bottom of frame.

Major Variations: barrel length, style of grips, style of cocking piece, frame and slide designs, markings.

Markings: left side of slide: Bonifacio Echeverria (Espana) Eibar, Pistola Automatica, Star (Caliber).
or: Automatic Pistol Star (Caliber).

Price(s):
Model I, 6.35mm, short barrel, very good—$195.00
Model I, 6.35mm, short barrel, excellent—$275.00
Model I, 6.35mm, long barrel, very good—$225.00
Model I, 6.35mm, long barrel, excellent—$300.00
Model I, 7.65mm, short barrel, very good—$225.00
Model I, 7.65mm, short barrel, excellent—$300.00
Model I, 7.65mm, long barrel, very good—$250.00
Model I, 7.65mm, long barrel, excellent—$345.00
Model I, 9mm K, short barrel, very good—$275.00
Model I, 9mm K, short barrel, excellent—$350.00
Model I, 9mm K, long barrel, very good—$300.00
Model I, 9mm K, long barrel, excellent—$425.00

History: The Star Model I was also called the Star Model of 1919 because of the date of its inception. Its history is quite confusing. The design stems from the Model 1908 Star and the Model 1914 Star, which superseded the Model 1908 Star; and the major change in the Model I was in the method of dismantling the pistol. On the early models, the trigger, the trigger guard, and the front end of the frame all formed a removable unit, which was pulled from the frame by pressing a serrated stud on the left side just behind the trigger. After this was removed, then the slide assembly could be disassembled. On the Model I, the trigger guard became an integral part of the frame and instead, at the front of the frame, there was a Mannlicher-style spring catch, which allowed the slide assembly to be disassembled. This pistol was available in 6.35mm, 7.65mm, and 9mm K; however, only the 6.35mm and the 7.65mm remained in production until the model's end in 1929. The 9mm K was discontinued in 1921, which makes the .380 quite collectible. The early models of this gun had checkered wooden grips, while the later models used hard rubber grips with various Star monograms, the most common being the word "Star" written in a band across the grip, with later models having the Star emblem located below it. All of these models had a lanyard ring located on the lower left side of the frame. The primary way to recognize these guns is by the round finger extension on the rear end of the slide just forward of the hammer and the cut-out over the breechblock in the same manner as the 1912 Steyr-Hahn. This entire series of pistols has a very Mannlicherish look to it.

Mechanical Functioning: The Star Model I series are blowback-operated, semiautomatic pistols using detachable box magazines inserted through the gripframe and retained by a catch located on the left side of the frame behind the trigger. They utilize a floating firing pin and an external hammer, and they operate in single action mode only. The hammers have a small spur at the end of the rounded piece at the top for easier cocking.

Star Model I 7.65mm

Bonifacio Echeverria Star SA
Eibar, Spain

Model: 1908/1914

Action Type: semiautomatic, blowback operated.

Caliber(s): 6.35mm, 7.65mm.

Barrel Lengths: varies from 3" to 6".

Finish: blue.

Manufacturing Dates: 1914–1919.

Stocks: wood or hard rubber.

Rifling: 6R.

Weight, Unloaded: about 32 oz.

Sights: fixed.

Serial Numbers: unknown, but appears to run to the 30,000s.

Major Variations: barrel length, style of grips, style of cocking piece, frame and slide designs, markings.

Markings: left side of slide: Automatic Pistol-Star Patent (caliber).

Price(s):
        Model 1908/14, 6.35mm, short barrel, very good—$225.00
        Model 1908/14, 6.35mm, short barrel, excellent—$300.00
        Model 1908/14, 6.35mm, long barrel, very good—$250.00
        Model 1908/14, 6.35mm, long barrel, excellent—$325.00
        Model 1908/14, 7.65mm, short barrel, very good—$250.00
        Model 1908/14, 7.65mm, short barrel, excellent—$325.00
        Model 1908/14, 7.65mm, long barrel, very good—$275.00
        Model 1908/14, 7.65mm, long barrel, excellent—$375.00

History: The Model 1908/1914 is an outgrowth of the Star Model 1908 patents, and from the transitional model between the 1908 and the 1919. It is most easily recognizable for its large, humpback fingerhold on the rear of the slide, which is milled in a circular pattern and then knurled, and the cut-out just forward of it resembling the Steyr-Hahn Model 1912. The difference between it and the Model 1908 is (1) in the shape of the hammer (the Model 1908 had a spur hammer, whereas this hammer is rounded) and (2) in the fact that it came in 7.65mm as well as 6.35mm. The Model 1908 came only in 6.35mm. There is also a takedown button just behind the grip on the Model 1908/14 which releases the trigger housing group for disassembly. When pushed, the entire trigger, trigger guard, and forward part of the frame can be removed. It can also be distinguished from the Model 1919, otherwise known as the Model I Star, because of the differences in the hammer. The Model 1919 has a round hammer with a spur on the end, and takedown is different. It also has a catch just forward of the trigger guard which releases the forward half of the frame, but not the trigger guard. This model was in production for only a short time, from 1914 through 1919, and it appears that perhaps only 20,000 of these pistols were made, making them in all calibers a scarce find for collectors.

Mechanical Functioning: The Star Model I series are blowback-operated, semiautomatic pistols using detachable box magazines inserted through the gripframe and retained by a catch located on the left side of the frame behind the trigger. They utilize a floating firing pin and an external hammer and they operate in single action mode only. The hammers have a small spur at the end of the rounded piece at the top for easier cocking. Takedown is accomplished on this model by making sure that the gun is unloaded and then pressing the small button on the left side of the frame just to the rear of the trigger guard. This allows the entire front end of the frame including the trigger and the trigger guard to be pulled off the gun. After this is done the rear of the slide is lifted slightly and the forward end pressed down. This slight rotation frees the slide from the recoil spring and allows it to be run over the barrel and off of the frame. Assembly is carried out in the reverse order. This model can be identified from the Models 1908 and 1919 by several key features. The Model 1908 had a standard spur-type hammer. The Model 1919 has the round hammer of the Model 1908/14 but has an additional spur added to the back portion. The takedown of the Model 1919 is different in that the release is on the underside of the frame forward of the trigger guard. The Model 1908 has neither type of takedown button.

Star Model 1908/14 7.65mm

Bonifacio Echeverria Star SA
Eibar, Spain
Importer: Interarms
Alexandria, VA

Model: 28

Action Type: semiautomatic, recoil operated, double action.

Caliber(s): 9mm Parabellum.

Barrel Lengths: 4½".

Finish: blue.

Manufacturing Dates: 1982–1984.

Stocks: plastic.

Rifling: 6R.

Weight, Unloaded: 40 oz.

Sights: rear adjustable for windage, ramp front.

Serial Numbers: n/a.

Serial Number Location: left side of frame.

Major Variations: none

Markings: right side of frame: Star Echeverria S.A. Eibar, Spain, Caliber 9mm.

Price(s):
   very good—$250.00; excellent—$325.00

History: The Star Model 28 is the latest in a long line of Star automatic pistols from Bonifacio Echeverria of Eibar, Spain. This is a radical departure from the standard Star series of pistols that were based on the Colt M1911 system. Following the trend of modern combat pistols, the Model 28 is double action, has a large magazine capacity of 15 rounds, and the forward part of the trigger guard is scalloped to provide a brace for a two-handed hold. The rear sight is adjustable for windage, and the pistol has a quick-draw ramp front. For combat use, it is provided with an ambidextrous safety which pushes the firing pin out of the way if the hammer unlocks it, so that the hammer can be safely lowered. An unusual feature of this pistol is that the only screws used in its construction are the windage screw in the sight, and the retaining screw in the magazine catch. You may have noticed in the last couple of years that a great many pistol makers have jumped into the market with some very fine combat pistols which have obviously had a great deal of thought and energy put into their design. They all seem to be of a type. They all have large magazine capacities and recurved, or at least serrated, forward portions of their trigger guards. They all seem to be double action with external hammers, and ambidextrous safeties also seem to be in vogue. Of course this may have something to do with the U.S. Military thinking about upgrading the U.S. issue handgun, and everyone wants to get into the act if they can. This does have one great benefit to the consumer: a wide choice of excellent state-of-the-art combat pistols to choose from!

Mechanical Functioning: The Star Model 28 is a double-action, recoil-operated, semiautomatic pistol with a 15-shot detachable box magazine that is inserted through the gripframe and retained by a spring-loaded catch just behind the trigger, level with the trigger guard on the left side of the frame. It possesses an external hammer and an ambidextrous safety which pushes the firing pin up out of the way of the failing hammer and locks it in place. The detachable magazine holds 15 rounds in a staggered fashion. The entire working parts of the lock are all located within the removable backstrap, and are disassembled as a single unit. The slide is mounted on the frame using the S.I.G. P.210 system, whereby the rails are machined in the slide, and the slide runs on the interior of the frame rather than on the exterior of it. It provides a much more solid bearing surface and a much smoother slide action. The Star Model 28 is roughly designed to approximate the external appearance of the Smith & Wesson Model 59 including the parallel milled grooves on the forward part of the gripstrap as well as the angle of the trigger guard. The ejection port is relieved both fore and aft and is slightly enlarged to reduce the chance of a jam from ejection failure. The grips are retained by a dovetailed slot in the gripframe. The trigger is wide and smooth for combat use. The extractor is of heavy strength and mounted on the exterior surface of the right hand side of the slide.

Stendawerke Waffenfabrik GmbH
Suhl, Germany

Model: Stenda

Action Type: semiautomatic, blowback operated.

Caliber(s): 7.65mm.

Barrel Lengths: 3″.

Finish: blue.

Manufacturing Dates: 1920 to about 1926.

Stocks: hard rubber.

Rifling: generally 6R, but some may be 5R.

Weight, Unloaded: 22 oz.

Sights: fixed.

Serial Numbers: from about 45,000 to the 70,000s.

Serial Number Location: left side of slide above trigger.

Major Variations: early model is the same as the Beholla.
late model has a different takedown system.

Markings: early pistols, left slide: Selbstlade Pistole "Stenda" Cal 7.65
early pistols, right slide: Stenda Werke G.M.B.H., Waffenbau, Suhl.
The left slide markings were next eliminated, and finally all markings
were omitted.
Some export models said "Germany" on left side.

Price(s):
early, Beholla type, very good—$175.00
early, Beholla type, excellent—$250.00
early, just Stenda marks, very good—$175.00
early, just Stenda marks, excellent—$250.00
early, no marks, very good—$175.00
early, no marks, excellent—$250.00
late, Stenda marks, very good—$200.00
late, Stenda marks, excellent—$175.00
late, no marks, very good—$175.00
late, no marks, excellent—$250.00
late, Germany marks, very good—$150.00
late, Germany marks, excellent—$225.00

History: The Beholla design was developed by Becker & Hollander Waffenbau at the beginning of World War I, and they must have had the war effort in mind as virtually the entire production went to the German military. However, it appears that after the war, the firm couldn't cope with peace, and in the middle of 1920 they apparently sold out. The new company, obviously using the same machinery, was named Stenda Werke GMBH Waffenbau, also of Suhl, Germany. Their early pistols were a continuation of the Beholla serial range, as some pistols even had Beholla marks on the left side of the slide.

Mechanical Functioning: This is a straight blowback, semiautomatic pistol with a seven-shot detachable box magazine. It is striker-fired and the manual thumb-operated safety intercepts the sear. The trigger is of pivoting type and is connected to the sear via a bar. There is no ejector per se, however at maximum opening, the firing pin protrudes and it knocks out the case. Because of this, whenever unloading the pistol or if running rounds through the chamber, be cautious not to use too much force or cycle the action too quickly, or the method of ejection may set off a sensitive primer. Takedown of the early style Stenda is accomplished by drifting out a pin through the openings in the slide sides, as on the Beholla series, which allows the removal of the barrel and slide. Later Stenda models eliminated the cross pin and instead had a takedown lever allowing the slide to be removed first. On these later models the barrel was drifted laterally out of the frame after the slide was removed. Assembly was in the reverse order. Like all of the guns in the Beholla series, the Stenda was ruggedly built, both in the early and late versions. Although the Stenda was made between the two World Wars, its predecessor, the Beholla, served well in military use.

Stenda 7.65mm, Late

Sterling Arms Corp.
Gasport, NY

Model: PPL

Action Type: semiautomatic, blowback operated.

Caliber(s): .380 A.C.P., or .22 L.R.

Barrel Lengths: 1".

Finish: blue.

Manufacturing Dates: 1971–1972.

Stocks: wood on the .22 L.R.
plastic on the .380 A.C.P.

Rifling: 6 L.

Weight, Unloaded: .22 L.R. is 24 oz.;
380 A.C.P. is 22½ oz.

Sights: fixed.

Serial Numbers: n/a.

Serial Number Location: right side of frame.

Major Variations: n/a.

Markings: caliber designation on left slide.
Sterling Arms Corp., made in U.S.A., Patents Pending, and the caliber
on the left frame over the barrel housing.

Price(s):
.22 L.R., very good—$125.00
.22 L.R., excellent—$150.00
.380 A.C.P., very good—$100.00
.380 A.C.P., excellent—$125.00

History: Sterling Arms Corp. was established in 1968 in Buffalo, N.Y., and in
about 1972 was purchased by E. & R. Machine and moved to Gasport, N.Y.

Mechanical Functioning: External-hammer, blowback-activated pistol based
on the high standard model HB Action, with a detachable box magazine.
The .22 L.R. has a ten-shot clip; the .380 A.C.P. has six shots.

Sterling Arms Corp.
Gasport, NY

Model: X-Caliber

Action Type: single-shot, single action, tip-up barrel.

Caliber(s): .22 L.R., .22 W.M.R., .357 Magnum, .44 Magnum, 7mm Int.R.

Barrel Lengths: 8″ or 10″.

Finish: blue.

Manufacturing Dates: introduced in 1982–1983.

Stocks: smooth Goncaco Alves wood grips and forearm.

Rifling: n/a.

Weight, Unloaded: 54 to 58 oz. with 8″ barrel; 58 to 62 oz. with 10″ barrel.

Sights: adjustable rear, barrel drilled and tapped for scope mount.

Serial Numbers: n/a.

Serial Number Location: n/a.

Major Variations: various calibers available in 8″ or 10″ barrel lengths.

Markings: n/a

Price(s):
    various calibers, very good—$175.00; excellent—$225.00
    extra barrels, very good—$25.00; excellent—$50.00

History: Sterling Arms Corp. was established in 1968 in Buffalo, N.Y., and in about 1972 was purchased by E. & R. Machine and moved to Gasport, N.Y.

Mechanical Functioning: Single-shot, single-action, tip-up barrel pistol with side lock. Side snap to change from rimfire to centerfire, finger groove on forward part of trigger guard for two-handed hold.

Sterling Arms Corp.
Gasport, NY

Model: 300

Action Type: semiautomatic, blowback.

Caliber(s): .22 L.R. or .25 A.C.P.

Barrel Lengths: 2³/₈".

Finish: blue or stainless steel.

Manufacturing Dates: .25 A.C.P. 1972–1983.
.22 L.R. 1973–1983.
stainless steel version 1976–1983.

Stocks: black plastic.

Rifling: 6R.

Weight, Unloaded: 13 oz.

Sights: fixed.

Serial Numbers: n/a.

Serial Number Location: right frame over trigger guard.

Major Variations: Model 300; blue, 25 A.C.P.
Model 300S: stainless steel, .25 A.C.P.
Model 302: blue, .22 L.R.
Model 302S: stainless steel, .22 L.R.

Markings: on left frame over trigger: Sterling Arms, Gasport, N.Y. or Lockport, N.Y.
on left slide: Sterling and caliber designation.

Price(s):
Model 300, very good—$65.00; excellent—$75.00
Model 300S, very good—$75.00; excellent—$100.00
Model 302, very good—$65.00; excellent—$100.00
Model 302S, very good—$75.00; excellent—$125.00

History: Sterling Arms Corp. was established in 1968 in Buffalo, N.Y., and in about 1972 was purchased by E. & R. Machine, and moved to Gasport, N.Y.

Mechanical Functioning: Blowback-actuated, striker-fired pistol with Galesi-style takedown and bottom magazine catch. The magazine is detachable box type and holds six rounds.

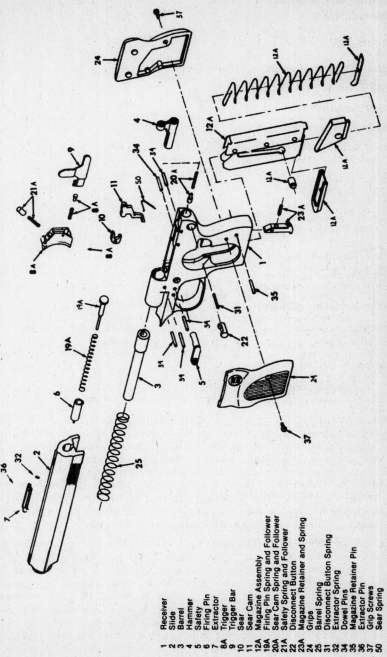

Model 300S/Model 302S

1 Receiver
2 Slide
3 Barrel
4 Hammer
5 Safety
6 Firing Pin
7 Extractor
8A Trigger
9 Trigger Bar
10 Sear
11 Sear Cam
12A Magazine Assembly
19A Firing Pin Spring and Follower
20A Sear Cam Spring and Follower
21A Safety Spring and Follower
22 Disconnect Button
23A Magazine Retainer and Spring
24 Grips
25 Barrel Spring
31 Disconnect Button Spring
32 Extractor Spring
34 Dowel Pins
35 Magazine Retainer Pin
36 Extractor Pin
37 Grip Screws
50 Sear Spring

Sterling Arms Corp.
Gasport, NY

Model: 400

Action Type: semiautomatic, blowback.

Caliber(s): .380 A.C.P.

Barrel Lengths: 3⁹/₁₆″.

Finish: blue or stainless steel.

Manufacturing Dates: Model 400 introduced in 1975. in stainless form, in 1977.

Stocks: checkered walnut.

Rifling: 8R.

Weight, Unloaded: 26 oz.

Sights: low profile adjustable rear, blade front.

Serial Numbers: n/a.

Serial Number Location: n/a.

Major Variations: Model 400, blue, .380 A.C.P.
Model 400S, stainless steel, .380 A.C.P.

Markings: caliber designation, double action, Sterling Arms, and Mark II on left slide;
Sterling Arms, Lockport, N.Y. and model number on left side of frame.

Price(s):
Model 400, very good—$175.00; excellent—$200.00
Model 400S, very good—$200.00; excellent—$250.00

History: Sterling Arms Corp. was established in 1968 in Buffalo, N.Y., and began manufacturing pistols similar to the High Standard H-D Military in styling and mechanical functioning. In about 1972 Sterling was purchased by E. & R. Machine and the factory moved to Gasport, N.Y. The Mark II Model 400 Series Pistol is slightly thinner than the early Model 400, and has a redesigned rear sight. The method of grip retention is with two screws rather than one center screw, as the early Model 400 had. The Model 400 Mk. II also has some strengthened internal parts to make the pistol function more reliably and last longer.

Mechanical Functioning: The Sterling Model 400 Mk. II series are blowback-operated semiautomatic pistols. They have an external hammer and mechanically are based on a somewhat modified Walther system. The manual safety is mounted on the slide, like the Walther, and prevents the hammer from touching the floating firing pin when it is engaged. The clip is of the detachable box magazine type and holds seven shots in .380 A.C.P. and eight shots in .32 A.C.P. The mechanism is double action, and the slide remains in the open position after the last shot is fired. The rear sight is adjustable for both windage and elevation, the front sight is of the ramp type. It is available in either blued steel or stainless style.

Model 400 Blue

Model 402S Stainless

Sterling Arms Corp.
Gasport, NY

Model: 450

Action Type: semiautomatic, recoil operated.

Caliber(s): .45 A.C.P.

Barrel Lengths: 4".

Finish: blue.

Manufacturing Dates: 1977–1980.

Stocks: smooth walnut.

Rifling: n/a.

Weight, Unloaded: 36 oz.

Sights: adjustable rear, blade front.

Serial Numbers: n/a.

Serial Number Location: n/a.

Major Variations: n/a.

Markings: left slide: .45 double action.

Price(s):
    very good—$250.00
    excellent—$300.00

History: When Sterling Arms Corp. was established in 1968 in Buffalo, N.Y., their early production was limited to virtual copies of the High Standard H-D Military–style single-action pistols complete with outside hammer and similar lockwork. In about 1972 Sterling Arms was purchased by E. & R. Machine and the facilities were moved to Gasport, N.Y. Sterling Arms has produced an interesting variety of pistols—most notably the Model 450 in 1977. This model was designed with law enforcement and the military in mind. Unfortunately, the idea didn't click, and in 1980 this model was discontinued. The exterior design was somewhat unique. It was one of the first pistols to have the recurved trigger guard that is now in vogue for two-handed combat shooting, and the safety was ambidextrous. It had double slide rails for smoother slide travel, and the locking system kept the barrel on the same plane as the bullet path until the projectile left the gun. The ejection port was sharply angled at the rear in contrast to the then acceptable designs, which had parallel slides. The extractor, because of the port angling, was placed in a milled slot just aft of the port on a level with the bottom of the port cut. The rear gripstrap, rather than being a somewhat flattened curve, as on most pistols, was sharply angled on the sides to bite into the hand and prevent slippage for (as they advertised) "better gun control."

Mechanical Functioning: The Sterling Model 450 is a double-action, recoil-operated pistol with an external hammer. It has a detachable eight-shot box magazine, which is retained by a spring-loaded catch located on the left side of the frame to the rear of the trigger guard. The safety is slide mounted and both locks the firing pin and blocks it from the hammer. It is of the cross-block type and can be reversed for left-handed shooters. The hammer is similar in style to the Walther PP in that it is rounded and serrated and somewhat hidden in a slide cut. The rear sight is adjustable for windage and elevation, and the front sight is of the quick-draw ramp type. The barrel is retained by a cross-pin at the rear, and in the front has a barrel bushing to give alignment. The recoil spring is located under the barrel, in a manner similar to the Colt/Browning M1911 system, but is in an integral recoil spring and guide assembly. There is a slide stop which holds the slide open on the last shot, and is also used as a takedown latch. The extractor is of the short pivot type with a spring-loaded plunger providing the pressure.

Model 450 .45 Double Action

J. Stevens Arms & Tool Co.
Chicopee Falls, MA

Model: No. 10

Action Type: single shot, tipping barrel.

Caliber(s): .22 L.R.

Barrel Lengths: 8″.

Finish: blue.

Manufacturing Dates: 1919 to about 1940.

Stocks: hard rubber.

Rifling: 6R.

Weight, Unloaded: 37 oz.

Sights: adjustable.

Serial Numbers: ran from about 1 to 10,000.

Serial Number Location: bottom of barrel and on top of frame near breech.

Major Variations: first type: 5/16″ diameter cocking piece with fine knurling. second type: 1/2″ cocking knob with coarse serrations.

Markings: left side of barrel: Stevens Arms Company, Chicopee Falls, Mass. U.S.A.
right side of barrel: Trademark Stevens, Reg. U.S. Pat. Off. & FGN.
first type had: Pat. App'd for on barrel top.
second type had: Pat'd, April 27, 1920 on barrel top.

Price(s):
first type, very good—$275.00
first type, excellent—$350.00
second type, very good—$250.00
second type, excellent—$325.00

History: The Stevens Arms Company had a long history of making single-shot, tipping-barrel pistols, dating all the way back to the 1880s. Right after World War I they decided to modernize their version of the tipping pistols and developed the #10 single shot. In external appearance it closely resembles an automatic pistol; however, upon examination it will be found that it has no provision for a magazine, and there is a catch on the left side of the pistol with which to unlock the barrel. There are two models of the #10. The first type had a small diameter cocking piece which was finely knurled and also had the "Patent Applied For" markings on the top of the barrel. Apparently when the patent was granted, the company also decided to change the cocking piece knob to something that was more easily grabbed, and enlarged the diameter to 1/2″ and knurled it a little more coarsely than the previous model. These pistols never sold very well; however, they were listed in company catalogs up to the beginning of World War II. About 10,000 of these pistols were said to have been made, 5,000 of each type.

Mechanical Functioning: The Stevens #10 in both variations is a single-shot, tip-up barrel pistol that utilizes a cocking piece on the rear end of the breech. To open the firearm, a pivoting catch on the left side of the frame is pulled, releasing the barrel to swing open. The extractor is a cam-actuated sliding variety, which gives manual extraction, rather than the spring-loaded type which pops the cartridge case out. There are no safeties on this pistol, since it was decided that whenever this pistol was loaded it would be fired almost immediately.

Stevens #10 Single Shot

Steyr
Oesterreichische Waffenfabriks Gesellschaft
Steyr, Austria

Model: 1909

Action Type: semiautomatic, blowback operated.

Caliber(s): 6.35mm.

Barrel Lengths: 2⅛".

Finish: blue.

Manufacturing Dates: 1909 to about 1914, and from 1921 to the mid-1930s.

Stocks: hard rubber.

Rifling: 6R.

Weight, Unloaded: 11⅝ oz.

Sights: fixed.

Serial Numbers: pistols have "A" suffix.

Serial Number Location: left side of frame above trigger guard.

Major Variations: early and late models.

Markings: left side of slide: Oesterr. Waffenfabriks-Ges. Steyr.
right side of slide: N. Pieper Patent.
grips have either OWG monogram or Steyr in target trademark.

Price(s):
Model 1909, early, OWG, very good—$225.00
Model 1909, early, OWG, excellent—$300.00
Model 1909, late, Steyr, very good—$200.00
Model 1909, late, Steyr, excellent—$275.00

History: The Steyr Model 1909 6.35mm pistol is sometimes called the Model 1908 because of the patent date stamped on the side, and because it was first commercially produced in 1909. Both model names have become synonymous with this pistol and both are probably correct. It is unknown at what point the serial numbers started on this pistol; however, it appears that all 6.35mm Steyrs have the suffix "A" attached to them, and numbering ran into the hundreds of thousands. The pistol is based on the Pieper patent and is identical to the Pieper Basculant pistols which have tip-up barrels. Like the later Le Francis, most of these pistols were made without extractors, relying on the blowback operation to knock the cartridge out.

Mechanical Functioning: The Steyr Model 1909 pistol is a straight blowback-operated, semiautomatic pistol with a six-round detachable box magazine which is retained by a spring-loaded catch at the rear of the gripframe. It utilized an external hammer bar extending back the left side of the frame over the top of the magazine to trip the sear. It had an internal concealed hammer and a floating firing pin. The recoil spring on this pistol was mounted above the barrel. The barrel assembly itself was hinged at the front and retained by a catch on the left side of the frame. Dropping the catch would allow the barrel to swing upward for loading, either as a single shot, or for cleaning. The magazine of this pistol is easily recognized because of the long tail at the base which extends back to the edge of the rear gripstrap. To take the pistol down, being sure the weapon is unloaded, remove the magazine, release the barrel catch tipping the barrel up. The slide can now move forward in order to remove the entire assembly, a screw located just behind the manual safety at the rear of the frame can be unscrewed allowing the entire upper assembly to be removed. The magazine catch on this pistol is slightly unusual. There are grooves cut in the rear of the magazine, about a half inch above the base, which lock into an internal spring-loaded catch pointing upward. The rear end of the magazine base extends back to the edge of the gripframe, forming a backward lip. The magazine release, located at the bottom rear of the gripframe, is pushed down, rotating against the magazine lock and at the same time, camming against the lip to push the magazine down and against the well, so that it can be grasped and removed from the gun. Assembly is in the reverse order.

Steyr Model 1909 OWG

Steyr
Oesterreichische Waffenfabriks Gesellschaft
Steyr, Austria

Model: 1911 Steyr-Hahn

Action Type: semiautomatic, recoil operated.

Caliber(s): 9mm Steyr.

Barrel Lengths: 5″.

Finish: blue.

Manufacturing Dates: 1911–1919.

Stocks: checkered wood.

Rifling: 4R.

Weight, Unloaded: 33¾ oz.

Sights: fixed.

Serial Numbers: started at 1 and ran in 4-digit blocks with a letter suffix after mid-1912, running into the "Z"s.

Serial Number Location: left side of frame on trigger guard.

Major Variations: Model 1911 Commercial, dovetailed rear sight, milled front. Model 1912, Austrian Military, milled rear sight, dovetailed front. Model 1912, Romanian Military, with Romanian crown on left side of slide. Model 1912, Chilean Military, with coat of arms on left side of slide and "Ejercito De Caile" on right. Model 1912, Nazi Military, chambered for 9mm Parabellum and marked "08" (1938).

Markings: left side of slide, Commercial: Oesterr, Waffenfabrik Steyr M1911 9mm.
left side of slide, Military: Steyr (and date).

Price(s):
    Model 1911, very good—$400.00
    Model 1911, excellent—$550.00
    Model 1912, Austrian, very good—$350.00
    Model 1912, Austrian, excellent—$450.00
    Model 1912, Chilean, very good—$450.00
    Model 1912, Chilean, excellent—$575.00
    Model 1912, Romanian, very good—$625.00
    Model 1912, Romanian, excellent—$700.00
    Model 1912, Nazi, very good—$450.00
    Model 1912, Nazi, excellent—$550.00

History: The Model 1911 and Model 1912 Steyr-Hahns were the development of Oesterreichische Waffenfabriks Gesellschaft of Steyr, Austria, and since they were designed to be used as military pistols, they added the name "Hahn," which means "hammer," to differentiate them from the 1907 Roth-Steyr, which they also manufactured, and which had no hammer. The first pistols made in early 1911 were strictly commercial. It differed from the Military version in several aspects. First it was very finely finished, and had a milled front sight. The later military models which were introduced in late 1911 or early 1912 had a dovetailed front sight. Conversely, the original rear sight for the Model 1911 Commercial was dovetailed in place, while the later military version was milled in place. Some very early military pistols will also be found with commercial slides, so be aware to watch for markings to differentiate between commercial and military. Several hundred thousand of these guns were made, and many of them remained in arsenal stock at the beginning of World War II. Knowing they needed quite a few weapons for the war, the Germans converted many of these pistols to 9mm Parabellum caliber and they are so indicated by the stamping "P.08," designating the cartridge on the side of the slide.

Mechanical Functioning: The Steyr 1911/1912 series of pistols were recoil-operated, semiautomatic pistols with an external hammer and a fixed magazine holding eight cartridges and loaded via a stripper clip from the top through guides. It had an unusual system for its recoil operation. Slide and barrel were locked together at battery via lugs at the front and the rear. Upon firing, the slide and barrel moved together as a unit for about a quarter of an inch, until a section of the barrel lug hit a cam on the frame, rotating the barrel about 20 degrees, and unlocking it from the slide. At this point the barrel and slide still moved back together again for a very minuscule distance until a second lug on the barrel struck a projection on the frame, holding the barrel in place while the slide continued to move backwards, cycling the action and cocking the hammer. On the forward push it stripped a cartridge out of its fixed magazine and threw the barrel forward, once again camming it 20 degrees in the reverse direction on its way to battery.

Model 1911 Steyr-Hahn

Steyr
Oesterreichische Waffenfabriks Gesellschaft
Steyr, Austria

Model: 1909 Solothurn

Action Type: semiautomatic, blowback operated.

Caliber(s): .32 A.C.P., 6.35mm, 7.65mm.

Barrel Lengths: 3³/₄".

Finish: blue.

Manufacturing Dates: 1909–1914 and 1921–1939.

Stocks: hard rubber.

Rifling: 6R.

Weight, Unloaded: 21¹/₄ oz.

Sights: fixed.

Serial Numbers: may have started at 1 and many have "P" suffix which may mean rework.

Serial Number Location: left side of frame above trigger guard.

Major Variations: early models had no extractor.
models were produced in Belgium, Austria, and Switzerland.
early models had serrations (slanted or straight) on top rear of block.
Solothurn Models had serrations on the lower block, had a fixed lanyard loop and a more massive block.

Markings: left side of slide: Oesterr. Waffenfabriks-Ges., Steyr. or: Oesterr. Waffenfabriks-Ges. Steyr made in Austria.
right side of slide: N. Pieper Patent.
late models just had patent dates on barrel.

Price(s):
early Steyr, no extractor, very good—$150.00
early Steyr, no extractor, excellent—$200.00
early Steyr, with extractor, slanted serrations, very good—$150.00; excellent—$200.00
early Steyr, with extractor, straight serrations, very good—$125.00; excellent—$175.00
Solothurn, early with short barrel finger piece, very good—$150.00; excellent—$200.00
Solothurn, late with long barrel finger piece, very good—$175.00
Solothurn, late with long barrel finger piece, excellent—$250.00
Solothurn, late with Nazi Police stamps, very good—$200.00
Solothurn, late with Nazi Police stamps, excellent—$275.00

History: In 1909 the Steyr factory concluded a deal with Nicholas Pieper of Liege, Belgium, to manufacture the Pieper-patent Basculant pistols under the Steyr name. These pistols, which came to be known as the

Model 1909 Steyr and later the Steyr Solothurn, were manufactured at first in Belgium and later in Austria and Switzerland and went through several changes. The very early pistols had no extractor, and later, when it was added, there were two styles of finger grooves located on the top of the firearm on the side where the rear sight was. The very early models had slanted serrations, and were later replaced by straight serrations. There were no lanyard loop on these pistols. It is said that nearly 60,000 of this type were made, many of them being used during World War I as a secondary martial pistol by the Austrians. After World War I, the Solothurn Works in Switzerland manufactured these pistols for Steyr. They were slightly redesigned, making them heavier and sturdier and also adding a fixed lanyard loop at the base of the butt. Rather than the OWG grips usually found on the early production, virtually all of the Solothurn pistols had the grips showing Steyr and a target, and having the slides unmarked as to maker. Within the Solothurn there were two different variations. The early models, like the Steyr-produced pistols, had a finger extension on the side of the barrel, which came within ¼" of meeting the frame. On the later Solothurns, this extended all the way down to the frame when the barrel was in the closed position. After the Anschluss in 1938, a great many of these pistols were used as police weapons for the Third Reich.

Mechanical Functioning: The Steyr Model 1909 and Solothurn variations were straight blowback-operated, semiautomatic pistols with a seven-shot detachable box magazine inserted through the gripframe and retained by a spring-loaded catch at the bottom rear of the gripstrap. The pistol is based on the Pieper Basculant patent, in which, by depressing a lever located just above the trigger on the left side of the frame, the barrel will pop open, either for single-shot loading or for cleaning.

Steyr Model 1909 Solothurn

Steyr
Oesterreichische Waffenfabriks Gesellschaft
Steyr, Austria

Model: SP

Action Type: semiautomatic, blowback operated.

Caliber(s): 7.65mm.

Barrel Lengths: 3½".

Finish: blue.

Manufacturing Dates: late 1959–1965.

Stocks: plastic.

Rifling: 6R.

Weight, Unloaded: 21⅞ oz.

Sights: fixed.

Serial Numbers: started at 1.

Major Variations: none.

Markings: left side of slide: Steyr-Daimier-Puch AG, Mod. SP, Kal 7.65mm. Made in Austria.
Year of manufacture marked on barrel and visible through the ejection port.

Price(s):
Model SP, very good—$450.00
Model SP, excellent—$575.00

History: Steyr had been out of the handgun business since the beginning of World War II; however, they had retained their rifle manufacturing capabilities, and had been doing quite well in the commercial market, with some good sales to the military. About 1958 the Steyr plant decided it was a good time to crack the American market for a good 7.65mm handgun, and their designers came up with the Model SP. It was a 7.65mm, blowback-operated pistol, which was double action only, using a concealed hammer. The pistol had a fine natural hold and good pointing qualities, and it was thought by the factory that this would make an excellent pistol for self-defense. Unfortunately, the American market is not what many Europeans think that it should be, with Americans preferring a good trigger pull and even target-like qualities on their pocket pistols. The first examples of this pistol seem to have hit the market in late 1959. Production continued through 1965, but very few models were produced. The double-action pull was just a little bit too rough for most people to be able to hit what they were shooting at, and though the pistol was well made, it did suffer from the fact that it had no single-action capability. The Model SP pistols are now fairly scarce.

Mechanical Functioning: The Model SP Steyr is a straight blowback-operated, semiautomatic pistol that functions as double action only, utilizing a concealed hammer and a floating firing pin. Takedown is accomplished by first making sure the pistol is unloaded, then removing the magazine. At this point the sleeve at the forward end of the slide can be removed in the same manner as on the Browning 1910, being very cautious to hold it firmly when turning it, because it is under heavy spring pressure from the recoil spring, and it can fly out. Upon removing it and the recoil spring, the slide may now be withdrawn fully to the rear, lifted slightly, and then run off the end of the barrel, which is fixed to the frame. The pistol is now field-stripped. Assembly is in the reverse order. The barrel is set into an extension of the frame and pinned in place. The magazine is of the detachable box type and is inserted through the gripframe and retained by a spring-loaded catch located at the bottom of the butt at the rear. The grips are formed of cast plastic and are held in place by a single screw on each side. The disconnector is integral with the sear connector and rests on the left side of the frame underneath the grip. The slide keeps the connector in the down position until it reaches battery and lets the disconnector slip into a cutout. The mainspring is of the coil type and rides on a guide in the Walther fashion. This pistol was neat and simple, two things that usually combine to spell success for a product. Unfortunately, when Steyr presented this pistol, the market wasn't quite ready for it.

Steyr Model SP

Franz Stock Maschinen u. Werkbaufabrik
Berlin, Germany

Model: Stock

Action Type: semiautomatic, blowback operated.

Caliber(s): .22 L.R., 6.35mm, 7.65mm.

Barrel Lengths: 2½" in 6.35mm, 3⅞" in 7.65mm, 4" to 6½" in .22 L.R.

Finish: blue or nickel.

Manufacturing Dates: 1923 to the 1930s.

Stocks: hard rubber.

Rifling: 4R in 6.35mm and 7.65mm, 6R in .22 L.R.

Sights: fixed.

Serial Numbers: in 6.35mm may have started at 1. 6.35mm and 7.65mm probably overlapped. 7.65mm numbers seen into the 20,000s.

Serial Number Location: left side of frame above grip.

Major Variations: calibers and finish.

Markings: left side of slide: Franz Stock, Berlin, and then generally caliber.

Price(s):
  .22 L.R., very good—$300.00
  .22 L.R., excellent—$350.00
  6.35mm, blue, very good—$200.00
  6.35mm, blue, excellent—$250.00
  6.35mm, nickel, very good—$200.00
  6.35mm, nickel, excellent—$275.00
  7.65mm, very good—$250.00
  7.65mm, excellent—$300.00

History: The Franz Stock pistol was developed by Franz Stock and manufactured by his company, the Franz Stock Maschinen u. Werkbaufabrik, in Berlin, Germany. It appears that production on the 6.35mm and the 7.65mm started about 1923 with the .22 L.R. being added to the line about 1925. Although virtually all the production seems to have been in blue, there has been observed one 6.35mm pistol which appeared to have factory plating. All three pistols are built on the same design, with the exception that the 6.35mm is built on a smaller frame, and everything reduced in size from the .22 L.R. and the 7.65mm. The .22 L.R. seems to share the same frame as the 7.65mm, and differs only slightly in slide construction. Where the 7.65mm has a sharp corner just under the barrel sleeve, the .22 L.R. is nicely radiused into the barrel sleeve. On the 6.35mm and the 7.65mm there were no choices as to barrel length, but apparently on the .22 L.R., barrels could be obtained anywhere from 4" to 6½" in length. This was an interesting pistol. It was fairly well made and of fairly unique design. It was quite safe to use, and it had not only the manual thumb safety locking the sear and preventing discharge, but also a magazine safety locking the action when the magazine was removed.

Mechanical Functioning: All of the Franz Stock pistols, regardless of frame size, are blowback-operated, semiautomatic pistols with detachable box magazines retained by a spring-loaded catch located at the base of the butt. The magazine capacity in 6.35mm automatic is seven shots, eight shots in 7.65mm automatic, and ten shots in .22 Long Rifle. It is striker-fired and utilizes a removable breechblock mounted into the slide. The barrel is fixed to the frame via a barrel extension, and the recoil spring is axially wound around the barrel, and retained by the barrel extension on the slide. Field stripping this pistol is accomplished by first making sure that the pistol is unloaded, removing the magazine and then retracting the slide to the rearward position, and locking it in place by flipping the safety up, engaging the safety in the notch cut into the left side of the slide just forward of the serrations for the finger grooves. With the slide thus locked in the rearward position, the breechblock can then be wiggled upward slightly and pushed out of the slide, using pressure on the rear screw, lifting the front at the same time. Once this is out, hold the slide firmly, allowing the slide to move forward under the pressure of the recoil spring and off the barrel, thus removing it from the receiver. The firing pin can then be removed from the breechblock by unscrewing the large screw located at its rear, and by removing the firing pin spring and firing pin. Assembly is in the reverse order.

Stoeger Arms Corp.
55 Ruta Court
South Hackensack, NJ 07606

Model: Luger

Action Type: semiautomatic, blowback operated.

Caliber(s): .22 L.R.R.F.

Barrel Lengths: 4½″, 5½″.

Finish: blue or blackened.

Manufacturing Dates: 1969 to date.

Stocks: smooth or checkered walnut.

Rifling: 6R.

Weight, Unloaded: 29½ oz.

Sights: fixed or adjustable rear.

Serial Numbers: starting number was CL01002.

Serial Number Location: right side above trigger.

Major Variations: early models had aluminum alloy frames, and were available in right (STLR, TLR) and left (STLL, TLL) hand versions, and in fixed sight (STLR or L) and target sight (TLR or L) versions. In 1980 the frame was made from forged steel, and in 1982 the frame was changed to investment cast steel.

Markings: on left and right side of frame: Luger.
on left side of the barrel extension: Cal. .22 LR.
on rear toggle link: Stoeger trademark.

Price(s):
    STLR-4, very good—$75.00
    STLR-4, excellent—$125.00
    STLL-4, very good—$75.00
    STLL-4, excellent—$125.00
    STLR-5, very good—$75.00
    STLR-5, excellent—$125.00
    STLL-5, very good—$75.00
    STLL-5, excellent—$150.00
    TLR-4, very good—$100.00
    TLR-4, excellent—$150.00
    TLL-4, very good—$100.00
    TLL-4, excellent—$150.00
    TLR-5, very good—$100.00
    TLR-5, excellent—$150.00
    TLL-5, very good—$100.00
    TLL-5, excellent—$150.00
    STLR-4, forged, very good—$95.00
    STLR-4, forged, excellent—$140.00

History: Stoeger Arms Corp. is in a unique situation. They own the copyright on the "Luger" name and trademark as it is applied to firearms (which explains why Mauser calls their newly issued "P.08" pistols "the Parabellums"). However, most people, upon seeing George Luger's pet pistol immediately state, "That's a Luger," and because of the beauty of the design, the P.08 has probably become the most recognized handgun in the world. In 1969 Stoeger decided to capitalize on this and introduced their .22 pistol. The original issue was supplied with beautifully checkered walnut grips impregnated with an epoxy resin for durability. Unfortunately, they were too perfect and because of the shininess, people assumed they were imitation! Stoeger corrected this in 1970 and supplied instead rather homely, plain wood grips. Current production had reverted back to checkered but without the shine.

Mechanical Functioning: The Stoeger Luger is a simple blowback-operated, semiautomatic pistol with a ten-shot detachable box magazine. Unlike the parent Parabellum pistol, the toggle does not lock the breech; rather it functions as a method of retracting the bolt and for decoration. The stationary barrel is retained in the frame with a cross pin, and in the early alloy guns, steel ways and guides provide strength and prevent wear.

STLR-4

Sturm, Ruger & Co.
Southport, CT 06490

Model: MK I and II

Action Type: semiautomatic, blowback operated.

Caliber(s): .22 L.R.

Barrel Lengths: 5½" or 6⅞".

Finish: blue.

Manufacturing Dates: 1982 to date.

Stocks: plastic, hard rubber, or wood.

Rifling: 6R.

Weight, Unloaded: 42 oz with 6⅞" barrel.

Sights: target rear.

Serial Numbers: n/a.

Serial Number Location: right side of frame.

Major Variations: Mark I.
    Mark II.
    barrel type.

Markings: right side: Ruger .22 Cal. Long Rifle Mark II Target.
    on MK I right side: Ruger .22 Cal. Long Rifle Mark I Target.

Price(s):
    Mark I, bull barrel, wood grips, very good—$150.00
    Mark I, bull barrel, wood grips, excellent—$175.00
    Mark I, Target, wood grips, very good—$175.00
    Mark I, Target, wood grips, excellent—$225.00
    Mark II, bull barrel, plastic grips, very good—$200.00
    Mark II, bull barrel, plastic grips, excellent—$250.00
    Mark II, Target, plastic grips, very good—$225.00
    Mark II, Target, plastic grips, excellent—$275.00

History: The Ruger Standard Model Automatic Pistol was first made in Target version in 1951. This differs from the Standard model in that it has adjustable rear sights and undercut target front sights. The 6⅞" barrel is tapered, while the 5½" is an untapered bull barrel. This variation of the Standard stayed in production until 1982 when it was replaced by the MK II version. Although the exterior of the MK I and MK II appear to be identical, there are internal differences, most noteworthy being the introduction of a bolt stop to hold the bolt open when the last shot is fired, or to manually hold the bolt open via a bolt stop catch on the left side of the receiver. The second most noteworthy feature is the enlarged magazine catch on the MK II to provide more positive functioning.

Mechanical Functioning: The Ruger MK II Target Model is a semiautomatic, blowback-operated pistol, chambered for .22 Long Rifle rimfire. It has a concealed internal hammer, a detachable ten-shot magazine which is fitted through the gripframe and is retained by a spring-loaded catch at the bottom base of the butt. The catch has been redesigned and enlarged.

Ruger MK II Target

Sturm, Ruger & Co.
Southport, CT 06490

Model: Blackhawk, New Model

Action Type: revolver, single action.

Caliber(s): .30 Carbine, .357 Magnum, 9mm Parabellum, .41 Magnum, .45 Long Colt, .45 A.C.P.

Barrel Lengths: 4⅝″, 6½″, 7½″.

Finish: blue.

Manufacturing Dates: 1973 to date.

Stocks: wood.

Rifling: 6R.

Weight, Unloaded: 40 oz. with 4⅝″ barrel.

Sights: adjustable.

Serial Numbers: n/a.

Serial Number Location: right side of frame.

Major Variations: conversion cylinders for 9mm Parabellum with .357 Magnum.
conversion cylinders for .45 A.C.P. with .45 Long Colt.

Markings: left side of barrel: Sturm Ruger & Co. Inc., Southport, Conn. USA.
left side of frame: Ruger (caliber) New Model Blackhawk.

Price(s):
    .30 Carbine—$300.00
    .357 Magnum—$300.00
    .357 Magnum Convertible—$325.00
    .41 Magnum—$300.00
    .45 Long Colt—$300.00
    .45 Long Colt Convertible—$350.00

History: The New Model Blackhawk began life in 1955 as the Ruger Black-hawk Single Action Revolver. The original Ruger Blackhawk had an action very similar to the Colt, in which the only safety was a half-cock notch and the fact that it had a floating firing pin so that it was safe to let down the hammer on the firing pin without the danger of the gun going off. However, because many people were carrying the firearm around with six shots in the chamber and the hammer on the half-cock notch, there was the danger of slippage, so in 1972 Ruger discontinued the old model and remanufactured it as the New Model with a built-in auto-matic hammer safety preventing discharge unless the hammer was first put in the full cock position and then the trigger pulled. The New Model has been made since 1972 and has been available in a variety of calibers and barrel lengths. In calibers .357 and .45 Long Colt, auxiliary cylin-ders are available to convert the caliber to 9mm Parabellum, and .45 A.C.P., respectively. Since 1978 this model has been stamped with a warning notice that says "Before using gun read warnings and instruction manual available free from Sturm, Ruger & Co., Inc., Southport, Conn. USA" along the side of the barrel. To celebrate the Bicentennial during 1976 all Ruger firearms carried the stamping "1776–1976" to celebrate the nation's birthday.

Mechanical Functioning: The New Model Ruger Blackhawk is a six-shot, single-action revolver based on a Western style. Loading and ejection are carried out by swinging open the cylinder port on the right rear side of the frame behind the cylinder. This releases the cylinder bolt, allowing the cylinder to spin freely. At this point the chambers can either be loaded, or using the rod ejector they can be unloaded, simply by aligning the chamber with the opening in the frame. There is no half-cock notch on this model; rather the safety is in the form of a transfer bar. Under carrying conditions, the face of the hammer rests against the rear wall of the frame above the firing pin out of contact with the firing pin. When the hammer is in the full cocked position and the trigger pulled, the transfer bar is lifted so that the force of the falling hammer may be transferred through it to the firing pin, allowing discharge. In this model of revolver, unlike many other single-action revolvers, it is safe to carry six shots in the cylinder. Normal cleaning can be accomplished by first opening the sidegate, making sure that the cylinder is unloaded, and then with the sidegate still open, pushing the locking pin forward of the cylinder on the side of the frame inward so that the center pin may be pulled out and the cylinder removed. Assembly is in the reverse order.

Ruger New Model Blackhawk

Sturm, Ruger & Co.
Southport, CT 06490

Model: Blackhawk, Stainless New Model

Action Type: revolver, single action.

Caliber(s): .357 Magnum, .45 Long Colt.

Barrel Lengths: 4⅝″, 6½″, 7½″.

Finish: stainless steel.

Manufacturing Dates: 1977 to date.

Stocks: wood.

Rifling: 6R.

Weight, Unloaded: 40 oz. with 4⅝″ barrel.

Sights: adjustable.

Serial Numbers: n/a.

Serial Number Location: right side of frame.

Major Variations: none.

Markings: left side of barrel: Sturm Ruger & Co., Inc., Southport, Conn. USA. left side of frame: Ruger (caliber) New Model Blackhawk .357 Stainless.

Price(s):
Blackhawk, Stainless, New Model, very good—$300.00; excellent—$375.00

History: The New Model Blackhawk Stainless began life in 1977. The original Ruger Blackhawk had an action very similar to the Colt, in which the only safety was a half-cock notch and the fact that it had a floating firing pin so that it was safe to let down the hammer on the firing pin without the danger of the gun going off. However, because many people were carrying the firearm around with six shots in the chamber and the hammer on the half-cock notch, there was the danger of slippage, so in 1972 Ruger discontinued the old model and remanufactured it as the New Model with a built-in automatic hammer safety preventing discharge unless the hammer was first put in the full-cock position and then the trigger pulled. Since 1978 this model has been stamped with a warning notice that says "Before using gun read warnings and instruction manual available free from Sturm, Ruger & Co., Inc., Southport, Conn. USA" along the side of the barrel.

Mechanical Functioning: The New Model Ruger Blackhawk .357 Stainless is a six-shot, single-action revolver based on a Western style. Loading and ejection are carried out by swinging open the cylinder port on the right rear side of the frame behind the cylinder. This releases the cylinder bolt, allowing the cylinder to spin freely. At this point the chambers can either be loaded, or using the rod ejector they can be unloaded, simply by aligning the chamber with the opening in the frame. There is no half-cock notch on this model; rather the safety is in the form of a transfer bar.

Under carrying conditions, the face of the hammer rests against the rear wall of the frame above the firing pin out of contact with the firing pin. When the hammer is in the full cocked position and the trigger pulled, the transfer bar is lifted so that the force of the falling hammer may be transferred through it to the firing pin, allowing discharge. In this model of revolver, unlike many other single-action revolvers, it is safe to carry six shots in the cylinder. Normal cleaning can be accomplished by first opening the sidegate, making sure that the cylinder is unloaded, and then with the sidegate still open, pushing the locking pin forward of the cylinder on the side of the frame inward so that the center pin may be pulled out and the cylinder removed. Assembly is in the reverse order.

Sturm, Ruger & Co.
Southport, CT 06490

Model: Police Service Six

Action Type: revolver, double action.

Caliber(s): .38 Special, .357 Magnum, 9mm Parabellum.

Barrel Lengths: 4″ or 2³/₄″.

Finish: blue.

Manufacturing Dates: 1973–1988.

Stocks: wood.

Rifling: 5R.

Weight, Unloaded: 33¹/₂ oz. in 4″ barrel.

Sights: fixed.

Serial Numbers: n/a.

Serial Number Location: bottom of butt.

Major Variations: heavy barrel available in 4″ .357 Magnum.

Markings: left side of barrel: Sturm Ruger & Co., Inc. Southport Conn USA.
right side of barrel: caliber
right side of frame: Ruger Police Service Six.

Price(s):
Police Service Six, very good—$200.00; excellent—$250.00
Bicentennial markings add 10%.
Pre-78 guns without warning stamp add 5%.

History: The Ruger Police Service Six was first introduced in 1973 to compete with Colt and Smith & Wesson for the police and military market both in the U.S. and abroad, and it was quite successful in achieving the same. It was a fixed-sight revolver, which is ideal for police service use, and comes in both 2³/₄″ and 4″ barrel versions. For rough use the heavy barreled 4″ version is available at no extra charge. For European and Mid-Eastern markets the 9mm Parabellum revolver was developed and for many years it was quite scarce in the United States. In 1976 Ruger stamped all the guns they made with "1776–1976" as a Bicentennial commemorative. These guns are now getting quite collectible, and while this model of firearm was primarily a duty gun, the Bicentennial markings will one day add even more value to it. In 1978 Ruger made a corporate decision to stamp every model of gun with a warning label, encouraging users to read the instruction manual for that particular model. Ruger firearms without that stamp are also becoming quite collectible.

Mechanical Functioning: The Ruger Police Service Six is a solid-frame, double-action revolver with a cylinder that swings out to the left. Ejection is manual and simultaneous on this six-shot cylinder, and the center pin locks both at fore and aft positions for positive alignment of the chamber with the barrel. The firing pin is of the floating type and is spring-loaded. There is an internal safety device incorporating a hammer transfer bar. Unless the trigger is pulled fully to the rear the firearm cannot discharge. Therefore, if the hammer is struck or the gun is dropped there is no fear of an accidental shooting. The mainspring is of a coil type and rides on a ball-ended guide that engages the hammer.

Ruger Police Service Six

Sturm, Ruger & Co.
Southport, CT 06490

Model: Police Service Six Stainless

Action Type: revolver, double action.

Caliber(s): .38 Special, .357 Magnum, 9mm Parabellum.

Barrel Lengths: 4" or 2³/₄".

Finish: stainless steel.

Manufacturing Dates: 1973–1988.

Stocks: wood.

Rifling: 5R.

Weight, Unloaded: 33¹/₂ oz. in 4" barrel.

Sights: fixed.

Serial Numbers: n/a.

Serial Number Location: bottom of butt.

Major Variations: heavy barrel available in 4" .357 Magnum.

Markings: left side of barrel: Sturm Ruger & Co., Inc. Southport, Conn USA. right side of barrel: caliber.
right side of frame: Ruger Police Service Six Stainless

Price(s):
very good—$225.00; excellent—$275.00

History: The Ruger Police Service Six Stainless was first introduced in 1973 to compete with Colt and Smith & Wesson for the police and military market both in the U.S. and abroad, and it was quite successful in achieving the same. It was a fixed-sight revolver which is ideal for police service use, and comes in both 2³/₄" and 4" barrel versions. For rough use the heavy-barreled 4" version is available at no extra charge. For European and Mid-Eastern markets the 9mm Parabellum revolver was developed, and for many years it was quite scarce in the United States. In 1976 Ruger stamped all the guns they made with "1776–1976" as a Bicentennial commemorative. These guns are now getting quite collectible, and while this model of firearm was primarily a duty gun, the Bicentennial markings will one day add even more value to it. In 1978 Ruger made a corporate decision to stamp every model of gun with a warning label, encouraging users to read the instruction manual for that particular model. Ruger firearms without that stamp are also getting quite collectible.

Mechanical Functioning: The Ruger Police Service Six Stainless is a solid-frame, double-action revolver with a cylinder that swings out to the left. Ejection is manual and simultaneous on this six-shot cylinder, and the center pin locks both at fore and aft positions for positive alignment of the chamber with the barrel. The firing pin is of the floating type and is spring-loaded. There is an internal safety device incorporating a hammer transfer bar. Unless the trigger is pulled fully to the rear, the firearm cannot discharge. Therefore, if the hammer is struck or the gun is dropped, there is no fear of an accidental shooting. The mainspring is of a coil type and rides on a ball-ended guide that engages the hammer.

Ruger Police Service Six Stainless

Sturm, Ruger & Co.
Southport, CT 06490

Model: Redhawk

Action Type: revolver, double action.

Caliber(s): .44 Magnum, .41 Magnum, .357 Magnum.

Barrel Lengths: 7½″.

Finish: stainless steel or blued steel.

Manufacturing Dates: 1979 to date (.44 Magnum only).

Stocks: walnut.

Rifling: 5R.

Weight, Unloaded: 46 oz.

Sights: adjustable rear, interchangeable front.

Serial Numbers: n/a.

Serial Number Location: bottom of butt.

Major Variations: interchangeable front sights.

Markings: left side of barrel: Sturm Ruger & Co., Inc. Southport, Conn, USA.
right side of barrel: .44 Magnum Cal.
right side of frame: Ruger Redhawk.

Price(s):
stainless—$450.00
blue—$400.00

History: The Ruger Redhawk double-action revolver is essentially an enlarged Security Six but more massive in every dimension. It is crafted entirely of stainless steel and is chambered for .44 Magnum. One of the intriguing features of this .44 Magnum is the interchangeable front sights. The standard front sight is of blade type with a red insert. The accessory sights consist of a bead front or blue, white, yellow, or red solid-plastic sights for greater visibility. The grips are plain and un-checkered for comfort, and this massive brute is primarily to be used, rather than to be looked at. Because of the nature of the metal, this gun can be used in the woods or in rough handling without worry about rust or corrosion.

Mechanical Functioning: The Ruger Redhawk is a double-action, solid-frame revolver with a cylinder that swings out to the left side and which holds six shots. Coil springs are used throughout the firearm and take-down can be accomplished using only a coin. Disassembly is as follows. Unload the revolver and close the cylinder. Remove the gripscrew and both grip panels with either a proper-size screwdriver or the rim of a cartridge case or coin. Cock the hammer and remove the disassembly pin from its storage position in the grip panel dowel, which is a hollow roll pin. Insert the disassembly pin about half its length into the hole in the hammer strut. Pull the trigger, holding the hammer, and remove the mainspring and strut assembly intact. Be very careful not to let the pin slip out and the mainspring come off of the strut. Pull the trigger to the rear and remove the hammer pivot from the right side of the frame. Pull the hammer out from the top of the frame while holding the trigger back. Use the top end of the hammer strut to depress the trigger guard lock plunger located inside the frame at the rear of the trigger guard. At the same time, pull out and remove the trigger guard assembly from the bottom of the frame. Open the cylinder and pull the cylinder and crane pivot assembly from the front of the frame as a unit. Remove the cylinder latch from the bottom of the frame. Assembly should be carried out in the reverse order.

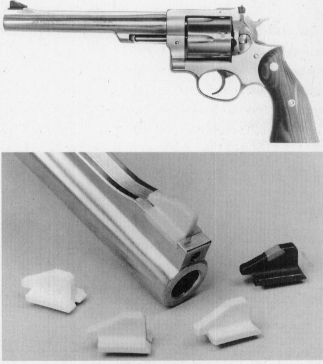

Ruger Redhawk

Sturm, Ruger & Co.
Southport, CT 06490

Model: Standard

Action Type: semiautomatic, blowback operated.

Caliber(s): .22 L.R.

Barrel Lengths: 4³/₄" or 6".

Finish: blue or stainless steel.

Manufacturing Dates: 1949 to 1981, superseded by Mark II in 1982.

Stocks: plastic or walnut.

Rifling: 6R.

Weight, Unloaded: 36 oz. with 4³/₄" barrel.

Serial Numbers: n/a.

Serial Number Location: forward part of receiver.

Major Variations: none.

Markings: right side of receiver. Sturm Ruger & Co., Southport Conn. USA. left side of receiver: Ruger .22 Cal Long Rifle Automatic Pistol.

Price(s):
Standard MK II—$200.00
Standard MK II, stainless—$250.00
Standard, very good—$125.00; excellent—$150.00
Standard Old model, serials under 25600, very good—$200.00
Standard Old model, series under 25600, excellent—$275.00

History: The Ruger Standard Automatic Pistol was a cornerstone of the Ruger company. First introduced in 1949, over a million pistols have been produced on its frame. At the end of 1981 the Standard pistol was discontinued and replaced by the MK II Standard. However, the final pistol off the production line of the Standard pistol was an all stainless steel version, limited to 5,000 issues, packed in a wood presentation case. The MK II version was almost identical in exterior appearance with most of the changes being with the action. For one, a bolt stop has been included in the MK II to hold the bolt in the open position after the last shot. A bolt stop front piece has also been added on the left side of the frame to manually lock the bolt open. The safety has also been changed to permit the pistol to be unloaded or to allow the bolt to be operated while the safety is in the "on" position, locking the sear.

Mechanical Functioning: The Ruger Standard and the Ruger MK II are semiautomatic, blowback-operated pistols chambered for .22 Long Rifle rimfire. They have a concealed internal hammer, a detachable ten-shot box magazine that is fitted through the gripframe and retained by a spring-loaded catch at the bottom base of the butt. On the MK II the catch has been redesigned and enlarged.

Ruger Standard .22 Pistol

Sturm, Ruger & Co.
Southport, CT 06490

Model: Security Six

Action Type: revolver, double action.

Caliber(s): .357 Magnum.

Barrel Lengths: 2¾", 4", 6".

Finish: blue.

Manufacturing Dates: 1970 to 1985.

Stocks: walnut service stocks or target stocks.

Rifling: 5R.

Weight, Unloaded: 33½ oz. with 4" barrel.

Sights: adjustable rear.

Serial Numbers: n/a.

Serial Number Location: on bottom of butt.

Major Variations: 4" heavy barrel.
large grips.

Markings: left side of barrel: Sturm Roger & Co., Inc. Southport Conn. USA.
right side of barrel: .357 magnum Cal.
right side of frame: Ruger Security Six.

Price(s):
2¾" barrel, very good—$250.00; excellent—$300.00
6" barrel, very good—$200.00; excellent—$250.00
4" heavy barrel, very good—$225.00; excellent—$275.00
with target grip, very good—$250.00; excellent—$325.00
Bicentennial markings add 10%.
pre-warning stamp add 5%.
lanyard loop add $10.00 to $20.00.

History: The Ruger Security Six was Ruger's first entry into the double-action revolver field and was first produced in 1970. Chambered for the .357 Magnum cartridge, this firearm has made excellent inroads into the police market for which it was designed. It has adjustable rear sights and a ramp front sight with a red insert, with the entire slide assembly sitting on an integral solid barrel rib. Different from most other double-action revolvers on the market, this is truly a solid-frame revolver with no sideplate, as the lockwork disassembles and comes off from either the bottom or the top. The only screws on this pistol that might work loose are the gripscrew and the sight-adjustment screw. All other retention is accomplished by either spring-loaded pins or friction fitting pins. A safe revolver, the Ruger Security Six will not discharge unless the trigger is fully pulled, raising the hammer transfer bar, and thus allowing the energy from the hammer to be transferred to the floating firing pin. Unless this is accomplished, a sufficient amount of energy to discharge the cartridge cannot be transmitted through the firing pin, even if the hammer is struck, or even though the revolver is dropped.

Mechanical Functioning: The Ruger Security Six is an adjustable-sighted, solid-frame, double-action revolver with a six-shot cylinder swinging out to the left. The cylinder latch is located on the left side of the frame, mounted on the flashguard and is depressed in order to release the cylinder lock. The cylinder center pin locks both at the rear and the forward end, insuring alignment of the chamber with the barrel. The same pin is also used for an ejector rod for a simultaneous manual ejection after the cylinder is swung out. Disassembly is simple and can be accomplished with either one screwdriver or a coin. Complete disassembly instructions are given in the Ruger Redhawk listing.

Ruger Security Six

Sturm, Ruger & Co.
Southport, CT 06490

Model: Security Six Stainless

Action Type: revolver, double action.

Caliber(s): .357 Magnum.

Barrel Lengths: 2³/₄", 4", 6".

Finish: blue.

Manufacturing Dates: 1970–1985.

Stocks: walnut service stocks or target stocks.

Rifling: 5R.

Weight, Unloaded: 33¹/₂ oz. with 4" barrel.

Sights: adjustable rear.

Serial Numbers: n/a.

Serial Number Location: on bottom of butt.

Major Variations: 4" heavy barrel.
  large grips.

Markings: left side of barrel: Sturm Ruger & Co., Inc. Southport Conn. USA.
  right side of barrel: .357 Magnum Cal.
  right side of frame: Ruger Security Six Stainless.

Price(s):
  2³/₄" barrel, very good—$275.00; excellent—$325.00
  6" barrel, very good—$200.00; excellent—$275.00
  4" heavy barrel, very good—$275.00; excellent—$300.00
  with target grip, very good—$275.00; excellent—$350.00
  Bicentennial markings add 10%.
  pre-warning stamp add 5%.
  lanyard loop add $10.00 to $20.00.

History: The Ruger Security Six Stainless was Ruger's first entry into the double-action revolver field and was first produced in 1970. Chambered for the .357 Magnum cartridge, this firearm has made excellent inroads into the police market for which it was designed. It had adjustable rear sights and a ramp front sight with a red insert, with the entire slide assembly sitting on an integral solid barrel rib. Different from most other double-action revolvers on the market, this is truly a solid-frame revolver with no sideplate, as the lockwork disassembles and comes off from either the bottom or the top. The only screws on this pistol that might work loose are the gripscrew and the sight-adjustment screw. All other retention is accomplished by either spring-loaded pins or friction fitting pins. A safe revolver, the Ruger Security Six Stainless will not discharge unless the trigger is fully pulled, raising the hammer transfer bar, and thus allowing the energy from the hammer to be transferred to the floating firing pin. Unless this is accomplished, a sufficient amount of energy to discharge the cartridge cannot be transmitted through the firing pin, even if the hammer is struck, or even if the revolver is dropped.

Mechanical Functioning: The Ruger Security Six Stainless is an adjustable-sighted, solid-frame, double-action revolver with a six-shot cylinder swinging out to the left. The cylinder latch is located on the left side of the frame, mounted on the flashguard and is depressed in order to release the cylinder lock. The cylinder center pin locks both at the rear and the forward end, insuring alignment of the chamber with the barrel. The same pin is also used for an ejector rod for a simultaneous manual ejection after the cylinder is swung out. Disassembly is simple and can be accomplished with either one screwdriver or a coin. Complete disassembly instructions are given in the Ruger Redhawk listing.

Ruger Security Six Stainless

Sturm, Ruger & Co.
Southport, CT 06490

Model: Speed Six

Action Type: revolver, double action.

Caliber(s): .38 Special, .357 Magnum, 9mm Parabellum.

Barrel Lengths: 2³/₄" or 4".

Finish: blue or stainless.

Manufacturing Dates: 1973 to date (9mm disc. 1984).

Stocks: walnut.

Rifling: 5R.

Weight, Unloaded: 31 oz. with 2³/₄" barrel.

Sights: fixed.

Serial Numbers: n/a.

Serial Number Location: bottom of butt.

Major Variations: spurless hammer.
heavy barrel.

Markings: left side of barrel: Sturm Ruger & Co., Inc., Southport, Conn. USA.
right side of barrel: Caliber.
right side of frame: Ruger Speed Six.

Price(s):
blue, .357 Magnum—$225.00
blue, .38 Special—$225.00
blue, 9mm Parabellum, very good—$225.00; excellent—$275.00
stainless, .357 Magnum—$250.00
stainless, .38 Special—$250.00
stainless, 9mm Parabellum, very good—$250.00; excellent—$300.00
Bicentennial markings add 10%.
no warning stamp add 5%.

History: The Ruger Speed Six was first introduced in 1973 and is available in blued steel or stainless steel versions. It is available in 2³/₄" or 4" barrel versions, and in calibers .357 Magnum, .38 Special, and 9mm Parabellum. The primary difference between the Speed Six and the Ruger Police Six is the fact that this is a round butt revolver for ease of concealability and greater carrying comfort. Designed primarily for law enforcement use, the 9mm Parabellum cartridge was added to the line primarily for overseas sales and is only now becoming widely sold in the United States. During the American Bicentennial in 1976, every Ruger produced that year carried the stamp "1776–1976." Firearms with these markings are slowly becoming quite collectible. Another item for collectors to look for are pre-warning stamp Rugers. In 1978 Ruger made a corporate decision to stamp every gun with a warning for the purchaser to obtain the instruction manual for that particular model and to read it.

Mechanical Functioning: The Ruger Speed Six is a double-action, solid-frame revolver with a six-shot cylinder that swings outward to the left. Ejection is manual and simultaneous via an ejector rod, which also served as the center pin and locks at both fore and aft positions for positive chamber alignment. A hammer transfer bar safety device is incorporated in this revolver. The hammer normally rests on the solid steel above the firing pin with that portion of the hammer that would ordinarily contact the firing pin being cut out. Only when the trigger is pulled fully to the rear will a transfer bar rise to the level of the firing pin, in order to transmit the energy from the falling hammer through the transfer bar into the firing pin allowing discharge. Unless this occurs, only insufficient energy can be transmitted to the firing pin and therefore, even if dropped, the revolver cannot discharge.

Sturm, Ruger & Co.
Southport, CT 06490

Model: Super Blackhawk, New Model

Action Type: revolver, single action.

Caliber(s): .44 Magnum.

Barrel Lengths: 4⅝", 5½", 7½", 10½".

Finish: blue or stainless.

Manufacturing Dates: 1973 to date.

Stocks: wood.

Rifling: 6R.

Weight, Unloaded: 48 oz.

Sights: adjustable rear.

Serial Numbers: n/a.

Serial Number Location: right side of frame.

Major Variations: none.

Markings: left side of barrel: Sturm Ruger & Co., Inc., Southport, Conn. USA, left side of frame: Ruger (caliber) Super Blackhawk.

Price(s):
blue, very good—$250.00; excellent—$300.00
stainless, very good—$300.00; excellent—$350.00

History: The New Super Blackhawk began life in 1959 as the Ruger Super Blackhawk. The original Ruger Super Blackhawk had an action very similar to the Colt, in which the only safety was a half-cock notch and the fact that it had a floating firing pin so that it was safe to let down the hammer on the firing pin without the danger of the gun going off. However, because many people were carrying the firearm around with six shots in the chamber and the hammer on the half-cock notch, there was the danger of slippage, so in 1972 Ruger discontinued the old model and remanufactured it as the New Super Blackhawk with a built-in automatic hammer safety preventing discharge unless the hammer was first put in the full cock position and then the trigger pulled. Since 1979 this model has been stamped with a warning notice that says, "Before using gun read warnings and instruction manual available free from Sturm, Ruger & Co., Inc., Southport, Conn. USA" along the side of the barrel. To celebrate the Bicentennial during 1976 all Ruger firearms carried the stamping "1776–1976" to celebrate the nation's birthday.

Mechanical Functioning: The Ruger New Super Blackhawk is a six-shot, single-action revolver based on a Western style. Loading and ejection are carried out by swinging open the cylinder port on the right rear side of the frame behind the cylinder. This releases the cylinder bolt, allowing the cylinder to spin freely. At this point the chambers can either be loaded, or using the rod ejector they can be unloaded, simply by aligning the chamber with the opening in the frame. There is no half-cock notch on this model; rather the safety is in the form of a transfer bar. Under carrying conditions, the face of the hammer rests against the rear wall of the frame above the firing pin out of contact with the firing pin. When the hammer is in the full cocked position and the trigger pulled, the transfer bar is lifted so that the force of the falling hammer may be transferred through it to the firing pin, allowing discharge. In this model of revolver, unlike many other single-action revolvers, it is safe to carry six shots in the cylinder. Normal cleaning can be accomplished by first opening the sidegate, making sure that the cylinder is unloaded, and then with the sidegate still open, pushing the locking pin forward of the cylinder on the side of the frame inward so that the center pin may be pulled out and the cylinder removed. Assembly is in the reverse order.

Ruger New Super Blackhawk

Sturm, Ruger & Co.
Southport, CT 06490

Model: Super Single Six, New Model

Action Type: revolver, single action.

Caliber(s): .22 L.R., .22 W.M.R.

Barrel Lengths: 4⅝", 5½", 6½", 9½".

Finish: blue or stainless steel.

Manufacturing Dates: 1972 to date.

Stocks: wood.

Rifling: 6R.

Weight, Unloaded: 34½ oz. with 6½" barrel.

Sights: adjustable rear.

Serial Numbers: n/a.

Serial Number Location: right side of frame.

Major Variations: convertible cylinders.

Markings: left side of barrel: Sturm Ruger & Co., Inc., Southport, Conn. USA. left side of frame: Ruger (caliber) Super Single Six.

Price(s):
  Super Single Six .22LR, blue—$225.00
  Super Single Six Combo, stainless—$300.00

History: The New Model Super Single Six began life in 1964 as the Ruger Super Single Six. The original Ruger Super Single Six had an action very similar to the Colt, in which the only safety was a half-cock notch and the fact that it had a floating firing pin so that it was safe to let down the hammer on the firing pin without the danger of the gun going off. However, because many people were carrying the firearm around with six shots in the chamber and the hammer on the half-cock notch, there was the danger of slippage, so in 1972 Ruger discontinued the old model and remanufactured it as the New Model with a built-in automatic hammer safety preventing discharge unless the hammer was first put in the full cock position and then the trigger pulled. Since 1978 this model has been stamped with a warning notice that says "Before using gun read warnings and instruction manual available free from Sturm, Ruger & Co., Inc., Southport, Conn. USA" along the side of the barrel. To celebrate the Bicentennial during 1976 all Ruger firearms carried the stamping "1776–1976" to celebrate the nation's birthday.

Mechanical Functioning: The Super Single Six is a six-shot, single-action revolver based on a Western style. Loading and ejection are carried out by swinging open the cylinder port on the right rear side of the frame behind the cylinder. This releases the cylinder bolt, allowing the cylinder to spin freely. At this point the chambers can either be loaded, or using the rod ejector they can be unloaded, simply by aligning the chamber with the opening in the frame. There is no half-cock notch on this model; rather the safety is in the form of a transfer bar. Under carrying conditions, the face of the hammer rests against the rear wall of the frame above the firing pin out of contact with the firing pin. When the hammer is in the full cocked position and the trigger pulled, the transfer bar is lifted so that the force of the falling hammer may be transferred through it to the firing pin, allowing discharge. In this model of revolver, unlike many other single-action revolvers, it is safe to carry six shots in the cylinder. Normal cleaning can be accomplished by first opening the sidegate, making sure that the cylinder is unloaded, and then with the sidegate still open, pushing the locking pin forward of the cylinder on the side of the frame inward so that the center pin may be pulled out and the cylinder removed. Assembly is in the reverse order.

Ruger New Super Single Six

Thompson/Center Arms
Box 2405
Rochester, NH 03867

Model: Contender

Action Type: single-shot, tip-up barrel.

Caliber(s): 5mm Rem. R.F.M., .22 L.R.R.F., .221 Rem., 7mm T.C.U., .22 W.M.R., .22 Hornet, .222 Rem., .223 Rem., .256 Win., .30 Herrett, .30 M-1 Carbine, .30-30 Win., .218 Bee, .22 Rem. Jet, .25-35, .38 A.C.P., .385 PEC., .357 Mag., 9mm Parabellum, .17 Hornet, .17 Mach IV, .17-.222, .17-.223, .357 Herrett, .357-44 B & D, .41 mag., .44 mag., .45 A.C.P., .45 Colt, .45 Win. Mag.

Barrel Lengths: 10″, 14″, 8¾″.

Finish: blue.

Manufacturing Dates: 1967 to date.

Stocks: walnut.

Rifling: generally 6R, however on calibers 5mm, .44, on .45 it is 8R.

Weight, Unloaded: 43 oz. in 10″ barrel.

Sights: target adjustable rear.

Serial Numbers: n/a.

Serial Number Location: top of frame behind hammer.

Major Variations: tapered octagon barrel, bull barrel, vent rib barrel, 14″ target barrel, detachable choice in .357 magnum and .44 magnum, left- or right-hand target grips.

Markings: top left side of barrel: Thompson Center Arms Rochester N.H. (caliber).

Price(s):
    various calibers, 10″ octagonal barrel—$300.00
    various calibers, Super 14″—$300.00
    various calibers, 10″ bull barrel—$300.00
    custom contender rifle conversion, long barrel, new factory—about $375.00 to $500.00

History: Thompson/Center was founded in 1966 by Kenneth Thompson and Warren Center. Center had developed a design for a single-shot pistol, and Thompson had the manufacturing capabilities to make the pistol and together they seem to have formed an excellent partnership. They developed one model, the Contender, and for many years it was the only thing that this company made. It was a single-shot pistol with an external hammer and the ability to interchange barrels and calibers rather quickly. By changing barrels, the shooter can have at his option almost any caliber in the world that will not break his arm through recoil, and even a few that come close to it. Always changing with the times, Thompson/

Center has brought out a wide range of calibers, both factory and wildcat, in order to gauge the public's mood and desires and sometimes to even shape it. It has been available in various barrel lengths. The 10″ and 14″ are still available. The 8¾″ is now discontinued. The standard barrel styles currently available are: tapered octagon, bull barrel, vent rib tapered barrel, or 14″ target barrel. Thompson/Center also developed cartridges known as "hot-shots" in which a plastic shot capsule is used in calibers .357 or .44 Magnum, and in both of those calibers, a detachable choke can be supplied for the end of the barrel. In .44 Magnum this gives the shooter the ability of essentially having the equivalent of a .410 gauge shotgun in the form of a pistol. These shot capsules have proved their worth on snakes many times over. Since this gun is so versatile, it is not unusual that in the mid-1970s custom stock and barrel makers began making long barrels and rifle stocks for it, but it is very important to remember that according to U.S. law, possessing a rifle stock and a short barrel for this pistol would make it illegal unless registered.

Mechanical Functioning: The Thompson/Center Contender is a single-shot pistol with an external hammer. The pistol can be easily converted to either rimfire or centerfire calibers by merely flicking the switch. To open the action, all that is required is to pull back on the trigger guard, unlocking the rear of the barrel allowing it to tip forward. To change barrels, have the pistol in the locked position and remove the fore end. Then unlock the barrel, swinging it forward and lifting it off the frame. The new barrel may then be installed. When changing the style of barrel, it may also be necessary to change the style of fore end used so that the internal inletting of the fore end will match the bottom of the barrel.

Contender, Vent Rib Barrel

Tokarev
Russian and other state arsenals

Model: TT-33

Action Type: semiautomatic, recoil operated.

Caliber(s): 7.62mm Tokarev.

Barrel Lengths: 4½".

Finish: blue.

Manufacturing Dates: 1930–1954.

Stocks: plastic.

Rifling: 4R.

Weight, Unloaded: 28⅛ oz.

Sights: fixed.

Serial Numbers: started at 1 with the TT-30 and continued the run with the TT-33. Two letter prefixes started around 1935. Runs made at other arsenals also seem to have started at 1.

Serial Number Locations: left side of frame above grip.

Major Variations: TT-30: has barrel locking lugs, and separate backstrap.
TT-33: has circumferential locking lug and integral backstrap.
TT-33: early slide serrations had 7 wide and 7 narrow alternating grooves. After about 1944 serrations were changed to 24 narrow spaced grooves.

Markings: proof marks, year of manufacture by serial number.

Price(s):
TT-30, very good—$450.00
TT-30, excellent—$600.00
TT-33, early, very good—$350.00
TT-33, early, excellent—$425.00
TT-33, late, very good—$325.00
TT-33, late, excellent—$375.00
M51 Chinese, very good—$250.00
M51 Chinese, excellent—$325.00
M54 Chinese, very good—$250.00
M54 Chinese, excellent—$325.00
48M Hungarian, very good—$300.00
48M Hungarian, excellent—$400.00
Pistolet TT Polish, very good—$300.00
Pistolet TT Polish, excellent—$400.00
M57 Yugoslavian, very good—$325.00
M57 Yugoslavian, excellent—$425.00

History: The Tokarev pistol was the invention Feodor Vassilevich Tokarev, who was the technical manager of the Tula Arsenal about World War I. About 1930 his design for a semiautomatic pistol was adopted by the Soviet Army, and it was called the TT-30, the TT standing for "Tula-

Tokarev." It was used throughout World War II, and at the end of the war was adopted as Warsaw Pact standard and manufactured in China, Hungary, Poland, and Yugoslavia. It was manufactured through the 1950s until finally replaced by the Makarov pistols. The primary way to tell these pistols apart is by the grip markings. The Russian pistols have a star on the grip with "CCCP" surrounding it. The Chinese pistols just have a plain star. The Polish pistols have a triangular panel with the letters "FB" like the Radom. The Hungarian pistols have sheaves of wheat. An interesting aside about the Tokarev pistol is that it was on this pistol that Petter based his design for his famous pistol, the French Model 1935, which was later used as the basis for the S.I.G. P.210.

Mechanical Functioning: The Tokarev pistols are recoil-operated, semi-automatic pistols utilizing an eight-shot detachable box magazine. They are in many ways a simplified Colt/Browning style 1911 design and utilize the same swinging link barrel operation. A major feature, however, of the Tokarevs is their reliability. Unlike many other automatic pistols that rely on perfect magazine lips for a short feeding, the magazine in the Tokarev might be slightly damaged, which would ordinarily jam another automatic. On this pistol, however, the guide rails are machined into the inside of the frame, allowing for feeding of the ammunition from a damaged magazine.

Tokarev TT-33 Early

Fab. Francais Societe Union
(M. Seytres)
St. Etienne, France

Model: Union

Action Type: semiautomatic, blowback operated.

Caliber(s): 7.65mm.

Barrel Lengths: 4½".

Finish: blue.

Manufacturing Dates: circa 1915.

Stocks: hard rubber.

Rifling: 6R.

Weight, Unloaded: 20½ oz.

Sights: fixed.

Serial Numbers: n/a.

Serial Number Location: right side of frame.

Major Variations: type 1: no grip safety.
　　type 2: grip safety.
　　type 3: full auto with selector switch on left rear of frame.

Markings: left side of slide: Pistolet Automatique Francais, Fabrique A St. Etienne, Cal. 7.65, Union.

Price(s):
　　type 1, very good—$150.00
　　type 1, excellent—$200.00
　　type 2, very good—$250.00
　　type 2, excellent—$350.00
　　type 3, very good—$350.00
　　type 3, excellent—$475.00
　　for horseshoe magazine add $250.00 to $375.00

History: The Union is an Eibar-pattern, semiautomatic pistol that is fairly undistinguished except for several items. The normal variation is of standard Ruby design with a concealed hammer, eight-shot magazine, and safety mounted above the trigger on the left side of the frame, and it is of normal heavy Ruby construction. The Model 2 variation has the added twist of having a grip safety, and generally, when used by the French army during World War I, was issued with a 32-round, horseshoe-shaped magazine that fitted through the gripframe as a normal magazine would, but the front end was shaped so it would clip to the front end of the frame when it was inserted. A third type of pistol, using the same frame and the same name, was like the type 2, only it had a small selector switch located on the left rear side of the frame in the area where a safety might ordinarily be located. When it was located around to the rear, the pistol turned into a selective-fire, full automatic. The horseshoe-shaped magazine, while unusual and very collectible, was not unique. It had been used on firearms before the Union, but it is on the Union that it is most popularized.

Mechanical Functioning: The Union semiautomatic pistols in .32 caliber are virtually exact copies of the Ruby, except for the last two types, which had a grip safety which intercepted the sear, and the final type, which had a full automatic selector switch that allowed the disconnector to be bypassed. The Ruby class of pistols was of standard Eibar based on the Browning 1906, and were blowback-operated, semiautomatic pistols with detachable box magazines. The average clip size was seven shots, although clips ranged up to 12 shots with the appropriate lengthening of the gripframe to cover the clip. Some postwar models held as many as 20 shots. For further variations, see also Astra Model 1915 and the Union pistol.

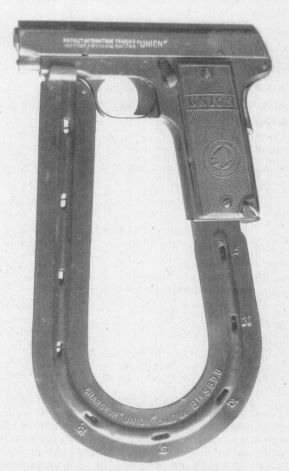

Union with Horseshoe Magazine

United Sporting Arms, Inc.
Tucson, AZ

Model: Seville

Action Type: revolver, single action.

Caliber(s): .45 Win. Magnum, .45 Colt, .44 Magnum, 9mm Win. Magnum, .357 Magnum, .357 Super Magnum, .41 Magnum, .454 Magnum, .357 Maximum.

Barrel Lengths: 4⅝″, 5½″, 6½″, 7½″, 10½″.

Finish: stainless or blue.

Manufacturing Dates: 1979–1986.

Stocks: walnut or Pachmayr.

Rifling: 6R.

Weight, Unloaded: 48 oz.

Sights: adjustable rear, red ramp or Patridge.

Serial Numbers: started at 2001 with the Sheriff's Model and Silhouette Model in the same series.

Serial Number Location: right side of frame.

Major Variations: this model features a quick change conversion kit to change barrels and cylinders for either different barrel lengths and front sights or different calibers.

Markings: on left side of frame: United Sporting Arms, Bisbee AZ.
on left side of barrel: caliber.
on right side of frame under serial number: Made in U.S.A.
on right side of barrel: Seville Model, and "stainless" on stainless barrels.

Price(s):
   stainless .357 Magnum, .41 Magnum, .44 Magnum, .45 L.C., .45 A.C.P., .45 Win. Magnum, very good—$300.00, excellent—$350.00
   stainless, 7½″ barrel, .357 Super Mag, .357 Maximum, very good—$400.00; excellent—$475.00
   stainless, 7½″ barrel, 454 Magnum, .45 L.C., very good—$300.00; excellent—$425.00
   blue, .357 Magnum, .41 Magnum, .44 Magnum, .45 L.C., .45 A.C.P., .45 Win. Magnum, very good—$300.00; excellent—$350.00
   blue, with brass backstrap, very good—$325.00; excellent—$375.00
   blue, with brass backstrap and brass ejector housing, very good—$300.00; excellent—$425.00

History: United Sporting Arms of Arizona was established in 1973. The first guns they made were in the Abilene series. They were Colt-style, single-action revolvers that they eventually sold to Mossberg, which is now the name under which they are produced. In 1979 they began experimenting and producing the Seville Model. It is essentially a standard, single action on a cross between the Ruger style and the Colt style, that incorporates the one feature that no one else does. Not only can the cylinders be interchanged to change the type of cartridge fired, but also the barrels can be interchanged quickly and easily, not only to change barrel lengths but also entire calibers. The revolvers have good heft and balance and broad-bladed adjustable target sights with either red ramp fronts, or Patridge target fronts. They could be purchased cased with various cylinders and barrels.

Mechanical Functioning: The Seville is a single-action revolver built on the Western style, and on the exterior it looks like a cross between the Ruger and the Colt. The action itself is similar to Colt; however, it has been modernized and a transfer bar added. When the trigger is pulled, the transfer bar raises so that the hammer hits it, and in turn, it strikes the firing pin, which is floating, thus striking the primer. Without the trigger being pulled, the transfer bar is in a lowered position, and away from the firing pin. This gun is safe to carry with all chambers loaded. In order to change calibers and barrels on this particular firearm, all you need are Allen wrenches, which are supplied with the gun. Changing cylinders is done in much the same manner as the Colt or the Ruger. To change barrels, you simply unscrew the ejector housing, lift it off, and then unscrew the barrel itself, and assemble in the reverse order. This gun is available in either 4140 steel or 416 stainless steel. The blued steel version is available with a brass trigger guard and a brass ejector housing.

United Sporting Arms, Inc.
Tucson, AZ

Model: Sheriff

Action Type: revolver, single action.

Caliber(s): .45 Colt, .45 A.C.P., .44/40, .44 Magnum.

Barrel Lengths: 3½″.

Finish: blue or stainless.

Manufacturing Dates: 1979–1986.

Stocks: walnut.

Rifling: 6R.

Weight, Unloaded: 42 oz.

Sights: adjustable rear, blade front or ramp front.

Serial Numbers: started at 2001 with the Seville Model and Silhouette Model in the same series.

Serial Number Location: right side of frame.

Major Variations: square butt with ramp front sight.
birdshead butt with blade front sight.

Markings: on left side of frame: United Sporting Arms, Bisbee AZ.
on left side of barrel: caliber.
on right side of frame under serial number: Made in USA.
on right side of barrel: Sheriff's Model.

Price(s):
stainless, square butt, very good—$350.00; excellent—$400.00
stainless, birdshead butt, very good—$325.00; excellent—$375.00
blue, square butt, very good—$325.00; excellent—$375.00
blue, birdshead butt, very good—$300.00; excellent—$350.00

History: United Sporting Arms of Arizona was established in 1973. The first guns they made were in the Abilene series. They were Colt-style, single-action revolvers that they eventually sold to Mossberg, which is now the name under which they are produced. In 1979 they began experimenting and producing the Sheriff Model. It is essentially a standard, single action on a cross between the Ruger style and the Colt style. The cylinders can be interchanged to change the type of cartridge fired. The revolvers have a good heft and balance, and broad-bladed adjustable target sights with either red ramp fronts or Patridge target fronts. They can be purchased cased with various cylinders.

Mechanical Functioning: The Sheriff is a single-action revolver built on the Western style, and on the exterior it looks like a cross between the Ruger and the Colt. The action itself is similar to Colt; however, it has been modernized, and a transfer bar added. When the trigger is pulled, the transfer bar raises so that the hammer hits it, and in turn, it strikes the firing pin, which is floating, thus striking the primer. Without the trigger being pulled, the transfer bar is in a lowered position, and away from the firing pin. This gun is safe to carry with all chambers loaded since the revolver cannot discharge without the trigger being pulled. Changing cylinders is done in much the same manner as the Colt or the Ruger. A spring-loaded reciprocating pin located in the frame forward of the cylinder and traveling laterally just beneath the center pin locks the center pin in place and prevents it from drifting out upon firing. By pushing in on this retaining pin the center pin can be unlocked and then pulled out. The cylinder can then be rotated out of the frame with the ratchet rolling through the loading gate. At this point the revolver can either be cleaned or the cylinder changed. The functioning of this model is single action only, which means that the hammer must be manually cocked each time you wish to fire. The revolver styling is Western, which aids the shooter when firing heavy calibers. Unlike double-action-style revolvers, which have a fairly straight backstrap angle, the Western style has a fairly rounded upper backstrap. Upon firing with a double-action revolver the emphasis is on a consistent hand hold, and therefore the frame is designed to prevent hand slippage. This in turn means that all of the recoil energy is transmitted directly to the shooter's hand. With the Western style, however, the hand hold has to be somewhat shifted each time the gun is fired because of the necessity to cock the revolver. When this style of handgun is fired, some of the recoil energy is used up rotating the gun in the shooter's hand lessening the felt recoil. This is also the reason that with heavy loads the gun usually winds up pointing straight up. This gun is available in either 4140 steel or in 416 stainless steel.

United Sporting Arms, Inc. Sheriff

U.S. Military

Model: M1911

Action Type: semiautomatic, recoil operated.

Caliber(s): .45 A.C.P.

Barrel Lengths: 5".

Finish: blue.

Manufacturing Dates: 1912–1925.

Stocks: wood.

Rifling: 6L.

Weight, Unloaded: 39 oz.

Sights: fixed.

Serial Numbers: Colt Military contract: 1–72570; 83856–102596; 107597–113496; 102567–125566; 133187 to an unknown number below 310000; 355001–629500.
Remington-UMC Military contract: 1–12,676 (1918–1919).
Springfield Armory: 72571–83855; 102597–107596; 113497–120566; 125567–133186; 310000–355000.

Serial Number Location: right side of frame above trigger.

Major Variations: none, however this covers only the M1911 variation.

Markings: Colt: left slide: Patented Apr. 20, 1897, Sept. 9, 1902, Dec. 19, 1905, Feb. 14, 1911, Colt's Pat. F.A. Mfg. Co., Hartford, Ct. USA.
Remington: Patented Dec. 19, 1905, Feb. 14, 1911, Aug. 19, 1913, Colt's Pat. F.A. Mfg. Co. Manufactured by Remington Arms UMC Co. Inc. Bridgeport, Conn. USA (and circular Remington Trademark).
left side of slide: Springfield: Patented Apr. 20, 1897, Sept. 9, 1902, Dec. 19, 1905, Feb. 14, 1911, Colt's Pat. F.A. Mfg Co., Springfield Armory U.S.A.
left side of frame forward of trigger guard: United States Property.
right side of slide: on Colt and Springfield: Model of 1911 U.S. Army.
right side of slide: on Remington: Model of 1911 U.S. Army Caliber .45.

Price(s):
M1911 Colt, very good—$1,000.00
M1911 Colt, excellent—$1,500.00
M1911 Springfield, very good—$1,200.00
M1911 Springfield, excellent—$1,750.00
M1911 Remington, very good—$1,750.00
M1911 Remington-UMC, excellent—$2,250.00

History: The mainstay of Colts during this century must be the Colt Model 1911 and its variants, which have been in constant use for over 70 years, and over 2½ million have been made. The U.S. Army in 1906 decided it was time to replace the revolver and put out word that it would hold trials for a new weapon. The requirements were stiff, including a solid rather than separate bolt; vertical ejection; locked breech; bullet weight minimum 230 grains; velocity minimum 800 f.p.s. It had to be simple to take down, reliable, and capable of reasonable accuracy. After the 1907 trials, several makers were given the chance to alter their arms to suit the military. After five years of development, the Colt design was chosen and designated the 1911. This model can be identified by its flat mainspring housing and long trigger. In 1922 Colt developed the 1911A1 type, and the army received it starting in 1924.

Mechanical Functioning: This recoil-operated pistol is based on the Browning designed Colt M1911A1. To disassemble this pistol, remove the magazine and check to make sure that the weapon is unloaded. Depress plug below the barrel far enough to allow the barrel bushing to be turned to the right until the plug can be eased out to the front. Remember that this plug is under spring tension, so remove carefully. Pull the slide back until the rear edge of the smaller of the two cuts near the center of the slide on the left hand side lines up with the rear end of the slide stock. Push the end of the slide stock in, right to left. This will push the slide stock out on the left-hand side far enough to be grabbed and pulled out entirely. When this is removed, the slide can be pulled directly forward off the receiver, taking the entire barrel assembly with it. The barrel bushing, recoil spring, recoil spring guide, and barrel may now be removed from the slide by turning the barrel bushing to the left as far as it will go, and withdrawing it to the front. Reassemble in the reverse order, making sure that the slide stop pin passes through the length at the bottom of the barrel, for this is the mechanism by which the pistol both locks and unlocks.

Carl Walther Waffenfabrik
Zella-Mehlis, Germany

Model: 5

Action Type: semiautomatic, blowback operated.

Caliber(s): 6.35mm.

Barrel Lengths: 2⅛".

Finish: blue.

Manufacturing Dates: 1913.

Stocks: hard rubber.

Rifling: 4R and 6R.

Weight, Unloaded: 10 oz.

Sights: fixed.

Serial Numbers: specimens seen from 20,000 to over 300,000.

Serial Number Location: left side of frame forward of grip, or right side of trigger guard.

Major Variations: sighting groove on the top of slide or raised solid rib with milled sights. Different slide groovings, different markings.

Markings: left side of slide: Walther's patent, Cal. 6.35.

Price(s):
    Model 5, wide slide serrations, very good—$300.00
    Model 5, wide slide serrations, excellent—$400.00
    Model 5, narrow slide serrations, very good—$350.00
    Model 5, narrow slide serrations, excellent—$450.00

History: To say that the early history of the Walther automatic pistol series is shrouded in confusion would be an understatement. When Carl Walther, assisted by his son Fritz and his cousin Friederich Pickert, developed his first semiautomatic pistol in 1908, they could not have guessed that by the time of their 50th anniversary in 1936 they would have produced over a million pistols. It was at that 50th anniversary that most of the confusion really came to a head. A Swiss firm by the name of W. Glaser Waffen put out a special, commemorative, 50th-anniversary catalog showing the complete Walther line. The advertising man who put the catalog together was not familiar enough with the line to do it justice, but he still tried, and he created a step chart, showing the various models as he saw them and the dates of their inception. Unfortunately, the chart leaves out several distinct model variations, and the Model 5 was one of those affected; therefore, it is often confused with the Model 2. The distinctions between the two models are: the Model 2 has a pop-up rear sight that acts as a loaded chamber indicator. The Model 5 is identical, except that it has two variations; one that is normally confused with the Model 2 has no sights at all, rather it just has an aiming groove milled on the top of the slide. The later type has a milled rib and sights. While externally it is distinctly different, the internal structure of both is the same.

Mechanical Functioning: The Walther Model 5 in both variations is a blow-back-operated, concealed-hammer, semiautomatic pistol with a six-shot detachable box magazine. The barrel is fixed to a frame extension, and the recoil slide is fitted axially around the barrel. A barrel bushing at the front end of the barrel connects with the slide and is retained by the pressure of the recoil spring, holding the slide in place. The trigger is pivoted at the top, and attached to it is a sear bar and disconnector, which runs along the left side of the frame. The magazine is retained by a spring clip at the bottom rear of the gripframe. The mechanical safety is located at the left rear side of the frame, and intercepts the sear blocking the hammer. The firing pin is of the floating variety. To disassemble, push the barrel bushing in, and turn a quarter of a revolution, slowly letting loose and easing it out. The slide can then be withdrawn fully to the rear, lifted up in the rear, and then slid off the end of the barrel. Assembly is in reverse order.

Carl Walther Waffenfabrik
Zella-Mehlis, Germany

Model: 9

Action Type: semiautomatic, blowback operated.

Caliber(s): 6.35mm.

Barrel Lengths: 2".

Finish: blue or nickel.

Manufacturing Dates: 1921 through World War II.

Stocks: plastic.

Rifling: 6R.

Weight, Unloaded: 9 oz.

Sights: fixed.

Serial Numbers: started at 420,000 and ran to 450,000. It then jumped to 500,000 and continued to about 650,000. Some Model 9s have numbers in the PPK 200,000 A range.

Serial Number Location: right side of frame to the rear of the grip.

Major Variations: finish and decoration only.

Markings: left side of slide: Walther Patent Model 9
right side of slide: "Waffenfabrik Walther, Zella-Mehlis (Thur.)".

Price(s):
blue, very good—$350.00
blue, excellent—$450.00
nickel, very good—$300.00
nickel, excellent—$550.00
engraved, very good—$450.00–$1,250.00
engraved, excellent—$750.00–$2,000.00

History: The Walther Model 9 was the last in the "number series" Pocket Pistols. It was designed to compete with the "Western Taschen" pistols so popular in the 1920s, and it accomplished its maker's objective. It was in production from 1921 through World War II, and during the war was very popular with Luftwaffe pilots to carry hidden as insurance. This was one of the most attractive, small .25s ever built, and other makers have copied the design, but no one seems to be able to match this pistol. At some point toward the end of its life, it was numbered in series with the PPK.

Mechanical Functioning: This is a straight blowback-operated, striker-fired, semiautomatic pistol with a six-shot detachable box magazine. The safety is manual and intercepts the sear. When the pistol is cocked, a small pin attached to the rear of the firing pin protrudes through a hole in the striker base assembly at the rear of the slide. The top of the barrel is exposed from the breech face forward, and it is mounted on the frame.

To accomplish takedown, remove the magazine and clear the chamber. Then, using the extension at the base of the clip, lever up the spring projection on the striker base at the rear of the slide. This assembly will pop out, then the slide can be slightly retracted and lifted up and slid off the barrel.

Walther Model 9

Walther Mark II
Mre de Machines du Haut-Rhin S.A. (Manurhin)
F68200 Mulhouse
Bourtzwiller, France

Model: PPK Mark II

Action Type: semiautomatic, blowback operated.

Caliber(s): .22 L.R., .32 A.C.P., .380 A.C.P.

Barrel Lengths: 3⅛".

Finish: blue or nickel.

Manufacturing Dates: 1950 to 1960s.

Stocks: plastic.

Rifling: 6R.

Weight, Unloaded: 23 oz.

Sights: fixed.

Serial Numbers: starting at 1001B. After a few hundred pistols were made, the suffix change to LR in .22 L.R.R.F. The .32 started at 10001 and went to 100,000 and started again at 300,001. .380 started at 10,001A.

Serial Number Location: right side of frame to the rear of the trigger.

Major Variations: caliber and finish.

Markings: left side of slide: Fabr. Manufacture De Machines Du Haut-Rhin, Lic. Excl. Walther Mod. PPK Cal.

Price(s):
    .22 L.R., blue, very good—$550.00
    .22 L.R., blue, excellent—$650.00
    .22 L.R., nickel, very good—$500.00
    .22 L.R., nickel, excellent—$750.00
    .32 A.C.P., blue, very good—$375.00
    .32 A.C.P., blue, excellent—$450.00
    .32 A.C.P., nickel, very good—$400.00
    .32 A.C.P., nickel, excellent—$500.00
    .380 A.C.P., blue, very good—$500.00
    .380 A.C.P., blue, excellent—$600.00
    .380 A.C.P., nickel, very good—$550.00
    .380 A.C.P., nickel, excellent—$700.00

History: At the end of World War II, Russian troops moved into the area of Thurngia, Germany, and into Zella-Mehlis where the Walther plant was located. Being rather intelligent, Carl Walther knew when to get out and move west. By 1950 he had made an agreement with Manufacture de Machines du Haut-Rhin, S.A. in Mulhouse-Bortzwiller, France, to produce his pattern pistols under license. The first pistols they produced were the Walther PP and the Walther PPK. Soon after Walther raised enough money to build a brand-new manufacturing plant in Ulm, West Germany, a few miles over the border from the Manurhin plant. Manurhin still makes pistols under license from Walther for French consumption with the Manurhin name, but most of their production is trucked to Germany to be assembled in the Ulm plant, and go out under the Walther label.

Mechanical Functioning: The Walther Manurhin PP is a straight blowback, double-action, hammer-fired, semiautomatic pistol with a detachable box magazine that holds eight rounds in .22 long rifle, seven rounds in .32 A.C.P., and seven rounds in .380 A.C.P. A signal pin mounted over the firing pin acts as a loaded chamber indicator, and protrudes at the top rear of the slide when the gun is loaded. The firing pin is of the floating variety, and there is an automatic functioning hammer safety, to prevent firing unless the trigger is actually pulled. The manual safety is located on the left side of the slide. When engaged, it not only mechanically blocks the firing pin, but also trips the sear and drops the hammer onto that block. Thus its secondary purpose is a safe way to lower the hammer over a loaded chamber. The recoil spring is axially mounted on the barrel. Takedown is accomplished by first making sure that the weapon is unloaded. Then, pivot the trigger guard downward, and warp it slightly to one side or the other so that the downward side rests against the frame. The slide is then retracted fully to the rear, lifted in the rear, and then it slides out over the barrel and off. The barrel itself is pinned to an extension milled into the frame. This is an extremely popular mechanical design, and it has been widely copied both under license and without license. Some notable examples are the Russian Makarov pistol, which is used by the Soviet forces in most Warsaw bloc countries, the Hege pistol, the Turkish N-KE, and the Hungarian Walan. All use essentially the exact same action, and some are virtually identical copies.

Carl Walther GmbH
Ulm/Donau, West Germany
Importer: Interarms
10 Prince St.
Alexandria, VA 22313

Model: P5

Action Type: semiautomatic, recoil operated.

Caliber(s): 9mm Luger.

Barrel Lengths: 3½″.

Finish: blue.

Manufacturing Dates: 1980 to date.

Stocks: black plastic or walnut.

Rifling: 6R.

Weight, Unloaded: 28 oz.

Sights: windage adjustable rear.

Serial Numbers: may have started at 1.

Serial Number Location: left side of frame above trigger guard, and above it on slide.

Major Variations: none.

Markings: left side of slide: Carl Walther Waffenfabrik, Ulm/Do. P5

Price(s):
    excellent—$650.00

History: The Walther P5 is the culmination of a long series of designs since 1938's adoption of the P.38. Many features of the P.38 are evident in the P5, notably, the upper frame design and the method of barrel locking. The world's first real notice of the P5 came when the German government held a competition to determine what the next German Federal Police pistol would be to replace the Walther P.1. The competition included such formidable weapons as the Ruger .357, the Smith & Wesson Combat .357, and the S.I.G. Sauer P.220. More than 5000 rounds were fired, and each weapon was judged for recoil, accuracy, reliability, and effectiveness. By the end of the competition, the Walther P5 stood out and was adopted to arm the entire Federal German police system. It has also been adopted by the Dutch police force and many other European police departments.

Mechanical Functioning: The Walther P5 is a recoil-operated, semiautomatic pistol with an external hammer and a double-action mechanism. The internal mechanism is very similar to the Walther P.38. Takedown is accomplished in the same manner. As with many of the earlier Walther products, ejection is on the left-hand side. One very unusual feature about this pistol is that there are no manual safeties. All are automatic. On the first shot, the Walther P5 functions as a revolver. The safety is in the long, heavy trigger pull. When the pistol is loaded and a round is put in the chamber, the hammer is cocked. The lever on the left side of the pistol behind the trigger acts both as a decocking lever and as a slide release lever. When it is pushed down, the hammer is automatically lowered, and when the last shot is fired, it also acts as a slide stop, locking the slide open. When a fresh magazine is inserted, the first push down will close the slide and send a round into the chamber. The second push down on it will safely lower the hammer. If you wish to lock the slide open manually there is a curve latch located just forward of the decocking lever. Push upward on it when you pull the slide back to lock it open. To release the slide either push down on the decocking lever or pull the slide back slightly and release it (as long as there is not an empty magazine in the gun). Another safety feature is that unless the trigger is completely pulled, the firing pin is in the lowered position and fits into a recess milled into the hammer, thereby obviating any chance of accidental discharge. The trigger must be pulled completely to the rear in order to fire the weapon. The magazine is of detachable box type, and is inserted through the frame and retained with a clip on the bottom of the gripframe. It holds eight rounds of 9mm × 19, a Plus P 9mm Parabellum. To field-strip this pistol first make sure that it is unloaded and remove the magazine. Then place the barrel against a hard surface and press into it slightly so that the takedown lever located on the left side of the frame forward of the trigger guard can be rotated down. The slide can now be removed from the frame. The barrel is removed by pressing the small button on the barrel extension and sliding the barrel out of the slide. Assembly is in the reverse order.

Walther Model P5
Photo courtesy of Interarms

Carl Walther GmbH
Ulm/Donau, West Germany
Importer: Interarms
10 Prince St.
Alexandria, VA 22313

Model: P-38

Action Type: semi-automatic, recoil operated.

Caliber(s): 9mm Parabellum, .30 Luger, and .22 L.R.

Barrel Lengths: 5″, 2³⁄₄″, 4³⁄₈″.

Finish: blue or nickel.

Manufacturing Dates: 1938 to date.

Stocks: plastic or wood.

Rifling: 6R.

Weight, Unloaded: 34 oz. with steel frame, 28 oz. with alloy frame.

Sights: fixed.

Serial Numbers: all serials are approximate. Military serials ran 4 digits with letter suffix; started at 1 and ran to about 26,000. Wartime: 480 code, 1-7300; ac code, 7300-9900; ac-40, 9900-9999a; ac-41-1, 1-9999; ac-42, 1-9999k; ac-43, 1-9999n; ac-44, 1-9999L; ac-45, 1-9999e. Other codes were byf and svw. Postwar serials started at 1001, export guns have "E" suffix.

Serial Number Location: left side of frame forward of trigger guard.

Major Variations: World War II: steel frame, commercial and military models.
postwar: alloy frame: P.1 (postwar P.38).
P.4 (4³⁄₈″ barrel, no safety, decocking lever).
P. 38K (2³⁄₄″ barrel).

Markings: wartime: left side of slide: P.38.
postwar: Carl Walther Waffenfabrik Ulm/Do. P.38 (Caliber).

Price(s):
9mm, military, very good—$600.00; excellent—$850.00
"480," 9mm, military, very good—$1,500.00; excellent—$2,000.00
ac, no date, 9mm, military, very good—$3,500.00; excellent—$3,000.00
ac-40, 9mm, military, very good—$1,000.00; excellent—$1,250.00.
ac-41, 9mm, military, very good—$800.00; excellent—$950.00
ac-42, 9mm, military, very good—$375.00; excellent—$450.00
ac-43, Police, 9mm, military, very good—$400.00; excellent—$500.00
ac-45, 9mm, military, very good—$325.00; excellent—$400.00
byf-43, 9mm, military, very good—$300.00; excellent—$400.00
byf-43 Police, 9mm, military, very good—$550.00; excellent—$750.00
cyq, 9mm, military, very good—$350.00; excellent—$450.00

svw-45, 9mm, military, very good—$300.00; excellent—$375.00
k, 9mm, short barrel, very good—$500.00; excellent—$650.00
IV (P.4), 9mm, very good—$500.00; excellent—$650.00

History: The Walther P.38 is a large-frame, military, automatic pistol that was developed by Walther to provide a replacement pistol for the Luger, or as in German designation, P.08. After tests in 1937 it was adopted in 1938 under the German nomenclature "P.38" and was the weapon of choice of Germans throughout World War II. By 1940 the German command had decided that codes, rather than factory names, should be used on all military articles. Therefore, the early code used was "480" meaning Walther, and in 1941 that was changed to "ac." As the war went on, other factories were authorized to make this pistol. They included the Mauser factory, with the code "byf," and in 1945 Mauser changed the code to "svw." At the end of the war, the French captured the plant and continued to produce the pistols with French markings and the code "svw-46." All of the wartime models have steel frames. After the war, when Walther finally built his factory in Ulm, Germany, he again tooled up to produce the P.38, this time with an alloy frame. Once again, the German military adopted it as its military pistol, this time designating it the P.1. Production on it began in 1957. In 1974 the P.38k was added to the line. It was a short-barreled version with the front sight mounted on the front of the slide. Also started in 1974 was the P.4 with a slightly shorter barrel, which eliminated the manual safety; instead, it just had an uncocking device.

Mechanical Functioning: The P.38 is a recoil-operated, semiautomatic pistol with an external hammer, and a detachable box magazine. It is a double-action pistol with left hand ejection and a loaded chamber indicator.

Walther Model P-38 "byf 44"
Photo courtesy of Orvel L. Reichert

Carl Walther GmbH
Ulm/Donau, West Germany
Importer: Interarms
10 Prince St.
Alexandria, VA 22313

Model: PP

Action Type: semiautomatic, blowback operated.

Caliber(s): .22 L.R., .25 A.C.P., .32 A.C.P., .380 A.C.P.

Barrel Lengths: 3⁷/₈″.

Finish: blue or nickel.

Manufacturing Dates: 1929 to date.

Stocks: plastic.

Rifling: 6R.

Weight, Unloaded: 23 oz.

Sights: fixed.

Serial Numbers: started at 750,000 numbered in series with the PPK. At 1,000,000 restarted with the "A" suffix.

Serial Number Location: right side of the frame forward of the grip.

Major Variations: steel or aluminum alloy frame.
military, police, or commercial.
various finishes, and various early mechanical changes.

Markings: on left side of slide: Waffenfabrik Walther, Zella-Mahlis (Thurs.) Walther's Patent (Caliber) Model PP.

Price(s):
.22 L.R., prewar, commercial, nickel, very good—$1,000.00; excellent—$1,500.00
.22 L.R., prewar, commercial, high-polish finish, very good—$650.00; excellent—$850.00
.25 A.C.P., prewar, commercial, high-polish finish, very good—$3,000.00; excellent—$4,000.00
.32 A.C.P., prewar, commercial, lightweight, high-polish finish, very good—$500.00; excellent—$750.00
.32 A.C.P., prewar, lightweight, very good—$450.00; excellent—$700.00
.32 A.C.P., prewar, commercial, nickel, very good—$750.00; excellent—$1,250.00
.32 A.C.P., prewar, commercial, high-polish finish, very good—$350.00; excellent—$450.00
.32 A.C.P., lightweight, very good—$450.00; excellent—$550.00
.380 A.C.P., prewar, commercial, high-polish finish, very good—$600.00; excellent—$750.00
.380 A.C.P., prewar, commercial, nickel, very good—$1,250.00; excellent—$1,750.00

.32 A.C.P., early, 90-degree safety, prewar, commercial, high-polish finish, very good—$550.00; excellent—$650.00

.380 A.C.P., early, bottom magazine release, prewar, commercial, high-polish finish, very good—$1,250.00; excellent—$1,750.00

.380 A.C.P., prewar, very good-$650.00; excellent—$850.00

.32 A.C.P., AC Police F, prewar, very good—$500.00; excellent—$625.00

.32 A.C.P., bottom magazine release, prewar, commercial, high-polish finish, very good—$600.00; excellent—$750.00

.22 L.R.R.F., Mark II Manurhin, high-polish finish, blue, very good—$400.00; excellent—$525.00

.32 A.C.P., Mark II Manurhin, high-polish finish, blue, very good—$375.00; excellent—$475.00

.380 A.C.P., Mark II Manurhin, high-polish finish, blue, very good—$375.00; excellent—$500.00

.32 A.C.P., NSKK, prewar, high-polish finish, very good—$1,500.00; excellent—$2,000.00

.32 A.C.P., PDM, prewar, high-polish finish, very good—$600.00; excellent—$750.00

.32 A.C.P., RFV, prewar, high-polish finish, very good—$500.00; excellent—$650.00

.22 L.R., SA, prewar, high-polish finish, very good—$1,000.00; excellent—$1,500.00

History: The Walther PP came into being in 1929. The PP was at first designed for the police market. When it was first introduced, it was only in .32 A.C.P. caliber. Later on, it became available in both .22 long rifle, and .380 automatic. The PP can be found in a wide variety of markings and finishes. It has been made both in steel frame and in lightweight versions. In the postwar period, the PP was made by Manurhin. When the U.S. importation was acquired by Interarms, the French-manufactured Walther was renamed "The Mark II" and was given full prewar markings, with an Ulm, Germany, address.

Mechanical Functioning: The Walther Manurhin PP is a straight blowback, double-action, hammer-fired, semiautomatic pistol with a detachable box magazine.

Walther PP German Military
Photo from Author's Collection

Carl Walther GmbH
Ulm/Donau, West Germany
Importer: Interarms
10 Prince St.
Alexandria, VA 22313

Model: PPK

Action Type: semiautomatic, blowback operated.

Caliber(s): .22 LR, 6.35mm, 7.65 mm, 9mm K.

Barrel Lengths: 3¹/₈".

Finish: blue or nickel.

Manufacturing Dates: 1929 to date.

Stocks: plastic.

Rifling: 6R.

Weight, Unloaded: 20 oz.

Sights: fixed.

Serial Numbers: started with the PP in the 750,000 range, following for a short time into the "A" suffix, then establishing the "K" suffix for itself.

Serial Number Location: right side of frame forward of grip.

Major Variations: steel or aluminum alloy frame.
military, police, or commercial.
various finishes.
various early mechanical changes.

Markings: on left side of slide: Waffenfabrik Walther, Zella-Mehlis (Thur) Walther's Patent (Caliber) Model PPK.

Price(s):
Amerian PPK, excellent—$450.00
.22 L.R., prewar, commercial, nickel, very good—$1,000.00; excellent—$1,500.00
.22 L.R., prewar, commercial, high-polish finish, very good—$850.00; excellent—$1,000.00
.25 A.C.P., prewar, commercial, high-polish finish, very good—$3,500.00; excellent—$4,750.00
.32 A.C.P., prewar, commercial, nickel, very good—$750.00; excellent—$1,250.00
.32 A.C.P., prewar, lightweight, high-polish finish, very good—$700.00; excellent—$900.00
.32 A.C.P., prewar, commercial, high-polish finish very good—$325.00; excellent—$475.00
.32 A.C.P., lightweight, postwar, very good—$400.00; excellent—$550.00
.380 A.C.P., prewar, commercial, high-polish finish, very good—$1,000.00; excellent—$1,500.00
.32 A.C.P., early, 90-degree safety, prewar, commercial, high-polish finish, very good—$600.00; excellent—$750.00

.380 A.C.P., early, bottom magazine release, prewar, commercial, high-polish finish, very good—$900.00; excellent—$1,400.00

.22 L.R., Mark II Manurhin, high-polish finish, blue, very good—$525.00; excellent—$700.00

.32 A.C.P., Mark II Manurhin, high-polish finish, blue, very good—$475.00; excellent—$625.00

.380 A.C.P., Mark II Manurhin, high-polish finish, blue, very good—$550.00; excellent—$650.00

.32 A.C.P., Party Leader, prewar, high-polish, very good—$1,750.00; excellent—$2,500.00

.32 A.C.P., RZM, prewar, high-polish finish, very good—$450.00; excellent—$1,000.00

.32 A.C.P., Verchromt, prewar, commercial, very good—$1,250.00; excellent—$1,750.00

.32 A.C.P., Waffenamt, prewar, high-polish finish, very good—$500.00; excellent—$650.00

History: The PPK was developed right about the same time as the PP, between 1929 and 1940, and it is essentially a PP with ¼″ lopped off the gripframe and the barrel shortened by ⁹⁄₁₆″. In order to reduce the weight of the gun, the entire backstrap of the gripframe was machined off and replaced by a wraparound plastic grip. The designation for it was "PPK," standing for "Polizei Pistole Kriminal" and was recommended for undercover use by police officers. As with the Model PP, the PPK was looked on as one of the finest guns of its time, and if imitation is the sincerest form of flattery, then as with the PP, the PPK was copied as well in both the Western world and in the Communist world. It has now been in production for 50 years, even though since 1968 its importation into the United States was banned by ¼″ in frame size.

Mechanical Functioning: The Walther PPK is a double-action, straight blowback, semiautomatic pistol, with an external hammer and a detachable box magazine. The magazine capacity in .22 was eight rounds; in .32 seven rounds; for .380 six rounds. Other specifications are the same as the Walther PP.

Walther Model PPK
Photo from Author's Collection

Carl Walther GmbH
Ulm/Donau, West Germany
Importer: Interarms
10 Prince St.
Alexandria, VA 22313

Model: PPK/S

Action Type: semiautomatic, blowback operated.

Caliber(s): .22 LR, .32 ACP, .380 ACP

Barrel Lengths: 3⅛″.

Finish: blue, nickel, stainless (American).

Manufacturing Dates: 1971–1983.

Stocks: plastic.

Rifling: 6R.

Weight, Unloaded: 23 oz.

Sights: fixed.

Serial Numbers: stainless models start at 1 with suffix "S."

Serial Number Location: right side of frame forward of the grip.

Major Variations: German make, American make, and stainless.

Markings: on left side of slide: under license of: Carl Walther Waffenfabrik Ulm/Donau Modell PPK/S (caliber).

Price(s):
    PPK/S, German, blue, .22, very good—$500.00
    PPK/S, German, blue, .22, excellent—$600.00
    PPK/S, German, blue, .32, very good—$300.00
    PPK/S, German, blue, .32, excellent—$425.00
    PPK/S, German, blue, .380, very good—$450.00
    PPK/S, German, blue, .380, excellent—$550.00
    PPK/S, German, nickel, .22, very good—$500.00
    PPK/S, German, nickel, .22, excellent—$650.00
    PPK/S, German, nickel, .32, very good—$325.00
    PPK/S, German, nickel, .32, excellent—$450.00
    PPK/S, German, nickel, .380, very good—$350.00
    PPK/S, German, nickel, .380, excellent—$475.00
    PPK/S, American Stainless—$400.00
    PPK/S, American Blue—$350.00

History: When Congress passed the Gun Control Act of 1968, they outlawed the importation of a great many fine pistols; one was the Walther PPK, of which there are already several hundred thousand in the country. However, not being able to import any more, the wise people at Inter-arms starting to do some research to see what they could create. They came up with the PPK/S, or as it is sometimes known, the PPK/Special, which is essentially the PPK slide assembly and the PP frame, and it just meets U.S. importation requirements. When first imported from Germany, they came in three calibers: .22 L.R., .32 A.C.P., and .380 A.C.P. Currently they are manufactured in the United States by Interarms in Alexandria, Virginia, and they come in blue, Nivel which is a matte-finish nickel, or stainless steel, and they are made to the same exacting requirements as the original PPK/S from Germany. They are also available in a variety of engraved models with fancy finishes from Interarms.

Mechanical Functioning: The Walther PPK/S is a straight blowback, double-action, hammer-fired, semiautomatic pistol. It has a detachable box magazine in all three calibers, holding seven rounds in .32 and .380 A.C.P., and eight rounds in .22 L.R. The magazine is inserted through the grip-frame and is retained by a spring-loaded catch located on the left side of the frame just aft of the trigger. The manual safety is located on the left side of the slide and when engaged blocks the firing pin and also trips the sear and safely lowers the hammer without risk of discharge. The firing pin is of the floating type, and the pistol can be safely carried with a round in the chamber with the hammer down and the safety on or off. Takedown is accomplished by first making sure that the pistol is unloaded, and removing the magazine. The trigger guard is then pulled down, pivoting on the rear section and the top is rested on the frame forward of the trigger. The slide is withdrawn all the way to the rear and then lifted slightly so that it clears the rails and is then run forward and off the frame. Assembly is in the reverse order.

Walther Model PPK/S
Photo courtesy of Interarms

Webley & Scott Ltd.
Park Lane
Birmingham B21 8LU England

Model: 1906 (.25)

Action Type: semiautomatic, blowback operated.

Caliber(s): .25 A.C.P.

Barrel Lengths: 2".

Finish: blue.

Manufacturing Dates: introduced in 1906 and produced up to World War II.

Stocks: hard rubber.

Rifling: 6R.

Weight, Unloaded: 12 oz.

Sights: none.

Serial Numbers: n/a.

Serial Number Location: right side of frame beneath the hammer.

Major Variations: 1906 hammer model.
1909 hammerless model.

Markings: left side of slide: Webley & Scott Ltd, London & Birmingham, 6.35mm Automatic Pistol.

Price(s):
Model 1906, 12 groove slide, very good—$150.00
Model 1906, 12 groove slide, excellent—$225.00
Model 1906, 8 groove slide, very good—$150.00
Model 1906, 8 groove slide, excellent—$200.00
Model 1909, hammerless, very good—$200.00
Model 1909, hammerless, excellent—$300.00

History: The Webley .25 Automatic with an external hammer is obviously an attempt by Webley to get into the competitive field of vest pocket automatic pistols. It is somewhat crude and appears to be fairly cheaply made, and yet it still functions very well and could be said to be a miniature of its .32 Automatic pistol. In 1909 Webley decided to go itself one better and built a .25 A.C.P. pistol virtually identical to its hammer version; however, with an interior concealed hammer, and at the same time reducing the weight of the pistol by 1 ounce. The 1909 version is more finely finished and has fixed sights mounted on the slide. Unlike the hammer version, the grips are retained by two screws per side, whereas the hammer version only has one center screw holding the grip in place.

Mechanical Functioning: The Webley & Scott .25 Automatics are both very similar. They are both straight blowback-operated, semiautomatic pistols, one having an externally mounted hammer and floating firing pin, the other having an internal hammer and floating firing pin. Both utilize six-shot detachable box magazines inserted through the gripframe and retained at the bottom of the butt by a spring-loaded catch. Takedown is accomplished in the same way on both pistols. After making sure the weapon is unloaded, pull downward and outward on the spring trigger guard, pivoting it to the farthest forward position. Pull the slide forward and off the gun, dropping the barrel out the bottom. The external hammer version of the pistol has a solid slide, no sights, and an ejection port located on the right side. The hammerless version has no ejection port, but rather has the entire top of the slide from the breech face to the front sight opened and exposed, showing the top of the barrel.

Webley Model 1906 .25 A.C.P.

Webley & Scott Ltd.
Park Lane
Birmingham B21 8LU England

Model: Metropolitan Police Automatic

Action Type: semiautomatic, blowback operated.

Caliber(s): .32 A.C.P., .380 A.C.P.

Barrel Lengths: 3½".

Finish: blue.

Manufacturing Dates: 1906–1940.

Stocks: hard rubber or wood.

Rifling: 7R.

Weight, Unloaded: 20 oz.

Sights: fixed.

Serial Number: n/a.

Serial Number Location: right rear side of frame.

Major Variations: 1905 prototype with safety mounted on hammer.
1906 model with small safety over left grip, ringed hammer.
1911 Police Model with long safety, raised rear sight, exposed trigger bar.
1913 Police Model with long safety, raised rear sight, thin trigger guard.
1913 Civilian with grooved slide instead of raised rear sight.
1913 late model with slide mounted safety.

Markings: left side of slide: Webley & Scott Ltd., London & Birmingham, 7.65mm .32 Automatic Pistol (date).

Price(s):
1905, very good—$250.00
1905, excellent—$350.00
1906, very good—$225.00
1906, excellent—$300.00
1911 Police, very good—$225.00
1911 Police, excellent—$300.00
1913 Police, very good—$200.00
1913 Police, excellent—$275.00
1913 Civilian early, very good—$175.00
1913 Civilian early, excellent—$250.00
1913 Civilian late, very good—$175.00
1913 Civilian late, excellent—$250.00

History: The Model 1906 Webley .32 A.C.P. started life in 1905 as the External Hammer 1905 Model. It was more of a prototype than a production pistol and featured an external trigger bar, a long trigger pull, and a hammer-mounted safety. In 1906 they simplified the pistol by mounting the safety on the left side of the frame below the slide in the center of the grip, and retained the concentric milled rings on the hammer. About 1911, when the police adopted this pistol, they elongated the safety and hinged it in the pattern that is more familiar to us. They eliminated the concentric rings on the hammer but kept the raised rear sight. In 1913 the Police Model retained the raised rear sight but no longer had the external trigger bar, and instead, had a shorter trigger pull. The trigger guard itself became a thin piece of spring steel instead of the thick heavy piece that had been used previously. The 1913 Civilian Model was the same as the Police Model with the exception of the rear sight being eliminated and instead a grooving was substituted on the top of the slide. The 1913 Late Model eliminated the safety located above the left grip and instead mounted the safety on the slide over the finger grooves, and let it act as a firing pin block. An additional way to recognize the Police Models, as opposed to the Civilian Models, are the police stamps used by the various departments and the lanyard loop located on the forward section of the butt.

Mechanical Functioning: The Webley & Scott Model 1906 and its variants are .32 A.C.P., straight blowback, semiautomatic pistols with eight-shot detachable box magazines inserted through the butt and retained by a spring catch at the bottom base of the butt. They are of the Webley quick-takedown pattern, and field stripping is accomplished merely by making sure the pistol is unloaded, cocking the hammer, removing the magazine and pulling downward and out on the trigger guard, rotating it forward, allowing the slide to be pulled off the front of the gun and the barrel dropped out of the slide.

Webley Model 1906 .32 A.C.P.

Webley & Scott Ltd.
Park Lane
Birmingham B21 8LU England

Model: MK I (M1913)

Action Type: semiautomatic, recoil operated.

Caliber(s): .455 Webley Auto.

Barrel Lengths: 5".

Finish: blue.

Manufacturing Dates: first made about 1909, adopted by the British Navy in 1913, and made through the war.

Stocks: hard rubber or wood grips.

Rifling: 6R, 5R (#2).

Sights: adjustable rear.

Serial Numbers: n/a.

Major Variations: Model MK I #1: fixed sights, no shoulder stock.
Model MK I #2: adjustable sights, ground for shoulder stock.
Model MK I #2: adjustable sights, no shoulder stock.

Markings: left side of slide: Webley & Scott, Ltd., Pistol Self-Loading .455 MK I n (date).

Price(s):
MK I #1, with grip safety, very good—$1,000.00
MK I #1, with grip safety, excellent—$1,250.00
MK I #1, without grip safety, very good—$1,250.00
MK I #1, without grip safety, excellent—$1,500.00
MK I #2, no cut for shoulder stock, very good—$2,500.00
MK I #2, no cut for shoulder stock, excellent—$3,000.00
MK I #2, cut for shoulder stock, very good—$3,000.00
MK I #2, cut for shoulder stock, excellent—$3,500.00
MK I #2, with shoulder stock, very good—$3,250.00
MK I #2, with shoulder stock, excellent—$4,500.00

History: The Webley .455 Automatic MK I was the final refinement in the series that began as the Model 1904. The pistol, as used by the British Navy during World War I, started development in 1906 based on the Model 1904 and was finally ready for production in 1909, and adopted in 1913. There were quite a few variants built on this frame. Pistols can be found with hard rubber grips and with checkered wood grips. They are available with and without grip safeties, although the majority have the grip safety, and they were available with an adjustable rear sight protected by raised ears, the latter being the MK I #2 variation. The Royal Flying Corps had an additional twist. In 1915 they ordered a production run of these pistols with a shoulder stock cut located on the lower left-hand side of the frame, which necessitated a short left grip.

These pistols were used primarily on the early war observation airplanes before the advent of the aerial machine gun. It provided something very handy, albeit something inaccurate, to shoot at your friendly opponent with.

Mechanical Functioning: The Webley MK I #1 series pistols are recoil-operated, external-hammer, semiautomatic pistols with seven-shot detachable box magazines inserted through the gripframe. The firing pin is of the floating type. The breechlock operates by engaging a locking shoulder at the top of the barrel against a shoulder in the slide when the breech is closed. During recoil, the barrel is forced out of a diagonal groove in the receiver, unlocking the slide, and allowing the slide to retract fully. The Webley MK I #2 pistol should not be confused with the Model 1904, which had a different construction than the MK I.

Webley MK I #2

Webley & Scott Ltd.
Park Lane
Birmingham B21 8LU England

Model: M & P (M1909)

Action Type: semiautomatic, blowback operated.

Caliber(s): 9mm Browning Long.

Barrel Lengths: 5″.

Finish: blue.

Manufacturing Dates: 1909–1930.

Stocks: hard rubber.

Rifling: 6R.

Weight, Unloaded: 34 oz.

Sights: fixed.

Serial Numbers: n/a.

Serial Number Location: left rear frame.

Major Variations: South African Police Model with manual safety. Standard Model with grip safety.

Markings: left side of slide: Webley & Scott Ltd., London, Birmingham, 9mm Automatic Pistol.

Price(s):
    Commercial, manual safety, very good—$750.00
    Commercial, manual safety, excellent—$900.00
    Commercial, grip safety, very good—$700.00
    Commercial, grip safety, excellent—$850.00
    South African Police, very good—$800.00
    South African Police, excellent—$950.00

History: The Webley Model 1909 Military and Police 9mm Browning Long semiautomatic pistol was first developed in 1908 and went into production in 1909. It was developed primarily to be a military and police model pistol, operating on a straight blowback design for customers in Europe who did not wish the heavy .455 caliber. Unfortunately for Webley, this pistol was not very well received because of its propensity to malfunction if the slightest amount of dirt got into the lockwork. Most European police departments avoided the pistol because of its unnecessary complexity and the tendency to malfunction. However, it was used by the South African police and possibly by the Egyptian police. There are two different styles which, although they are the same model, they are distinctly different. The early model, which is the model that the South African Police used, had a manual safety located on the left side of the slide and had no grip safety. The lanyard loop was mounted on the rear side of the frame, and was an attached loop. The later model dispensed with the manual safety on the slide, and substituted instead a grip safety, and also dispensed with the attached lanyard loop, substituting instead a fixed, solid loop located on the bottom, left-hand side of the butt. There was some discrepancy over the rifling pattern on this pistol. It appears that the most common variant is 6 Right; however, models have been reported with 7 Right, but have not been confirmed to this author.

Mechanical Functioning: The Webley Model 1909 Military and Police in all variations is a blowback-operated, semiautomatic pistol with a seven-shot detachable box magazine inserted through the grip. Depending on the variation, it either utilizes a manual safety to lock the firing pin, or a grip safety to prevent disengagement of the sear. The hammer is external. The firing pin is floating. This pistol utilizes Webley and Scott's quick takedown design. To dismount the pistol, first make sure that it is unloaded, and then remove the magazine, leaving the hammer cocked. Grasping the bottom end of the trigger guard, pull down and forward, releasing the spring guard from the frame and rotating it along a pin at the top forward end of the trigger guard. The slide can now be pulled forward and the barrel dropped out of the bottom. Assembly is in the reverse order. The late variation of this pistol, except in size, is nearly identical to the Model 1906 .32 A.C.P. Webley, and to the Model 1906 .25 Automatic Webley with the external hammer.

Webley Model 1909 M & P

Webley & Scott Ltd.
Park Lane
Birmingham B21 8LU England

Model: Fosbery Automatic Revolver

Action Type: revolver, semiautomatic.

Caliber(s): .455 Webley, .38 A.C.P.

Barrel Lengths: 4″, 6″, 7½″.

Finish: blue.

Manufacturing Dates: 1901–1939.

Stocks: hard rubber or wood.

Rifling: 7R.

Weight, Unloaded: 38 oz.

Sights: fixed.

Serial Numbers: n/a.

Serial Number Location: on barrel forward of cylinder on front.

Major Variations: Models 1901 and 1902 available in .38 or .455 calibers in standard or target versions.

Markings: on left top of barrel extension above cylinder: Webley Fosbery or Webley Fosbery Automatic.
on left side of frame: caliber.
on barrel: Made by the Webley & Scott Revolver & Arms Co., Ltd.

Price(s):
Model 1901, .455, Target, 7½″ barrel, very good—$3,750.00
Model 1901, .455, Target, 7½″ barrel, excellent—$4,750.00
Model 1901, .455, Civilian, 6″ barrel, very good—$3,000.00
Model 1901, .455, Civilian, 6″ barrel, excellent—$4,000.00
Model 1901, .38, Civilian, 6″ barrel, very good—$4,000.00
Model 1901, .38, Civilian, 6″ barrel, excellent—$5,000.00
Model 1902, .455, Target, 7½″ barrel very good—$2,750.00
Model 1902, .455, Target, 7½″ barrel, excellent—$3,500.00
Model 1902, .455, Civilian, 6″ barrel, very good—$2,250.00
Model 1902, .455, Civilian, 6″ barrel, excellent—$3,000.00
Model 1902, .455, Civilian, 4″ barrel, very good—$2,500.00
Model 1902, .455, Civilian, 4″ barrel, excellent—$3,250.00
Model 1902, .38, Civilian, 6″ barrel, very good—$3,250.00
Model 1902, .38, Civilian, 6″ barrel, excellent—$4,000.00
Model 1902, .455, Military, 6″ barrel, very good—$2,000.00
Model 1902, .455, Military, 6″ barrel, excellent—$2,750.00

History: The Webley Fosbery was the brainchild of Colonel George Fosbery, V.C. He worked on this invention throughout the 1890s, finally perfecting it about 1900. This is best described as a semiautomatic, top-break revolver. The cylinder rotates by virtue of zig-zag cuts milled into the periphery of the cylinder, which allows a guide located in the frame to rotate the cylinder as the entire barrel cylinder assembly reciprocates back and forth. This was considered to be a delightful revolver to shoot, because the action absorbed most of the recoil; however, if it was held too lightly, then there was not enough force on the frame to allow the barrel to slide back and forth, and instead, took the frame with it on recoil, meaning that the cylinder would not be rotated, nor would the hammer be cocked. It was available in two calibers, .455, which was the military caliber, and for target shooting in particular, .38. The .38 is sometimes known as the Winans' Model named for Walter Winans, a top pistol shot of the day and one of the major proponents of the Fosbery. Although popular, the Fosbery did not make a fine service weapon because the slightest amount of dirt would jam the track along which the barrel assembly had to move, thus jamming the pistol and rendering it inoperative. The Model 1901 and 1902 are essentially the same with minor differences which were adopted primarily for manufacturing ease. The Model 1901 was much more finely made and is recognizable externally by a screw located directly above the trigger forward of the safety and by the cylinder release assembly located forward of the cylinder on the left side of the barrel extension. The Model 1902 eliminated these niceties, as well as slightly changing the contour of the grip and the barrel.

Mechanical Functioning: The Webley Fosbery was a semiautomatic revolver firing six shots in .455 caliber, eight shots in .38 caliber, with a hinged barrel and automatic simultaneous ejection. It was single action, and a manual thumb safety was provided on the left side of the frame above the grip.

Webley Model 1902 .455

Whitney Firearms Co.
Hartford, CT

Model: Wolverine

Action Type: semiautomatic, blowback operated.

Caliber(s): .22 L.R.

Barrel Lengths: 4⁵⁄₈″.

Finish: blue or nickel.

Manufacturing Dates: 1955–1963.

Stocks: plastic.

Rifling: 6R.

Weight, Unloaded: 23 oz.

Sights: fixed.

Serial Numbers: appeared in the 30,000 range.

Major Variations: early model had Pat. Pending Mark and was made of "210 aluminum alloy."
late model was made of "318 aluminum alloy."

Markings: on left side of slide: Whitney.
on right side of slide, early: Caliber .22 LR, Patents Pending, The Whitney Firearms Co. Hartford Conn USA.
on right side of slide, late: Whitney Firearms Co. New Haven Conn USA.
last models had "Wolverine" on right side of slide above address.

Price(s):
Wolverine, blue, very god—$350.00
Wolverine, blue, excellent—$450.00
Wolverine, nickel, very good—$350.00
Wolverine, nickel, excellent—$500.00

History: The Whitney Wolverine was developed by Robert Hillberg. It was first manufactured in Hartford, Connecticut, about 1955, possibly under the name "Lightning." Sometime shortly afterward the company was moved to New Haven, Connecticut, and there lasted until about 1963. The chief feature of this pistol was its light weight, and its extremely raked grip making for excellent pointing qualities, and it made a very fine plinking handgun. About 1958 the alloy used in the pistol was changed from 218 aluminum to 318 aluminum, and for its size, it was a very lightweight pistol. The serial number range on these pistols is somewhat confusing, as pistols observed with the "Patent Pending" marks on them sometimes appear to have a higher number than those that have already had the patents granted. It is not known if these pistols ran in descending order in the 30,000 range.

Mechanical Functioning: The Whitney pistols are blowback-operated, semi-automatic pistols with a ten-shot detachable magazine that is inserted through the gripframe and retained by a spring-loaded catch at the base of the butt. Field-stripping the Wolverine is accomplished by first making sure the weapon is unloaded, depressing the locking plunger located under the barrel nut at the front of the frame, and unscrewing the barrel nut counterclockwise. Cocking the hammer, withdraw the operating tube assembly from the frame towards the rear by pulling back on the cocking piece. The cocking piece is attached to the bolt and retained by a pin. By pulling forward on the barrel to hold tension on the recoil spring and relieving it from the bolt, punch out the pin which holds the bolt to the operating tube. The bolt, barrel, and recoil spring can now be removed from the tube. Assemble in the reverse order.

Whitney Wolverine

Fab. De'Armes Zaragoza
Zaragoza, Mexico

Model: Corla

Action Type: semiautomatic, blowback operated.

Caliber(s): .22 L.R.

Barrel Lengths: 4½".

Finish: blue.

Manufacturing Dates: unknown.

Stocks: plastic.

Rifling: 8R.

Weight, Unloaded: 24¾ oz.

Sights: fixed.

Serial Numbers: possibly 1 to about 400.

Serial Number Location: right side of frame above trigger.

Major Variations: first type: Colt system design including slide stop.
second type was simplified, eliminating Colt features.

Markings: right side of frame: Zaragoza Hecho En Mexico.
left side of frame: Modelo Corla, Cal .22 L.R. Automatica.
on the second type these markings are on opposite sides.

Price(s):
first type, very good—$300.00
first type, excellent—$450.00
second type, very good—$200.00
second type, excellent—$350.00

History: Very little is known about the Zaragoza Corla pistols. The manufacturing dates are unknown, and about all that is known is that they were made in Mexico in the town of Zaragoza. They came in two distinct variations. The first type, of which it is approximated that only 65 were made, was a very good copy in miniature of the Colt Model 1911A1, with the primary difference between it and the 1911A1 being an extractor mounted on the right side of the frame which extended through the frame, but located below and slightly behind the ejection port which had rounded sides as in the Colt. The second model, however, was quite different. In place of the floating barrel retained by a cross pin, which also formed the slide stop, it was solidly mounted to a frame extension. The ejection port was redesigned and squared off with the extractor coming up level with the bottom of the port and extending into it. Of the second type it is assumed that in excess of 300 pistols were made and the two serial number ranges for each type are presumed to have been run in sequence.

Mechanical Functioning: The first type of Zaragoza Corla is an identical copy in miniature of the Model 1911A1 Colt. It is, however, a blowback-operated, semiautomatic pistol with a ten-shot detachable box magazine inserted through the butt and retained in Colt fashion by a spring-loaded catch on the left side of the frame behind the trigger. The barrel is of the floating type, retained by the slide stop pin extending through the frame from left to right. It has an external hammer and a floating firing pin, a manual safety locking the sear on the left side of the firearm, and a grip safety. The mainspring housing is a miniature of the Model 1911. Takedown is accomplished in the same method. First, making sure the weapon is unloaded, turn the barrel bushing to release the spring and plunger located underneath the barrel, and then withdraw the slide until the notch lines up with the slide stop, so that the slide bar can be pushed out from the right side going towards the left and pull the entire assembly out. At this point the slide can be removed from the frame just as on the original Colt. The second model is slightly different. In order to take it down, first remove the barrel bushing in the same manner, and then all that is necessary is running the slide straight off the frame. There is no cross pin to link the barrel, as the barrel is firmly attached to a frame extension and permanently mounted. Most other aspects of the firearm are the same as the first model, including the presence in the slide of cuts for where the earlier slide stop would have been located. The extractor bar is longer, extending all the way through to the rear of the finger grooves on the right-hand side of the frame and extending forward into a cut in the side of the barrel.

Zaragoza Corla First Type

E. Zehner Waffenfabrik
Suhl, Germany

Model: Zehna

Action Type: semiautomatic, blowback operated.

Caliber(s): 6.35mm.

Barrel Lengths: 2³/₈".

Finish: blue.

Manufacturing Dates: 1919–1928.

Stocks: hard rubber.

Rifling: 4R.

Weight, Unloaded: 13 oz.

Sights: fixed.

Serial Numbers: ran from 1 to about 5,000 for the first type.
continued in series to around 20,000.

Serial Number Location: right side of frame above trigger.

Major Variations: early style was more crudely made.
late style was more finely finished.

Markings: left side of slide: Zehna Cal. 6.35 D.R.P. a E. Zehner, Suhl, Made
in Germany.
early models had "Zehna D.R.P.a" on right side of slide.

Price(s):
early model, very good—$275.00
early model, excellent—$325.00
late model, very good—$325.00
late model, excellent—$375.00

History: The Zehna pistol was invented by Emil Zehner around 1919 and
was first put into production sometime shortly afterwards in his own
plant in Suhl, Germany. The first pistols he produced were quite crude
and not very well finished. It appears though, that around serial number
5,000 he decided to modify the pistol somewhat, and clean up the lines
and make it a little more finely finished. This was accomplished and it
appears that he sold about another 5,000 pistols in addition to the previous 5,000. Production continued on into about 1927 or 1928 when the
worldwide Depression was really starting to take hold. The Zehna was a
fine little pocket pistol with several unusual features. The slide mated
precisely at breech face to barrel, with the barrel top exposed and the
slide running to the side of it and slightly underneath it. The recoil
spring was located beneath the barrel, and was instrumental in retaining
the barrel in place. It had a manual safety located at the left rear of the
frame which blocked the sear. The Zehna was another of the fine pocket
pistols manufactured in Germany during the 1920s, and Zehner was
another one of the manufacturers to cash in on the rising tide of anarchy

present in Germany at the time, by manufacturing a pistol that the average man could use for self-defense, a very necessary commodity during those times.

Mechanical Functioning: The Zehna is a .25 A.C.P., straight blowback-operated, semiautomatic pistol utilizing a detachable box magazine holding six rounds. The clip is inserted through the gripframe through the bottom and is retained by a spring-loaded catch at the base of the butt. The pistol is striker-actuated, and the safety is of the type that intercepts the sear, and when engaged, locks the striker. Takedown is accomplished by first making sure the weapon is unloaded, pulling the trigger, removing the magazine, and turning the safety catch around until it is in the rearmost position and pointing up. Withdraw the slide until the safety engages the small notch cut within the finger groove pattern on the left side of the slide. At this point, pull the flat plate on the forward part of the frame under the barrel outward against the pressure of the recoil spring until the small pin is fully exposed. At this time, you can rotate that flat plate until that pin rests on the frame. The barrel can now be lifted straight up and clear of the pistol. Holding the slide firmly against the pressure of the recoil spring, lower the safety unlocking the slide. The slide can now go forward and off the frame of the gun, and the recoil spring assembly removed, as well as the striker assembly. Assembly is in the reverse order.

Zehna Late Model

M. Zulaica y Cia.
Eibar, Spain

Model: 1914

Action Type: semiautomatic, blowback-operated.

Caliber(s): 7.65mm.

Barrel Lengths: 3³/₈".

Finish: blue.

Manufacturing Dates: 1915–1916.

Stocks: checkered wood.

Rifling: 6R.

Weight, Unloaded: 21⅞ oz.

Sights: fixed.

Serial Numbers: may have started at 1.

Serial Number Location: on left side of slide.

Major Variations: 7- to 20-shot magazines with matching gripframe length.

Markings: on left side of slide: 7.65 1914 Model Automatic Pistol, M. Zulaica & Co. Eibar.

Price(s):
Model 1914, very good—$125.00
Model 1914, excellent—$175.00

History: Zulaica y Cia. of Eibar, Spain, was one of the prime subcontractors for Gabilondo when the French placed their orders in 1915 for an inexpensive 7.65mm automatic for use in the trenches. The generic term for this type of pistol is the Ruby, and Zulaica was one of the prime manufacturers both during the war and afterward. After the war, these same pistols were made under the trade name "Royal" and used fancier grips than the checkered wood. They were also available in various frame lengths to accommodate different-size magazines. The most noteworthy production came under the Royal Z Novelty trade name, which is also mentioned in this book. The term "Ruby," even though a trade name of Gabilondo y Cia., now denotes an entire class of pistols used by the French Army during World War I. These pistols were first designed around 1910 and based on the design of Browning for 1903. They featured concealed internal hammers and straight blowback operation with recoil springs mounted under the barrel, with takedown done in much the same manner as the Browning 1903. As a class, they were fairly heavy pistols and designed to be rapidly and inexpensively made. At the outbreak of the war, when the French were caught napping and in dire need of a great many handguns, they turned to the Spanish firms to help them out of their plight. The primary contract went to the firm of Gabilondo, and by the middle of 1915 with orders already running at 30,000 pistols per month, the French decided that they needed even more. Not being able to keep up with the work, Gabilondo called on about a dozen other firms in Spain to help make pistols on their pattern, and thus as a class, Rubys can be found with a variety of names, and some differences of design, because they are made by so many different firms. It is possible, considering the commercial variants as well as the French military variants, to be able to have a hundred-pistol collection of Rubys with no two pistols being alike.

Mechanical Functioning: The Zulaica class of pistols was of standard Eibar based on the Browning 1906. They were blowback-operated, semi-automatic pistols with detachable box magazines. The average clip size was seven shots, although clips ranged up to 12 shots with the appropriate lengthening of the gripframe to cover the clip. Some postwar models held as many as 20 shots. For further variations, see also Astra Model 1915 and the Union pistol.

Zulaica Model 1914

M. Zulaica y Cia.
Eibar, Spain

Model: Royal (Z Novelty)

Action Type: semiautomatic, blowback operated.

Caliber(s): 6.35mm, 7.65mm.

Barrel Lengths: in 7.65mm, 3", in 6.35mm, 2".

Finish: blue.

Manufacturing Dates: circa 1920.

Stocks: hard rubber.

Rifling: 6R.

Weight, Unloaded: in 7.65mm, 21⅝ oz; in 6.35mm 13 oz.

Sights: fixed.

Serial Numbers: n/a.

Serial Number Location: right side of frame.

Major Variations: .25 A.C.P.
.32 A.C.P.

Markings: left side of slide: The Royal Patent Automatic Pistol (Caliber).
on grips: Royal Z Novelty.

Price(s):
6.35mm, very good—$100.00
6.35mm, excellent—$150.00
7.65mm, very good—$125.00
7.65mm, excellent—$175.00

History: M. Zulaica y Cia. of Eibar, Spain, was one of the firms that benefited by the French lack of preparedness for World War I. This firm had always tried to do a good job even making inexpensive guns, so it was to firms like this that Gabilondo y Cia. had to turn to when the pressures of World War I caught up to them. Zulaica was a prime subcontractor for Gabilondo in the manufacture of Ruby pistols for the French military. Quite naturally after the war when the orders were canceled, they had to turn their production instead to commercial variations. And since they already had the tooling set up they just modified the frame slightly, and continued to make what was essentially a Ruby pistol. In the early 1920s they came out with what they called their Novelty line, and the grips were marked, "Royal Z Novelty." In both of these pistols they tried to slightly modify the Eibar pattern but they did not get too far. While Zulaica could not be accused of fostering the pioneering spirit among Eibar arms makers, they did do a creditable job of manufacturing a standard product, and they generally were proud enough of their handiwork to affix their name to it. The most adventurous they became was in the late 1920s when they attempted to copy the Mauser C-96 Broomhandle. Of course it must be borne in mind that Europe in the early 1920s was something like the wild west, and if it could shoot it was in demand.

Mechanical Functioning: The Royal Z Novelties are straight blowback, semiautomatic pistols with an internal concealed hammer and a detachable box magazine inserted through the butt with a spring-loaded magazine catch at the base of the butt retaining them. Internally, they are of standard Eibar pattern with few original features. The 6.35mm. model has the safety catch just behind the trigger and works as a sliding plate instead of the normal rotating bar. The 7.65mm model has a redesigned gripframe with a small butt and enlargements behind the trigger to improve the grip. Takedown is accomplished by first making sure that the pistol is unloaded, removing the magazine, and withdrawing the slide until the barrel lugs can be lined up with a cut visible just beneath the ejector port on the slide. The barrel is then rotated about 120 degrees to the right, unlocking it from the slide. The slide can now be withdrawn forward and off the gun. Assembly is in the reverse order. There were three other models in the Royal series, none of them being named "Novelty." Two of them were rather uninspired copies of the Ruby, one being of standard size, the other enlarged with a 12-shot clip. The last Royal, which was the most original, was a copy of the Mauser C-96 but was poorly made. The Royal C-96 copy was made of soft metal and poorly finished, but it was available in either semiautomatic or full automatic with a selector switch. Of the entire line, the Novelties were perhaps the best.

Royal

GLOSSARY

A.C.P. Abbreviation for Automatic Colt Pistol, which is part of a caliber designation.

ACTION. That part of the firearm made up of the breech and the parts designed to fire in-cycle cartridges.

ADAPTER. A device that inserts into the chamber (known as an auxiliary chamber) and that may extend into the barrel, which allows the firing of smaller-caliber and/or lower-powered ammunition.

ALLOY FRAME: A term generally applied to handguns having a non-ferrous frame. Generally made of aluminum or zamak.

ANTIQUE. A legal classification that in the U.S. is applied to weapons manufactured in or before 1898 and replicas that do not fire fixed ammunition.

ARSENAL. A military installation that stores and usually upgrades and modifies military weapons; sometimes applies to governmental weapon-manufacturing facilities.

AUTOMATIC. Action type that ejects a spent cartridge and brings a fresh cartridge into the firing position without manual intervention and has the capability of firing more than one shot with each pull of the trigger.

AUTOMATIC REVOLVER. Firearm action that resembles a conventional revolver except that on firing, the cylinder is rotated and the hammer cocked by the recoil energy of the fired cartridge.

AUTOMATIC SAFETY. A device on some handguns, generally incorporated in the grip safety, that prevents discharge unless the firearm is actually held in firing position.

BACKSTRAP. The rear of the frame at the grip, generally made of metal.

BACKTHRUST. The force exerted on the breechblock by the head of the cartridge case during discharge.

BARREL. Tube through which the bullet passes on firing.

BARREL CATCH. The catch on the rearmost part of the barrel on hinge-frame firearms that locks the barrel in the closed position.

BARREL, INTERCHANGEABLE. A barrel that may easily be exchanged with the original barrel upon field stripping.

BARREL LENGTH. On pistols, the distance between the muzzle and the face of the closed breechblock. On revolvers, the overall length of the barrel itself.

BARREL LINER. A thin steel tube, usually permanently inserted into the barrel, either to change the caliber, restore the gun, or to make the gun more functional when the barrel is formed from softer material.

BARREL REFLECTOR. A device for examining the bore and chamber of a handgun, generally consisting of a small mirror to reflect light through the action toward the muzzle for viewing the interior of the bore.

BARREL RETAINER. A grooving on the barrel and frame that is used to retain the barrel in the firearm.

BARREL, RINGED. A circumferential bulge in a barrel caused by excessive radial pressure from firing with an obstruction in the bore.

BARREL WEIGHT. A small weight that is attached to a barrel, generally on target handguns to change the center of balance.

BATTERY. A condition in which the action is properly closed and the firearm ready for firing.

BLOWBACK ACTION. An action in which the breechblock is held forward only by spring pressure and cycled from the rearward gas thrust of the fired cartridge. In ammunition, this is a rearward leakage of gas on firing.

BLOWFORWARD ACTION. An action that has a fixed breechblock in which spring pressure secures a barrel that reciprocates and cycles the action from the pressure of expanding gasses when a cartridge is fired.

BLOW, LIGHT. Description of a condition caused either by insufficient firing pin energy or protrusion resulting in a misfire.

BLUE. An artificial oxidation process that yields some rust protection and leaves steel surfaces with a blue-black color. The term is also applied to blackened alloys used on firearms.

BORE. The inside of a barrel, or diameter. The diameter of a circle formed by the tops of the lands.

BRASS. Fired cartridge cases.

BREAKTOP. A hinged frame action that exposes the breech by unlocking and the barrel tipping downward, rotating on a point just forward of the breech.

BREECH. Rear end of the barrel, or that part of the action that contacts the rear of the cartridge.

BREECHBLOCK. The locking and cartridge-head-supporting mechanism of a firearm that does not operate in line with the access of the bore.

BREECHBOLT. The locking and cartridge-head-supporting mechanism that operates in line with the access of the bore.

BREECHFACE. The part of the breech that is against the head of the cartridge case during firing.

BUFFER. Any part designed to absorb shock and reduce recoil.

BULL BARREL. A heavy barrel, usually with no taper, generally found on target handguns.

BUTT. The bottom part of the grip and/or the grip frame.

CALIBER. Bore diameter, usually measured land to land in decimals of an inch, or in millimeters. In ammunition, a term naming the cartridge and not necessarily the bore diameter.

CARTRIDGE. A self-contained unit of ammunition consisting of the case, primer, propellent, and projectile.

CARTRIDGE INDICATOR. Sometimes known as a chamber indicator. A device on a handgun that protrudes, showing that when the firearm is in battery, it is loaded.

CASE HARDENED. A surface hardening that on firearms is usually done so as to leave a broad spectrum of colors on the metal.

CENTER FIRE. Cartridge that contains a primer in the center of the base of the case.

CHAMBER. Portion of the gun in which the cartridge is placed.

CHAMBER, FLOATING. A movable chamber that operates the mechanism of a handgun.

CHAMBER, FLUTED. A chamber that has longitudinal grooves cut into it to assist in extraction.

CHECKERING. Geometric carving in the shape of parallel lines that cross to form diamonds, used both for beauty and to provide a better hand grip.

CLIP. A detachable box that holds and feeds ammunition into the firearm by spring pressure. See Magazine.

COMPENSATOR. A device attached to or integral with the muzzle of the barrel, to redirect escaping gas on firing to reduce recoil. It is also called a muzzle break.

CONDITION. This is the state of the newness or wear of a gun. See Introduction for a complete description.

CONVERSION. Converting a firearm to use a different cartridge or changing the general configuration of the gun.

CRANE. On a solid frame revolver, the part on which the cylinder rides and swings out on. Also called a yoke.

CURIO. Curios and relics are a legal subclassification of modern arms. See Introduction for complete definition.

CYLINDER. The rotating container with cartridge chambers in a revolver.

DAMASCENE. An overlay of metal, usually gold leaf, sometimes combined with light engraving and used for decoration.

DAMASCENING. Also called engine turning or jeweling, this is an ornamental polishing consisting of repeated and overlapping circles.

DELAYED BLOWBACK. A blowback action in which there is a mechanical delay to retard the action cycling until the chamber pressure has been reduced.

DERINGER. A small percussion pistol developed by Henry Deringer.

DERRINGER. A copy of the Deringer, now meaning any small manually operated pistol.

DEWAT. An acronym for deactivated war trophy.

DISCONNECTOR. A device on semiautomatic firearms to prevent full automatic firing.

DOUBLE ACTION. The ability to both cock and fire a gun by the single pull of a trigger.

EJECTION. The act of expelling a cartridge or a cartridge case.

EJECTION PORT. An opening through which the cartridge or cartridge case ejects.

EJECTOR. A metal stud or rod that forcibly knocks the cases out of the firearm.

ENGRAVING. Metal carving for decoration.

ESCUTCHEON. A metal or plastic reinforcement around a screw hole on grips, or the part of a grip that displays a company name or trademark.

EXTRACTOR. The metal part that lifts the case out of the chamber.

FEED RAMP. The surface toward the rear of the chamber on which the cartridge rides when it slips from magazine to chamber.

FINISH. Materials used to coat wood grips, or the treatment of metal parts.

FIXED SIGHTS. Nonadjustable sights.

FLASH HIDER. A device that reduces the amount of muzzle flash.

FLUTED BARREL. A barrel with longitudinal grooves cut into it for decoration and/or strength.

FORCING CONE. A tapered section at the breech end of a revolver barrel.

FRAME. The metal part of the gun that contains the action.

FREE PISTOL. A handgun designed for certain types of target shooting.

FRONT STRAP. The exposed metal portion of the grip frame to the front of the grips.

GRIP. The portion of the gun to the rear of the trigger that is held by the firing hand.

GRIP ADAPTER. A filler attached to the front of the gripframe.

GRIPFRAME. On handguns, that portion of the frame that is held by the hand.

GRIPS. On handguns, the stocks.

GRIP SAFETY. A mechanical block that is released when the gun is held by hand in the firing position.

GRIPSTRAP. The exposed metal portion of the gripframe to the front or rear of the grips.

HAMMER. The part of the mechanism that hits and imparts thrust to the firing pin.

HAMMERLESS. A term applied to both striker-actuated guns and guns with hammers hidden within the action.

HAMMER SHROUD. A device that covers the sides of the hammer, while leaving the top exposed.

HANDGUN. A firearm designed to be held and fired with one hand.

HARDBALL. A slang term for full metal-jacketed ammunition.

HOLSTER STOCK. A holster usually made of wood, or wood and leather, that attaches to a handgun for use as a shoulder stock.

INLAY. Decoration made by inlaying patterns on wood or metal.

LAND. The raised portion in a rifled bore.

LANYARD RING. A ring used to secure the gun by a lanyard to the shooter so that it won't be lost or dropped.

LOADING GATE. On revolvers, a hinged piece attached to the frame that is opened to permit loading.

LOCKING BLOCK. A sliding block that locks the breechblock closed.

MAGAZINE. In repeating arms, a storage device that feeds cartridges into the breech.

MAGAZINE SAFETY. A device that prevents firing unless the magazine is inserted into the handgun.

MAGNUM. Usually refers to arms or cartridges that are more powerful than normal or that utilize higher pressure.

MATTE FINISH. A dull finish that does not reflect light.

MISFIRE. The failure of a cartridge to discharge after being struck by the firing pin.

MODERN. A legal term applied to cartridge firearms manufactured after 1898. Also see Introduction.

MUZZLE. The most forward end of the barrel.

MUZZLE BLAST. The noise and flash that occurs at the muzzle upon firing.

MUZZLE BRAKE. See Compensator.

PARABELLUM. A name used in cartridge designation, from the German word meaning "for war."

PARKERIZED. A matte, phosphated finish that is highly rust-resistant and is usually placed on military arms.

PISTOL. A handgun in which the chamber is part of the barrel.

PISTOL GRIP. The grip on a pistol.

POCKET REVOLVER. A small revolver.

PORT. An opening into the action for ejected cases to pass through, or an opening for gasses to flow through.

PORTING. The removal of metal around an ejection port on combat guns to aid in extraction and prevent malfunctions.

PROOF. The testing of a gun to see if it stands the stress of firing.

PROOFMARK. A stamp applied to show that the weapon has undergone proof testing.

RECEIVER. The part of the frame that houses the bolt or breechblock.

RECOIL. The rearward push of the gun when fired.

RECOIL OPERATED. An action that is cycled by the recoil from the fired cartridge.

REVOLVER. A handgun with a revolving cylinder containing multiple chambers.

RIB. A raised surface used as a sighting plane.

RIFLING. Helical grooves cut into the bore to impart rotary motion to a projectile.

RIMFIRE. Cartridges containing the priming compound in the rim.

ROTATING BARREL. A system in which the barrel, slide, and receiver are locked together by heavy, interrupted threads and on firing, the barrel rotates to unlock the breech.

ROUND. A military term for cartridge.

SAFETY. A mechanical block that prevents the firearm from firing.

SEAR. That part of the action that engages the striker or hammer and allows them to fall when released by the trigger.

SEMIAUTOMATIC. Action type that ejects the spent case and cycles a new round into the chamber with the energy of the fired round, and fires only one shot with each pull of the trigger.

SERIAL NUMBER. A number applied to a firearm in order to identify the individual firearm.

SIDEPLATE. A removable plate in the frame that allows access to internal parts.

SIGHT. A device that allows precise aim.

SILENCER. A device that reduces the noise of firing.

SINGLE ACTION. An action type that requires manual cocking for each shot.

SINGLE-SHOT. A gun capable of firing only one shot and having no magazine.

SLIDE. The reciprocating part of a semiautomatic pistol containing the breechblock.

SMOOTH BORE. Firearm with an unrifled bore.

SOLID FRAME. A revolver that does not have a hinged frame.

SOLID RIB. A raised sighting plane on a barrel.

SPUR TRIGGER. A trigger with no guard, but protected by a sheath.

STRIKER. A spring-activated firing pin held in place by a sear, which when released has enough energy to fire a primer.

STIPPLING. Small marks and raised portions of metal caused by repeated striking over a wide area with prick-punch and hammer to form a rough surface, used as background for engraving or, when it is coarser, to provide a better grip, usually on the grip straps. Sometimes used to break reflections along the sighting plane.

STOCK. Grip.

STRIPPER CLIP. A folded piece of sheet metal that holds five to ten cartridges, used to load cartridges quickly into fixed magazines.

TAKEDOWN. Disassembly.

TAKEDOWN LATCH. A catch device used to facilitate disassembly.

TARGET. Designed for target shooting.

TARGET STOCK. A stock designed for target shooting.

THUMB REST. A ledge on the side of target grips for the thumb to rest on.

TIP-UP. A revolver with a frame hinged at the upper rear portion, or a single-shot pistol that has a break-top action.

TOGGLE ACTION. A semiautomatic action with a toggle joint that locks the breechblock.

TOP STRAP. The portion of a solid-frame revolver above the cylinder.

TRIGGER. The exterior sear release.

TRIGGER GUARD. A band, usually of metal, that encircles the trigger, preventing accidental discharge.

TRIGGER PULL. The amount of force that must be applied to the trigger to cause sear release.

TRIGGER SHOE. An accessory attached to the trigger to give wider bearing surface.

VENT RIB. A raised sighting plane on barrels with air vents between it and the barrel.

WADCUTTER. A bullet used for target shooting with a sharp-shouldered nose, intended to cut paper cleanly.

ABBREVIATIONS

Throughout this book and in most other books, as well as manufacturers' catalogs and ballistic tables, you will find various abbreviations, sometimes making no sense in the real world. For instance, the abbreviation for "barrel" that is most commonly accepted throughout the firearms trade is "bbl." How or why this particular practice started, I do not know, since barrel has only one *b*. So that we can avoid confusion, both in this text and in your other reading, the following are generally acceptable abbreviations for various firearm terms:

A.C.P. Automatic Colt Pistol. A name applied to cartridges.

A.P. Armor piercing.

AUTO. Automatic.

BBL. Barrel.

BLK. Black, as in black powder.

BL-C. Ball-C, as in powder.

B.P. Black powder.

BT. Boattail, as in boattail bullet.

CAL. Caliber.

CF. Center fire.

CHEM. Chemical examination or test.

C.I.L. The Canadian manufacturer Canadian Industries Limited.

CM. Centimeter.

C.M.S. Case mouth seal. This is the color of the lacquer identification that is sometimes used on military cartridges at the base of the bullet, sealing the cartridge case.

C.N. Cupro-nickel bullet jacket, or type of tear gas.

CTG. Cartridge.

CU. Copper.

CYL. Cylinder.

DBL. Double.

D.C. Dual core, as in bullets.

DUP. FACT. BALL. Duplicates factory ballistics, as in ammunition.

D.W.M. Deutsche Waffen und Munition, a German cartridge and handgun maker.

E. Energy, generally in foot pounds, unless it is in a European Ballistic Table, in which case it will be measured in joules.

EJT. Ejector.

EXT. Extractor.

F. Function.

F. & F. Full and full choke designation.

F. & M. Full and modified choke designation.

F/L. Flintlock.

F.L. Factory load, as in ammunition.

F.M.C. Full metal case, as in a full jacketed bullet.

F.M.J. Full metal jacket; also known as full patch, applying to jacketed bullets.

F.P. Firing pin; or foot pounds; as an energy measurement.

F.P.S. Feet per second, as in velocity.

G.C. Gas check.

GR. Grain, a unit of measurement (1 oz. = 437.5 gr., 7,000 gr. = 1 lb.).

H/R. Hard rubber, as in grips.

H. & H. English manufacturer Holland & Holland.

H.B. Heavy ball, a manufacturer's term for round-nose bullets; or heavy barrel.

H.E. High explosives.

H.M.G. Heavy machine gun.

H.P. Hollow point, as in an open-faced bullet.

I. Incendiary.

I.C. Improved cylinder choke.

I.C.I. Imperial Chemical Industries, a Canadian ammunition manufacturer.

IM/C Improved cylinder choke.

I.P. Inside primed.

J.H.P. Jacketed hollow point, as in bullet.

J.S.P. Jacketed soft point, as in bullet.

L.R.N. Lead round-nosed bullet, a manufacturer's designation.

L.S. Lacquered steel, a type of finish used on cartridge cases.

LUB. Lubaloy, a trade name for a lubricated lead bullet.

LW. Lightweight.

M. Meter.

MAG. Magnum; sometimes used as magazine.

MANN. Mannlicher.

MAX. Maximum.

M.C. Metal cased, as in bullet.

M.E. Muzzle energy.

MFG. Manufacture or manufacturer.

M.G. Machine gun.

MM. Millimeter.

M.R.T. Midrange trajectory.

M.-S. Mannlicher-Schoenauer, a manufacturer in Austria.

M.V. Muzzle velocity.

N.I.B. New in box.

O/A. Overall.

OCT. Octagon, as in barrel.

O.P.E. English term for "open point expanding," the equivalent of hollow point.

O/U. Over/under.

P. In ammunition meaning "pointed bullet."

P.A. Primer annulus, the color-identification lacquer that sealed primers on some commercial and military ammunition.

Pb. Lead.

PERC. Percussion.

P.P. Paper patch, a term for paper-wrapped bullets that were used in the black powder era.

P.S.I. Pounds per square inch, measurement of relative pressure.

R.B. Round barrel.

REM. Remington Arms Company.

REV. Revolver.

RF. Rimfire.

R.N. Round nose, a term used to describe bullets.

R.W.S. An ammunition trade name used by Dynamit Nobel on ammunition.

S. & W. Smith & Wesson.

S.A. Semiautomatic.

SGT. Sight.

S.L. Self-loading, another term for semiautomatic.

S.M.G. Submachine gun.

S.N. Soft nose, describing an exposed-lead-tipped bullet.

S.P. Soft point; essentially the same as soft nose, except at a sharper point.

SPL. Special, as in .38 Special, an ammunition designation.

S.S. Single shot, a type of firearm action.

S.S.T. Single selective trigger.

S.T. Single trigger.

S.W.C. Semi-wad cutter, a bullet shape.

SxS Side by side.

T. Tracer.

T.B. Top break.

T.C. Truncated cone, a bullet shape.

T.G. Trigger guard.

T.S. Target sights.

T.T. Target trigger.

V. Velocity.

V.R. Ventilated rib over barrel.

W/ With.

W.C. Wad cutter, a bullet shape.

W.C.F. Winchester center fire, an ammunition designation.

WIN. Winchester.

W.M.R. Winchester Magnum rimfire, an ammunition designation.

WT. Weight.

W-W. Winchester Western, an ammunition manufacturer.

YDS. Yards.

MODEL INDEX

Adams, Robert, biographical information, 9

Advantage Arms U.S.A., Inc., Model, 422

Albini, Augusto, biographical information, 9

American Derringer Corp., Models, 1, 7, and 3, 40–41

AMT (Arcadia Machine & Tool), Back Up, 36–37

Arizaga, Gaspar, Mondial, 42–43

Arminex, Ltd., Tri-Fire, 44–45

Hijos de Calixto Arrizabalaga, Sharp Sooter, 46–47

Astra-Unceta y Cia., S.A.
  A-80, 48–49
  200 Firecat, 53–54
  357, 55–56
  400 (1921), 57–58
  900, 59–60
  1911, 61–62
  2000 Cub, 51–52
  Constable, 50

Auctions, selling guns, 20

Auto Mag, Corp., Auto Mag, 63–64

Auto Ordnance Corp.
  M1911A1!, 65–66
  1927 A-5 (pistol/carbine), 67–68

Bargmann/Bayard, 1908, 1910, and 1910/21, 97–98

Bauer Firearms Corp. 25-SS, 71–72

Bayard
  1908, 73–74
  1923, 75–76

Manufacture D'Armes Automatiques Bayonne (MAB)
  Model B, 77–78
  Model D, 79–80
  Model F, 81–82

Becker & Hollander Waffenbau, Beholla, 83–84

Berdan Gunmakers Ltd., Britarms 2000 Mark II, 85–86

Berdan, Hiram, biographical information, 9

Theodor Bergmann Waffenfabrik
  1896 #'s 2, 3, and 4, 95–96
  Taschen, 93–94

Borchardt, Hugo, biographical information, 9

B.R.F, Junior, 69–70

Browning Arms Co.
  1903, 103–104
  1910, 105–106
  1922, 107–108
  Challenger, 99–100
  High Power, 101–102

Browning, John Moses, biographical information, 10

Budischowski, TP 70, 109–110

Campo Giro, 1913–16, 111–112

Cartridges, pistol and revolver, listing of, 28–34

Charter Arms
  Bulldog, 113–114
  Pathfinder, 115–116
  Target Bulldog, 117–118
  Undercover, 119–120

Witold Chylewski, Brevet, 121–122

Cleaning guns, 27–28

Charles P.H.Clement, 1910, 123–124

Colt
  1902 Sporting and Military, 167–168
  1903 Pocket, 169–170
  1903 Pocket Hammerless, 171–172
  1908 Hammerless, 173–174

Colt *(cont'd)*
  1909 New Service
    (Army/Navy/U.S.M.C.),
    175–176
  Ace, 125–126
  Agent, 127–128
  Bankers' Special, 129–130
  Bisley, 131–132
  Camp Perry, 133–134
  Cobra, 135–136
  Commando, 137–138
  Detective Special, 139–140
  Diamondback, 141–142
  Gold Cup National Match MK IV
    Series 70, 143–144
  Government MK IV Series 70,
    145–146
  Junior, 147–148
  Lawman MK III, 149–150
  Metropolitan MK III, 151–152
  National Match, 153–154
  New Pocket, 155–156
  Police Positive, 157–158
  Python, 159–160
  Trooper MK III, 161–162
  Trooper MK V, 163–164
  Woodsman/Huntsman, 165–166
Colt, Samuel, biographical
  information, 10
Commemoratives, buying
  guidelines, 21–22
Coonan Arms, Inc., 357, 177–178
Counterfeits, buying guidelines, 19
CZ (Ceska Zbrojovka)
  VZ 27, 179–180
  VZ 38, 181–182

Deringer, Henry, biographical
  information, 10
Detonics Manufacturing Corp.
  Mark I, 192–193
  Mark V/Mark VI/Mark VII/MC-
    1/MC-2, 194–195
  Scoremaster, 196–197
Dreyse
  1907, 200–201
  Vest Pocket Model 2, 198–199
DWM-Deutsche Waffen and
  Munitions Fabriken
  Luger 1900, 183–184
  Luger 1904 Navy, 185–186
  Luger 1906, 187–188
  Luger 1908 (P.08), 189–191

Echave & Arizmendi, Fast, 206–207
E.M.F.
  1875 Outlaw, 204–205
  Dakota, 202–203

Firearms, legal classification of,
  13–14
French Government Arsenals
  M1935A (Pistolet Automatique
    Modele 35A), 208–209
  1935S, 210–211
  1950, 212–213
Frommer/Fegyvergyar
  1910, 218–219
  Liliput, 214–215
  Stop Pocket Auto, 216–217
Frommer, Rudolf, biographical
  information, 10

Gabilondo y Cia., Ruby, 220–223
Soc. Siderurgica Glisenti, Glisenti,
  224–225
Gun shops
  buying guns, 18
  selling guns, 19
Gun shows
  buying guns, 18
  selling guns, 20
Gustloff Werke Waffenfabrik,
  Gustloff, 226- 227

C.G. Haenel, Schmeisser Model I,
  228–229
Hafdasa, Ballester-Molina, 230–231
Handguns
  abbreviations related to, 517–520
  buying guidelines, 17–19
  cleaning guns, 27–28
  collecting as investment, 17
  condition, categories of, 16
  designers/inventors of, 9–13
  historical view, 3–8
  identifying features, 20–21
  inspection for functioning, 26–27
  legal classifications of firearms,
    13–14
  limited edition guns, 21–23
  pistol/revolver cartridges, 28–34

restoration of, 23–26
selling guidelines, 19–20
terms related to, 510–516
value, determining factors, 14–17
Harrington & Richardson,
  Self-Loading Pistol, .32 cal.,
  232–233
Hartford Arms & Equipment Co.,
  Target Pistol (single shot,
  repeater, and 1925), 234–235
Heckler & Koch
  HK4, 236–237
  P9S, 238–239
High Standard Manufacturing
  Corporation
  Derringer, 240–241
  H-D Military, 242–243
  Olympic I.S.U. Military, 244–245
  Sentinel (series), 246–247
  Supermatic Citation (series),
    248–249
  Victor, 250–251
Hispano-Argentine Fabricas de
  Automoviles S.A., Hafdasa,
  252–253
Husqvarna Vapenfabrik, Lahti,
  Swedish Model 40, 254–255
Husqvarna Vapenfabrik Aktiebolag,
  1907, 256- 257

Interarms, Virginian, 258–259

Jager Waffenfabrik, Jager, 260–261
Japanese Military
  Nambu, Papa, and Grandpa,
    264–265
  Nambu, Type 14, 262–263

J. Kimball Arms Co., Standard,
  266–267
Korriphila GMBH, TP-70, 268–269
Krnka, Karel, biographical
  information, 10

Langenhan Gewehre v.
  Fahrradfabrik, F.L. Model I,
  272–273
Le Francis Manufacture Francais
  D'Armes et Cycles Manufrance
  28 "Armee," 274–275
  Pocket, 276–277

Legal classifications, for firearms,
  13–14
Manufacture D'Armes LePage, S.A.,
  LePage Auto Pistol, 278–279
L.E.S., , Inc., Rogak P–18, 270–271
Akt. Ges Lignose
  2 and 2A, 280–281
  3A, 282–283
Limited edition guns
  commemoratives, 21–22
  short production arms, 22–23
  special purpose markings, 22
Llama Gabilondo y Cia, S.A., Omni,
  284–285
Luger, VOPO, 286–287
Luger, Georg, biographical
  information, 11

Magnum Research, Inc., Desert
  Eagle, 288–289
Mail order
  buying guns, 17–18
  selling guns, 19
Mannlicher, Ferdinand Ritter von,
  biographical information, 11
Mann-Werke AG, Pocket Pistol,
  290–291
Margolin, Michael, biographical
  information, 11
Mauser
  1878 (Zig Zag), 302–303
  1896 "Broomhandle" Pistol,
    292–293
  1910/1914/1934, 296–297
  1914/1934, 298–299
  HSc, 294–295
  WTP Model 1 (Westentaschen
    Pistole), 300–301
Mauser, Peter Paul, biographical
  information, 11
August Menz Waffenfabrik, Menta,
  304–305
Waffenbabrik August Menz, I and II,
  306–307
O.F. Mossberg & Sons, Inc.,
  Brownie, 308–309
Myska, Frantisek, biographical
  information, 11

Nagant, Emile and Leon,
  biographical information, 11

Fabrique D'Armes Nagant, 1878 and 1883, 310–311

Nagant Freres, Russian M1895, 312–313

Necas, Augustin, biographical information, 12

Norwegian Military, M1914, 314–315

Cooperativa Obrera, Longines, 316–317

Heinrich Ortgies & Co., H.O. and D., 318–319

P.A.F. (Pretoria Arms Factory), Junior, 320–321

Pawn shops, buying guns, 18

Anciens Etablissements Pieper, Demontant and Basculant, 322–323

Pieper, Nicholas, biographical information, 12

Pietro Beretta
1915/1919, 89–90
1934/1935, 91–92
Bantam (418), 87–88

Fabryka Broni w Radomiu, Radom, 324–325

Randall Firearms Mfg. Corp., Service and Compact, 326–327

Refinished guns, buying guidelines, 18

Remington Arms Co.
Double Derringer (Model 95), 328–329
M51, 330–331

Restoration of handguns, 23–26
burred metal, 24
metalwork, 23–24
and missing parts, 24
refinishing guns, 24–25
and wood and grips, 24
wood refinishing, 25–26

Retolaza Hermanos, 1924 Liberty, 332–333

Rheinische Metallwaren u. Maschinenfabrik, Rheinmetall, 334–335

Romerwerke, Romer, 336–337

Roth-Steyr, 1907, 338–339

Russian State Arsenal, Makarov, 340–341

Sanford, Harry, biographical information, 12

J.P. Sauer & Sohn
M1913 Pocket Automatic, 344–345
Roth-Sauer, 346–347

J.P. Sauer & Sohn GMBH, 38 H, 348–349

Savage Arms Corp.
1907, 350–351
M1917, 352–353

Schmeisser, Louis, biographical information, 12

August Schueler, Reform, 354–355

Schwarzlose, Andreas Wilhelm, biographical information, 12

A.W. Schwarzlose GMBH, M1908, 356–357

SIG (Schweizerische Industrie Gesellschaft), P 210, 342–343

Short production arms, buying guidelines, 22–23

Waffenfabriken Simson & Co., Vest Pocket, 358–359

Smith & Wesson
10: M & P, 360–361
19; .357 Combat Magnum, 362–363
29, 364–365
.32 Safety Hammerless (Lemon Squeezer), 400–401
34; 1953 .22/.32 Kit Gun and 1935 .22/.32 Kit Gun, 366–367
.35 Automatic Pistol (1913), 396–397
36: .38 Chief's Special, 368–369
38; Bodyguard Airweight, 370–371
41, 372–373
49; Bodyguard, 374–375
52: .38 Master, 376–377
58: .41 Military and Police, 378–379
59, 380–381
60; Stainless Chief's Special, 382–383
61; Escort, 402–403
65: Stainless .357 Military and Police, 384–385

66: .357 Combat Magnum Stainless, 386–387
547: 9mm Military and Police, 388–389
559, 390–391
586: Distinguished Combat Magnum, 392–393
629, 394–395
Straight Line Target, 398–399
Bonifacio Echeverria Star SA
28, 412–413
1908/1914, 410–411
BM, 404–405
I, 408–409
PD, 406–407
Stendawerke Waffenfabrik GmbH, Stenda, 414–415
Sterling Arms Corp.
300, 418–419
400, 420–421
450, 422–423
PPL, 416
X-Caliber, 417
Stevens, Joshua, biographical information, 12
J.Stevens Arms & Tool Co., No. 10, 424–425
Steyr
1909, 426–427
1909 Solothurn, 430–431
1911 Steyr-Hahn, 428–429
SP, 432–433
Franz Stock Machinen u. Werkbaufabrik, Stock, 434–435
Stoeger Arms Corp., Luger, 436–437
Sturm, Ruger & Co.
Blackhawk, New Model, 440–441
Blackhawk, Stainless New Model, 442–443
MK I and II, 438–439
Police Service Six, 444–445
Police Service Six Stainless, 446–447
Redhawk, 448–449
Security Six, 452–453
Security Six Stainless, 454–455
Speed Six, 456–457
Standard, 450–451
Super Blackhawk, New Model, 458–459
Super Single Six, New Model, 460–461

Thompson/Center Arms, Contender, 462–463
Tokarev, TT-33, 464–465

Tokarev, Feodor Vassilevich, biographical information, 12
Tomiska, Alois, biographical information, 12

Fab. Francais Societe Union, Union, 466–467
United Sporting Arms, Inc.
Seville, 468–469
Sheriff, 470–471
Upgrades, buying guidelines, 19
U.S. Military, M1911, 472–473

Carl Walther Waffenfabrik
5, 474–475
9, 476–477
Carl Walther GmbH
P5, 480–481
P-38, 482–483
PP, 484–485
PPK, 486–487
PPK/S, 488–489
Walther Mark II, PPK Mark II, 478–479
Webley & Scott Ltd.
1906 (.25), 490–491
Fosbery Automatic Revolver, 498–499
M & P (M1909), 496–497
Metropolitan Police Automatic, 492–493
MK I (M1913), 494–495
White, Rollin, biographical information, 12
Whitney Firearms Co., Wolverine, 500–501

Fab. De'Armes Zaragoza, Corla, 502–503
E. Zehner Waffenfabrik, Zehna, 504–505
M. Zulaica y Cia
1914, 506–507
Royal (Z Novelty), 508–509

ABOUT THE AUTHOR

ROBERT H. BALDERSON, MBA, authors several books on antiques and collectibles including: *The Official Price Guide to Antique and Modern Firearms* and *The Official Guide to Gunmarks.*

Mr. Balderson holds a BA in economics with a minor in history, and a Masters of Business Administration. He teaches classes at the California State University, encompassing economics, investments, marketing, and appraisal.

For twenty years Robert Balderson has been involved in the area of antiques and collectibles, as a collector, dealer, appraiser, writer, and bookseller.

Robert Balderson resides in Sacramento, California, is a business consultant, and continues to sell collectibles and related books, as well as writing and editing.

Respected sources, including the Smithsonian Institution and *Maloney's Antiques and Collectibles Resource Directory,* list Mr. Balderson as an authority in several areas of the antiques and collectibles field. Robert H. Balderson may be contacted as a consultant or appraiser at P.O. Box 254886, Sacramento, CA 95865. For appraisals, he requests as much information (description, photographs, etc.) as possible be included with the first correspondence.

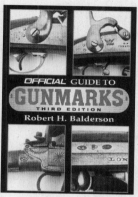

HOUSE OF COLLECTIBLES

THE OFFICIAL® IDENTIFICATION AND PRICE GUIDES TO

AMERICAN INDIAN
ARROWHEADS
1st edition
John L. Stivers
876-37913-7 $17.50

ANTIQUE
AND MODERN
FIREARMS
8th edition
Robert H. Balderson
876-37907-2 $17.00

ANTIQUE AND
MODERN TEDDY
BEARS
1st edition
Kim Brewer and Carol-
Lynn Rossel Waugh
876-37792-4 $12.00

ANTIQUE CLOCKS
3rd edition
876-37513-1 $12.00

ANTIQUE JEWELRY
(ID) 6th edition
Arthur Guy Kaplan
876-37759-2 $21.00

ARTS AND CRAFTS
*The Early Modernist
Movement in
American Decorative
Arts, 1894–
1923* (ID)
2nd edition
Bruce Johnson
876-37879-3 $12.95

AUTOMOBILIA
1st edition
David K. Bausch
676-60030-1 $19.95

THE BEATLES
*Records and
Memorabilia*
1st edition
Perry Cox and Joe
Lindsay, with an
introduction by Jerry
Osborne
876-37940-4 $15.00

BEER CANS
5th Edition
Bill Mugrage
876-37873-4 $12.50

BOTTLES
11th edition
Jim Megura
876-37843-2 $14.00

CIVIL WAR
COLLECTIBLES
1st edition
Richard Friz
876-37951-X $17.00

COLLECTIBLE TOYS
(ID), 5th edition
Richard Friz
876-37803-3 $15.00

COLLECTOR CARS
8th edition
Robert H. Balderson
676-60024-7 $17.00

COLLECTOR
HANDGUNS
5th edition
Robert H. Balderson
676-60038-7 $17.00

COLLECTOR KNIVES
11th edition
C. Houston Price
876-37973-0 $17.00

COLLECTOR PLATES
6th edition
Rinker Enterprises
876-37968-4 $17.00

COMPACT DISCS
1st edition
Jerry Osborne
876-37923-4 $15.00

COUNTRY MUSIC
RECORDS
1st edition
Jerry Osborne
676-60004-2 $15.00

ELVIS PRESLEY
RECORDS AND
MEMORABILIA
1st edition
Jerry Osborne
876-37939-0 $14.00

FINE ART
2nd edition
Rosemary and
Michael McKittrick
876-37909-9 $20.00

FRANK SINATRA
RECORDS AND CDs
1st edition
Vito R. Marino and
Anthony C. Furfero
876-37903-X $12.00

GLASSWARE
1st edition
Mark Pickvet
876-37953-6 $15.00

OLD BOOKS
1st edition
Marie Tedford and
Pat Goudey
876-37915-3 $15.00

ORIENTAL RUGS
2nd edition
Joyce C. Ware
676-60023-9 $15.00

POSTCARDS (ID)
1st edition
Diane Allmen
876-37802-5 $9.95

POTTERY
AND PORCELAIN
8th edition
Harvey Duke
876-37893-9 $15.00

ROCK AND ROLL—
MAGAZINES,
POSTERS, AND MEM-
ORABILIA (ID), 1st
edition
David K. Henkel
876-37851-3 $12.50

STAR TREK
COLLECTIBLES
4th edition
Sue Cornwell
and Mike Kott
876-37994-3 $19.95

WATCHES
10th edition
Cooksey Shugart &
Tom Engle
876-37808-4 $18.00

BECKETT GREAT SPORTS HEROES

TROY AIKMAN
676-60035-2 $15.00

WAYNE GRETZKY
676-60032-8 $15.00

ANFERNEE
HARDAWAY
676-60033-6 $15.00

MICHAEL JORDAN
876-37979-X $15.00

DAN MARINO
676-60034-4 $15.00

JOE MONTANA
876-37981-1 $15.00

SHAQUILLE O'NEAL
876-37980-3 $15.00

FRANK THOMAS
676-60029-8 $15.00

More listings and order form on following page